OMNES CIRCUMADSTANTES

OMNES CIRCUMADSTANTES

Contributions towards a history of the role of the people in the liturgy

Presented to Herman Wegman
on the occasion of his retirement
from the chair of History of liturgy and theology
in the Katholieke Theologische Universiteit Utrecht

Edited by Charles Caspers and Marc Schneiders

UITGEVERSMAATSCHAPPIJ J.H. KOK – KAMPEN 1990

CIP-GEGEVENS KONINKLIJKE BIBLIOTHEEK, DEN HAAG

Omnes

Omnes Circumadstantes: contributions towards a history of the role of the people in
the liturgy: presented to Herman Wegman on the occassion of his retirement from the
chair of History of liturgy and theology in the Katholieke Theologische Universiteit
Utrecht / ed. by Charles Caspers and Marc Schneiders. – Kampen: Kok
Met bibliogr., index.
ISBN 90-242-5442-6
SISO 239.3   UDC 264(091)   NUGI 636
Trefw.: liturgie; geschiedenis.

© Uitgeversmaatschappij J.H. Kok – Kampen, 1990
Omslag Bas Mazur
Zetwerk: Elgraphic bv, Schiedam
ISBN 90 242 5442 6
NUGI 636 W-boek

Contents

Preface

ואמר כל־העם אמן

(Ps. 106, 48)

In 1985 Herman Wegman gave an address during the annual 'academic session' of the *Katholieke Theologische Universiteit* (in those days still called *Hogeschool*) *Utrecht*, which was printed in the same year (no. 192 in his bibliography in this *Festschrift*). In this address professor Wegman raised a number of critical questions regarding liturgical studies. In the summary he put one of the questions thus:

Has the history of worship not been described too exclusively from the part the clergy plays in it? The clergy's liturgy seems to have changed little over the ages, whereas the faith experience of the Lord's community has pursued other paths. Further, has there ever been a community liturgy?

And in the main text he said to himself:

[...] the direction of research in the history of liturgy must be given a twist. I should post myself in the nave of the church, lend my ear to what I may hear, and keep my eyes wide open. What kind of liturgy will I discover there? The liturgy around the confessional e.g., or what is happening at the statues of the Mother of God and of the saints [...]

We have tried to take up this challenge which Herman Wegman provided for himself. Not because it is 'new' and fashionable in historical research nowadays to pay attention to the 'ordinary people'. Herman Wegman's attention – for many years now – for the people's part in the liturgy cannot have escaped anyone who knows his works. To us, his pupils, his attention for the people, both in the classroom and in the supervision of our work, may have seemed almost a preoccupation at times. This preoccupation may be healthy in research, but it does not make it easier for a liturgist, certainly not when his work is mainly historical. The sources for a history of the role of the people are meagre, especially for the first *millennium*, because so very few of the small enough number of people who could write did post themselves in the nave of the church and left a record of what they saw and heard. Moreover, it is often very difficult to reach an agreement among scholars on what the sources which we have really say. Nevertheless we have chosen to make Herman Wegman's preoccupation the theme of this *Festschrift*, simply because we expect he will like it.

The **illustration** on the cover, which is printed in its entirety on page IX, is taken from an emblem book from 1603 which is the work of the Flemish Jesuit John David.[1] The purpose of the illustration is to support chapter 36 in which David explains that there are no better means for a virtuous life 'than often to listen to God's word, often to go to confession and to Communion'.[2] The contents of this apologetic book from the Counter Reformation are not the reason, however, why we found the engraving appropriate to adorn the cover of professor Wegman's *Festschrift*. On the contrary, it is rather our purpose to present the picture – against every rule of historical scholarship – outside its context. Why?

First, because we spent quite some time searching for an illustration of the *circumadstantes* from the medieval period, but in vain. We were happy when at last we found an early modern art product in which the people stand, if perhaps not exactly around, in any case near the priest. The presence of the *circumadstantes*, whom one would not look for in the liturgy so shortly after the Council of Trent, makes the engraving in a way ageless.

The picture has another interesting feature: the austerity of the church furniture and the small distance between priest and people, which sooner evoke the atmosphere of the Reformation than that of the Counter Reformation. When faith is expressed in a way which transcends denominational frameworks and conventions, Christian unity may be within reach. From this point of view the engraving is not only ageless but also universal, even if David's intentions must have been entirely different.

Which brings us back to the man to whom this volume is dedicated. For this historian of liturgy more than for anyone else the unravelling of what is 'timeless' and memorable (in the liturgical sense which this word also has!) from the historically determined liturgy kept pace with his repeated pleas for ecumenism, or should we say they went hand in hand?

In the middle of the month of February 1989 we were informed about the early retirement of Herman Wegman in the spring of 1990. On April 12, 1989 we could sent out letters of invitation to the contributors of this volume. We want to thank them all for their willingness to contribute despite the very short time available and the extra burden which we put upon them by setting a theme. We are very sorry that we could not ask scholars from other countries to write for this volume. We hope that Herman Wegman's friends outside the

---

1. Ioannes DAVID: *Christeliicken Waerseggher. De principale stucken van t' Christen Geloof en Leven int cort begrijpende* [...] (T'Antwerpen: Inde Plantijnsche Druckerije, by Ian Moerentorf, 1603). De *Christeliicken Waerseggher* ('The true Christian') contains some hundred allegorical engravings of Théodore GALLE. A Latin version of David's work was printed two years earlier than his Dutch text under the title *Veridicus Christianus* also by Plantijn-Moerentorf. For David's life and works, cf.: Roger MOLS: David (Jean), in *Dictionnaire d'histoire et de géographie ecclésiastique* 14 (Paris 1960) 1485-1490.
2. *dan dickmael t'woordt Godts te hooren, dickmael te biechte ende ten H. Sacramente te gaen* (DAVID: *Christeliicken Waerseggher* 96).

Quid mage Christiadas Virtutis ad ardua ducit?
Concio: Rite piare animum: et sacro sancta Synaxis.

Seght, wat den Christen gheest, in deughden doet vermeeven,
D'woordt Godts ô: de Biecht: en meest, theylich Lichaem onô Heeven.

Quel poinct nous auance, Plus a l'eminence, De perfection?
Confesser au prestre, De Dieu le repaistre, Hanter le sermon.

Netherlands will understand that it would have been impossible to get this *Festschrift* ready within a year, when we would have asked them too.

Although we would have preferred to present an 'international' *Festschrift*, the fact that only Dutch colleagues and pupils of Herman Wegman could contribute does have one result which is perhaps not a disadvantage. We like to think that this book is also a presentation for the international *forum* of what is going on in liturgical research in the Netherlands. We are happy that all contributions, except for one, which is on a specific Dutch subject, are presented in a 'foreign' language. We thank those who assisted authors and editors in curtailing the number of errors in the three 'foreign' languages as much as was possible in the short time available.

We also thank those who through substantial grants made possible this volume financially: the *Kollege van Kuratoren* and the *Universiteitsraad* of the *Katholieke Theologische Universiteit Utrecht*; the provinces of the four religious orders and congregations which participate in the *Katholieke Theologische Universiteit Utrecht*: the Dutch Augustinians (O.S.A.), Franciscans (O.F.M.), Marists (S.M.) and Passionists (C.P.); the *Radboudstichting*.

Ch.C.
M.S.

H.A.J. Wegman: A bibliography

COMPILED BY CHARLES CASPERS AND MARC SCHNEIDERS

Herman Antoon Joseph Wegman was born on April 10, 1930 in Soesterberg, the Netherlands. He was educated in the seminaries of the Archdiocese of Utrecht in Apeldoorn (located for two years during the Second World War in Ootmarsum) and Driebergen (Rijsenburg). He studied in Rome (Gregoriana, Pontifical Institutes for Christian Archaeology and of Oriental Studies, 1955-1957) and Paris (Institut Liturgique, École des Hautes Études (H. Marrou), 1957-1959) and completed his studies with a dissertation on Easter week (1959; published in 1968, see no. 57 below).

From the very beginning of the Katholieke Theologische Universiteit Utrecht in 1967 professor Wegman taught the history of liturgy and theology in this institution and in the Theological Department of Utrecht State University. For many years he has also been involved in the development of present-day liturgy, both in Catholic and ecumenical contexts.

An account of his published work (until December 31, 1989) is given below.

Six series of articles which were published in the local Church periodical *Mededelingen Arca pacis* during the years 1978-1979 (on Easter), 1979-1980 (on the Eucharist), 1980-1981 (on the Church), 1981-1982 (on Councils), 1982-1983 (on Sacraments) and 1983-1984 (on the Ministry) have not been included in this bibliography.

Editions of the two eucharistic prayers written by professor Wegman are listed in an appendix.

1960
1. De katechese voor de neophyti en de gezangen van de paasweek, in *Nederlandsche katholieke stemmen* 56 (1960) 83-94.
2. De zielzorg voor de dopelingen in de vasten en de paasweek, in *Tijdschrift voor liturgie* 44 (1960) 134-144.

1961
3. *Gedachten over prefatie en canon*, Hilversum: Gooi en Sticht, 1961, [i,] 8 pp.

1962
4. *Gedachten over de communieritus*, Hilversum: Gooi en Sticht, 1962, [i,] 11 pp.
5. [With J.P.N. Rokebrand:] *Bijbel, godsdienst, liturgie. Stempels voor het godsdienstonderwijs op de R.K. school*. Samengesteld en van tekst voorzien. Met tekeningen van J.B. v.d. Beld, Groningen: Noord Ned. Stempel- en Leermiddelenfabriek, 1962, 72 pp.

6. Grotere invloed van de bisschoppen in liturgicis?, in *Tijdschrift voor liturgie* 46 (1962) 140-147.

1963

7. *Gedachten over de offerande*, Hilversum: Gooi en Sticht, 1963, [i,] 11 pp.
8. De werking van de H. Geest in de initiatio christiana, in *Tijdschrift voor liturgie* 47 (1963) 169-178.

1964

9. *Gedachten over de gestalte der eucharistieviering*, Hilversum: Gooi en Sticht, 1964, [i,] 14 pp.
10. *Vraag en antwoord*, Driebergen: Nederlandse Commissie voor Liturgie, 1964, 16 pp.
11. L'histoire de l'octave de Pâques, in *Octave de Pâques*. Présenté par J. Aubry, B. Guillard, E. Haulotte, M. Huftier, P. Vanbergen, A. Vanhoye, H.A.J. Wegman (= Assemblées du Seigneur 43), Brugge: Biblica, 1964, 7-15.
12. Lessen der historie, in *Getuigenis* 8 (1963-1964) 294-304.

1965

13. *Gedachten over gebed en lezing*, Hilversum: Gooi en Sticht, 1965, [i,] 10 pp.
14. De concelebratie, in *Pastorale gids* 1-9-1965, 8 pp.
15. 'De mis is korter geworden', in *Tijdschrift voor liturgie* 49 (1965) 167-172.
16. 'Hij is ons aller brood geworden'. Voorstel tot rekonstruktie van de communie-ritus, in *Tijdschrift voor liturgie* 49 (1965) 381-403.
    With a summary in French (401-403).

1965-1968

17. [Co-editor of:] *Liturgisch woordenboek* II, Roermond: Romen & zonen, 1965-1968, xvi pp., cc. 1311-3026.
18. Kopten, in *idem*, cc. 1377-1378.
19. Lans, in *idem*, c. 1432.
20. Megalynarion, in *idem*, c. 1691.
21. Menologion, in *idem*, c. 1701.
22. Mesonyktikon, in *idem*, cc. 1704-1705.
23. Metania, in *idem*, c. 1705.
24. Morgenofficie V, in *idem*, cc. 1793-1794.
25. Nachtwake I-III, in *idem*, cc. 1851-1853.
26. Paasweek, in *idem*, cc. 2116-2121.
27. Paramenten, in *idem*, cc. 2142-2145.
28. Petrus en Paulus, in *idem*, cc. 2190-2195, plate lxxi.
29. Pinksteren III. C. 2, in *idem*, c. 2202.
30. Prein, Joannes Adrianus Maria, in *idem*, cc. 2262-2263.
31. Reservatie I, in *idem*, cc. 2389-2393.
32. Rubrieken, in *idem*, cc. 2456-2459.
33. Sacramentarium, in *idem*, cc. 2491-2493.
34. Schuldbelijdenis, in *idem*, cc. 2531-2533.
35. Subdiaken, in *idem*, cc. 2599-2601.
36. Uitstelling/Lof, in *idem*, cc. 2738-2740.
37. Veertigurengebed, in *idem*, cc. 2772-2773.
38. Verrijzenis, in *idem*, cc. 2784-2787.
39. Verzaking, in *idem*, cc. 2792-2794.

40. Vigilius, in *idem*, cc. 2824-2825.
41. Volksdevotie, -vroomheid, in *idem*, cc. 2830-2835.
42. [With R. Dijker:] Voorbereiding der doopleerlingen, in *idem*, cc. 2848-2854.
43. Vormsel I-II, in *idem*, cc. 2862-2871.
44. Witte Donderdag, in *idem*, cc. 2923-2929.
45. Zondag, in *idem*, cc. 2996-3001.
46. Zondagsrust, -plicht, in *idem*, cc. 3002-3003.

1966
47. [With P.G. van Hooijdonk and W.J. Veldhuis (eds.):] *Osmose. Gedachten over leven in kerk en wereld*, Utrecht: Ambo, 1966, 335 pp.
48. De kerk in ceremonieel tenue, in *idem*, 286-307.
49. De gebedsdienst bij een crematie, in *Pastorale gids* [1966] 4 pp. (417-420).

1966-1975
50. [Contributions in the field of 'liturgie' to:] *Grote Winkler Prins*, zevende geheel nieuwe druk, Amsterdam-Brussel: Elsevier, 1966-1975, 20 vols.
    Cf. no. 163.

1967
51. *De liturgie en het onderwijs*, Driebergen: s.n., 1967, [i,] 26 pp.
52. [With P.J.M. van den Berg, M.R. van den Bosch and J.A.W. van Eupen:] *Woorden van welkom. Thematische modellen voor de welkomsgroet bij de zondagsviering*. Onder redactie van Kerugma, Hilversum: Gooi & Sticht, 1967, 104 pp.
53. De gezongen Nederlandse prefaties, in *Pastorale gids* 3-1-1967, 2 pp. (91-92).
54. [Review of:] H.B. Meyer, *Luther und die Messe*. [...] Paderborn [...] 1965 [...], in *Tijdschrift voor theologie* 7 (1967) 211-212.
55. [Review of:] *Liturgie der Gemeinde* [...] Wenen [...] 1966, in *Tijdschrift voor theologie* 7 (1967) 214-215.
56. [Review of:] C.W. Mönnich, *Antiliturgica. Enige kanttekeningen bij de viering van kerkelijke feesten* [...] Amsterdam [...] 1966 [...], in *Tijdschrift voor theologie* 7 (1967) 215.

1968
57. *Het paasoktaaf in het Missale Romanum en zijn geschiedenis*, Assen: Van Gorcum, 1968, [vi,] 144 pp.
    With a summary in English (134-137). Shortened version of unpublished dissertation: *Pâques, du premier jour au huitième. Étude sur l'histoire de la semaine de pâques en occident*, Roma: pro manuscripto, 1959, X, 170, 28 pp.
58. [Contributions in the field of 'liturgie' to:] A.M. Heidt (ed.): *Catholica. Informatiebron voor het katholieke leven*, [2nd edition], Hilversum: Stichting Catholica, 1968, 2 vols.
59. Ter inleiding, in *Directorium voor de Nederlandse kerkprovincie in het jaar 1969*, s.l.: Nederlandse Commissie voor Liturgie, 1968, 3-4.
60. Neue Eucharistiegebete in Holland, in *Liturgisches Jahrbuch* 18 (1968) 44-60.
61. 'Wat is dan de mens, dat Gij aan hem denkt?' Het gebed in de liturgie, in *Theologie en pastoraat* 64 (1968) 96-111.
    Same article: no. 100.
62. [Review of:] L.A. van Buchem, *L'homélie pseudo-eusébienne de pentecôte. L'origine de la confirmatio en Gaule Méridionale et l'interprétation de ce rite par Fauste de Riez*, Nijmegen [...] 1967, in *Tijdschrift voor theologie* 8 (1968) 454-455.

63. [Review of:] *Jeudi Saint*, présenté par C. Florin, N. Lazure, e.a. [...] Parijs [...] 1967, in *Tijdschrift voor theologie* 8 (1968) 467.

1969

64. Monde d'aujourd'hui et liturgie d'hier, in *Communauté chrétienne* 8 (1969) 117-130.
65. Hoe beoordeel ik de waarde van een eucharistisch gebed?, in *G en S* 5 (1969) 62-64.
66. 'Waarom is deze nacht zo anders dan de andere nachten?' De geschiedenis van het christelijk paasfeest, in *Getuigenis* 13 (1968-1969) 162-178.
67. De vernieuwing van de liturgie in de rooms katholieke kerk; een stand van zaken, in *Ministerium* 3 (1969) 145-152.
68. Een reflexie op liturgisch spraakgebruik, in *Schrift* 1 (1969) no. 3, 108-110.
69. Liturgie met zieken en stervenden, in *Tijdschrift voor liturgie* 53 (1969) 179-196.
70. [Review of:] *Ostern. Fest der Auferstehung heute*, hrsg. v. Th. Bogler [...] Maria Laach [...] 1968 [...], in *Tijdschrift voor theologie* 9 (1969) 468.
71. [Review of:] *Das Sakrale im Widerspruch*, hrsg. v. Th. Bogler [...] Maria Laach [...] 1967 [...], in *Tijdschrift voor theologie* 9 (1969) 468.
72. [Review of:] *Deutsche Liturgie? Sind wir auf dem Weg dahin?*, hrsg. v. Th. Bogler [...] Maria Laach [...] 1967 [...], in *Tijdschrift voor theologie* 9 (1969) 468.
73. [Review of:] H. Leeb, *Die Psalmodie bei Ambrosius* [...] Wenen [...] 1967 [...], in *Tijdschrift voor theologie* 9 (1969) 468.

1970

74. De betekenis van de decreten van het Tweede Vaticaans Concilie voor de liturgie, in A. Hollaardt (ed.): *Liturgisch woordenboek, supplement. Liturgische oriëntatie na Vaticanum II*, Roermond: Romen & zonen, 1970, 17-18.
75. De sacramenten. 1. Sacramententheologie en liturgie, in *idem*, 34-36.
76. 'De avond voor Pasen spelen wij met vuur', in *Bijdragen. Tijdschrift voor filosofie en theologie* 31 (1970) 261-293.
    With a summary in English: Liturgy on Eastereve (292-293).
77. Het sacrament voor zieken en stervenden, in *De heraut* 101 (1970) 277-281.
    Same article: no. 78.
78. Het sacrament voor zieken en stervenden, in *De nieuwe boodschap* 97 (1970) 260-264.
    Same article: no. 77.

1971

79. *Een uitzicht vanuit de Romeinse liturgie op het gezamenlijk verstaan van het avondmaal door de kerken.* Rede uitgesproken bij de aanvaarding van het ambt van buitengewoon hoogleraar in de geschiedenis van het dogma en de liturgie in de Faculteit der Godgeleerdheid aan de Rijksuniversiteit te Utrecht op maandag 22 november 1971, Assen: Van Gorcum, 1971, 34 pp.
80. Avondmaal en eucharistie II. Elkaar verstaan en herkennen, in *Kosmos en oecumene* 5 (1971) 180-182.
81. De vernieuwing van de rooms katholieke eredienst, in *Ministerium* 5 (1971) 209-215.
82. Han Fortmann in memoriam, in *Tijdschrift voor liturgie* 55 (1971) 1-4.
83. [Review of:] B. Bürki, *Im Herrn entschlafen*, Heidelberg [...] 1969 [...], in *Tijdschrift voor theologie* 11 (1971) 336.

1972

84. [With P.G. van Hooijdonk:] *Zij breken hetzelfde brood. Een kritische wegwijzer bij de viering van de eucharistie op basis van een liturgie-historische en -sociologische analyse* (= De kerk van morgen 9), s.l.: Pastoraal Instituut van de Nederlandse Kerkprovincie/Katholiek Archief, 1972, 144 pp.

85. [Editor of:] *De bijbelse achtergronden van eucharistie-avondmaal. Discussienota*, Amersfoort: Commissie Intercommunie en Ambt van de Raad van Kerken in Nederland/Archief van de Kerken, 1972, 16 pp.

86. Besnijdenis en doopsel in de jonge kerk, in *Christus en Israel* 15 (1972) no. 1, 18-22.

87. Kanttekeningen bij de bespreking, in *Inzet* 1 (1972), Besproken, 7-8.
    Remarks to H. Jorna: Samenvatting van de bespreking van de Werkgroep 'Katechese Basisscholen' Arnhem op 26 januari 1972. Gesprek met H. Wegman, in *idem*, Besproken, 6-7.

88. Die Ostertage. Neue Formen der Osterfeier in Holland, in *Liturgisches Jahrbuch* 22 (1972) 42-48.
    Translation of no. 93.

89. De lezing van de H. Schrift in de christelijke gemeente, in *Ministerium* 6 (1972) 279-283.

90. De menselijke mens en zijn eer, in *Spes* 3 (1972) 86-92.

91. De mysteriespelen van Herman Verbeek, in *Theologie en pastoraat* 68 (1972) 15-27.

92. De gelovige mens en zijn eredienst, in *Tijdschrift voor liturgie* 56 (1972) 4-14.

93. De dagen van Pasen: nieuwe vormen voor de viering van het oude feest, in *Tijdschrift voor liturgie* 56 (1972) 88-94.
    German translation: no. 88.

94. [Review of:] U. Wickert, *Sacramentum unitatis. Ein Beitrag zum Verständnis der Kirche bei Cyprian* [...] Berlijn [...] 1971, in *Tijdschrift voor theologie* 12 (1972) 468-469.

95. [Review of:] W. Simonis, *Ecclesia visibilis et invisibilis. Untersuchungen zur Ekklesiologie und Sakramentenlehre in der afrikanischen Tradition von Cyprian bis Augustinus* [...] Frankfurt [...] 1971, in *Tijdschrift voor theologie* 12 (1972) 469.

1973

96. Woorddienst en eucharistisch gebed, in *Inzet* 2 (1973), Weloverwogen, 22-24.

97. Erfahrungen mit neuen Hochgebeten in Holland, in *Liturgisches Jahrbuch* 23 (1973) 21-29.

98. Terug naar de vleespotten?, in *Tenminste* 92 (1973) no. 10, 8-12.

99. [Review of:] H. Jongerius O.P., Orationale, delen I en II, uitgave KBS Boxtel 1972/73, in *Inzet* 2 (1973), Besproken, 21-22.
    Cf. no. 111.

1974

100. 'Wat is dan de mens, dat Gij aan hem denkt?' Het gebed in de liturgie, in *Bidden maakt anders*, Hilversum: Gooi en Sticht, 1974, 79-99.
     Same contribution: no. 61.

101. De nieuwe Romeinse orde van dienst voor de kinderdoop, in *Bijdragen. Tijdschrift voor filosofie en theologie* 35 (1974) 129-147.
     With a summary in English: The Roman rite for the baptism of children (146-147).

Abstract: The roman rite for infant baptism, in *Theology digest* 23 (1975) 127-133.

102. Op doortocht naar het leven, in *Getuigenis* 19 (1974-1975) 100-104.
103. Missaal voor zon- en feestdagen: bruikbaar? belangrijk?, in *Inzet* 3 (1974) 11-16.
104. Overpeinzing bij de zondagsliturgie, in *Inzet* 3 (1974) 82-85.
105. [Review of:] *Archiv für Liturgiewissenschaft*, Band XIV, hrsg. v. E. [von] Severus OSB, Regensburg [...] 1972 [...], in *Tijdschrift voor theologie* 14 (1974) 202.
106. [Review of:] P. Oskamp, *Liturgische broedplaatsen*, Kampen [...] 1973 [...], in *Tijdschrift voor theologie* 14 (1974) 203.

1975
107. De zeven sacramenten, in *Inzet* 4 (1975) 106-108.
108. De voorlezing van de H. Schrift in de Romeinse liturgie, in *Tenminste* 95 (1975) no. 1, 9-13.
109. Het waaien van de Geest?, in *Tijdschrift voor liturgie* 59 (1975) 213-225.
110. [Review of:] D.A. Bertrand, *Le baptême de Jésus: Histoire de l'exégèse aux deux premiers siècles* [...] Tübingen [...] 1973 [...], in *Tijdschrift voor theologie* 15 (1975) 205.
111. [Review of:] H. Jongerius, *Orationale: Gebeden voor de viering van de eucharistie op weekdagen*, 3, de vierendertig weken door het jaar (jaar 2), Boxtel [...] 1973 [...], in *Tijdschrift voor theologie* 15 (1975) 222. Cf. no. 99.

1976
112. *Geschiedenis van de christelijke eredienst in het westen en in het oosten. Een wegwijzer*, Hilversum: Gooi en Sticht, 1976, 294 pp. Second edition: no. 179. Translation: no. 153.
113. [Editor of:] *Intercommunie en ambt. Bijbelse achtergronden en kerkelijke perspectieven*. Uitgave van de Commissie Intercommunie en Ambt van de Raad van Kerken in Nederland, 's-Gravenhage: Boekencentrum, 1976, 124 pp.
114. [Editor of:] *Goed of niet goed? Het eucharistisch gebed in Nederland. Een reeks bijdragen* (= BreedBoek), Hilversum: Gooi en Sticht, 1976, 165 pp.
115. Over het samengaan van woord en rite, in *idem*, 21-24.
116. Eucharistisch gebed 14 [H. Oosterhuis: *In het voorbijgaan*, 171-174], in *idem*, 86-90.
117. Eucharistisch gebed 21 [J. Duin: *Wiens brood men breekt*, 45-46], in *idem*, 116-118.
118. Eucharistisch gebed 30 [Ph. Stein: *De dienst van de maaltijd*, 26-28], in *idem*, 156-158.
119. Het presbyterium: bisschop en priesters, in *Het bisschopsambt* (= Annalen van het Thijmgenootschap 64, 3), Baarn: Ambo, 1976, 78-96.
120. Een vaste paasdatum voor de christenen?, in *Saamhorig* 1 (1976) no. 4, 6-7.
121. [Review of:] K. Hein, *Eucharist and Excommunication: A study in early Christian doctrine and discipline* [...] Bern/Frankfurt [...] 1973 [...], in *Tijdschrift voor theologie* 16 (1976) 87.
122. [Review of:] *Kult in der sekularisierten Welt*, Regensburg [...] 1974 [...], in *Tijdschrift voor theologie* 16 (1976) 105.
123. [Review of:] H. Fischer, *Thematischer Dialog-Gottesdienst*, Hamburg [...] 1975 [...], in *Tijdschrift voor theologie* 16 (1976) 105-106.

124. [Review of:] J. Straver, *Dopen? Wat een vraag: Pastorale ervaringen rond de kinderdoop* [...] Hilversum [...] 1975 [...], in *Tijdschrift voor theologie* 16 (1976) 340-341.

125. [Review of:] A.G. Luiks, *Baptisterium: De bediening van de doop in de oudchristelijke kerk*, Kampen [...] 1975 [...], in *Tijdschrift voor theologie* 16 (1976) 429.

126. [Notice of:] Th. Maas-Ewerd, *Fürbitten beim Gedächtnis der Heiligen: Modelle für die Messfeiern zur Kirchweihe und zu den Commune-Messen der Heiligen; Modelle für die Heiligenfeste und Gedenktage in den Monaten Dezember bis April*, Regensburg [...] 1975 [...], in *Tijdschrift voor theologie* 16 (1976) 351.

1977

127. [With J. Droste:] De uitvaartliturgie, in *Analecta aartsbisdom Utrecht* 50 (1977) 19-24.

128. De schriftlezingen van Goede Vrijdag in de huidige Romeinse liturgie, in *Bijdragen. Tijdschrift voor filosofie en theologie* 38 (1977) 28-43.
    With a summary in English: The readings of the Scripture at Good Friday in the Roman liturgy today (43).

129. Klooster-liturgie, in *Franciscaans leven* 60 (1977) 93-100.

130. Oekumenische schriftlezing, in *Kosmos en oecumene* 11 (1977) 288-290.

131. 'Procedere' und Prozession. Eine Typologie, in *Liturgisches Jahrbuch* 27 (1977) 28-41.

132. De taal van ons bidden, in *Saamhorig* 2 (1977) no. 1, 3-5.

133. Liturgieviering: vindplaats van oecumene?, in *Tenminste* 97 (1977) no. 10, 4-8.

134. 3 april 1977. Palm- of passiezondag: toegang tot de lijdensweek, in *Tijdschrift voor verkondiging* 49 (1977) 93-97.

135. Het doopsel van kinderen volgens de Romeinse ritus, in *Werkmap voor liturgie* 11 (1977) 93-109.
    Same article: no. 228.

136. [Review of:] *Archiv für Liturgiewissenschaft*: Bd. XVII/XVIII, hrsg. v. E. v. Severus, Regensburg [...] 1975/1976 [...], in *Tijdschrift voor theologie* 17 (1977) 316.

137. [Review of:] S. Krikke, *Veranderd levensbesef en liturgie: Een verkenning van godsdienstwijsgerige en liturgische aspecten der randkerkelijkheid* [...] Assen/Amsterdam [...] 1976 [...], in *Tijdschrift voor theologie* 17 (1977) 316-317.

138. [Review of:] G. Hoenderdaal, *Riskant spel: Liturgie in een geseculariseerde wereld* [...] Den Haag [...] 1977 [...], in *Tijdschrift voor theologie* 17 (1977) 317.

1978

139. [Editor of:] *Goed of niet goed?-2. Het eucharistisch gebed in Nederland*. Aangeboden aan [...] H. Manders [...] (= BreedBoek), Hilversum: Gooi en Sticht, 1978, 218 pp.

140. Tafelgebeden in 'Onze Hulp'; uitgegeven op verzoek van de Gereformeerde Deputaten voor de eredienst en de Commissie-Dienstboek, van de Hervormde Raad voor de Eredienst, door de Professor van der Leeuwstichting (1978), in *idem*, 103-139.

141. Herkenning tijdens het breken van het brood. Fantasie op een bekend thema, in *idem*, 209-218.

142. Liturgie aan de oppervlakte, in *Analecta aartsbisdom Utrecht* 51 (1978) 91-100.
    Same article: no. 146.

143. 4. Liturgie und Klassenkampf, in Artur Waibel: Liturgie und Politik. Notizen zu einigen neueren Veröffentlichungen, in *Liturgisches Jahrbuch* 28 (1978) 249-255, on 253-255.
144. Geordend voorlezen uit de schriften: een lange geschiedenis, in *Rondom het woord* 20 (1978) no. 2, 9-16.
145. Bij stukjes en beetjes..., in *Schrift* 10 (1978) no. 56, 68-71.
146. Liturgie aan de oppervlakte, in *Tijdschrift voor liturgie* 62 (1978) 97-105. Same article: no. 142.
147. De initiatie van volwassenen, in *Tijdschrift voor liturgie* 62 (1978) 184-199.
148. Wie zegt Willem Barnard dat Jezus is?, in *Tijdschrift voor theologie* 18 (1978) 390-412.
    With a summary in English: Jesus in the hymns of Willem Barnard (412).
149. [Editor of:] Zegel van de Geest. Het sacrament van het vormsel, in *Werkmap voor liturgie* 12 (1978) 115-215.
150. Inleiding, in *idem*, 119.
151. De liturgie van het vormsel, in *idem*, 197-215.
152. [Review of:] R. Schaeffler/P. Hünermann, *Ankunft Gottes und Handeln des Menschen: Thesen über Kult und Sakrament* [...] Freiburg/Bazel/Wenen [...] 1977 [...], in *Tijdschrift voor theologie* 18 (1978) 98-99.

1979
153. *Geschichte der Liturgie im Westen und Osten*, Regensburg: Pustet, 1979, 300 pp. German translation of no. 112. Translated by Michael Grütering.
154. Pleidooi voor een tekst: de anaphora van de apostelen Addai en Mari, in *Bijdragen. Tijdschrift voor filosofie en theologie* 40 (1979) 15-43.
    With a summary in English: Plea for a text. The anaphora of Addai and Mari (43).
155. In ons midden, in *Inzet* 8 (1979) no. 2, 32-33.
156. Schriftlezing op de zondagmorgen, in *Kosmos en oecumene* 13 (1979) 124-127.
157. De kerkinwijding volgens de vernieuwde Romeinse ritus, in *Tijdschrift voor liturgie* 63 (1979) 306-314.
158. De liederen van Huub Oosterhuis over Jezus van Nazaret, in *Tijdschrift voor theologie* 19 (1979) 124-146.
    With a summary in English: Jesus in the lyrics of Huub Oosterhuis (146).
159. [Review of:] *Elke morgen nieuw. Inleiding tot de Joodse gedachtenwereld aan de hand van de sjemoné esré; het achttiengebed* [...] 1978, in *Tijdschrift voor liturgie* 63 (1979) 171.
    Same review: no. 161.
160. [Review of:] W. Jetter, *Symbol und Ritual: Anthropologische Elemente im Gottesdienst*, Göttingen [...] 1978 [...], in *Tijdschrift voor theologie* 19 (1979) 205.
161. [Review of:] *Elke morgen nieuw: Inleiding tot de Joodse gedachtenwereld aan de hand van een van de centrale Joodse gebeden; Achttiengebed*, samengesteld d. D. v.d. Sluis e.a. [...] z.pl. (Amsterdam/Arnhem) [...] 1978 [...], in *Tijdschrift voor theologie* 19 (1979) 205-206.
    Same review: no. 159.
162. [Review of:] J. Davies, *New Perspectives on Worship Today*, London [...] 1978 [...], in *Tijdschrift voor theologie* 19 (1979) 205.

1979-1984
163. [Contributions in the field of 'theologie' to:] *Grote Winkler Prins encyclopedie in*

25 delen. Achtste geheel nieuwe druk, Amsterdam-Brussel: Elsevier, 1979-1984, 25 vols.
Cf. no. 50.

1980

164. Kerkwijding van Sint Jan van Lateranen, in *Getuigenis* 24 (1979-1980) 273-276.
165. Généalogie hypothétique de la prière eucharistique, in *Questions liturgiques* 61 (1980) 263-278.
166. De viering van paasnacht, in *Tijdschrift voor liturgie* 64 (1980) 40-42.
167. [Review of:] *Das Recht der Gemeinde auf Eucharistie: Die bedrohte Einheit von Wort und Sakrament*, hrgb. v. Solidaritätsgruppe katholischer Priester (SOG) der Diözese Speyer [...] Trier [...] 1978 [...], in *Tijdschrift voor theologie* 20 (1980) 121.

1981

168. Deux strophes de la prière eucharistique III du missel romain, in *Fides sacramenti, sacramentum fidei. Studies in honour of Pieter Smulders*, Assen: Van Gorcum, 1981, 309-320.
169. Une anaphore incomplète? Les fragments sur Papyrus Strasbourg Gr. 254, in R. van den Broek and M.J. Vermaseren (eds.): *Studies in gnosticism and hellenistic religion, presented to Gilles Quispel on the occasion of his 65th birthday* (= Études préliminaires aux religions orientales dans l'empire romain 91), Leiden: Brill, 1981, 432-450.
170. De dood verkondigen is het leven vieren. Soms tegen beter weten in verwachten dat de machten niet het laatste woord hebben, in *De bazuin* 64 (1981) no. 15, 4-5.
171. Het hemd van de pastoor, in *Inzet* 10 (1981) no. 4, 24-27.
172. Samen bidden in de avond, in *Kosmos en oecumene* 15 (1981) 134-137.
173. De nieuwe liturgie: waarom eigenlijk?, in *Tijdschrift voor het gezin. De rozenkrans* 99 (1981) 53-56.
174. 'Wij gedenken de dood van de Heer'. Enige gedachten over de eucharistie als offer, in *Tijdschrift voor theologie* 21 (1981) 48-62.
   With a summary in English: Commemorating the death of the Lord: the Eucharist as sacrifice (62).
175. [Review of:] *Archiv für Liturgiewissenschaft*, Bd. XX/XXI, hrsg. v. A. Häussling, Regensburg [...] 1978/1979 [...], in *Tijdschrift voor theologie* 21 (1981) 338.
176. [Review of:] G. Lukken, *De onvervangbare weg van de liturgie*, Hilversum [...] 1980 [...], in *Tijdschrift voor theologie* 21 (1981) 338.

1982

177. The rubrics of the institution-narrative in the Roman Missal 1970, in Pierre Jounel, Reiner Kaczynski and Gottardo Pasqualetti (eds.): *Liturgia opera divina e umana. Studi sulla riforma liturgica offerti a S.E. Mons. Annibale Bugnini in occasione del suo 70° compleanno* (= Bibliotheca 'Ephemerides liturgicae', 'Subsidia' 26), Roma: Edizioni Liturgiche, 1982, 319-328.
178. De geschiedenis van Goede Vrijdag, in *Werkschrift voor leerhuis en liturgie* 2 (1981-1982) no. 5, 21-28.

1983

179. *Geschiedenis van de christelijke eredienst in het westen en in het oosten. Een wegwijzer* [Second edition], Hilversum: Gooi en Sticht, 1983, 290 pp.
   Second revised edition of no. 112. Translation: no. 190.

180. Significante effecten van insignificante veranderingen, in *Concilium* 19 (1983) no. 2, 66-71.
   Translations of this article appeared in the different language editions of *Concilium*.
181. Persoonlijke voorkeur: Lied aan het licht, in *Werkschrift voor leerhuis en liturgie* 4 (1983-1984) no. 1, 148-149.
182. [Notice of:] W. Blasig, *Für einen menschengerechten Gottesdienst: Anregungen zur liturgischen Praxis und zur Fortführung der Liturgiereform*, München [...] 1981 [...], in *Tijdschrift voor theologie* 23 (1983) 331.
183. [Notice of:] *Werkboek voor een doopviering*, door de Universitaire Parochie Leuven, Westerlo [...] 1981² [...], in *Tijdschrift voor theologie* 23 (1983) 331.

1984
184. [With L. van Tongeren:] *De kerndagen van het christelijk geloof. Achtergronden van het paasfeest, zoals christenen dat jaarlijks vieren*, Hilversum: Gooi en Sticht, 1984, 46 [, 2] pp.
185. De zesde van de achtste maand, in *Van gerechtigheid tot liturgie* (= Theologie en samenleving), Hilversum: Gooi en Sticht, 1984, 11-21.
186. De geestelijke. Vroeg-middeleeuwse wortels van het traditionele priesterbeeld, in *Tijdschrift voor theologie* 24 (1984) 374-387.
   With a summary in English: Liturgical roots of the traditional view of the priest (387).
187. Inhoudelijke criteria voor het gebruik van Nederlandstalige liturgische gezangen; een voorbeeld, in *Werkmap voor liturgie* 18 (1984) 81-93.
188. [Review of:] G. Lukken, *Geen leven zonder rituelen: Antropologische beschouwingen met het oog op de christelijke liturgie* [...] Baarn [...] 1984 [...], in *Tijdschrift voor theologie* 24 (1984) 430.
189. [Notice of:] *Oecumenische Liturgie: Handreiking bij samenstellen van oecumenische diensten*, door T. Exel-Wieninga e.a., Assen [...] 1983 [...], in *Tijdschrift voor theologie* 24 (1984) 437.

1985
190. *Christian worship in East and West. A study guide to liturgical history*, New York: Pueblo, 1985, xvii, 390 pp.
   Translation of no. 179. Translated by Gordon W. Lathrop.
191. De liturgie is geen huis geworden om in te wonen (= Verder met Vaticanum II), in *De bazuin* 68 (1985) no. 39, 1-2.
192. De komaf van het liturgisch gedenken. Anamnese gespiegeld aan menselijk ervaren, in *Tijdschrift voor theologie* 25 (1985) 163-175.
   With a summary in English: The background of the anamnesis in the liturgy (174-175).
193. [With Gerard Lukken:] De viering van Pasen, in *Werkmap liturgie* 19 (1985) 353-363.
194. Verbaal, in *Werkschrift voor leerhuis en liturgie* 6 (1985-1986) no. 1, 31.
195. Bien étonné, in *Werkschrift voor leerhuis en liturgie* 6 (1985-1986) no. 2, 35-36.
196. Positie, in *Werkschrift voor leerhuis en liturgie* 6 (1985-1986) no. 3, 36-38.
197. [Review of:] Auf der Maur, Hansjörg. *Feiern im Rhythmus der Zeit I* [...] Regensburg [...] 1983 [...], in *Bijdragen. Tijdschrift voor filosofie en theologie* 46 (1985) 206.
198. [Review of:] J.D. Laurance, *'Priest' as Type of Christ: The Leader of the Eucha-*

rist in Salvation History according to Cyprian of Carthage [...] New York [...] 1984 [...], in *Tijdschrift voor theologie* 25 (1985) 423.

1986

199. Theologie en piëteit, in *De gelovige Thomas. Beschouwingen over de hymne Sacris sollemniis van Thomas van Aquino* (= Annalen van het Thijmgenootschap 74, 2), Baarn: Ambo 1986, 36-49.
200. De datum van Pasen, in *Hervormd Utrecht* 1986, 552-553.
201. Bidprentjes als liturgische bron. De mentaliteitsgeschiedenis (Kort verslag derde sessie), in *Jaarboek voor liturgie-onderzoek* 2 (1986) 22-31.
202. Aan de hand van Ida Gerhardt, in *Werkschrift voor leerhuis en liturgie* 6 (1985-1986) no. 4, 25-28.
203. 'Het andere', in *Werkschrift voor leerhuis en liturgie* 6 (1985-1986) no. 5, 21-23.
204. De schriftuitleg wordt verzorgd door..., in *Werkschrift voor leerhuis en liturgie* 7 (1986-1987) no. 1, 8-9.
205. Speciale talenten, in *Werkschrift voor leerhuis en liturgie* 7 (1986-1987), no. 2, 22-23.
206. [Review of:] Kleinheyer, Bruno; Emmanuel v. Severus; Reiner Kaczynski. *Sakramentliche Feiern II* [...] Regensburg [...] 1984 [...], in *Bijdragen. Tijdschrift voor filosofie en theologie* 47 (1986) 79-80.
207. [Review of:] G. Martelet, *Deux mille ans d'Eglise en question: Crise de la foi, crise du prêtre*, Parijs [...] 1984 [...], in *Tijdschrift voor theologie* 26 (1986) 96-97.
208. [Review of:] A. Adam, *Grundriss Liturgie*, Freiburg/Bazel/Wenen [...] 1985 [...], in *Tijdschrift voor theologie* 26 (1986) 316-317.
209. [Review of:] A. Bouley, *From Freedom to Formula* [...] Washington DC 1981, in *Vigiliae christianae* 40 (1986) 192-193.
210. [Review of:] A. Gerhards, *Die griechische Gregoriosanaphora* [...] Münster [...] 1984 [...], in *Vigiliae christianae* 40 (1986) 304-305.
211. [Review of:] *The Origins of the Liturgical Year.* By Thomas J. Talley. New York [...] 1986 [...], in *Worship* 60 (1986) 461-463.
212. [Notice of:] *Theologie und Ästhetik*, Hrsg. G. Pöltner/H. Vetter, Wenen/Freiburg/Basel [...] 1985 [...], in *Tijdschrift voor theologie* 26 (1986) 324.
213. [Notice of:] *De liturgische viering op zondag* [...] Leuven/Amersfoort [...] 1985 [...], in *Tijdschrift voor theologie* 26 (1986) 324.

1987

214. Dit is uw opgang naar Jerusalem, waar Gij uw vrede stelt voor onze ogen, vrede aan allen die uw naam verhogen: heden hosanna, morgen kruisigt Hem! (W. Barnard). De liturgie van Palmzondag, in *Jaarboek voor liturgie-onderzoek* 3 (1987) 1-40.
    With a summary in English (39-40).
215. De eerste en de laatste, in *Liturgiekrant. Pax Christi/InterKerkelijk Vredesberaad* 1987, 3.
216. De la pesanteur de la liturgie catholique romain, in *Praxis juridique et religion* 4 (1987) 168-175.
217. Ik zag een troon, in *Schrift* 19 (1987) no. 114, 235-237.
218. Klemtoon, in *Werkschrift voor leerhuis en liturgie* 7 (1986-1987) no. 3, 23-24.
219. Het moest niet mogen, in *Werkschrift voor leerhuis en liturgie* 7 (1986-1987) no. 4, 23-24.
220. In alle talen, in *Werkschrift voor leerhuis en liturgie* 7 (1986-1987) no. 5, 16-17.

11

221. Dank je feestelijk, in *Werkschrift voor leerhuis en liturgie* 8 (1987-1988) no. 2, 7-9.

222. [Review of:] W. Rordorf, *Liturgie, foi et vie des premiers chrétiens: Études patristiques* [...] Parijs [...] 1986 [...], in *Tijdschrift voor theologie* 27 (1987) 110.

223. [Review of:] *Liturgie – ein vergessenes Thema der Theologie?*, Hrsg. K. Richter [...] Freiburg/Bazel/Wenen [...] 1986 [...], in *Tijdschrift voor theologie* 27 (1987) 218.

224. [Review of:] *Die Feier der Sakramente in der Gemeinde: Festschrift für Heinrich Rennings*, Hg. M. Klöckener/W. Glade, Kevelaer [...] 1986 [...], in *Tijdschrift voor theologie* 27 (1987) 420.

225. [Notice of:] *Ambt en avondmaalsmijding: Herderlijk schrijven van de generale synode der Nederlandse Hervormde Kerk ten aanzien van avondmaalsmijding door gemeenteleden en ambtsdragers*, 's-Gravenhage [...] 1986 [...], in *Tijdschrift voor theologie* 27 (1987) 427.

226. [Notice of:] F. Reckinger, *Gott begegnen in der Zeit: Unser Kirchenjahr*, Paderborn [...] 1986 [...], in *Tijdschrift voor theologie* 27 (1987) 427.

227. [Notice of:] W. Barnard, *Hebdomadarium of Zevendagenboek – Een dagboek bij de Schriftlezingen uit het aloude brevier: Lezingen voor de zomertijd, de eerste helft/de tweede helft* [...] Voorburg [...] 1986 [...], in *Tijdschrift voor theologie* 27 (1987) 427-428.

1988

228. Het doopsel van kinderen volgens de Romeinse ritus, in A. Blijlevens, W. Boelens and G. Lukken (eds.): *Dopen met water en geest. Doopliturgieën, elementen voor vieringen en achtergrondbeschouwingen uit 20 jaar werkmap Liturgie (1966-1985)*, Hilversum: Gooi en Sticht, 1988, 30-43.
Same contribution: no. 135.

229. Erkenning en verkenning, in *Toespraken academische zitting 1988*, Utrecht: Katholieke Theologische Universiteit Utrecht, 1988, 3-13.

230. De Romeinse euchologie in de Quadragesima. Verandering van paradigma?, in *Jaarboek voor liturgie-onderzoek* 4 (1988) 5-40.
With a summary in English (39-40).

231. De gebeden van de paastijd in het missaal van 1970. Tekstanalyse in het kader van liturgie als verbeelding van geloof, in *Tijdschrift voor theologie* 28 (1988) 349-370.
With a summary in English: The prayers for Easter in the Roman Missal of 1970: Analysis and evaluation (370).

232. Het jaar van de burger en van de gelovige, in *Werkmap voor liturgie* 22 (1988) 78-87.

233. [Review of:] H. Zweck, *Osterlobpreis und Taufe: Studien zu Struktur und Theologie des Exultet und anderer Osterpraeconien unter besonderer Berücksichtigung der Taufmotive* [...] Frankfurt/Bern/New York [...] 1986 [...], in *Tijdschrift voor theologie* 28 (1988) 322-323.

234. [Review of:] K. Küppers, *Diözesan-, Gesang- und Gebetbücher des deutschen Sprachgebietes im 19. und 20. Jahrhundert* [...] Münster [...] 1987 [...], in *Tijdschrift voor theologie* 28 (1988) 412.

1989

235. 'Schau, der Bräutigam! Geht aus, ihm zu begegnen!' Die Theologie der Vigil, in Martin Klöckener and Heinrich Rennings (eds.): *Lebendiges Stundengebet. Vertiefung und Hilfe* (= Pastoralliturgische Reihe in Verbindung mit der Zeitschrift 'Gottesdienst'), Freiburg-Basel-Wien: Herder, 1989, 442-461.

236. De witte hostie, in R.E.V. Stuip and C. Vellekoop (eds.), *Licht en donker in de Middeleeuwen* (= Utrechtse bijdragen tot de mediëvistiek 9), Utrecht: H&S, 1989, 107-120.

237. De toekomst van de theologiebeoefening in Nederland, in *Verslag van Stegonsymposium over het verkenningsrapport Godgeleerdheid. 19 mei 1989*, Den Haag: Stegon, 1989, 28-31.

238. De Eerste Dag na twaalf jaren, in *De Eerste Dag* 12 (1989) no. 3, 1-4. Same article: nos. 239, 243.

239. 'De Eerste Dag' na twaalf jaren, in *Eredienstvaardig* 5 (1989) 66-71. Same article: nos. 238, 243.

240. De moeder van de nachtwaken: de vigilie van pasen, in *Eredienstvaardig* 5 (1989) 293-297.

241. Aankomst en toekomst. Theologie van de advent, in *Jaarboek voor liturgieonderzoek* 5 (1989) 165-188.
With a summary in English: Coming: theology of Advent (188).

242. Het laat-middeleeuwse lijdensverhaal. Verslag studiedag liturgiedocenten 14 juni 1989; De heimelike passie, in *Jaarboek voor liturgie-onderzoek* 5 (1989) 333-334; 353-361.
With a summary in English (361).

243. De Eerste Dag na twaalf jaren, in *Kosmos en oecumene* 23 (1989) 102-109. Same article: nos. 238, 239.

244. Steenrots en stroom, in *Mara* 3 (1989-1990) no. 1, 21-25.

245. De eerste en de achtste dag. De viering van de zondag, in *Schrift* 21 (1989) no. 121, 20-24.

246. Duplex ordo, een simpele keus, in *Wending. Tijdschrift voor evangelie, cultuur en samenleving* 44 (1989) 256-260.

247. [Review of:] K.-P. Jörns, *Der Lebensbezug des Gottesdienstes: Studien zu seinem kirchlichen und kulturellen Kontext*, München [...] 1988 [...], in *Tijdschrift voor theologie* 29 (1989) 191.

248. [Review of:] C. Grethlein: *Taufpraxis heute: Praktisch-theologische Überlegungen zu einer theologisch verantworteten Gestaltung der Taufpraxis im Raum der EKD*, Gütersloh [...] 1988 [...], in *Tijdschrift voor theologie* 29 (1989) 313.

249. [Notice of:] F. Stuhlhofer, *Symbol oder Realität? Taufe und Abendmahl* [...] Berneck [...] 1988 [...], in *Tijdschrift voor theologie* 29 (1989) 207.

APPENDIX: EUCHARISTIC PRAYERS

Two eucharistic prayers written by professor Wegman were printed in different missals and collections. Here we list those publications in which we found a revised version as well as the German translation of one of the prayers.

A. 'Waardig zijt Gij onze lofprijzing te ontvangen'/ 'Waardig zijt Gij, dat wij U aanbidden'.

250. Proeve van een anaphora, te gebruiken tijdens de eucharistieviering op een zondag, in *Tijdschrift voor liturgie* 51 (1967) 99-108.

251. Verbeterde proeve..., in *Tijdschrift voor liturgie* 51 (1967) 254-255.
Revised version of no. 250.

252. Eucharistisch gebed XVI, in *Missaal, deel 1: Ordo missae*, s.1.: Nederlandse Commissie voor Liturgie, 1969, 140-145.
    Revised version of no. 251.

253. Kanon 11 (Höllandischer Kanon 16), in *Elf Eucharistie Gebete (Holländische Kanontexte)*. Deutsche Studienausgabe von Alfred Schilling, Essen: Driewer, 1972, 44-47.
    German translation of the text of no. 252. The translator used the text printed in *11 eucharistische gebeden (Nederlandse canons)*, Hilversum: Gooi en Sticht, 1970.

254. Eucharistische gebeden: [F], in *Missaal voor zon- en feestdagen*, Utrecht: Nationale Raad voor Liturgie, 1973, 985-988.
    Revised version of no. 252.

255. *Eucharistisch gebed. God van mensen*. Tekst: Herman Wegman. Muziek: Floris van der Putt. Voor celebrant, gemengd koor, volkszang en orgel, Hilversum: Gooi en Sticht, 1975, 8 pp.
    Issued simultaneously in two formats.
    Revised version of no. 254, with musical notation.

B. 'Heer God, almachtige Vader, U prijzen en aanbidden wij'.

256. [Unsigned:] Eucharistische gebeden: [H] (naar de Anaphora van St. Jacobus), in *Missaal voor zon- en feestdagen*, Utrecht: Nationale Raad voor Liturgie, 1973, 990-991.

Les transformations du rôle liturgique du peuple: la contribution de la sémiotique à l'histoire de la liturgie[1]

GERARD LUKKEN

En 1986 Herman Wegman a écrit que son initiation à l'histoire des mentalités imposait l'apprentissage d'une nouvelle méthode de recherche.[2] Cette nouvelle méthode de recherche prit forme entre autres dans son programme de recherche 'Contributions héortologiques'. En outre, ces dernières années Herman Wegman portait de l'intérêt à la sémiotique, tant à celle d'A.J. Greimas[3] qu'à celle de C.S. Peirce.[4] Mais cet intérêt ne serait pas approfondi. Pour l'historien de la liturgie le chemin de l'histoire des mentalités devait être plus évident.

Alors, dans cette contribution-ci je veux mettre en rapport les deux domaines d'études, celui de la sémiotique et celui de l'histoire. Je veux montrer ce que la sémiotique, en particulier celle de Greimas et de son école de Paris, pourrait apporter à l'histoire des mentalités. Je vais illustrer cet apport à l'aide de la thématique de ce recueil.[5]

1. LA SÉMIOTIQUE ET L'HISTOIRE DES MENTALITÉS

En 1981 W. Frijhoff a publié un article, *Van 'histoire de l'église' naar 'histoire religieuse'* (De l''histoire de l'église' à l''histoire religieuse').[6] Dans cet article il encourageait ses collègues, historiens néerlandais, de prendre plus d'intérêt à l'histoire des mentalités. Il signalait l'influence du structuralisme sur l'histoire

---

1. Je veux exprimer ma reconnaissance à Laetitia van den Heuvel et Frans Hoppenbrouwers qui ont corrigé ma traduction.
2. H.A.J. Wegman: De mentaliteitsgeschiedenis, dans *Jaarboek voor liturgie-onderzoek* 2 (1986) 22-31, p. 23.
3. Comparez la thèse chez H. Wegman de L. van Tongeren: *Semiotische tekstanalyse. De beschrijving en bestudering van een structurele analysemethode en een toepassing daarvan op de poëtische tekst van de eerste prefatie van pasen* (Thèse Katholieke Theologische Hogeschool Utrecht, pro manuscripto) (Utrecht 1981).
4. H. Wegman: The rubrics of the institution-narrative in the Roman Missal 1970, dans P. Jounel, R. Kaczynski et G. Pasqualetti (éds.): *Liturgia opera divina e umana: Studi sulla riforma liturgica offerti a S.E. Mons. Annibale Bugnini in occasione del suo 70° compleanno* (Roma 1982) 319-328.
5. Pour les concepts de la sémiotique d'A.J. Greimas, voir: A.J. Greimas et J. Courtés: *Sémiotique. Dictionnaire raisonné de la théorie du langage* 1-2 (Paris 1979-1986); G. Lukken (éd.): *Semiotiek en christelijke uitingsvormen. De semiotiek van A.J. Greimas en de Parijse school toegepast op bijbel en liturgie* (Hilversum 1987).
6. W. Frijhoff: Van 'histoire de l'église' naar 'histoire religieuse'. De invloed van de 'Annales'-groep op de ontwikkeling van de kerkgeschiedenis in Frankrijk en de perspectieven daarvan voor Nederland, dans *Nederlands archief voor kerkgeschiedenis* 61 (1981) 113-153.

des mentalités et son intérêt pour les structures de surface et les structures profondes de l'histoire. Pourtant la sémiotique comme telle n'est pas mentionnée dans cet article et j'ai d'ailleurs l'impression qu'elle continue de jouer même aujourd'hui un rôle minime dans l'histoire des mentalités de notre pays. Mais, c'est précisément la sémiotique et spécialement celle de l'école de Paris qui signale fréquemment qu'elle peut contribuer d'une façon pertinente à l'histoire des mentalités.[7] Mais de la part des historiens le malentendu persiste que la sémiotique ne s'intéresse qu'à la synchronie et qu'elle ne peut pas contribuer pour cette raison à la discipline de l'histoire. D'abord je veux discuter ce malentendu et ensuite je vais tracer le chemin à parcourir d'une façon plus positive.

1.1. La synchronie et la diachronie

A juste titre on peut se demander comment un système d'analyse dont le caractère essentiel est la synchronie, pourrait-il se rendre compte de son contraire qui est la diachronie. D'abord il faut remarquer l'existence d'un malentendu réel. Si l'on suppose que la synchronie concerne l'ensemble d'événements ayant lieu en même temps, dans ce cas-là, la description d'une synchronie impliquerait, à la limite, l'enregistrement de toutes les paroles prononcées et de tous les actes accomplis, dans un même instant, par des milliers de sujets.[8] Mais chez F. de Saussure cela n'a jamais été l'objet de la synchronie. Selon lui elle a pour objet tous les éléments et tous les facteurs qui appartiennent à un seul et même moment d'une seule et même langue, c'est à dire à un seul état de cette langue.[9] La diachronie au contraire fait intervenir des éléments et facteurs appartenant à des différents états de développement d'une même langue.[10]

Greimas indique que le concept de synchronie n'a été opératoire que dans la mesure où elle a permis de fonder celui de système linguistique conçu comme une organisation interne. Et Haidu signale qu'il s'agit du caractère synchronique du procès dans lequel on comprend la signification des événements successifs.[11] La synchronie concerne la simultanéité des relations qui indiquent les différences et qui constituent la signification. La signification est constituée par la coprésence des éléments qui signifient: *any grasp of meaning per se is a shift of the sequential, the temporal, into a synchronic and atemporal mode of*

---

7. A.J. GREIMAS: Sur l'histoire événementielle et l'histoire fondamentale, dans A.J. GREIMAS: *Sémiotique et sciences sociales* (Paris 1976) 161-174, p. 162; P. HAIDU: Semiotics and history, dans *Semiotica* 40 (1982) 187-228, p. 222; P. HAIDU: La sémiotique socio-historique, dans H. PARRET et G. RUPRECHT (éds.): *Exigences et perspectives de la sémiotique. Recueil d'hommages pour Algirdas Julien Greimas* 1 (Amsterdam 1985) 215-228, p. 225.
8. A.J. GREIMAS: Structure et histoire, dans A.J. GREIMAS: *Du sens. Essais sémiotiques* (Paris 1970) 103-115, p. 107.
9. GREIMAS et COURTÉS: *Sémiotique. Dictionnaire raisonné* 1, 97-98 et 374 (s. vv. Diachronie et Synchronie); O. DUCROT et T. TODOROV: *Dictionnaire encyclopédique des sciences du langage* (Paris 1972) 178.
10. DUCROT et TODOROV: *Dictionnaire encyclopédique* 189-190.
11. HAIDU: Semiotics and history 189.

understanding.[12] Il est intéressant de constater que Haidu a introduit en dehors du terme synchronique le terme achronique (atemporel). Alors Greimas estime que la notion de synchronie est vraiment imprécise et qu'elle n'est plus opératoire. Il faut la remplacer par la notion d'achronie.[13] Les structures sémiotiques profondes ont un caractère atemporel. Cela peut être éclairci à l'aide du carré sémiotique qui montre la structure de la signification au niveau profond. Le carré sémiotique est la représentation atemporelle des valeurs en relation de contrariété (A ↔ B), de subcontrariété (B̄ ↔ Ā), de contradiction (A ↔ Ā et B ↔ B̄) et d'implication (B ← Ā et A ← B̄):[14]

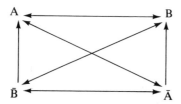

Maintenant on pourrait se poser la question suivante: comment un système de valeurs achronique peut-il se rendre compte de la diachronie, la diachronie étant tellement caractéristique pour l'histoire? Avec Haidu on pourrait répondre de la façon suivante: le carré sémiotique est à la fois une représentation atemporelle et une représentation d'une dynamique.[15] Dans l'ordre épistémologique, l'analyse procède par réductions successives des moments temporels, jusqu'à ce qu'elle atteigne le noeud des moments essentiels à la systématisation logique de l'histoire. Le carré sémiotique incorpore simultanément la captation statique-achronique des valeurs qui sont en jeu et en conflit, ainsi que la virtualité de leur dynamique, c'est-à-dire le potentiel de leur actualisation en suite conflictuelle et narrative selon la syntaxe profonde. Ainsi le carré sémiotique montre aussi la structure élémentaire des opérations et des transformations narratives. Dans le carré sémiotique on peut lire comment il y a des transformations d'une valeur à l'autre: de A via Ā à B et de B via B̄ à A. Ainsi le carré sémiotique est la conjonction de l'analyse achronique et de l'analyse diachronique, introduisant le concept même de l'histoire. On se trouve devant un tableau achronique qui est traversé par des lignes de forces constitutives du développement proprement historique. De cette manière l'ensemble d'étapes statiques et dynamiques du carré sémiotique représente le processus historique. Car, dans le conflit interne des éléments historiques, où l'un succède à l'autre, leur coprésence doit, par définition, précéder la victoire de l'un sur l'autre.[16]

12. HAIDU: Semiotics and history 189.
13. GREIMAS et COURTÉS: Sémiotique. Dictionnaire raisonné 1, 2 et 374 (s. vv. Achronie et Synchronie); GREIMAS: Structure et histoire 107-108.
14. LUKKEN: Semiotiek en christelijke uitingsvormen 48-49.
15. HAIDU: La sémiotique socio-historique 224-225.
16. HAIDU: La sémiotique socio-historique 225.

1.2. L'histoire événementielle

Frijhoff fait remarquer que l'histoire des mentalités s'oppose à une conception courante de l'histoire qui la considère comme un simple enchaînement d'événements isolés et d'individus et d'institutions particuliers.[17] Du point de vue de la sémiotique l'histoire événementielle se déroule au niveau de la manifestation c'est-à-dire au niveau immédiatement aperçu. Une infinité de micro-événements se produit à ce niveau, par milliers, à chaque instant et partout. Cette infinité n'est pas susceptible d'une description exhaustive ou systématique, quelle qu'elle soit.[18]

A partir de cette multiplicité de micro-faits l'historien effectue une sélection d'événements qu'il juge significatifs et qui acquièrent ainsi la dignité d'événements historiques. L'enchaînement de ces événements historiques constitue l'histoire événementielle. Elle est située à un niveau plus abstrait que le niveau de la manifestation. Dans le parcours génératif de Greimas on peut situer l'histoire événementielle au niveau de surface.[19] Ce niveau de surface est situé entre le niveau de la manifestation et le niveau profond qui est le niveau de l'histoire fondamentale. Dans le parcours génératif, entre le niveau de surface et le niveau de la manifestation, on trouve encore le niveau des structures discursives. C'est à ce niveau qu'il faut situer la thématisation qui touche en partie les questions du rôle thématique dont nous parlerons ci-dessous.

Greimas a élaboré un métalangage. A l'aide de ce métalangage il est possible d'analyser d'une façon plus précise le niveau de surface de l'histoire.[20] Le point de départ de ce métalangage est cette question-ci: quels sont les éléments constitutifs de l'événement historique?

Il y en a qui estiment que l'événement historique est constitué par l'inscription des événements dans leurs coordonnées spatio-temporelles. Cependant cela ne suffit pas. Le temps et l'espace ne sont, pour employer un terme linguistique, que les circonstants de ces événements. Ils ne déterminent pas la signification de l'événement historique d'une manière constitutive. Ils peuvent être totalement absents et souvent ils sont trop imprécis. Si la mesure quantitative des événements, construit à l'aide du temps chronométrique, est possible dans certains cas, il n'en est plus de même de la mensuration de l'espace en latitudes et longitudes. Car toute introduction d'indications topologiques constitue une référence à des entités sociologiques et non à la coordonnée spatiale abstraite. Il est donc nécessaire de distinguer l'événement historique de son ancrage dans le temps et l'espace.

D'autres par contre prétendent que l'événement historique peut être défini comme une dénotation de la réalité. Mais c'est une prétention positiviste. Les choses ne sont pas d'une telle simplicité. La réalité historique comme telle

---

17. Frijhoff: Van 'histoire de l'église' naar 'histoire religieuse' 119.
18. Greimas: Sur l'histoire événementielle et l'histoire fondamentale 163.
19. La dénomination 'niveau de surface' peut prêter à confusion. A.J. Greimas n'est pas très satisfait de cette dénomination qui quand-même s'est acclimatée (Greimas et Courtés: *Sémiotique. Dictionnaire raisonné* 1, 372 (s. v. Surface (structure de)).
20. Greimas: Sur l'histoire événementielle et l'histoire profonde 167-174.

n'est pas présente à l'historien. L'historien ne peut pas connaître la réalité historique que par intermédiaires. Il ne dispose que des textes, des documents et des chroniques d'une certaine époque. Et aussi ces médiations ne sont que des traductions plus ou moins libres des programmes somatiques de sujets réels. Les textes historiques et les textes de l'historien ne sont que des référents des suites événementielles réelles.

Ce qui est constitutif pour l'énoncé historique, ce sont le faire comme fonction (F) et un sujet (S) et un objet (O) de ce faire, reliés entre eux par la fonction de relation ($\rightarrow$):

$$\text{F faire (S} \rightarrow \text{O).}$$

Cette formule ne signifie rien d'autre que: 'quelqu'un fait quelque chose'. Ainsi on peut formuler tous les événements historiques d'une façon univoque et formelle. Ensuite des contenus spécifiques peuvent être investis dans cet énoncé, selon les valeurs qui jouent un rôle décisif.

Il est possible de définir le sujet historique à un niveau individuel, mais aussi à un niveau collectif. Le sujet collectif est l'ensemble des hommes, dans la mesure où ils participent à un faire commun. Il s'agit donc d'un collectif d'hommes considérés seulement en tant qu'agents d'un faire programmé. Lorsque quelqu'un dit que la faculté de théologie fait quelque chose, il veut dire entre autres que le sujet de faire est l'ensemble des hommes dans la mesure où ils participent à un faire commun de cette faculté. De cette façon l'historien peut structurer les différents sujets et anti-sujets et leurs programmes de faire historique selon les différents niveaux: le niveau économique, le niveau social ou le niveau culturel. Du point de vue du sujet collectif on pourrait en outre préciser ce qu'on entend par l'indication de 'la foule'. Quand on parle de la foule (par exemple: la foule dans la rue), il ne s'agit pas là d'une simple collection numérique d'individus. Dans ce cas-là un élément essentiel est l'intégration du vouloir-faire partagé par tous et la constitution d'un pouvoir-faire collectif. Une telle 'foule' peut réaliser un événement historique, parce qu'elle représente un actant collectif – par exemple une classe sociale – dont elle est le mandataire. Ainsi l'attaque et la prise de la Bastille par la foule est un événement historique.

Pour la syntaxe historique l'enchaînement chronologique des événements est moins important que l'enchaînement qui organise les relations causales entre énoncés historiques. Cela veut dire que la présentation de l'histoire sous la forme d'une finalité *a posteriori* à l'heure actuelle semble plus neutre que la présentation chronologique dans laquelle on pourrait facilement lire le *post hoc* comme un *propter hoc*. En effet, la construction de l'histoire est toujours une re-construction qui pénètre dans les profondeurs de l'histoire à partir du *hic et nunc*.

Il n'est pas difficile d'ajouter aux actants du sujet de faire et de l'objet les autres actants du grammaire narratif de l'école de Paris comme le sujet d'état, le destinateur, le destinataire et finalement l'observateur dont nous parlerons encore ci-dessous.[21]

---

21. Lukken: *Semiotiek en christelijke uitingsvormen* 38-40.

1.3. L'histoire fondamentale

Je vous ai parlé du carré sémiotique qui représente au niveau profond le processus historique dans ses étapes statiques et dynamiques. C'est là que le niveau de l'histoire fondamentale, la préoccupation principale de l'histoire des mentalités, est situé. L'histoire fondamentale a pour objet la dimension profonde de l'histoire comme lieu d'organisations taxinomiques des valeurs et comme lieu de transformations structurelles.[22] Ce niveau est donc plus profond et plus abstrait que le niveau de l'histoire événementielle. Au niveau de l'histoire fondamentale il s'agit de ce qu'on appelle couramment les éléments de 'la longue durée' (Braudel): le conflit entre des valeurs plutôt épochales qu'immédiates; on y trouve assez souvent des investissements sémantiques qu'on n'a pu pas formuler à l'époque où le texte lui-même a été écrit.[23]

La notion de 'longue durée' n'est pas opératoire parce qu'elle est trop relative. On peut se poser cette question: quelle est l'amplitude décisive de la longueur d'une durée. Et en outre: pourqoi un événement qui dure longtemps serait-il plus essentiel que celui qui ne dure qu'un instant. Il me semble qu'il vaut mieux parler des valeurs profondes ou structurelles.[24]

Au niveau profond on peut réaliser à la fois un comparatisme historique et achronique entre de différentes structures. Il y a des changements profonds qui consistent en une transformation de structures et en une succession de deux états tout à fait différents. On parle d'une rupture dans le cours de l'histoire, dès que le modèle déjà existant ne rend plus compte des événements nouvellement manifestés et qu'un nouveau modèle doit être postulé.[25]

Ultérieurement le niveau profond peut être structuré par la dimension de différents niveaux: le niveau économique, social et culturel. Ce sont aussi le conflit et la coopération de ces différents niveaux, qui jouent un rôle dans l'histoire fondamentale. Selon Greimas plusieurs modèles appartenant d'abord aux différents états et, surtout, aux différents niveaux de l'histoire profonde (le niveau économique et cetera), concourent à produire un événement ou un objet historique. Eh bien, s'il y a plusieurs structures qui convergent en vue de la production d'un même objet événementiel, elles peuvent manifester entre elles des incompatibilités. Il est possible qu'elles s'excluent. Mais elles peuvent partager de vastes espaces de compatibilité aussi. Alors, il paraît que dans ces zones de compatibilité structurale, la liberté historique des hommes est située. C'est dans ces zones-là que les choix originaux de l'histoire se manifestent. C'est par ces vastes zones d'incompatibilité et de compatibilité que les événements historiques peuvent être dits significatifs et qu'ils peuvent être distingués parmi l'infinité de micro-événements quotidiens.[26] C'est ainsi que l'histoire profonde sélectionne les événements selon leur signification

22. GREIMAS: Sur l'histoire événementielle et l'histoire fondamentale 162-163.
23. HAIDU: La sémiotique socio-historique 227.
24. GREIMAS: Structure et histoire 106-107.
25. GREIMAS: Structure et histoire 112.
26. GREIMAS: Sur l'histoire événementielle et l'histoire fondamentale 166-167.

comme des événements historiques. Et l'historien de sa part va chercher à faire une sélection délibérée parmi les innombrables événements et à donner une interprétation correcte des événements et de leur enchaînement qui correspond à ce qui a été inscrit dans l'histoire même.[27]

2. LES TRANSFORMATIONS DU RÔLE LITURGIQUE DU PEUPLE

Je n'ai pas l'intention de faire ici une recherche historique originelle sur le rôle du peuple dans la liturgie du passé. Mon point de départ, c'est l'historiographie. Je pars des données communément acceptées par les historiens de la liturgie. Je veux démontrer que la sémiotique peut contribuer à une meilleure intelligibilité de ces données et qu'elle peut proposer une distribution plus organique de ces données, tout en tenant compte de ce qui est dit ci-dessus sur l'histoire événementielle et l'histoire fondamentale.[28] Cependant l'ampleur de cet article ne me permettra pas d'élaborer tous les éléments mentionnés dans la première partie. Mais ce que je ferai sera suffisant pour notre projet.

2.1. L'église ancienne
Dans son livre *La liturgie des premiers siècles jusqu'à l'époque de Grégoire le Grand* J. Jungmann écrit:[29]

Le grand changement qui intervient dans la pratique liturgique, le plus grand changement peut-être dans toute l'histoire de la messe fut l'abandon du repas comme support de celle-ci. Avec l'enrichissement progressif de la prière d'action de grâces, et, en même temps, l'accroissement continu par les conversions de communautés qui devenaient trop importantes pour se réunir autour de la table familiale, le repas caractéristique de l'assemblée chrétienne pouvait disparaître, et disparut en effet, et la célébration devint réellement une célébration eucharistique. Ce changement s'était déjà produit vers la fin du premier siècle.

Ce changement entraîne à sa suite de grandes modifications dans la forme extérieure de la célébration. Les tables disparurent de la salle, toutes excepté celle où présidait l'évêque ou le prêtre. La salle à manger s'élargit en une salle suffisamment vaste pour contenir toute la communauté, avec pour centre d'intérêt la table unique qui était maintenant de façon plus évidente la table du Seigneur, la *mensa Domini*: l'autel. Les participants ne furent plus couchés ou assis pour le souper; ils devinrent les *circumstantes*, debout devant Dieu pour le culte. Et l'idéal, déjà formulé par saint Ignace au début du second siècle, fut pour tous de se rassembler pour une Eucharistie commune.

---

27. GREIMAS: Sur l'histoire événementielle et l'histoire fondamentale 163.
28. Je veux signaler ici l'analyse intéressante du livre de J. DELUMEAU: *Le péché et la peur. La culpabilisation en Occident: XIIe-XVIIIe siècles* (Paris 1983) par J. COURTÉS dans son article: Sémiotique et théologie du péché, dans H. PARRET et G. RUPRECHT (éds.): *Exigences et perspectives de la sémiotique. Recueil d'hommages pour Algirdas Julien Greimas* 2 (Amsterdam 1985) 863-903.
29. J. JUNGMANN: *La liturgie des premiers siècles jusqu'à l'époque de Grégoire le Grand* (Lex orandi 33) (Paris 1962) 66. (Édition originale: *The early liturgy to the time of Gregory the Great* (Notre Dame 1959).)

J. Jungmann suggère que dans l'église ancienne des transformations historiques se sont réalisées, qui touchent l'histoire fondamentale. Elles peuvent être
placées dans un carré sémiotique:

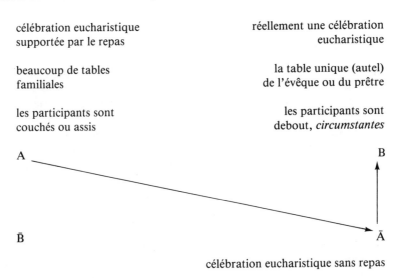

célébration eucharistique supportée par le repas	réellement une célébration eucharistique
beaucoup de tables familiales	la table unique (autel) de l'évêque ou du prêtre
les participants sont couchés ou assis	les participants sont debout, *circumstantes*

A   B

B̄   Ā

célébration eucharistique sans repas

La première transformation est celle de la célébration supportée par le repas
ou dans le cadre d'un repas (A)[30] à une célébration sans repas (Ā) qui est
nommée réellement une célébration eucharistique (B). H. Wegman parle de la
transformation du repas eucharistique à un repas rituel et une consommation
rituelle.[31]

La deuxième transformation est celle de plusieurs tables à une table unique
du président: l'autel, de A via Ā à B.

La troisième transformation est celle des participants couchés ou assis à des
participants qui restent debout autour de la table unique, de A via Ā à B.

Quant à notre thématique la deuxième et la troisième transformation qui
sont liées l'une à l'autre, sont d'importance. Là il s'agit du rôle du peuple. La
sémiotique distingue le rôle actantiel et le rôle thématique. Le rôle actantiel
concerne les positions syntaxiques comme sujet de faire, sujet d'état, objet,
destinateur, destinataire et observateur. Le rôle thématique est la formulation
actantielle de thèmes ou de parcours thématiques au niveau des structures discursives: par exemple le parcours thématique royal, pastoral et cetera devient
actantiellement le rôle du roi, du pasteur et cetera.[32]

Quant au rôle actantiel on trouve un sujet de faire collectif. Là il s'agit de

30. JUNGMANN: *La liturgie des premiers siècles* 54.
31. H. WEGMAN: *Geschiedenis van de christelijke eredienst in het westen en in het oosten. Een wegwijzer* (Hilversum 1983²) 40.
32. GREIMAS et COURTÉS: *Sémiotique. Dictionnaire raisonné* 1, 318-319 (s. v. Rôle).

l'ensemble des chrétiens dans la mesure où ils participent au faire liturgique. Le sujet collectif participe d'une façon active au repas eucharistique, seulement rituel ou non. Le sujet collectif est un sujet de faire qui est lié à un autre sujet de faire à savoir le président du repas, qui est en même temps le destinateur du faire du peuple qui est, de sa part, le destinataire.

Le rôle thématique du peuple est de rester debout autour de la table: *circumstantes*; la source originelle parle de *circumadstantes*.[33] Ce terme-ci semble indiquer que le peuple se trouvait non seulement autour de l'autel, mais aussi tout près de l'autel. Au lieu du rôle on parle souvent de la 'place' du peuple. Dans cette expression 'place' est une métaphore avec des connotations spatiales. Mais il s'agit de plus que d'une métaphore dans notre cas. Le rôle thématique indiqué du peuple implique la topologie du peuple dans la célébration eucharistique et en outre la proxémique qui vise les dispositions des sujets et objets dans l'espace.

Alors, selon Jungmann, dans le cadre de la transformation du repas réel au repas rituel qu'il caractérise comme 'peut-être le plus grand changement dans toute l'histoire de la messe', il y a aussi une 'grande' modification du rôle du peuple. La sémiotique pourrait éclaircir cet adjectif 'grande' qui est assez flou et vague.

Il est évident qu'on ne peut pas parler d'une modification du rôle actantiel du peuple. Tant au repas eucharistique qu'à l'eucharistie réduite à sa fonction rituelle, le peuple est le sujet de faire et le destinataire. Le changement doit donc se rapporter au rôle thématique. Ce rôle touche le parcours thématique du niveau des structures discursives; au niveau de surface il concerne – en plus du rôle actantiel et précisément dans la ligne de la thématique, mais d'une façon plus abstraite – la valeur investie dans l'objet; et au niveau profond il touche la taxinomie des valeurs. Eh bien, puisque le rôle thématique est indiqué d'une façon topologique et proxémique, c'est à partir de la sémiotique de l'espace qu'on pourrait éclaircir cette modification.

Par le moyen de l'induction, c'est-à-dire en étudiant des discours concrets, la sémiotique de l'espace distingue trois différentes configurations: a) la configuration contractuelle, b) la configuration polémique et c) la configuration polémique-contractuelle.[34]

a) La configuration contractuelle a la forme d'une cercle ou d'un carré autour d'une place vide. En dessin avec les variantes:

33. B. Botte: *Le canon de la messe romaine. Édition critique, introduction et notes* (Textes et études liturgiques 2) (Louvain 1935) 32.
34. Comparez G. Lukken: De semiotiek van de kerkruimte als semiotiek van het visuele, dans *Jaarboek voor liturgie-onderzoek* 5 (1989) 275-299; M. Hammad: L'architecture du thé, dans *Actes sémiotiques. Documents* 9 (1987) no. 84-85, 30-31.

Dans cette configuration contractuelle il y a une juxtaposition topique d'équivalence. Cette position topique est liée aux compétences d'équivalence de ceux qui occupent une place dans la configuration. Ils sont conjoints à cette compétence d'équivalence comme à une valeur investie dans l'objet. Au niveau profond on trouve la taxinomie structurelle d'/égal/ et /inclusif/ versus /hiérarchique/ et /exclusif/.

b) La configuration polémique a la forme de deux topoi face à face qui sont séparés par une ligne de démarcation réelle ou imaginaire.
Schématiquement:

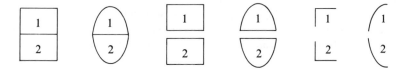

Dans cette configuration il y a une opposition absolue entre les deux topoi. Cette position topique est liée à des compétences opposées de ceux qui occupent les topoi de cette configuration. La compétence de la personne qui se trouve dans le topos 1 est exclusive. La personne qui se trouve dans le topos 1 est conjointe à la compétence comme à une valeur investie dans l'objet et la personne qui se trouve dans le topos 2 en est disjointe. Au niveau profond il y a la taxinomie structurelle de /polémique/ et /exclusif/ versus /égal/ et /inclusif/.

c) La configuration polémique-contractuelle prend forme, quand on remplit la place vide de la configuration contractuelle sous a).
Schématiquement:

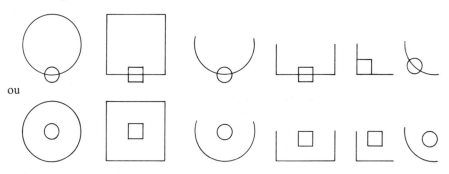

ou

Cette configuration représente une opposition relative. On peut la situer entre la configuration contractuelle et la configuration polémique. D'une part il y a une juxtaposition, d'autre part une opposition. Ces positions sont liées à des compétences qui sont d'une part des compétences d'équivalence et d'autre part des compétences d'opposition. Cela veut dire d'un côté que les sujets sont conjoints à la même compétence comme à une valeur investie dans l'objet, mais de l'autre côté que les sujets sont en opposition et que l'un des sujets est conjoint à une compétence spécifique comme à une valeur dont l'autre est disjoint. Au niveau profond on trouve la taxinomie structurelle d'/égal-polémique/ et /inclusif-exclusif/ soit versus /polémique/ et /exclusif/ soit versus /égal/ et /inclusif/.

Alors, comment me faut-il interpréter le changement du rôle du peuple qui s'est réalisé dans l'église ancienne? Le peuple qui était d'abord couché ou assis autour des tables familiales est ensuite debout autour de la table unique de l'autel. Dans les deux cas on remarque la configuration polémique-contractuelle, comportant sa valeur et sa taxinomie fondamentale. Bien qu'il soint moins marqué, il y a le topos spécial du président du repas encore autour de la table familiale. Le changement du rôle thématique du peuple est donc moins grand et radical que Jungmann ne suggère. Tout au plus on peut dire qu'il y a un changement à l'intérieur de la configuration polémique-contractuelle. Car dans ce modèle-ci il est possible que l'accent porte soit sur le pôle contractuel soit sur le pôle polémique. J'ai l'impression que l'accent est mis sur l'élément contractuel dans l'eucharistie comme repas familial et sur l'élément polémique dans l'eucharistie avec les *circumstantes*. On peut donc parler d'un changement qui est moins important qu'on ne le pense. Ce changement peut être présenté de la façon suivante (de A via Ā à B):

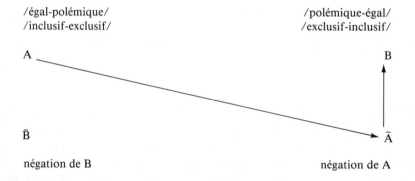

/égal-polémique/
/inclusif-exclusif/

/polémique-égal/
/exclusif-inclusif/

A

B

Ā

Ā

négation de B

négation de A

2.2. L'église du Moyen Age
F. van der Meer a caractérisé la différence entre la liturgie de l'église ancienne et celle du Moyen Age de la façon suivante:[35]

Et tous qui restent dedans pour les mystères saintes, restent debout autour de l'autel [...] Quand le service communal est abandonné au bout de tant de siècles et qu'on ne perçoit plus la communauté qui reste debout et qui écoute autour de l'autel, mais seulement une communauté qui voit et qui écoute ce qui s'accomplit sur l'autel de manière

---

35. F. van der Meer: *Christus' oudste gewaad. Over de oorspronkelijkheid der oud-christelijke kunst* (Utrecht-Brussel 1949) 109.

incompréhensible [...], alors l'autel est déplacé dans le lointain [...] Au début il y avait l'unité: ún autel, ún Seigneur, úne communauté, úne foi. Et le miracle de la basilique était cet espace central unique, vide et rempli, orienté mais s'étendant dans toutes les directions, orienté vers l'orient mais ouvert par un espace qui coule sans fin autour d'un petit autel vide. Et le pain et le vin ne venaient qu'après l'encerclement de l'autel par la *familia dei* et devenait ainsi la table du Seigneur.

Et Th. Klauser a écrit dans une paragraphe de son livre sous le titre 'La décomposition de l'assemblée liturgique':[36]

Bien entendu l'église ancienne avait laissé la direction de l'action liturgique et l'accomplissement des actions décisives consécratoires ou sacramentelles à l'évêque ou à son remplaçant sacerdotal, mais elle n'a jamais abandonné la participation du peuple à la prière et à l'action. Il fallait que le peuple pouvait suivre la prière et l'action dans tous les détails et que de cette manière il était non seulement de simples spectateurs attentifs, mais aussi des partenaires participants [...] La transition à la récitation murmurée inaudible du canon était une démarche d'un poids extrêmement lourd. Le lien entre prêtre et peuple a été rompu sur un point central; la partie décisive de la célébration devenait une affaire exclusive de l'évêque ou du prêtre; le peuple a été forcé dans le rôle du spectateur passif. Et si l'on éliminait le peuple ici, pourquoi ne ferait-on pas disparaître sa participation [...] pendant les parties non-consécratoires aussi? Ainsi on s'est mis en chemin, c'était un chemin plein de conséquences. Et l'évolution ultérieure montre qu'on a suivi conséquemment ce chemin jusqu'au bout.

La célébration eucharistique devenait ainsi un *mysterium depopulatum*.[37] Et le peuple cherchait une issue. Il la trouvait dans la messe allégorique c'est à dire dans la messe comme mystère (représentation dramatique) de la passion, et surtout dans l'élévation de l'hostie, qui a été préscrite en 1209 ou en 1215 par une synode parisienne et qui fut répandue partout en quelques décennies. L'eucharistie serait déterminée essentiellement par l'élévation de l'hostie à partir de ce moment-là jusqu'à Vatican II. La messe était restructurée dans une théophanie visuelle. Et ainsi le peuple trouvait un nouveau rôle: on contemplait l'hostie, montrée par le prêtre, et dans la communion avec les yeux (*Augenkommunion*) le peuple réalisait une *manducatio spiritualis*.[38] Ces changements-ci concernent plusieurs aspects du rôle du peuple. Trois éléments sautent aux yeux: d'abord le changement d'un peuple actif en peuple qui reste plutôt non-actif, puis le changement d'un peuple *circumstans* en peuple *distans*, et finalement le changement d'un peuple pleinement engagé dans l'action

---

36. Th. KLAUSER: *Kleine abendländische Liturgiegeschichte. Bericht und Besinnung* (Bonn 1965) 100-101.
37. A.L. MAYER: Liturgie und Geist der Gothik, dans *Jahrbuch für Liturgiewissenschaft* 6 (1926) 68-97, p. 93; O. NUSSBAUM: *Die Aufbewahrung der Eucharistie* (Bonn 1979) 120; G. SNOEK: *De eucharistie- en reliekverering in de Middeleeuwen. De middeleeuwse eucharistie-devotie en de reliekverering in onderlinge samenhang* (Amsterdam 1989) 50, 371, 385, 390, 396.
38. Comparez entre autres: P. BROWE: *Die Verehrung der Eucharistie im Mittelalter* (München 1933 = 1967ʳ) 46-48; H.B. MEYER: Die Elevation im deutschen Mittelalter und bei Luther, dans *Zeitschrift für katholische Theologie* 85 (1963) 162-217; NUSSBAUM: *Die Aufbewahrung der Eucharistie* 127; SNOEK: *De eucharistie- en reliekverering* 50-53 et 371-373.

liturgique en peuple spectateur. A vue d'oeil on devine ici un changement du rôle du peuple qui est plus grand que celui dans l'église ancienne. Je vais éclaircir cela ci-dessous.

Un changement véritable s'est accompli en ce qui concerne le rôle actantiel, de sorte que le peuple n'est plus le sujet collectif de faire du programme liturgique. Au moins on doit dire que ici se réalise une opposition de contradiction: du sujet opérateur au sujet non-opérateur. Mais ensuite il faut se poser cette question-ci: quel autre rôle actantiel le peuple joue-t-il désormais? Celui de destinataire, celui d'observateur? Peut-être nous pouvons y répondre après avoir éclairci la deuxième et la troisième transformation.

En fait du rôle thématique du peuple il y a une modification des *circumstantes* dans l'ancienne église en *distantes* dans l'église du Moyen Age. Cette modification touche immédiatement la topologie et la proxémique et elle est manifestée d'une façon évidente par l'architecture. Dans l'architecture de l'église ancienne le sanctuaire était en partie impliqué dans la nef, soit dans la basilique romaine, soit la basilique africaine du temps de saint Augustin ou soit la basilique syrienne. Il y avait une disposition intérieure dans laquelle une assemblée hiérarchisée pouvait participer à l'action commune, conformément à l'affirmation de saint Cyprien: 'L'église est un peuple qui ne fait qu'un avec son prêtre.'[39] Cette disposition destinait la proxémique des *circumstantes*, et nous avons vu qu'elle constituait une configuration polémique-contractuelle. Eh bien, les architectes du Moyen Age par contre ont dissocié au maximum le sanctuaire de la nef. On y trouve deux topoi face à face, et une frontière entre les deux qui est fortement marquée par le jubé. Ainsi une transformation s'est accomplie: de la configuration polémique-contractuelle à la configuration polémique. Dans cette configuration seulement la personne qui se trouve dans le sanctuaire, l'évêque ou le prêtre, est conjoint à la valeur de la compétence liturgique. Le peuple *distans* en est disjoint. Au niveau profond on trouve la transformation de /polémique-égal/ et d'/exclusif-inclusif/ à /polémique/ et /exclusif/. C'est vraiment une transformation au niveau de l'histoire fondamentale. La conséquence est que le peuple devient un sujet de faire exclu au niveau événementiel, c'est-à-dire un non-sujet de faire. Ainsi le rôle actantiel, que nous avons formulé en partant de la première transformation, est confirmé par cette transformation. On ne peut pas parler du rôle actantiel que d'une façon négative, comme c'était le cas dans la première transformation: le peuple devient un nón-sujet de faire. Il est donc toujours impossible d'éclaircir le rôle actantiel du peuple d'une manière positive.

La troisième transformation est celle du peuple pleinement engagé dans l'action liturgique au peuple spectateur. Le peuple joue depuis lors le rôle thématique de spectateur. Cela est une transformation radicale.

L'ethnosémiotique et la sociosémiotique distinguent trois phases: la phase

---

39. S. CYPRIEN: Lettre 66, 8: *Ecclesia plebs sacerdoti adunata*. Voir P. JOUNEL: L'assemblée chrétienne et les lieux du rassemblement humain au cours du premier millénaire, dans *La maison-Dieu* 136 (1978) 13-37, p. 26.

du mythique, du folklorique et du spectaculaire.[40] La phase mythique est caractérisée par une participation communautaire. Cette participation communautaire est marquée du syncrétisme des manifestations narratives (récit mythique), poétiques, musicales et gestuelles (la danse, les gestes et cetera). Cette activité mythique n'a pas de spectateurs. Elle n'est pas un spectacle s'adressant à un public et cherchant à communiquer du sens à ceux qui l'observent. Au contraire on y trouve une intentionnalité transformant le monde en tant que telle et s'adressant à un destinateur mythique (Dieu), cherchant à établir et à entretenir avec lui des liens contractuels. Le faire mythique est l'expression d'axiologies collectives et effectue l'intégration de l'individu dans le groupe et l'instauration d'un sujet de faire collectif.

Dans la phase folklorique on ne trouve plus ni récit mythique ni danse sacrée ou musique sacrée. Cette deuxième phase est marquée du conte merveilleux, de la danse folklorique et de la musique folklorique, au lieu du récit mythique, de la danse sacré et de la musique sacré. D'une part cette phase entraîne toujours des éléments mythiques: elle peut comporter un certain faire mythique qui veut réaliser une participation communautaire et qui n'a pas l'intention de communiquer quelque chose. D'autre part on y trouve un spectacle ayant l'intention de communiquer le sens à ceux qui l'observent. On regarde la danse folklorique et on écoute le récit et la musique folklorique.

Les représentants principaux de la phase spectaculaire sont le récit littéraire, le théâtre, le ballet, l'opéra et le film.[41] Ici l'intention primaire est de communiquer du sens aux spectateurs. Le faire sémiotique est détourné en objet d'un regard ou de l'oreille. Chez les spectateurs on trouve l'attitude passive, réceptrice de l'individu. Et, tandis que le mythique est l'expression d'axiologies collectives, le spectaculaire manifeste des systèmes de valeurs individualisées. Dans ce contexte Greimas interprète la réforme liturgique de Vatican II d'une manière précise: c'est la réforme d'une église 'qui cherche à transformer la messe devenue spectacle pur en lui reconférant le statut d'une participation communautaire mythique'.[42] Quant au rôle du peuple la transformation la plus radicale est donc assurément celle qui s'est accomplie au Moyen Age, celle du mythique au spectaculaire. En carré sémiotique: p. 29.

Cette transformation de A via Ā à B est inversée après Vatican II de B en passant de B̄ à A. Pour ma part, je suppose que, dans les phases de transition, aussi les positions de Ā et B̄ ont été dramatisées. Ainsi on peut se rendre compte du fait que l'on trouve des tentatives pour réaliser une liturgie non-mythique (Ā) déjà avant Vatican II et que l'on trouve encore aujourd'hui la

---

40. A.J. GREIMAS: Réflexions sur les objets ethno-sémiotiques, dans GREIMAS: *Sémiotique et sciences sociales* 175-185; A.J. GREIMAS: Conditions d'une sémiotique du monde naturel, dans GREIMAS: *Du sens. Essais sémiotiques* 49-91, p. 79. Ici Greimas fait la même distinction, mais elle est indiquée comme respectivement sacré, ludique et esthétique.
41. GREIMAS et COURTÉS: *Sémiotique. Dictionnaire raisonné* 1, 392-393 (s. v. Théâtrale (sémiotique-)); E. DE KUYPER: *Pour une sémiotique spectaculaire* (Thèse de troisième cycle EHSS, pro manuscripto) (Paris 1979).
42. GREIMAS: Conditions d'une sémiotique du monde naturel 80.

mythique spectaculaire

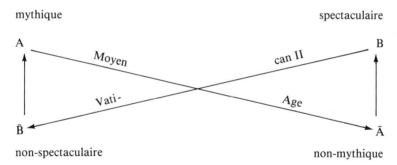

A B

Moyen can II

Vati- Age

B̄ Ā

non-spectaculaire non-mythique

position du non-spectaculaire (B̄) dans la réception de Vatican II, à côté de l'ancienne position B. Je ne peux pas élaborer cette pensée dans le cadre de cet article.

La sémiotique spectaculaire peut éclairer aussi le rôle actantiel du peuple au Moyen Age. Dans la sémiotique spectaculaire il y a trois différents points de vue en ce qui concerne le rôle actantiel du spectateur.

D'abord, Greimas suggère que la communication qui s'accomplit entre les acteurs du spectacle et les spectateurs, est une communication dans laquelle les acteurs sont les destinateurs et les spectateurs sont les destinataires.[43] Le spectateur est un observateur, c'est-à-dire un 'sujet cognitif délégué par l'énonciateur et installé par lui [...] dans le discours-énoncé où il est chargé d'exercer le faire réceptif et, éventuellement, le faire interprétatif'.[44] Les spectateurs sont les destinataires de la manipulation, exercée par les acteurs comme destinateurs.

Un deuxième point de vue est celui de E. de Kuyper.[45] Il nuance les pensées de Greimas. Selon lui, le spectateur est non seulement un destinataire, mais aussi un destinateur qui, en ce qui concerne l'objet spectaculaire, délègue son pouvoir à des représentants spécialistes qui sont les acteurs.[46] Le spectateur est donc plus qu'un réceptacle bienveillant, puisqu'il est également un destinateur. Ainsi dans le spectacle il y a une dynamique participative qui relativise la relation étroitement communicationnelle que l'on suppose en général.[47]

Une troisième opinion importante est celle de S. Alexandrescu.[48] Dans le spectacle il y a une absence de relation entre les acteurs et les spectateurs: aucun énoncé ni verbal ni gestuel ne passe entre eux. Leurs regards ne se croisent pas. Il n'y a pas de communication proprement dite entre l'acteur et

43. GREIMAS: Réflexions sur les objets ethno-sémiotiques 175-185; GREIMAS: Conditions d'une sémiotique du monde naturel 68-82.
44. GREIMAS et COURTÉS: Sémiotique. Dictionnaire raisonné 1, 259-260 (s. v. Observateur).
45. DE KUYPER: Pour une sémiotique spectaculaire.
46. DE KUYPER: Pour une sémiotique spectaculaire 103.
47. DE KUYPER: Pour une sémiotique spectaculaire 104.
48. S. ALEXANDRESCU: Observateur, dans GREIMAS et COURTÉS: Sémiotique. Dictionnaire raisonné 2, 156-158; S. ALEXANDRESCU: L'observateur et le discours spectaculaire, dans: PARRET et RUPRECHT: Exigences et perspectives de la sémiotique 2, 553-574.

29

l'observateur. L'observateur reste à l'extérieur: il ne participe pas à la communication. Dès que l'observateur est manipulé par l'acteur, il entre dans le jeu des autres. Mais, en même temps il cesse d'être observateur et il devient interlocutaire. Donc, du moment que l'acteur et l'observateur se rencontrent vraiment, le statut de l'observateur n'existe plus et ils deviennent interlocuteurs et interlocutaires remplissant respectivement le rôle actantiel de destinateur et de destinataire. Donc, selon Alexandrescu, le spectateur qui n'est qu'une spécification de l'observateur, reste par définition hors du discours spectaculaire. Le spectateur observe toute la situation de communication. C'est un actant spécial, distingué des autres actants comme le sujet de faire, le destinateur et le destinataire.

Lorsqu'on se rend compte du rôle actantiel du peuple dans l'église ancienne, on doit avouer tout au moins qu'une transformation considérable s'est accomplie au Moyen Age. Maintenant il est possible de discuter cette transformation non seulement d'une façon négative, à savoir que le peuple n'est plus sujet de faire, mais aussi d'une façon positive: le peuple devient destinataire ou destinateur/destinataire ou actant observateur, selon le point de vue que l'on adopte. Bien qu'il n'y ait pas d'unanimité dans ce domaine d'études, il faut dire que la sémiotique peut nuancer le parler quelque peu simpliste dans la littérature liturgique courante. Elle invite à une réflexion plus profonde. Il est évident que la transformation selon la troisième opinion (S. Alexandrescu) est plus considérable que la transformation selon la première opinion (A.J. Greimas), et que la transformation la plus modeste est représentée par la deuxième opinion (E. de Kuyper), bien qu'elle soit toujours considérable!

Après avoir mis en évidence les aspects de la thématique que j'ai voulu exposer, je vais terminer cet article, tout en sachant que je n'ai pas pu épuiser le sujet. En ce qui concerne les transformations signalées on pourrait encore étudier la relation précise entre les différents niveaux de l'histoire fondamentale (le niveau économique, social et culturel) et chercher les destinateurs, les sujets de faire, les anti-destinateurs et les anti-sujets de faire de l'histoire événementielle. J'espère quand-même que j'ai pu convaincre le lecteur de la contribution que la sémiotique peut faire à l'histoire de la liturgie.

John Bossy and the study of liturgy[1]

PAUL POST

I. INTRODUCTION

As recent surveys demonstrate, the Dutch study of liturgy is in a state of flux.[2] Though I think it is too early for a balanced analysis of the situation, a few 'lines of force' can be distinguished. In this contribution I would like to follow on these lines, which revolve around two points: on the one hand an upswing in border traffic with other disciplines, on the other hand a shift in the questions and themes presented in research, new phrases being, for instance: 'popular participation in liturgy', 'experience and reception', 'popular religion', 'mentalities', 'bottom-up approaches', 'attention for the average worshipper'.[3] The two points are closely related, while various other lines of development in the Dutch study of liturgy touch on these two aspects in one way or another. However, the relation between the two would be oversimplified by supposing that liturgists were brought into contact with a host of neighbouring fields of scholarship simply by a new phrasing of questions and themes.

A certain distinction in this causal relation could be made by observing that the study's traditional bedding in theological and Church curricula is being questioned. One might say that the study of liturgy has developed a canon, which is indeed reflected in many handbooks, and it is proving hard for new fields of research to become accepted. Moreover, it is the established Christian inner-Church mainstream of worship that forms the core of this canon. A further factor is that liturgists have become aware of the fact that many researchers outside our discipline are devoting themselves to 'our' themes. Philosophers, scholars in the study of religion, anthropologists, folklorists and (European) ethnologists, (art) historians and social scientists have long taken an interest in Christian feasts and rituals in past and present. Yet the study of liturgy has

---

1. A very abridged version of this contribution was presented as a paper on the 12th International Congress of the Societas Liturgica held from August 14 to 19, 1989 at York.
2. G. LUKKEN: Het Genootschap voor Liturgiestudie in een nieuw spanningsveld, in *Jaarboek voor liturgie-onderzoek* 4 (1988) 91-106; G. ROUWHORST: Onderzoeksactiviteiten en -plannen op het terrein van de liturgiewetenschap in Nederland, in *Jaarboek voor liturgie-onderzoek* 1 (1985) 173-185; G. ROUWHORST: Recente ontwikkelingen op het terrein van de liturgiewetenschap en hun mogelijke betekenis voor de liturgische praktijk, in *Tijdschrift voor liturgie* 72 (1988) 382-394.
3. These phrases I took from a journalistic presentation of the heortological research programme directed by H. WEGMAN: Tekst en context van de christelijke feesten, in *KTUU-Info* no. 12 (1989) 10-12.

hardly sought cooperation with other disciplines. Only in a few areas there have been contacts: with the phenomenology of religion and with various disciplines which are concerned with the study of rituals, signs and symbols.[4] Another element in the field of forces between multidisciplinarity and the shifting of questions and themes is the way in which sciences and arts are organized, or rather the way in which they are being reorganized. For reasons of administration as well as content, the academic practice in the Netherlands is in turmoil. Research is being subjected to scrutiny, networks and research groups are set up, research programmes are introduced and so on.

However complex the situation may be, a change in the formulation of questions, in the selection of themes and hence in the source material used, does seem to be decisive for the change in climate in the Dutch study of liturgy. The research of H. Wegman may illustrate this. The Church is no longer assumed to be the only producer of liturgy; it is also being explored now how the celebrators themselves become producers of the ceremony, or in other words, how the process of initiative and reception works out. Unfortunately the balance for the celebrators often turns out to be uncertain: new sources and new methods are called for. The traditional sources do not provide more than indirect information on this point, so the study of liturgy is trying to find partners outside the territory of theology. Summing up, it may be said that on the one hand the ideology and the functions and values of liturgy are explored and on the other hand the way in which people experience liturgical rites and symbols; the question, in short, of functions and values, of initiative and reception.[5]

This question and this balance of the study of liturgy will be the basis for my further reasoning. I would like to center my argument around the work of one

---

4. See in general: G. LUKKEN: *Geen leven zonder rituelen. Antropologische beschouwingen met het oog op de christelijke liturgie* (Baarn 1984); G. LUKKEN: *De onvervangbare weg van de liturgie* (Hilversum 1984²); *Gestalt des Gottesdienstes* (= Gottesdienst der Kirche. Handbuch der Liturgiewissenschaft 3) (Regensburg 1987). Another good example of the border traffic referred to is: W. SENTENIE: *De werkzaamheid van de ritus. Antoon Vergote over structuur en werkzaamheid van de christelijke ritus*, in *Jaarboek voor liturgie-onderzoek* 4 (1988) 41-66. See also the references in P. POST: Het liturgische spel: implikaties en voorwaarden vanuit omgang met symbolen, in *Werkmap voor liturgie* 20 (1986) 157-173. For a summary of the multidisciplinarity referred to, see: P. POST: Onderweg. Tussentijdse notities met betrekking tot bedevaartonderzoek, in M. VAN UDEN and P. POST (eds.): *Christelijke bedevaarten. Op weg naar heil en heling* (Nijmegen 1988) 1-38; P. POST: Bedevaart zonder grenzen, in *Tijdschrift voor liturgie* 73 (1989) 135-156; P. POST: 'Het suizen van een zachte koelte.' Het weer en christelijke rituelen: terreinverkenning en pleidooi voor wetenschappelijk grensverkeer gethematiseerd via palmzondagriten, in *Volkskundig bulletin* 15 (1989) 177-200.
5. Cf. among others H. WEGMAN: De zesde van de achtste maand, in *Van gerechtigheid tot liturgie* (= Theologie en samenleving) (Hilversum 1984) 11-21; H. WEGMAN: De liturgie van palmzondag, in *Jaarboek voor liturgie-onderzoek* 3 (1987) 1-40; H. WEGMAN: De romeinse euchologie in de Quadragesima. Verandering van paradigma?, in *Jaarboek voor liturgie-onderzoek* 4 (1988) 5-40; H. WEGMAN: De gebeden van de paastijd in het missaal van 1970, in *Tijdschrift voor theologie* 28 (1988) 349-370. See for a general sketch POST: 'Het suizen van een zachte koelte' 177-182.

researcher, as I did before with P. Brown and S. Sinding-Larsen.[6] This time I have singled out the work of John Bossy. Through Bossy I want to outline the prospects of border traffic between the studies of liturgy and social history and raise a few fundamental methodical points that one comes across when delving into the roots of liturgy in the experience of people in past and present. Bossy's work is an excellent point of departure because Christian liturgy occupies a key position in his quest for the heart of everyday religious life.

2. BRIEF OUTLINE OF BOSSY'S WORK

My starting-point is a bibliography of 20 titles encompassing the period from 1959 to 1985.[7] I will not go into biographical detail; it is enough to note here that Bossy was born in London in 1933, read history in Cambridge, took his Ph.D. in 1961 and was associated with the Queen's University of Belfast from 1966 to 1978, in which year he was appointed professor of history at the University of York, where he held his inaugural lecture in 1981. His name has long been associated with the famous journal *Past and present*; for years he sat on the editorial board of this journal, which featured several of his important studies.

For further orientation at the present stage I might note that two main lines can be distinguished in his research: first and foremost the history of English Catholicism (roughly speaking from the sixteenth to the eighteenth and nineteenth centuries), and secondly the social history of Western Christianity both before and after the Reformation. To put it in other words: Bossy is concerned with the transition from the later Middle Ages towards the early-modern period, though he may considerably extend this key period in Western history by including in a study an introduction that starts in c. 1200 and an aftermath that runs well into the nineteenth century. One of the central themes in his enquiries is the Roman Catholic liturgy, particularly that of the Counter Reformation. Geographically his focus is on France and (Northern) Italy as

---

6. Cf. P. POST: Heiligen tussen hemel en aarde. Kanttekeningen bij de reconstructie van opkomst, bloei en functie van de laat-antieke heiligencultus door Peter Brown, in *Jaarboek voor liturgie-onderzoek* 2 (1986) 119-162; P. POST: Iconografie en hagiografie. Enige kanttekeningen bij Peter Brown, in A. HILHORST (ed.): *De heiligenverering* (Nijmegen 1988) 193-202; P. POST: Bedevaart, liturgie en artes. Methodische notities vanuit een onderzoeksprogramma bij S. Sinding-Larsen's 'Iconography and Ritual', in *Jaarboek voor liturgie-onderzoek* 3 (1987) 111-138.

7. See annex to this contribution. I have left the numbers 1, 2, 4, 6, 8 and 11 in the context of this contribution out of account. I have used the first edition of no. 13. No. 16 will not be referred to because this study was largely retracted in no. 17. References to Bossy's work in this contribution will be made by a short indication of the title, without year and place of publication. Bossy was brought to my attention through the work of my colleague H. Roodenburg; cf. H. ROODENBURG: 'Splendeur et magnificence.' Processions et autres célébrations à Amsterdam au XVIe siècle, in *Revue du Nord* 69 (1987) no. 274, 515-533; H. ROODENBURG: *Onder censuur. De kerkelijke tucht in de Gereformeerde gemeente van Amsterdam 1578-1700* (Hilversum 1990) (in the press).

well as on England. Two works in his *oeuvre* stand out from all the others: his vast study *The English Catholic community (1570-1850)* from 1975 and the book *Christianity in the West*, which was published ten years later and aimed to present a sort of synthesis of his research since the 1950's.

Bossy's inquiries circle around a fixed set of mainly liturgical themes: the Eucharist (the *canon missae*, the Host, the feast of *Corpus Christi*, the *pax* ritual), confession (sin and penance) and, to a lesser extent, baptism, fraternities, the role and position of the parish church, marriage, pilgrimage, saints and holiness, death and burial rites. His questions always hinge on the relation between religious and social experience. This is most evident in his inaugural speech (1981), in which he successively goes into the concept of 'society', the concept of 'religion' and the relationship between the two. Subsequently he views the phrasing of this question and the objective of his research against the background of processes of cultural change, particularly those in the period of transition from the Middle Ages to early-modern society in Europe. The social history of liturgy presents Bossy with a fruitful line of approach to chart this transformation process.

Meanwhile Bossy's work has also been pigeonholed in many ways. Particularly in critical reviews of *Christianity in the West* labels like 'functionalistic', 'reductionalistic', 'uniformistic' and 'phenomenological' abound.[8] To me it makes little sense to use labels like these, unless they are associated with Bossy's complete *oeuvre* and with a critical presentation of his research design.

3. ELABORATION OF SOME ASPECTS OF BOSSY'S WORK

3.1. Research context and research design

Bossy can be considered an exponent of the broad tradition of social history, which in turn is embedded in a tradition of cultural research. Bossy seems to be in keeping with a number of developments within social history. It was not until relatively late that social history had an eye for religion in general and Christian liturgy in particular. This interest may have been stimulated greatly by the contacts with cultural anthropology, where the investigation of rituals and social change has been prominent since the beginning of this century. Another stimulus has been the increasing tendency for historical research to look at popular culture. Religious image and rituals prove to be an extremely valuable line of approach here. Evidently this links up with the said general interest in popular religious themes.[9]

8. Cf. A. PROSPERI and A. TORRE: 'Christianity in the West' di John Bossy, in *Quaderni storici* no. 66 [a. XXII no. 3] (1987) 961-986. Two other reviews: *Revue d'histoire ecclésiastique* 82 (1987) 182-183 and *The times literary supplement* 2.5.1986 no. 4, 335, p. 480 (by B. BRADSHAW).
9. I simply refer to a few works that provide good bibliographical surveys: S. CLARK: French historians and early modern popular culture, in *Past and present* no. 100 (1983) 62-99 (literature in note 1 on p. 62); M. INGRAM: Ridings, rough music and the 'reform of popular culture' in

For the relationship between rituals and social change as it took shape in influential anthropological studies, I refer to an essay recently published in *Worship* by C. Bell.[10] She distinguishes two general approaches. First the approach which is focussed on the role of ritual in the maintenance of social groups; the ritual is seen as a mechanism for stability, identity and continuity; it is a way of countering social change. Important names in this context are V. Turner and M. Douglas.[11] The other approach focusses on how groups change through ritual: ritual is seen as integral to the way in which the ideals and traditions of a social group are adapted to changing circumstances. Names here are E. Durkheim and C. Geertz.[12] As Bell points out, the contrast between these two approaches should not be overemphasized. This is confirmed by the cultural-historical research of the last few decades, in which both roads have proved extremely fruitful. I am thinking here of the work of K. Thomas, P. Burke, N.Z. Davies, M. Vovelle, J. Delumeau, R. Muchembled, A. Dupront, C. Ginzburg, E. Le Roy Ladurie, R. Scribner, R. Briggs.[13] And Bossy's name could certainly be added to this list. A few times, moreover, Bossy explicitly refers to the sketched anthropological orientations around ritual and social change.[14]

It should be pointed out, though, that Bossy has a special and somewhat isolated position in social history. A first aspect of this special position is Bossy's reticence in formulating theories and in devising large coherent patterns for interpreting historical processes. His reticence is not so much due to a lack of methodical interest as to his belief that, because of the complexity of the interactive factors and processes, the utmost care should be taken in reconstructing the past, not to mention interpreting it. He feels that many of the current models of interpretation (notably the one of popular and élite culture)

early modern England, in *Past and present* no. 105 (1984) 79-113, in particular 79-81 notes 1-6; A. BLIJLEVENS, A. BRANTS and E. HENAU (eds.): *Volksreligiositeit: uitnodiging en uitdaging* (= HTP-studie 3) (Averbode 1982) 180ff.; G. ROOIJAKKERS and Th. VAN DER ZEE (eds.): *Religieuze volkscultuur. De spanning tussen de voorgeschreven orde en de geleefde praktijk* (Nijmegen 1986) 137ff. In a more general sense I may refer to: H. PEETERS, M. GIELIS and Ch. CASPERS (eds.): *Historical behavioural sciences: a guide to the literature* (Tilburg 1988).

10. C. BELL: Ritual, change and changing rituals, in *Worship* 63 (1989) 31-41.

11. I only refer to a too little noticed article of V. TURNER: Ritual, tribal and Catholic, in *Worship* 50 (1976) 504-526, and to the influential M. DOUGLAS: *Natural symbols* (New York 1973).

12. Cf. the classical work from 1912: E. DURKHEIM: *Les formes élémentaires de la vie religieuse* (Paris 1912) (English translation: *The elementary forms of the religious life* (London 1915[1] 1976[2]) cf. Some elementary forms); and C. GEERTZ: *The interpretation of cultures* (New York 1973).

13. Cf. note 9 above; here I will only refer to P. BURKE: *Popular culture in early modern Europe* (London 1978); R. MUCHEMBLED: *Culture populaire et culture des élites dans la France moderne, XVe-XVIIIe siècles* (Paris 1978); see also the recent works: R. SCRIBNER: *Popular culture and popular movements in Reformation Germany* (London 1987); R. BRIGGS: *Communities of belief. Cultural and social tension in early modern France* (Oxford 1989).

14. Cf. Some elementary forms, passim; Holiness and society (particularly for the connection with N. DAVIES); *Christianity in the West* vi-ix, 13, 42; The Mass 30-32.

are useless and anachronistic and do not justice to the complex reality of the past. Bossy does not want to think in terms of charged polarities such as Roman Catholic versus Protestant, élite versus popular, magic versus belief. An exception to this is the bipolarity of public and private, which Bossy, as we shall see, uses as an important heuristic instrument. The sophistication of Bossy's studies lies in the ingenuity with which his description is interwoven with explanation and analysis. Theoretical backgrounds and explanatory models are implicit in his description.

Briggs points at a second aspect of Bossy's work that marks his special position. Unlike scholars like Delumeau and Muchembled, Bossy does not try to find external causes to explain processes of change in Christian practice, but 'is working outwards from the ritual and social acts which lay at the heart of everyday religious life, he seeks to identify their meanings, and the ways in which these codes were changed'.[15] Once again, Bossy consciously opts for a narrow and carefully defined line of approach, giving at the very most an internal account of the fundamental processes of changes that were taking place in Europe from the fifteenth to the seventeenth century.

3.2. Social history and the study of liturgy

After this short sketch of the research context it is appropriate to add a short note about the contribution of the study of liturgy within social history in general and within Bossy's work in particular. The role of the study of liturgy can be considered relatively small. Most of the names mentioned above are hardly ever encountered in studies on liturgy, whereas social historians on their part appear to be reasonably well acquainted with liturgist literature. What is striking here, however, is the rather critical attitude towards research into the history of liturgy. Existing research is usually disregarded or disputed by social historians on the ground of their own research. Generally they go to the sources themselves, and at the most they are prepared to base themselves on the older classics, especially those by J. Jungmann, A. Franz and G. Dix.[16] A good example of this is the work of R.W. Scribner.[17] Scribner's distance from the study of liturgy is the more conspicuous because he focuses on the German situation in roughly the same period that is central in Bossy's work (the transition from the later Middle Ages to the early modern period). This period in

---

15. Briggs: *Communities of belief* 389.
16. A characteristic example is The Mass, passim, in particular: 30, 32 note 4, 42ff.; the same is true for other authors, such as Scribner and Briggs. Disciplines like the study of liturgy are usually also unfamiliar to historians specialized in the industrial era: cf. E. Hobsbawm: Introduction: Inventing traditions, in E. Hobsbawm and T. Ranger (eds.): *The invention of tradition* (= Past and present publications) (Cambridge 1983) 4.
17. From Scribner's *oeuvre* I particularly mention in this connection: R.W. Scribner: Cosmic order and daily life: Sacred and secular in pre-industrial German society, in *Popular culture* 1-16; R.W. Scribner: Ritual and popular religion in Catholic Germany in the time of the Reformation, in *Popular culture* 17-47; judgments on research into the history of liturgy: 18f. note 10 (indirectly), 22 note 21, 26 note 35, 28f., 39 note 99! and (indirectly) the final paragraph on 47.

Germany cannot be said to have been underexposed in liturgical research from Roman Catholic and Protestant sides. Scribner and Bossy are remarkably alike in their rejection of recent studies of the history of liturgy. About the liturgical research into 'sacramentals' (*sacramentalia*) Scribner claims succinctly: 'Works by Bartsch, Dinkel and Probst are more concerned to justify their modern use in the Catholic Church',[18] which leads him to fall back on the standard work by Franz from 1909.[19] Bossy too has a clear-cut opinion about the value of what is contributed by liturgists:

They [i.e. the historians] will not be much helped by the existing literature on the subject (at least in English), arising as it does out of the liturgist's concern to reveal the ideal Christian community existing somewhere in the past, or the apologist's interest in theological or practical abuses...[20]

He too falls back on Jungmann and Franz and seeks the support of 'the anthropologically minded historians'.[21] This is the more remarkable because, as far as the method goes, Bossy's article is a most traditional analysis of the *canon missae*, in which text and context meet; a study which links up closely with a long tradition in the study of the history of liturgy. It may be objected by historians of liturgy, however, that some are rather too quick in dismissing contributions from liturgists. On further consideration many relevant studies, particularly into the history of liturgy, turn out to be unknown. Standard works, old and more recent handbooks, publications of sources and monographs would certainly have helped ahead this sort of socio-historical research on certain points.

If we take a close look at this attitude towards the study of the history of liturgy which we find in Bossy's work and that of the other researchers mentioned, we see a sort of double suspicion of liturgical research. They sense or suppose – often quite rightly – a strong ecclesiastical allegiance or involvement in the research and, in line with this, an almost exclusive orientation on the prescribed official ecclesiastical ritual.

Socio-historical research into rituals, in contrast with this, are works with a very open and broad conception of liturgy, with schemes of the interaction between élite and popular culture, and hence the interaction between official and popular religion.

3.3. The social setting of Christian liturgy

For those who are willing to meet the challenge which border traffic with other disciplines presents for exploring the role of all celebrators, it is expedient that we dwell here on the specific character of Bossy's research design and its interest for the study of liturgy. These can be adequately illustrated by working out

18. SCRIBNER: Popular culture 39 note 99.
19. A. FRANZ: *Die kirchlichen Benediktionen im Mittelalter* 1-2 (Freiburg i. Br. 1909 = Graz 1960ʳ).
20. The Mass 30.
21. The Mass 30, cf. particularly note 4 on p. 32.

the attention he pays to the social roots of liturgy. First it must be noted that in Bossy's view the Christian ritual is not the primary subject of investigation. He is not a historian of liturgy; to him liturgy is a means of tracing the combined action of social and religious experience. Only twice – in an elaborate review article following the publication of the volume *The pursuit of holiness* and in his inaugural speech[22] – does he explicitly enlarge on his method and formulation of questions and does he analyse the concepts and terms he uses. But even if his work is not explicitly theoretical and methodical, Bossy's model of investigation is lucid and transparent: presuming that social and religious sentiments and experiences will only be there when there are social institutions to support them, he seeks to reconstruct the social role or function of Christian rituals. Key questions are how rites change functions, how certain functions are passed on when the context has changed, etc. Bossy wants to know the narrative behind liturgy, the experience, the interaction of initiative and reception, of religion and society. It is with approval therefore that Bossy quotes sociological or anthropological views on religion, for instance the description of religion as 'the extension of social relations beyond the frontiers of merely human society'.[23] In the analyses of rituals Bossy proves to by typically 'functionalistic'. Religious institutions are continually investigated for their social function or functions. In this context liturgy is a definite expressive 'vehicle' of Christian sentiments, an unsuppressible moment in social history. In view of this 'functionalistic research design' it is not surprising to see him approvingly quote P. Brown, who in Bossy's eyes applies a similar model of investigation to the period of early Christianity and the early Middle Ages. In negative terms, the criticism of Brown's method could be directed against Bossy as well. I will not work out this point here, but simply refer to the review of *Christianity in the West* by A. Torre.[24]

In my opinion the 'functionalistic approach' is extremely fruitful when Bossy tries to show how a ritual both reflected and affected its social milieu. While referring to my earlier observations about ritual and social change, I must stress the fact that both sides – reflection as well as affection – are considered. The background is what has been called 'the economy of the Holy'.[25] The essential question is to what extent large groups in the community

22. Holiness and society; Some elementary forms.
23. Besides Some elementary forms, passim: *Christianity in the West* (quotation from p. 13).
24. For a survey of Brown's work see POST: Heiligen tussen hemel en aarde; POST: Iconografie en hagiografie; in addition: P. BROWN: *The body and society* (London-Boston 1989); Bossy frequently refers to Brown, either directly, as in Holiness and society 132 note 43!, or indirectly when he speaks of humanization of the sacred, holiness, saints, of God's human friends, *patronus/patrinus* etc. On this point see particularly: Holiness and society; Elementary forms of Durkheim; *Christianity in the West*. Cf. the notes by TORRE: 'Christianity in the West' 978ff. sub 3; for criticism of Brown's 'functionalistic' approach see Ch.M. RADDING: Superstition to science: Nature, fortune, and the passing of medieval ordeal, in *American historical review* 84 (1979) 945-951.
25. I derive this terminology from SCRIBNER: *Popular culture* 129, who in turn refers back to Bossy (cf. 129 notes 1 and 2).

have access to the Holy: how are vehicles of the Holy used, by whom, when, why and what for? This 'economy of the Holy', this interest in the social setting of Christian rituals, comes to light in Bossy's work through a fixed set of themes.

First and foremost is the confraternity.[26] By means of this important institution of the later Middle Ages the complex interaction between social and religious experiences can be charted, for the confraternities were great inventors of ritual. Here Bossy joins N.Z. Davies, who claimed:

> The history of confraternities might better be related, not to economic contraction and short-range political disorder, but to the more slowly changing features of life that influence people's sense of community, of boundaries between the self and the others, and of the character of social relationships.[27]

Bossy calls these words: 'words of gold'.[28]

Another liturgical subject recurrent in Bossy's work is the *pax* rite (kiss of peace).[29] This ritual of exchanging a kiss in the Mass after the sacrifice (before the fifth century in the West before the sacrifice as a greeting at the offertory) is seen by Bossy as a locus for the extrapolation of social violence. The wholeness of the community is central here. Bossy underlines that no distinction should be made between sacral and secular, between the official ritual in church and the life of the community. Study of the development and the function of the *pax* ritual shows how these liturgical phrases and acts around peace and justice are not an abstract or theological condition, but a state of social relations. Bossy works out this exceedingly concrete role of the *pax* ritual particularly for urban communities with a great deal of tension among districts, kinships (*maagschappen*) etc.

Similarly Bossy tells us how the Host rites essentially had a unity-seeking background and how the feast of *Corpus Christi* eventually came to incorporate the socially integrative powers of the Host in the later Middle Ages, when liturgical reforms tended to separate this sort of social functions from the ordinary Eucharist.[30]

Thus Bossy interprets and explains the function of Christian rituals in social

26. Cf. in particular The Counter-Reformation 58ff.; Holiness and society 122; *Christianity in the West* 57ff.
27. N.Z. DAVIES: Some tasks and themes in the study of popular religion, in Ch. TRINKHAUS and H.A. OBERMAN (eds.): *The pursuit of holiness in late mediaeval and Renaissance religion* (= Studies in mediaeval and Renaissance thought 10) (Leiden 1974) 307-336 (quotation from p. 318).
28. Holiness and society 122.
29. This ritual and the 'state of peace' comes up in: Holiness and society 131ss.; The Mass 52ff.; *Christianity in the West* 21, 72, 141; *Disputes and settlements* passim (indirectly). Liturgists could point at additional literature, cf. A. HOLLAARDT: Vredeskus, in *Liturgisch woordenboek* 2, 2882-2883. In my opinion Bossy's sketch of the development of the *pax* ritual's place in the Eucharist is in need of qualification. He seems to have based his study either exclusively on the general sketch by Jungmann or on a few very specific sources, i.e. sources from a definite place and time.
30. Cf. The Mass 58ff. (cf. bibliography 59 n. 85); *Christianity in the West* 74f., 141ff.

terms: saints' lives are brought back to human size and transformed into the recognizable pattern of friendships between God and human beings; the liturgy for the dead is described as in essence a cult of living friends in the service of dead ones. Hence Bossy's analysis of the Latin *canon missae* (eucharistic prayer) results in a refined sociology of salvation, the social framework of which classifies people into four categories: living friends and foes and dead friends and foes.[31] The ascent and development of the cult around Jesus' family is also explained from social patterns in the community.[32] In the fifteenth century it was propagated through the cult of St. Anne that Christ was not a foundling but had a family tradition, with Mary and Anne as protagonists and initially with Joseph and Joachim in supporting roles. By the end of the Middle Ages (notably from c. 1500 onwards) the carpenters' guilds helped to spread the cult of Joseph, which was completed with his own feast. This means that one thing was unequivocally propagated in the later Middle Ages: Christ belongs to a family! In addition there is an intricate network of friends: the procession of saints, the corpus of God's human friendship (a good many of whom once again appear to be relatives!). Through this functional analysis Bossy is able to make processes of change transparent. The social function of the Christian cult and the humanization of the expression and celebration of the divine were reorganized during the period he describes. He points out how this can seldom be done with impunity, and how people tried to find ways of maintaining social functions and combining sociability with the worship of God. Attention to the social setting and the function of Christian symbols and rites may give a better understanding of the origin and context of reform movements. The Reformation, for instance, queried the said network of relatives and friends around Christ. In the period concerned a drastic reconstruction of Christianity was intended, particularly as an outcry against the humanization of the social universe, effected in traditional belief by the reconciliation of man and God.[33] I will now elaborate on this important theme of processes of change.

3.4. Pastoral-liturgical strategies or offensives

We have noted various times that ritual and social change form an important line of approach in cultural history, and Bossy too is concerned with this theme. He tries to envisage the complex process of transition between roughly 1400 and 1700 A.D. Bossy approaches the aspect of ritual and social change mainly through the theme of pastoral-liturgical strategies, or, to use an adapted wording of a well-known model, 'liturgical civilizing offensives'.[34] Of course these are not Bossy's own phrases; once again he avoids the use of gen-

31. See in particular: The Mass 43ff.
32. See in particular: *Christianity in the West* 3-13.
33. Authoritatively expressed in: *Christianity in the West* 95.
34. On 'civilizing offensives' in general, notably the origin of the term: C.A. DAVIDS: Aristocraten en juristen, financiers en feministen, in *Volkskundig bulletin* 13 (1987) 157-159.

eral interpretation models and lays all the emphasis on the description of specific historical processes. His analysis of the processes of change concentrates entirely on the mainstream of Christian worship and connects the changes with pastoral-liturgical strategies. Bossy has elaborated this pastoral-liturgical policy notably for the Counter Reformation.[35] The bishops were aiming at a uniform and strictly centralized parochial ritual practice. The liturgical practice played a key role in their policy, since ceremonies like baptism, marriage, burial, the Easter ritual (Easter communion), confession, the Eucharist and the use of the parish church provided excellent means of steering and controlling parish life. This policy drastically reorganized the liturgical supply and affected the existing social functions and effects; as a result the social implications of the rituals are laid bare. Through numerous examples Bossy sketches how efficient and effective these 'liturgical civilizing offensives' were, and he has an eye not only for the policy makers (bishops, councils, synods, liturgists, theologians) and the executives (local bishops, parish clergy with additional training) but also for the experience of the celebrators. The policy was intended particularly to direct all the widely diverging streams of popular religion into one single parochial channel. They were – says Bossy – 'obsessed with the problem of distinguishing liturgical from non-liturgical'.[36] Cornerstone in this strategy was the parish church. The various fraternities had to be centralized. They were not allowed to mingle with the parish and parochial liturgy: Christians should be parishioners first of all; membership of fraternities came second. Bossy shows that this is where the history of 'the parish' started. Though this pastoral-liturgical strategy can be considered successful, it must not be concluded as a matter of course that the parish community was a homogeneous entity with a homogeneous liturgical practice. It may very well be that there was a sense of community only at special moments of ritual festivity and that precisely rituals – as demonstrated above – had a uniting and stabilizing effect. The parish community is one that includes friends as well as foes; it is a socially stratified community composed of various districts, occupational groups, associations and families in constant interaction. This process of reorganization and introduction of discipline is concerned not so much with abolition of rituals as with a top-down distinction between various forms of liturgy; only a few rites received the designation 'Christian liturgy'.

It is particularly the development of the sacrament of penance and confession in the sixteenth and seventeenth centuries that accentuates this process of change for Bossy. This development is well known in the circle of liturgists; a succinct summary has recently been published by F. Heggen.[37] At certain

35. See: The character of Elizabethan Catholicism; *The spirit*; The social history of confession; *The English Catholic community*; The Counter-Reformation; The Mass; *Christianity in the West*.
36. The Counter-Reformation 62.
37. For a good historical synopsis and bibliographical survey on guilt, penance and rituals: F. HEGGEN: *Omgaan met schuld in de christelijke geloofsgemeenschap* (Hilversum 1988) 75-118, literature 208ff. See also the papers of the 11th Congress of the Societas Liturgica 1987, published in *Studia liturgica* 18 (1988) 1-116.

points, e.g. the occurrence of the confessional, Bossy strikes a different note. According to him, the reversal occurs notably as the social implications change and as the experience of guilt changes, which becomes apparent in the fact that the role of the restitution became less and less significant in the sacrament.[38]

To conclude this aspect of pastoral-liturgical policy I would like to point out that four elements recur in Bossy's analyses of such 'liturgical civilizing offensives'. In my opinion these elements also illustrate the close connection between the various aspects that I have highlighted in Bossy's work.

– First of all, as I have noted, he observes that the policy was given shape particularly by liturgical means.

– Secondly, that eucharistic devotion was latched onto in order to clear obstacles in this offensive of parochial control and centralization.

– Thirdly, that the status of the secondary fields of devotion or popular devotion was reduced, because they were uncontrollable, taking place as they did in the family or in fraternities.

– And finally, that elements of popular and public or communal participation were increasingly eliminated from the official ritual in the course of this process. This was not a preconceived objective of the 'liturgical civilizing offensives' but it came along with the incorporation of the various forms of domestic and private *pietas* in the mainstream of official public liturgy. Whether it is possible to extract a more general model of change for these processes from Bossy's work will be examined when I discuss the closely related aspect of religion and popular culture.

3.5. Public versus private, community versus individual

The element of elimination of public or communal and popular participation, which we just saw, deserves elaboration. Bossy regards changes in the relationship between public and private and between community and individual as a fundamental feature of the process of change that started in the Middle Ages and reached its full growth in the Counter Reformation.[39]

The use of these oppositions must be seen in the light of the scholarly context that was outlined above. Besides attention for the combination of ritual and change in social history we often find the model of bipolarity, as it has been formulated in circles of structuralists and cultural anthropologists (cf. C. Lévi-Strauss and the concept of the unity-in-opposition of the pair).[40] Bossy has a double track in mind: he is concerned both with the form of the ritual (public or private) and with its function and the way in which it is experienced. Though very public and common in form, a ritual may be extremely

---

38. About penance and confession: *The English Catholic community* 268-272; The Counter-Reformation 63ff.; Holiness and society 127f.; *Christianity in the West* 35-56, in particular 45ff.
39. See: The Counter-Reformation; Holiness and society; The Mass 51ff.; *Christianity in the West*.
40. See for instance the explicit reference to Lévi-Strauss in the analysis of Carnival in *Christianity in the West* 42.

private in function and experience. Once again the Mass is illustrative of this.[41] To Bossy the medieval Eucharist is a composition of two ritual traditions which were taken over from early Christianity, which in turn was rooted in the antique world: the tradition of public worship practised by communities and that of the private, family or domestic cult. In this connection it should be pointed out too that the Jewish roots are evident. In Judaism bipolarity was frequently seen between temple and family rites.[42] Bossy associates the concepts of sacrament and sacrifice with this distinction between private and public. The element of sacrifice reflects the aspect of the public cult, while the eucharistic or sacramental element reflects that of the domestic cult. The development of the eucharistic ritual from early Christianity onwards is showing a slow incorporation of the domestic aspect of sacrament into the public rite. Here Bossy aims at sketching the form of the ritual. The process of change that occurred at the end of the Middle Ages, however, touched primarily on function and experience. According to Bossy, the pastoral-liturgical offensive of the Counter Reformation, though collective in form, was a process of individualization in effect, a process which was confronted time and again with the tension between *pia exercitia* at home (domestic) and in church (public). The medieval harmony between private and collective rites was disturbed in many places, often unintentionally, and a décor for collective rites was called for. Apart from the example of the Mass and the theme of the attitude towards death – a theme which has repeatedly been worked out by others as well (Ph. Ariès!)[43] – Bossy sketches the changes in the relation between individual and community chiefly through the rituals of guilt and penance.[44] In the Middle Ages these rites were more social than private acts, both in form and in impact, but after the Reformation the various forms of public penance disappeared. The social bedding of the sacrament, its communal character, became increasingly a point of issue. Confession as a collective rite with unmistakable social implications gradually faded away, which is evident in particular from the ritual form of the auricular confession, officially introduced at the Fourth Lateran Council in 1215. It appears that form, function and experience do not necessarily run parallel. The auricular confession had to take place in the accessible part of the parish church, not in the sacristy or the presbytery, and there were still communal tactile rites (imposition of hands). What undermined the communal aspect, however, was not so much the ritual form as the experience of sin and guilt, plus the fact that the

---

41. The Mass passim, in particular 51ff.; see also: *The English Catholic community* 369-377.
42. Cf. for instance the description of the tension between public-temple and private-family in the sketch of the Passover in: H.-J. AUF DER MAUR: *Feiern im Rhythmus der Zeit* 1. *Herren-feste in Woche und Jahr* (= Gottesdienst der Kirche. Handbuch der Liturgiewissenschaft 5) (Regensburg 1983) 56ff. and R. CANTALAMESSA: *Ostern in der alten Kirche* (= Traditio christiana 4) (Bern-Frankfurt a.M.-Las Vegas 1981) XIII-XXXIV.
43. The attitude towards death is summed up in: *Christianity in the West* 26ff. Actually Bossy is very critical of Ariès, *Christianity in the West* 26.
44. See note 38 above.

rite was rooted in the community through the aspect of restitution, which liturgists and theologians considered less and less a significant (i.e. sacramentally effective) part of the ritual. Eventually a rite emerged that was very much geared to the individual, both in function and in experience. The motives for giving this rite a most individual form (cf. confession box) did not originate primarily from the theology of sacraments or from changing ideas about social function, sin or sense of guilt, but from the role of corporality in liturgy.

Elsewhere Bossy demonstrates these changes in rites and experience by means of the Carnival rituals.[45] He places Carnival in this broad process of sin, guilt and penance rites. It was a public and communal separation rite through which man came into his penitential state. Starting from this connection with the Christian fasting and penance ritual, Bossy emphasizes the Christian and medieval character of Carnival and reacts against theories that it would reflect some kind of pre-Christian cult. Following in the footsteps of J. Caro Baroja[46] Bossy is very positive on this point: he is certain that there is no specific indication of Carnival rites before 1200. He even derives the term 'Carnival' from Christian religion, *domenica carnelevalis* being the day when the clergy in Rome and Milan began the penance regime of Lent. The basic idea of the Carnival ritual was always associated with fasting: 'the world was turned upside-down to see what was crawling about underneath'.[47] To fathom the essence and the function of Carnival it is crucial, according to Bossy, to find an explanation for the geographical spread. Why did the feast take root in some parts (Italy, Spain, most of France, Switzerland and a part of Germany) and not in others (Holland, apart from a small part of the South, the British Isles, the North of Germany and Scandinavia)? It is obvious that the Reformation here cannot be an argument, because the origin and spreading of Carnival have taken place in an earlier period. Bossy finds the explanation in the penance ritual. Carnival came into existence where the long tradition of public confession and penance had been left in the air by the further progress of privacy after 1215 (the official introduction of auricular confession). The areas without Carnival celebrations are the parts where the penitential tariff had been invented and where penance rites had had a more individual character of old. Carnival was the inverted image of the traditional machinery of penance and also provided the required channel for a collective ritual. The affections of the multitude, the element of community were attached to certain points of concentration, such as the feast of Corpus Christi and Carnival.

---

45. Summing up: *Christianity in the West* 42-45.
46. See the rarely noted work of J. Caro Baroja: *Le carnaval* (= Bibliothèque des histoires) (Paris 1979).
47. *Christianity in the West* 44.

3.6. Religion, social change and popular religion

Bossy has been criticized for hardly or not explaining processes of change by placing them in the interplay between élite culture and popular culture.[48] As a conclusion I would like to highlight this point in particular. I think it is very relevant and in line with what I have said about social change and the 'pastoral-liturgical civilizing offensives'.

In my eyes it is not true that the 'popular-versus-élite-culture' model is entirely absent in Bossy's work; it is only given a very specific interpretation, which is rather different from the way in which it is used by authors like Burke, Muchembled, Scribner and Delumeau. Bossy consciously avoids phrases like 'popular culture' and 'official, learned or élite culture' because the model which uses these distinctions is under a heavy burden. As the terminology would mark reality with an anachronistic image from the start, he does away with it. Similarly he claims that he prefers not to work with the concept of 'Reformation' because by a long historiographical tradition this phrase evokes a chain of causal argumentations. Parallel to this, Bossy wants to get round the image of popular culture as both entirely distinct from élite culture and in opposition to the axioms of the Christian faith:

Among disfigurements of this piece of the past I count the idea that medieval Christianity was a burden which most of the population of the West was delighted to shake off; or that there was something you can call 'popular culture' and distinguish radically from something called 'élite culture', especially where that popular culture is held by axiom to be non-Christian.[49]

Of course the distinction that researchers using the popular-versus-élite-culture model have in mind may not be so rigid at all. Burke, Scribner and Briggs, for instance, handle the model with much more flexibility than Delumeau and Muchembled, and so they are much closer to Bossy than the latter two. This differentiation applies to all of the following observations.

It is very important, in my opinion, to see that Bossy, unlike for instance S. Schama, does not radically denounce the popular-versus-élite-culture model. Rather he applies it in a very individual and creative manner and thus contributes considerably to the debate about the practical use of the model. Two lines can be distinguished in this process of translation: 'popular culture', generally focussing on 'popular religion', is first of all 'translated' by Bossy into phrases like 'the average Christian', 'traditional Christianity', 'everyday life', 'conventional behaviour', 'conformistic life' and subsequently into 'communally based religion', 'instinctive or intuitive religion', 'natural and spontaneous religiosity', 'common sense'.[50]

48. Cf. with the necessary modifications ROODENBURG: Onder censuur; cf. BRIGGS: Communities of belief 390-392.
49. *Christianity in West* viii. See also: The Counter-Reformation about 'popular reception' and the critical notes by PROSPERI and TORRE: 'Christianity in the West' 965ff., 980.
50. I refer particularly to the phrasing in *Christianity in the West* 27, 29 ('natural religion'), 30 ('common-sense view'), 45 ('spontaneous(ly)') etc. See also: The Counter-Reformation; Holiness and society; Some elementary forms.

By choosing an internal and functionalistically descriptive point of view, he examines the social status and implications of the very widely celebrated Christian rituals, and thus quite naturally distinguishes between the various segments and vehicles of culture from the start. The Eucharist is described by Bossy in its 'high-liturgical' and theological dimensions, but is also viewed in its social functions and values; besides the dimensions of sacrament and sacrifice he also has an eye for the fact that in the experience of large groups of people the Mass in part belongs to the 'category of magical rites'.[51] In his analysis of liturgy he deals with the objectivity and massiveness of the doctrine as well as with everyday social experience, often in sharp contrast. Bossy is after the popular religion, the common behaviour of ordinary people. That is the starting point for his selection of research themes. He opts for the conformistic code of behaviour; he wants to find, in his own words, the 'silent revolution'.[52] The reader is challenged to bear this angle of view in mind. In the preface to *Christianity in the West* he claims: 'Supposing that your account of what you call traditional Christianity is roughly correct, what difference does it make to the conventional narrative of sixteenth-century reformations, Protestant or Catholic?'[53]

Bossy's suspicion of the phrase 'popular culture' or 'popular religion' is also evident in passages where he denies the supposed contrast between popular religion and official religion or puts it in perspective, for instance when the question comes up to what extent there was a difference between doctrine and practice. Where many liturgists have supposed that there was a contrast between the silent, private priest's Mass in a foreign and ritual language and the community-building function of the Eucharist, there need not be such contrast according to Bossy: 'Despite the complaints of liturgists and reformers, it was not a contradiction that the mass should be offered by the priest alone, in a ritual language, largely in silence and partly out of sight, and yet embody or create the sense of collective identity.'[54] Further he puts in perspective the supposed gap between eucharistic popular devotion and official eucharistic theology. He demonstrates that people on the whole were reasonably acquainted with eucharistic theology: 'We need not suppose that congregations were ignorant of what the priest was doing on the altar, if only his performance was frequently criticised. The average parishioner, who would probably not be up to that, nevertheless knew what he needed to know.'[55]

And it remains a fact, also in Bossy's view, that the doctrine may well be in contradiction with how it is experienced.

Bossy implicitly blames many historians for focussing on non-conformistic and deviant behaviour by stressing the gap between élite and popular culture

---

51. The Mass 33 (but Bossy qualifies 'magic' and he prefers to speak of 'powerful work').
52. The Counter-Reformation 54.
53. *Christianity in the West* viii.
54. *Christianity in the West* 67.
55. *Christianity in the West* 67.

and thus paying too little attention for instance to the study of the Counter Reformation and its social implications. His starting-point is the mainstream of liturgical practice. Therefore he encounters prominent and leading individuals from the élite such as Charles Borromeo of Milan (1538-1584) as well as more 'popular' liturgical impulses from the fraternities and from the affections of the masses. In this way the interaction and interwovenness of élite culture and popular culture is frequently considered in his work, though – typically! – in other phrases and spread over many other distinctions, such as lay and clerical initiatives, secular and regular clergy, higher and lower clergy, town and country, nobility and common people. He never uses these distinctions as a general model, but always links them to a specific historical process. The model, according to Bossy, should emanate from the description and not function like a straitjacket.

Sometimes Bossy even hints at the impossibility of an adequate reconstruction of processes of change. This seems to be the case particularly when the historian tries to trace motives and incentives. Even in the quite often examined phenomenon of pilgrimage the ultimate incentives of the pilgrim remain in the dark. Was it primarily a penance ritual imposed on the pilgrim with legal as well as penitential and sacramental dimensions? Or was it rather a spontaneous initiative to redeem promises made in exchange for favours prayed for and received? Was it the attraction of the holy places, or of the saints themselves? Or was a mere change of air the most important motive after all?[56]

Another observation can be made about the static character that Bossy discerns in the scheme of élite versus popular culture. He is interested in processes of change; one senses his feeling that the sketch based on the élite-versus-popular-culture scheme by authors like Delumeau and Muchembled, and even by Burke and Scribner, is too general and too schematic, in spite of the fact that the said authors do not regard the two as strictly separate circuits either but as closely interfering and interwoven segments. But Bossy does not feel it incumbent on him (as Burke does) to recognize 'recurrent problems' that call for treatment at a more general and abstract level than that of the concrete local or regional historical process. Yet in his work Bossy does develop something like an implicit 'model of change' in which the interaction of élite and popular culture is important. Here Bossy's work is closely connected with that of Scribner and Briggs. For this relationship and a description of this model I would like to refer to Briggs. In a recently published volume of essays with an elaborate theoretical epilogue, Briggs frequently refers to Bossy's work.[57] In comparison with his review of Delumeau and Muchembled he is remarkably mild towards Bossy. In his exploration of the relationship between religion and popular culture he repeatedly sketches a model of change

---

56. *Christianity in the West* 52.
57. BRIGGS: *Communities of belief*, in particular 381-413, review of Bossy 389ff.; cf. also ch. 7 (The sins of the people. Auricular confession and the imposition of social norms).

that he has derived almost directly from Bossy.[58] Thus Briggs' criticism of Bossy seems to be chiefly that Bossy is too unassuming to make certain generalizations. Briggs himself is more daring. Inspired by Bossy, he assumes in his model of change that a certain distinction can be made between

a. the official code, the theological doctrine, the recorded and prescribed liturgy etc., and

b. beside or against this the popular code, the popular interpretation and experience, or social function.

Now everything revolves around the interaction between the two; the boundaries between a. and b. are never fixed, they keep moving and overlapping. All kinds of strategies and civilizing offensives have been set out to affect and change the relationship between a. and b. Looking at the liturgical change campaigns to which I have referred, Briggs sees a general pattern of causation which is entirely confirmed by Bossy's work on the Counter Reformation. This pattern refers to the interaction between three developments occurring mainly within the Church:

a. A drive for doctrinal purity.

b. An important movement to discipline and educate the clergy in order to make them follow and propagate the purified doctrine themselves. The first concern here is the purging of liturgical practice, that is: the elimination of popular superstitions.

c. The general strategy of large-scale banning of wrong practices. In fact this is a schematic rendering of what I said sketching 'the pastoral-liturgical civilizing offensives'.

4. CONCLUSION

At the end of this contribution I would like to formulate some perspectives for research in the study of liturgy. I intentionally say 'perspectives', to indicate, in the footsteps of O. Löfgren and N.-A. Bringéus, that it is neither the Utopia of a holistic approach nor a segmentation of historical reality or of the scholarly trade that I have in mind.[59]

– The first important perspective, and one that I have brought forward here more than once, is that an internal approach will not suffice in the study of liturgy. Liturgy is part of broader cultural practices. Rituals have a place in the search for the completest possible model for the interpretation of cultural history. This perspective touches on the often very dominant relation of research with the Church as well as on the more contextual approach that is desirable.

– Closely related with this first is, in my opinion, a second perspective: it is

58. BRIGGS: *Communities of belief* 280ff., 391f.
59. O. LÖFGREN: On the anatomy of culture, in *Ethnologia Europaea* 12 (1981) 26-46; N.-A. BRINGÉUS: Perspektiven des Studiums materieller Kultur, in *Jahrbuch für Volkskunde und Kulturgeschichte* 29 (1986) 159-174. See also: POST: 'Het suizen van een zachte koelte'.

necessary that we stop focussing our attention exclusively on the form of the rite. Even if the primary objectives are making comparisons and tracing patterns of development (as e.g. in the work of A. Baumstark),[60] and even if this research extends beyond the boundaries of the official liturgical mainstream, a research perspective that is concerned predominantly with the technical aspects of rites and with their diffusion in time and place will stand in the way of a more contextual, communicative and functional research perspective. The attention will have to shift from form and development towards function and social context. Liturgy cannot be regarded directly and unmistakably as a mirror of mentalities. Contextual analyses demonstrate a very intricate and at times contradictory relationship between a ritual form and its development on the one hand and the functions and values which are supposedly associated with a form and development on the other hand. Christian rituals have sometimes most surprising roots in society. As a matter of fact, this picture is confirmed in numerous other studies. Research in social sciences shows how ideas about the function and operation of rituals in many cases need adjusting.[61] Studies like Bossy's make us aware of the relativity and the complexity of liturgy as a source for research in culture.

– Finally I would point once more at the importance of seeing the rituals under analysis in the context of the interaction between theology and devotion, between élite and popular culture. A first step towards this perspective is to use 'Christian ritual and liturgy' in a broad and open sense instead of narrowing it down to the prescribed order of the official ecclesiastical books. To sum up: a broad and open conception of liturgy which covers a broad area without strict limitations. Maybe I should add that this does not by any means deny the importance of further discussion about the twin concepts 'popular' and 'devotion' (cf. *Volksfrömmigkeit*), but in principle our research shall not be restricted in any way. There shall be neither a lower limit (for instance the transition from religion to magic, as is sometimes suggested) nor an upper limit (such as the transition to strictly intellectual practices established by Church and theology).

Only with this outlook can questions about the attitude of all the participants in Christian rituals towards liturgy be tackled successfully and can the multidisciplinary, contextual and functional research perspectives that I have outlined above really have an impact on the study of liturgy.

---

60. A. BAUMSTARK: *Liturgie comparée* (Chevetogne 1953³).
61. After the important impulse of H. WEGMAN and P. VAN HOOIJDONK: *Zij breken hetzelfde brood. Een kritische wegwijzer bij de viering van de eucharistie op basis van een liturgie-historische en -sociologische analyse* (Rotterdam 1972) this empirical research is hesitantly beginning to take shape. I would mention the pilgrimage research (summaries may be found in: VAN UDEN and POST: *Christelijke bedevaarten*) and a large-scale research project in Nijmegen (cf. A. SCHEER: De beleving van liturgische riten en symbolen, in J. VAN DER VEN (ed.): *Pastoraal tussen ideaal en werkelijkheid* (Kampen 1985) 105-120).

ANNEX

SELECT BIBLIOGRAPHY OF JOHN BOSSY

1. English Catholics and the French marriage, in *Recusant history. A journal of research in post-Reformation Catholic history in the British Isles* 5 (1959) 2-16.
2. *Elizabethan Catholicism: The link with France* (= Cambridge University Ph.D. thesis 1961) (Cambridge 1961).
3. The character of Elizabethan Catholicism, in *Past and present. A journal of historical studies* no. 21 (1962) 39-59 (reprint: no. 5).
4. A propos of Henry Constable, in *Recusant history* 6 (1962) 228-237.
5. The Character of Elizabethan Catholicism, in: T. ASTON (ed.): *Crisis in Europe, 1560-1660. Essays from 'Past and present'* (London 1965 1975²) 223-246 (reprint of no. 3).
6. Four Catholic congregations in rural Northumberland, 1750-1850, in *Recusant history* 9 (1967) 88-119.
7. J. BOSSY and H.O. EVENNETT: *The spirit of the Counter-Reformation* (= The Birkbeck lectures in ecclesiastical history given in the University of Cambridge in May 1951) ed. with postscript by J. BOSSY (Cambridge 1968).
8. More Northumbrian congregations, in *Recusant history* 10 (1969-1970) 11-34.
9. The Counter-Reformation and the people of Catholic Europe, in *Past and present* no. 47 (1970) 51-70 (= lecture on the *Past and present* Conference on 'Popular Religion' 1966; cf. also paper to the 9th Irish Conference of Historians May 1969).
10. Blood and baptism: Kinship, community and Christianity in Western Europe from the fourteenth to the seventeenth centuries, in D. BAKER (ed.): *Sanctity and secularity* (= Studies in Church history 10) (Oxford 1973) 129-143.
11. The English Catholic community 1603-25, in: A.G.R. SMITH (ed.): *The reign of James VI and I* (London 1973) 91-105.
12. The social history of confession in the age of the Reformation, in *Transactions of the Royal Historical Society* 5th series 25 (1975) 21-38 (read in the Royal Historical Society on March 8, 1974).
13. *The English Catholic community, 1570-1840* (London 1975 1979²).
14. Catholic Lancashire in the 18th century, in: J. BOSSY and P. JUPP (eds.): *Essays presented to Michael Roberts, sometime professor of modern history in the Queen's University of Belfast* (Belfast 1976) 54-69.
15. Holiness and Society, in *Past and present* no. 75 (1978) 119-137 (= review article with reference to: Ch. TRINKHAUS and H.A. OBERMAN (eds.): *The pursuit of holiness in late mediaeval and Renaissance religion* (= Studies in mediaeval and Renaissance thought 10) (Leiden 1974)).
16. Essai de sociographie de la messe 1200-1700, in *Annales ESC* 36 (1981) 44-70 (slightly revised English version: no. 17).
17. The Mass as a social institution, 1200-1700, in *Past and present* no. 100 (1983) 29-61 (Slightly revised version of no. 16).
18. Some elementary forms of Durkheim, in *Past and present* no. 95 (1982) 3-18 (= Inaugural lecture University of York, 11 February 1981).
19. Postscript, in J. BOSSY (ed.): *Disputes and settlements. Law and human relations in the West* (= Past and present publications) (Cambridge 1983) 287-293.
20. *Christianity in the West, 1400-1700* (= Oxford University Press, Series Opus) (Oxford-New York 1985).

La célébration de l'eucharistie selon les Actes de Thomas[1]

GERARD ROUWHORST

Dans les dernières années plusieurs liturgistes, parmi lesquels il faut compter Herman Wegman,[2] ont plaidé en faveur d'un élargissement de l'horizon dans la recherche sur l'histoire de la liturgie. Ils ont - à mon avis à juste titre - appelé l'attention sur les limites qu'a l'approche 'classique', qui depuis très longtemps a eu presque le monopole; ils ont souligné le fait que cette approche concernait trop exclusivement la liturgie 'officielle' telle qu'elle est décrite et prescrite dans les sources liturgiques normatives. D'après ces liturgistes, il serait nécessaire de remplacer cette manière classique d'aborder l'histoire de la liturgie par une approche plus large qui ne se rapporte pas seulement à la liturgie officielle, mais également aux rites moins officiels ou même marginaux - par exemple aux traditions liturgiques qui sont parfois rangées sous l'étiquette de la 'paraliturgie' ou de la 'religion populaire' ou aux rites pratiqués par des chrétiens 'hétérodoxes' - et surtout à la réception de la liturgie 'officielle' par le 'peuple' chrétien, c'est à dire pas les différentes catégories de chrétiens dont ce 'peuple' est constitué.

Le bien-fondé de cette critique adressée à la science liturgique classique n'est guère sujet à discussion. De fait, qui oserait ne pas s'intéresser à 'l'histoire vécue du peuple chrétien', en l'occurrence à la façon dont ce peuple a vécu la liturgie? La question est pourtant de savoir comment il faut réaliser ce projet de recherche à première vue si passionnant. Où trouve-t-on, par exemple, les sources qui nous renseignent sur la participation, soit active, soit passive, du 'peuple' à la liturgie? On constate plutôt que le plus souvent les sources connues sont très peu communicatives sur ce point ou gardent un silence complet.

D'autre part, une fois qu'on s'est rendu compte du problème esquissé, on peut parfois faire des découvertes surprenantes. Il peut alors, par exemple, se révéler qu'il existe des sources qui jusqu'à présent, pour une raison ou une autre, n'ont guère retenu l'attention des liturgistes, mais qui, dans la perspective d'une approche renouvelée, plus large de la science liturgique, vont prendre tout à coup un intérêt inattendu, précisément parce qu'elles nous aident à nous former une idée, ne fût-ce que très imparfaite, de la façon dont certains (groupes de) chrétiens ont participé à la liturgie ou l'ont vécue. Il nous

1. Je tiens à remercier ici particulièrement le père F. Bourdeau qui a lu, corrigé et amélioré le texte français de la plus grande partie de cette contribution. De même, je suis très reconnaissant au père A. Hollaardt qui a revu le texte français des premières et dernières pages et des annotations.
2. Voir par exemple H. WEGMAN: Bidprentjes als liturgische bron. De mentaliteitsgeschiedenis, dans: *Jaarboek voor liturgie-onderzoek* 2 (1986) 22-31.

semble qu'à cette catégorie de sources appartiennent, entre autres, les actes apocryphes des apôtres. En effet, les passages liturgiques que renferment certains de ces écrits - notamment les Actes de Jean et de Thomas - ont été en général négligés par les liturgistes - cela vaut notamment pour les descriptions de l'eucharistie qu'on y rencontre -[3] soit parce que ces liturgistes ont été troublés par l'odeur d'hérésie que, durant des siècles, les actes apocryphes ont eu,[4] soit qu'ils ont été mis dans l'embarras par certaines particularités des rites qui y sont décrits, particularités qui semblent difficiles à concilier avec certaines idées plus ou moins généralement admises sur le caractère et le développement de la liturgie aux premiers siècles du christianisme. Néanmoins, ces sources nous paraissent incontestablement revêtir un intérêt particulier. En effet, les passages liturgiques des actes apocryphes comptent parmi les sources les plus anciennes qui nous renseignent sur la célébration de la liturgie chrétienne. En outre, ces écrits ont joui d'une popularité considérable et ont été connus de différentes communautés chrétiennes, tant orthodoxes que hétérodoxes.[5] Ce qui signifie qu'il ne peut pas y avoir été un trop grand écart entre, d'une part, les traditions liturgiques de ces communautés et la 'mentalité' ou, si on veut, la 'spiritualité' liturgique de celles-ci et, d'autre part, les rites décrits dans les actes apocryphes.

Dans le but de montrer l'importance qu'ont les actes apocryphes pour la recherche sur l'histoire de la liturgie et la façon dont elle a été vécue par le 'peuple' chrétien, je me propose d'examiner dans cette contribution une série de passages qui sont tirés d'un de ces écrits apocryphes, les Actes de Thomas, et qui contiennent des descriptions, en partie assez détaillées, de quelques célébrations eucharistiques. A vrai dire, ce n'est pas la première fois que je traite ce sujet. Je l'ai déjà abordé il y a dix ans à l'occasion d'un colloque à Louvain et en collaboration avec Herman Wegman.[6] Cette fois-ci je voudrais pourtant

---

3. Parmi les auteurs qui font exception à cette règle, il faut en tout cas mentionner H. LIETZMANN: *Messe und Herrenmahl* (Berlin 1926) 234-237. On trouve en outre quelques observations intéressantes au sujet de ces célébrations eucharistiques dans J. BETZ: *Die Eucharistie in der Zeit der griechischen Väter* 1, 1 *Die Aktualpräsenz der Person und des Heilswerkes Jesu im Abendmahl nach der vorephesinischen griechischen Patristik* (Freiburg 1955) 324-325; G. KRETSCHMAR: Abendmahl, dans *Theologische Realenzyklopädie* 1 (Berlin 1977) 68; C. VOGEL: Anaphores eucharistiques préconstantiniennes. Formes non-traditionnelles, dans *Ecclesia orans. Mélanges offerts au Père Adalbert G. Hamman OFM* (= Augustinianum 20, 1-2) (Paris 1980) 401-410; H.B. MEYER: *Eucharistie: Geschichte, Theologie, Pastoral* (= Gottesdienst der Kirche. Handbuch der Liturgiewissenschaft 4) (Regensburg 1989) 95-96. Voir également G. ROUWHORST: Bénédiction, action de grâces, supplication. Les oraisons de la table dans le Judaïsme et les célébrations eucharistiques des chrétiens syriaques, dans *Questions liturgiques* 61 (1980) 211-240, surtout 221-229.

4. Cf. E. JUNOD: Actes apocryphes et hérésie: le jugement de Photius, dans F. BOVON: *Les actes apocryphes des apôtres.Christianisme et monde païen* (Genève 1981) 11-24; G. POUPON: Les actes apocryphes des apôtres de Lefèvre à Fabricius, dans BOVON: *Les actes* 25-47; J.-D. KAESTLI: Les principales orientations de la recherche sur les actes apocryphes des apôtres, dans BOVON: *Les actes* 49-67.

5. Pour la diffusion des Actes de Thomas, voir par exemple P.H. POIRIER: *L'hymne de la perle des Actes de Thomas. Introduction, texte, traduction, commentaire* (= Homo religiosus 8) (Louvain-la-Neuve 1981) 227-283.

6. Cf. ROUWHORST: Bénédiction, action de grâces, supplication.

étudier ces passages d'une manière plus systématique que je ne l'ai fait il y a dix ans et, en outre, en partant d'un point de vue quelque peu différent.

La plus grande partie de cette contribution consistera en une analyse détaillée des passages concernés des Actes de Thomas. Je ne m'occuperai pas de la question posée par la relation entre la liturgie 'officielle' – adjectif que d'ailleurs pour la période dont datent les Actes de Thomas, on ne peut utiliser que sous réserve! – et la réception de celle-ci par les chrétiens, le 'peuple' qui l'a célébrée: cette question ne reviendra qu'à la fin de cette contribution. En outre, comme les Actes de Thomas ne semblent pas être très bien connus parmi les liturgistes et qu'ils suscitent, en plus, un certain nombre de problèmes, nous ferons d'abord quelques remarques préalables sur cet ouvrage.

1. LES ACTES DE THOMAS

Les Actes de Thomas appartiennent à un genre littéraire qui, pendant plusieurs siècles, a connu une grande popularité dans des communautés chrétiennes diverses, tant orthodoxes que hétérodoxes. Malgré les différences de style et de contenu qu'on peut déceler parmi ces différents actes, ceux-ci n'en ont pas moins ceci de commun qu'ils portent tous sur l'activité missionnaire de l'un des apôtres, par exemple Jean, Paul, André, et que le récit de ces actes suit en gros toujours le même trame: la prédication de l'apôtre qui comporte en règle générale un appel à la chasteté absolue et est appuyée par des miracles parfois fort sensationnels, d'où résultent assez vite des conversions, surtout parmi les femmes de la haute société, mais aussi la colère de ceux qui sont moins convaincus par le message de l'apôtre, notamment si celui-ci convertit leurs femmes, leurs fiancées ou leurs amantes à la continence sexuelle, et cela finit toujours, sauf dans le cas des Actes de Jean, par le martyre de l'apôtre.[7]

Dans les Actes de Thomas il s'agit de l'activité missionnaire de l'apôtre Thomas – appelé aussi 'Jude Thomas' ou 'Jude'[8] – en Inde (indication de lieu qui demeure quelque peu vague et fait encore l'objet de discussions savantes).[9] La plus grande partie de l'ouvrage porte sur la prédication de Thomas dans ce pays et sur les miracles qu'il y accomplit. Les Actes se terminent par le récit du martyre de Thomas qui est tué par quelques soldats du roi Mazdai après qu'entre autres Mygdonia, la femme d'un officier, et la femme du roi lui-même ont été gagnées par Thomas au christianisme.

Des multiples problèmes que suscitent les Actes de Thomas, on peut dire que la solution d'un certain nombre a rallié le consensus des spécialistes. Ainsi

---

7. Cf. pour cette caractérisation des actes apocryphes des apôtres F. MORARD: Souffrance et martyre dans les actes apocryphes des apôtres, dans BOVON: *Les actes* 95-108, p. 96. Voir également A. KLIJN: *The Acts of Thomas* (= Supplement to Novum Testamentum 5) (Leiden 1962) 18.

8. Cf. pour les questions relatives au nom de l'apôtre: KLIJN: *The Acts* 158-159; G. BORNKAMM: The Acts of Thomas, dans E. HENNECKE et W. SCHNEEMELCHER: *New Testament apocrypha* 2 (London 1975²) 426.

9. KLIJN: *The Acts* 27-29.

il y a pratiquement unanimité sur la date de composition et sur le milieu d'origine. Les spécialistes s'accordent pour dater les Actes de Thomas du troisième siècle et pour situer leur milieu d'origine dans la région d'Edesse.[10] De même, on tend à prendre pour acquis que la langue originelle est le syriaque, mais que la version syriaque dont nous disposons actuellement a été révisée dans un sens orthodoxe, et qu'en règle générale la teneur originelle a été mieux préservée par la traduction grecque.[11]

A côté de ces questions qui ont trouvé des solutions plus ou moins communément acceptées et à notre avis effectivement très vraisemblables, il y en a d'autres qui font encore l'objet de discussions et de divergences d'opinion. Un problème qui demeure encore irrésolu, est celui de la composition interne des Actes de Thomas. En effet, il paraît clair que cet écrit a un caractère composite,[12] qu'il est par exemple formé d'une série de récits qui, au moins en partie, donnent l'impression d'ensembles autonomes et qu'ensuite ces récits eux-mêmes semblent formés de nombreux éléments disparates, par exemple de discours, de prières et d'hymnes – que l'on songe à la fameuse 'Hymne de la perle' qui fait d'ailleurs défaut dans la plupart des manuscrits –[13] sans liens constitutifs étroits avec la narration. Il faut pourtant ajouter qu'il est très difficile sinon impossible de reconstruire la préhistoire du texte, de dégager par exemple les 'sources' qui y sont utilisées ou les tendances d'un éventuel rédacteur (voire de plusieurs rédacteurs). En tout cas, on ne peut pas attendre pour l'étude des célébrations eucharistiques des Actes de Thomas le jour où l'on aura résolu tous les problèmes posés par la composition interne de cet écrit: cela reviendrait probablement à renvoyer cette étude aux kalendes grecques.

Le dernier problème que nous voulons mentionner est celui du milieu théologique dont les Actes de Thomas sont issus. A dire la vérité, il n'est pas dans notre propos de traiter à fond cette question fort débattue et qui a déjà fait couler beaucoup d'encre. Il nous paraît pourtant nécessaire de faire observer que, dans le passé, on a associé les Actes de Thomas avec une trop grande facilité à l'hérésie, en particulier au gnosticisme,[14] ce qui, comme nous l'avons

10. Ainsi par exemple KLIJN: *The Acts* 26, 30-33; BORNKAMM: The Acts 440-441; G. QUISPEL: *Makarius, das Thomasevangelium und das Lied von der Perle* (= Supplements to Novum Testamentum 15) (Leiden 1967) 6; H. PUECH: *En quête de la Gnose* 2 (Paris 1978) 42; POIRIER: *L'hymne* 275-276.

11. KLIJN: *The Acts* 13-16; BORNKAMM: The Acts 428, 442; R. MURRAY: *Symbols of Church and kingdom* (Cambridge 1975) 26.

12. KLIJN: *The Acts* 28; BORNKAMM: The Acts 428-429; Y. TISSOT: Les Actes apocryphes de Thomas: exemple de recueil composite, dans BOVON: *Les actes* 223-232.

13. Cf. P.H. POIRIER: L'hymne de la perle des Actes de Thomas: étude de la tradition manuscrite, dans *Symposium syriacum 1976* (= Orientalia Christiana analecta 205) (Roma 1978) 19-29; POIRIER: *L'hymne* 171-184.

14. La thèse de l'origine gnostique des Actes de Thomas a été notamment défendue par R. LIPSIUS: *Die apokryphen Apostelgeschichten und Apostellegenden* (Braunschweig 1883, 1887, 1884 = Amsterdam 1976ʳ) (voir pour les Actes de Thomas: 1, 225-347) et par BORNKAMM: The Acts 429-442. Elle a été partagée par de nombreux autres savants, par exemple par des liturgistes comme H. Lietzmann (LIETZMANN: *Messe und Herrenmahl* 244) et J. Betz (BETZ: *Die Eucharistie* 324).

déjà constaté, pourrait expliquer en partie le silence dont les liturgistes ont entouré cet écrit. A notre avis, la plupart des arguments qu'on a allégués pour montrer le caractère 'hétérodoxe' des Actes de Thomas, ne sont pas convaincants et au moins faut-il constater qu'on n'a pas réussi à rattacher ces Actes avec certitude à aucun système ou groupe 'hétérodoxe' particulier,[15] si ce n'est l'encratisme[16] (très répandu dans l'église ancienne et surtout dans le christianisme syriaque primitif).[17] Du reste, on ne peut guère trop insister sur le fait que, dans le milieu où les Actes de Thomas ont pris naissance, celui du christianisme syriaque d'Edesse du troisième siècle, les lignes de démarcation entre l'orthodoxie et l'hétérodoxie étaient beaucoup plus floues qu'elles ne le seraient plus tard, par exemple après les grands conciles des quatrième et cinquième siècles.[18]

Ayant relevé les données les plus essentielles concernant les Actes de Thomas et nous étant prononcés sur quelques questions débattues regardant cet écrit, voyons maintenant quelles indications on peut en tirer sur la célébration de l'eucharistie.

2. LA CÉLÉBRATION DE L'EUCHARISTIE SELON LES ACTES DE THOMAS

Pour la clarté nous voulons d'abord donner quelques précisions sur la méthode que nous nous proposons de suivre. Puis nous examinerons successivement les passages des Actes de Thomas qui renferment une description d'une célébration eucharistique. Notre intention est de traduire un par un ces passages. Parce qu'il y a parfois des différences sérieuses entre la version grecque et le texte syriaque, nous donnerons les traductions des textes grec et syriaque sous forme d'une synopse.[19] Les commentaires dont nous ferons

---

15. A remarquer que des auteurs tels que Lipsius et Bornkamm, qui défendent la thèse de l'origine gnostique, ont une conception très vague et parfois même erronée du 'gnosticisme' (cela vaut notamment pour le premier de ces deux auteurs; cf. KAESTLI: Les principales orientations 54).
16. Cf. par exemple: Y. TISSOT: Encratisme et actes apocryphes, dans BOVON: Les actes 109-119, pp. 118-119; P. BROWN: The body and society (New York 1988) 97-100.
17. Voir par exemple QUISPEL: Makarius 6-7; G. QUISPEL: The Study of encratism: a historical survey, dans U. BIANCHI (éd.): La tradizione dell'enkrateia. Atti del Colloquio Internazionale - Milano 20-23 aprile 1982 (Roma 1985) 35-82, pp. 55-63; BROWN: The body 83-102.
18. Cf. par exemple W. BAUER: Rechtgläubigkeit und Ketzerei im ältesten Christentum (Tübingen 1964²) 6-48; H. DRIJVERS: Rechtgläubigkeit und Ketzerei im ältesten syrischen Christentum, dans Symposium syriacum 1972 (= Orientalia Christiana analecta 197) (Roma 1974) 291-308.
19. Pour le texte syriaque voir: W. WRIGHT: Apocryphal acts of the apostles 1-2 (London-Edinburgh 1871 = Amsterdam 1968ʳ). Pour le texte grec: R. LIPSIUS et M. BONNET: Acta apostolorum apocrypha 2, 2 (Leipzig 1903 = Hildesheim 1972ʳ) 99-291. Wright avait pourvu son édition d'une traduction anglaise qui a été reproduite par A. Klijn (KLIJN: The Acts). Une traduction de la version grecque se trouve dans HENNECKE et SCHNEEMELCHER: New Testament apocrypha (traduction allemande de G. Bornkamm dans la version originale et traduction anglaise de R.McL. Wilson dans l'édition anglaise). A remarquer encore que la subdivision en chapitres est empruntée à l'édition de Lipsius et Bonnet. (Cf. pour d'autres détails relatifs à cette question KLIJN: The Acts 2, note 3.)

suivre les traductions auront pour but, d'une part, de reconstituer des versions aussi anciennes que possible des passages traduits – en nous basant évidemment surtout sur une comparaison entre les deux versions – et, d'autre part, d'éclaircir certains problèmes que ces passages susciteront, et surtout de dégager la forme et le caractère de la célébration eucharistique sous-entendue par les versions originelles reconstituées.

2.1. Fraction et manducation du pain eucharistique

On trouve la première mention d'une célébration eucharistique aux chapitres 26 et 27 où est décrite l'initiation du roi Gundaphore et de son frère. Après que les deux convertis ont demandé à (Jude) Thomas de leur donner le sceau,[20] l'apôtre leur répond dans l'affirmative, en ces mots:

(Chapitre 26)

G	S
Moi aussi je me réjouis et je vous demande de recevoir ce sceau et de participer avec moi à cette eucharistie et à cette bénédiction du Seigneur et d'être rendus parfaits par celle-ci. Car c'est Lui le Seigneur et le Dieu de tous, Jésus-Christ que je proclame et il est le Père de la vérité, en qui je vous ai enseigné à croire.	Moi aussi je me réjouis et je vous demande de participer à l'eucharistie et aussi à la bénédiction de ce Christ que je proclame.

Dans le récit d'initiation qui suit maintenant il existe des écarts sérieux entre les deux versions qui tiennent surtout au fait que dans le texte syriaque le mot 'sceau' a un autre sens que dans la version grecque (voir ci-dessus, note 20). Dans les deux récits l'initiation s'achève pourtant par une célébration eucharistique qui est décrite comme il suit:

(Chapitre 27)

G	S
Et lorsque l'aube parut et le jour se leva, il (Thomas) rompit le pain et les fit participer à l'eucharistie du Christ. Et ils se réjouirent et jubilèrent.	Et lorsque l'aube parut et qu'il fit jour, il rompit l'eucharistie et les fit participer à la table du Christ. Et ils se réjouirent et jubilèrent.

Enfin, un peu plus loin, à la fin du chapitre 29, à nouveau il est fait mention d'une célébration eucharistique qui cette fois-ci n'a aucun lien avec le rituel de

---

20. Syriaque *rushma*, grec *sphragis*, terme que la version grecque interprète au sens de 'baptême', mais qui à l'origine s'est sans nul doute référé à une onction prébaptismale, comme c'est encore le cas dans la version syriaque. Cf. pour cette question TISSOT: Les Actes 225-226; KLIJN: The Acts 55-57.

l'initiation. Cette célébration qui a lieu à la fin de la nuit du samedi au dimanche, est évoquée en ces termes:

(Chapitre 29)

G	S
Et ayant parlé ainsi, il (Thomas) leur imposa ses mains et les bénit.	Et ayant parlé ainsi, il leur imposa sa main
Et ayant rompu le pain de l'eucharistie,	et il rompit l'eucharistie
il le leur donna,	et la donna à eux tous,
en disant:	en disant:
'Que cette eucharistie vous serve à la miséricorde et à la clémence et non au jugement et à la vengeance.'	'Que cette eucharistie vous serve à la miséricorde et à la clémence et non au jugement et à la vengeance.'
Et ils dirent: 'Amen.'	Et ils dirent: 'Amen.'

Comme la synopse que nous avons faite, permet de le voir tout de suite, il y a quelques différences entre les deux versions.

Premièrement, on est frappé par le fait que, dans le passage tiré du chapitre 26, le texte de la version syriaque est plus court que celui de la traduction grecque. Comment expliquer cet écart? Le traducteur grec a-t-il ajouté quelques mots à l'original syriaque? Ou bien, la version syriaque serait-elle le résultat de l'abrègement d'un texte syriaque plus ancien? La dernière solution paraît la plus probable. En fait, on ne voit pas quelle raison le traducteur grec pourrait avoir eu pour ajouter les phrases qui manquent dans le texte syriaque. Du reste, on peut partir du principe que, sauf preuve du contraire, la version grecque est plus proche de l'original syriaque perdu que le texte syriaque actuel, révisé.[21]

Ensuite, dans les passages tirés des chapitres 27 et 29 on peut relever quelques divergences dans la terminologie qui est utilisée pour la fraction du pain eucharistique. La version grecque parle d'abord de 'rompre le pain' et ensuite de 'rompre le pain de l'eucharistie'. Le texte syriaque, par contre, donne à deux reprises l'expression 'rompre l'eucharistie' (elle utilise le mot grec en se contentant de le transcrire). A première vue, on tendrait à croire que l'auteur grec a voulu éviter l'emploi du mot grec *eucharistia* au sens de 'pain eucharistique' qui aurait pu sembler étrange au lecteur grec. Tel ne semble cependant pas être le cas, parce qu'ailleurs (chapitre 158, voir plus loin) la version grecque aussi utilise l'expression 'rompre l'eucharistie'[22] et que du reste, les mots 'participer (*koinonein*) à l'eucharistie' dont le traducteur grec se sert dans ce même chapitre – en s'écartant du texte syriaque! –, ne peuvent signi-

---

21. Cf. ci-dessus, par. 1.
22. A remarquer d'ailleurs que l'expression intervient également dans un écrit composé originairement en grec, à savoir l'homélie pseudo-clémentine XI (chapitre 36; cf. B. REHM et J. IRMSCHER: *Die Pseudoklementinen* 1. *Homilien* (= Die griechischen christlichen Schriftsteller der ersten Jahrhunderte 42²) (Berlin 1969²) 172). Voir aussi KLIJN: *The Acts* 218.

fier qu'une seule chose: 'se nourrir du pain eucharistique'. Une autre solution semble dès lors préférable. C'est que la version syriaque trahit une prédilection particulière pour l'expression 'rompre l'eucharistie'. Or, il ne serait pas difficile de trouver une explication pour une telle prédilection: la tournure 'rompre l'eucharistie' intervient à deux reprises dans la *Peshitta*, à savoir dans Actes 2, 42 et 20, 7. C'est pourquoi nous formulons l'hypothèse que, sur le point aussi de la terminologie utilisée pour indiquer la fraction du pain eucharistique, la version grecque est plus primitive que le texte syriaque, qui a subi ici l'influence de la *Peshitta*.

En ce qui concerne les parties que les deux versions ont en commun, il paraît indiqué d'attirer l'attention sur la signification précise qu'y revêtent quelques mots et expressions qui pourraient prêter à des malentendus ou dont du moins la connotation pourrait facilement nous échapper.

a. Comme nous l'avons déjà signalé, le mot 'eucharistie' signifie tout d'abord 'pain eucharistique (consacré)'. A remarquer notamment que ce terme n'a certainement pas la connotation d''action de grâces' (ce n'est même pas le cas dans la version grecque). En effet, l'un des traits les plus étonnants des célébrations eucharistiques décrites dans les Actes de Thomas est précisément que l'action de grâces n'y joue aucun rôle.[23]

b. Comme nous l'avons également déjà fait observer, 'participer (grec: *koinonein*, syriaque: *shawteef*) à l'eucharistie' signifie: 'se nourrir du pain eucharistique', 'communier'. Du reste, il est intéressant de relever qu'ailleurs dans les Actes de Thomas ce verbe et ses dérivés sont utilisés pour désigner l''union' sexuelle[24] tellement détestée par l'auteur (ou le rédacteur) de cet écrit. Il ne paraît pas trop téméraire de supposer que dans la conception 'encratite' de l'auteur ou du rédacteur des Actes il y a une parenté contrastée entre la 'communion' et l'union sexuelle!

c. Nous signalons d'emblée que plus loin[25] il se révélera à l'évidence que le mot 'bénédiction' (grec: *eulogia*, syriaque: *burkta*) a lui aussi un sens particulier et en tout cas très précis: il se réfère à la prière qui précède la fraction du pain eucharistique et la communion, prière qui, nous le verrons encore, a le caractère et la forme d'une invocation, d'une 'epiclèse'.

Ceci étant, nous sommes en mesure de nous former une certaine idée de la célébration eucharistique telle qu'elle est sous-entendue par la version 'originelle' de cette partie des Actes de Thomas. Celle-ci a comporté les éléments suivants: une 'bénédiction', la fraction du pain eucharistique, une brève formule précédant la communion (chapitre 29) et la communion elle-même, la manducation du 'pain de l'eucharistie', c'est à dire du pain eucharistique. Dans la suite, il apparaîtra que tels sont effectivement les moments essentiels, les points culminants de la célébration eucharistique des Actes de Thomas.

23. Cf. ROUWHORST: Bénédiction, action de grâces, supplication 221-224.
24. Cf. chapitres 12, 43, 88 et, en outre, chapitres 51, 52, 55, 135 de la version syriaque.
25. Voir notamment chapitres 49 et 133 et, en outre, ROUWHORST: Bénédiction, action de grâces, supplication 223-224.

2.2. L'invocation de la mère

Dans le cinquième acte (chapitres 42-50) on peut lire comment l'apôtre libère une femme d'un démon qui l'habitait. L'exorcisme est suivi de l'initiation de la femme exorcisée et de beaucoup d'autres qui ont été impressionnés par le pouvoir et le message de Thomas. Cette initiation se termine, elle aussi, par une célébration eucharistique.

(Chapitre 49)

G	S
L'apôtre ordonna à son diacre d'apporter une table et ils apportèrent un petit banc qu'ils trouvèrent là, il étendit une nappe et mit le pain de la bénédiction dessus.	Et l'apôtre ordonna à son diacre de préparer le (pain) rompu et il apporta un banc qui était là et il disposa dessus le pain de la bénédiction qu'il avait apporté.
Et l'apôtre se mit à côté (de ce banc) et dit:	Et l'apôtre se mit à côté et dit:
'Jésus qui nous a rendu dignes de participer à l'eucharistie de ton saint corps et sang,	'Jésus qui nous a rendu dignes de nous approcher de ton saint corps et de participer à ton sang vivifiant.
voici	Voici qu'à cause de la confiance que nous avons en Toi,
que nous osons nous approcher de ton eucharistie et invoquer ton saint nom.	nous osons nous approcher et invoquer ton saint nom qui fut proclamé par tes prophètes comme ta divinité l'a voulu, et Tu es prêché par tes apôtres dans le monde entier, selon ta bonté et par ta miséricorde Tu as été révélé aux justes.
Viens et sois en communion avec nous.'	Nous te demandons de venir et d'être en communion avec nous en vue de (nous) aider et de (nous) apporter la vie et pour que tes serviteurs se convertissent à Toi, afin qu'ils marchent sous ton joug agréable, dans ta force victorieuse et qu'ainsi ils obtiennent pour leurs âmes la santé et pour leurs corps la vie dans ton monde qui est (plein) de vie.'
Et il commença à dire:	Et il commença à dire:

'Viens, compassion parfaite!
Viens, communion du mâle!
Viens, (Toi) qui
connais les mystères de l'élu!

Viens, (Toi) qui prends part
à tous les combats
du noble athlète!

Viens, silence qui révèles les hauts
faits de toute grandeur!
Viens, (Toi) qui montres
ce qui est caché et fais
connaître ce qui est ineffable!
Colombe sainte, qui enfantes des
jumeaux!
Viens, mère cachée!
Viens, (Toi) qui te montres
dans tes actions et procures
la joie et le repos
à qui s'unissent avec Toi!

Viens et sois en communion avec
nous dans cette eucharistie
que nous célébrons en ton nom
et dans l'agape
(ou: dans l'amour?) dans laquelle
nous sommes unis, par ton appel!'
Et après avoir dit ces mots,
il marqua le pain du signe
de la croix et le rompit
et commença à le distribuer.
Et il en donna d'abord
à la femme, en disant:
'Que par ce (pain)
vous obteniez la rémission des
péchés et des fautes éternelles.'

Et après elle,
il en donna aussi à tous les autres
qui avaient reçu le sceau.

'Viens, don du (très-) haut!
Viens, compassion parfaite!
Viens, Saint-Esprit!
Viens, (Toi) qui
révèles les mystères de l'élu
parmi les prophètes!
Viens, (Toi) qui par tes apôtres
proclames les combats
de notre athlète victorieux!
Viens, trésor de la majesté!
Viens, bien-aimée de la
miséricorde du très-haut!
Viens, silencieuse qui révèles les
mystères du (très-)haut!
Viens, (Toi) qui énonces
les choses cachées et montres les
oeuvres de notre Dieu! Viens
(Toi,) qui donnes la vie dans le
secret et les révélations par
Tes actions!
Viens, (Toi) qui donnes

la joie et le repos
à tous ceux qui s'unissent avec
Toi!
Viens, puissance du Père
et sagesse du Fils
qui êtes un en tout.
Viens et sois en communion avec
nous dans cette eucharistie
que nous célébrons et dans
cette offrande que nous offrons
et dans cette commémoraison
que nous célébrons!'
Et après
il marqua le pain du signe
de la croix

et il en donna d'abord
à cette femme, en lui disant:
'Que par (ce) pain
vous obteniez la rémission des
péchés et la résurrection
pour l'éternité.'
Et après elle
il en donna à toutes les personnes
qui avaient été baptisés avec elle
Puis il en donna à tout le monde,
en leur disant:

60

'Que cette eucharistie vous serve
à la vie et au repos
et non au jugement et à la
vengeance.'
Et ils dirent: 'Amen.'

A propos de ce long passage qui constitue un admirable complément de la description de l'eucharistie rencontrée aux chapitres 26 et 27, surgissent deux questions qui sollicitent une attention particulière.

Premièrement, en comparant les deux versions, on constate quelques divergences qui concernent la structure de la célébration eucharistique. Dans la version grecque il est d'abord fait mention de la préparation de la 'table' – un petit banc trouvé sur place – et après suivent successivement la prière adressée à Jésus, la longue invocation du nom – sur laquelle nous reviendrons encore –, la fraction du pain eucharistique qui auparavant a été marqué avec le signe de la croix, et finalement la communion de la femme exorcisée et des autres convertis. Dans ses grandes lignes, le texte syriaque concorde avec la version grecque à ceci près pourtant que le rite y commence par la préparation non de la table, mais du 'pain de la bénédiction' – le pain qui va être béni par l'invocation du nom – et en outre que ce pain se trouve déjà être rompu et dès lors n'est plus rompu à la fin, avant la communion.

Il n'est pas douteux qu'en tout cela ce soit à nouveau la version grecque qui est la plus proche de la rédaction primitive. En effet, l'ordonnance décrite dans cette version grecque inspire déjà la confiance pour la seule raison qu'elle est entièrement conforme à celle que nous avons rencontrée aux chapitres 26 et 27, tandis que la structure de la célébration supposée par le texte syriaque s'en écarte. En plus, le mot que le texte syriaque emploie pour désigner le pain rompu (qesta)[26] est connu de la liturgie syrienne où il est utilisé pour le pain non-consacré. En d'autres termes, la version syriaque porte à coup sûr les traces d'une adaptation à la liturgie syrienne et est donc sans aucun doute secondaire.

En second lieu, il convient de s'arrêter un instant à l'élément qui, dans cette description, fait l'impression la plus originale et en même temps, force est bien de l'admettre, fait aussi mystère: la longue invocation du nom de Jésus qui est identifié au nom d'une entité divine féminine, voire avec cette entité elle-même.

Disons d'avance qu'il ne nous sera pas possible d'étudier à fond toutes les questions que pourrait susciter cette invocation, cette 'épiclèse'. Signalons notamment que nous n'aurons pas le temps de discuter au long et au large toutes les attaches (juives, chrétiennes, judéo-chrétiennes, païennes) de cette prière.[27] Nous sommes obligés de nous borner à quelques remarques rapides dont le but principal est d'éclairer la fonction que cette invocation prend dans

---

26. Cf. KLIJN: *The Acts* 244.
27. Cf. pour ses attaches KLIJN: *The Acts* 213-217; A. KLIJN: *Edessa, die Stadt des Apostels Thomas* (Neukirchen 1965) 123.

l'ensemble de la célébration eucharistique dont elle fait partie. La première question qui se pose est à nouveau celle de la relation entre les deux versions qui présentent quelques carts sérieux. De ces deux recensions quelle est la (plus) primitive?

La réponse à cette question est simple. Il est hors de doute que la teneur originelle a été mieux conservée par la traduction grecque. En effet, dans le texte syriaque tel que nous l'avons devant nous, on décèle incontestablement une tendance à réviser la prière dans un sens 'orthodoxe'. Preuve en est notamment l'insertion d'allusions aux prophètes et aux apôtres, ainsi qu'à l'offrande et à la commémoraison qui manquent dans le texte (à notre avis donc originel) de la version grecque. Pareillement, il semble clair que la préoccupation d'orthodoxie de l'auteur de la version syriaque a amené celui-ci à introduire certains titres divins tels que 'Saint-Esprit', 'Puissance du Père' et 'Sagesse du Fils', et d'autre part à omettre l'invocation adressée à la 'Colombe sainte enfantant des jumeaux'!

Autre problème celui de l'identité de la 'mère divine' qui est invoquée et à qui sont attribués des titres divins en partie assez originaux et parfois même étonnants. Qui est cette 'mère' divine?

Impossible, bien entendu, de retracer la provenance de tous les titres qui sont mentionnés et, par voie de conséquence, aussi de dire le dernier mot sur l'identité de cette entité divine féminine. Signalons pourtant que dans une autre invocation des Actes de Thomas,[28] très apparentée à celle que nous rencontrons ici – sauf qu'elle est prononcée non sur le pain eucharistique, mais sur l'huile de l'onction prébaptismale –, cette 'mère' divine est identifiée avec le Saint-Esprit. A quoi on peut ajouter que le titre 'Colombe sainte' omis dans le texte syriaque, suggère également une telle solution[29] et qu'en outre dans le christianisme syriaque le Saint-Esprit fut effectivement représenté comme une mère.[30] Des indices indéniables donc que l'invocation s'adresse au nom du Saint-Esprit ou, ce qui apparemment revient au même pour l'auteur des Actes de Thomas, au Saint-Esprit lui-même qui, à son tour, est associé, identifié au nom de Jésus. Pour le reste, il paraît clair que le Saint-Esprit dont il s'agit dans cette invocation, a emprunté certains de ses titres et de ses particularités à une autre entité divine féminine, connue du judaïsme et du christianisme, la Sagesse. Autrement dit, l'insertion secondaire des titres 'Saint-Esprit' et 'sagesse' va bel et bien dans le sens du texte primitif.

S'imposent encore quelques observations concernant le caractère de l'invocation, notamment sa forme littéraire et sa relation avec la célébration liturgique à laquelle elle est destinée, la célébration de l'eucharistie.

28. Voir chapitre 27.
29. Etant donné qu'une colombe intervient dans le récit évangélique du baptême du Christ au Jourdain (cf. Matthieu 3, 16; Marc 1, 9; Luc 3, 22). A remarquer que déjà J. THILO: *Acta S. Thomae apostoli* (Leipzig 1823) 186 et suiv. et LIPSIUS: *Die apokryphen Apostelgeschichten* 314 ont cru reconnaître dans ce titre une allusion à la colombe du baptême du Christ au Jourdain.
30. Cf. par exemple MURRAY: *Symbols* 312-320.

En ce qui concerne la forme littéraire, à remarquer d'abord que, sur ce point, l'invocation présente des parallèles étroits avec certaines prières d'incantation magiques païennes (grecques) qui se caractérisent également par de longues énumérations de noms divins ainsi que par des appels réitérés et instants à une divinité ou à des divinités et commençant par des impératifs de verbes qui signifient 'venir' (par exemple *elthe*, le mot qui intervient dans la version grecque des Actes de Thomas).[31] D'autre part, il y a une différence très frappante avec la catégorie de prières (chrétiennes) qui, du point de vue de leur fonction (liturgique), sont le plus proches de cette invocation, à savoir les prières eucharistiques, les anaphores connues de l'église ancienne. Dans notre invocation manquent à peu près tous les éléments qui sont essentiels dans ces anaphores: l'action de grâces, la louange adressée à Dieu, pour ne pas parler du récit de l'institution. Dans la version grecque (primitive) on ne trouve même pas la moindre allusion à la commoraison (ou l'offrande). Le seul élément que notre prière a en commun avec (une partie) des prières eucharistiques classiques est précisément l'invocation du Saint Esprit, l''épiclèse'.

Ensuite, force est de constater qu'au moins dans la version grecque, qui est sans nul doute la plus ancienne, il n'y a presque pas de liens constitutifs entre cette invocation et la célébration dont elle fait partie. Sauf à la fin, aucune allusion n'y est faite à l'eucharistie ou à un motif ou un élément qui y est lié. Qui plus est, comme nous l'avons déjà signalé, ailleurs dans les Actes de Thomas, au chapitre 27, on rencontre une invocation très similaire, mais qui cette fois-ci n'est pas prononcée sur le pain eucharistique, mais sur l'huile de l'onction prébaptismale. Ceci donné, il y a deux possibilités: ou bien il s'agit d'une prière d'un caractère général, pouvant servir à la 'bénédiction' de plusieurs éléments qui jouent un rôle dans la liturgie, ou bien nous avons affaire à un texte qui plonge ses racines dans la liturgie baptismale, mais a été légèrement adapté à la célébration de l'eucharistie. Il est difficile de se décider pour l'une de ces deux solutions, mais nous n'en voulons pas moins signaler que, dans la seconde hypothèse, on aurait trouvé une explication pour le problème posé par la mention de la 'colombe sainte enfantant des jumeaux', élément qui détonne dans un contexte eucharistique, mais ne le fait pas du tout dans un cadre baptismal.[32]

Quoi qu'il en soit de la solution qu'on préfère adopter pour ce problème, il ne nous paraît pas probable que dans cette invocation nous ayons affaire à une insertion tardive dans le texte des Actes de Thomas.[33] S'il faut admettre que le

---

31. Cf. certains des textes magiques grecs édités par K. PREISENDANZ: *Papyri Graecae magicae* 1-2 (Stuttgart 1973² et 1974²), notamment le no. VIII (2, 45-50), texte qui commence par les mots: *elthe moi, kyrie Herme*. La parenté entre ce texte et les épiclèses des chapitres 27 et 50 des Actes de Thomas a déjà été remarquée par LIETZMANN: *Messe und Herrenmahl* 244.

32. Cf. ci-dessus, note 29.

33. Ainsi pourtant W. BOUSSET: Manichäisches in den Thomasakten, dans *Zeitschrift für die neutestamentliche Wissenschaft und die Kunde des Urchristentums* 18 (1917-1918) 1-39, pp. 34-39, qui considère cette épiclèse comme une interpolation manichéenne. Cette hypothèse est pourtant réfutée d'une manière convaincante par TISSOT: *Les Actes* 227-228.

lien entre cette invocation et le rituel de l'eucharistie n'est pas très étroit, il n'en reste pas moins qu'une fois éliminée cette invocation, il manquerait à la célébration eucharistique un élément essentiel: une espèce de prière sur le pain eucharistique. D'ailleurs, sans cette 'épiclèse' aussi la bénédiction dont il est question au début du passage – où il est fait mention du 'pain de la bénédiction', c'est à dire du 'pain qui est à bénir' – perdrait son sens. Cette allusion à une bénédiction, à quoi devrait-elle se référer si ce n'est précisément à l'invocation précédant la distribution du pain eucharistique?

Dernier détail. A la fin de l'épiclèse, telle qu'elle est transmise par la version grecque, apparaît le mot *agape*. Evidemment, il est possible que ce terme doive se traduire tout simplement par 'amour', mais on ne peut d'autre part pas exclure la possibilité d'une signification plus spécifiquement liturgique, d'un renvoi à la célébration d'une 'agape'[34] (dans cette hypothèse, l'omission de ce mot et de la phrase dont il fait partie, serait d'autant plus remarquable!).

2.3. Du pain et de l'eau

On trouve une troisième évocation d'une célébration eucharistique – cette fois-ci plus rapide et aussi plus fragmentaire – au début du dixième acte, aux chapitres 120 et 121 où est décrit le baptême – ou peut-être faudrait-il plutôt dire l'initiation – de Mygdonia. Celle-ci a été gagnée par Thomas à l'évangile et refuse désormais d'avoir des relations sexuelles avec son mari, un officier du roi Mazdai. Ce dernier a fait jeter Thomas en prison, mais l'apôtre en est sorti d'une manière miraculeuse et baptise Mygdonia, à sa demande, dans la maison de celle-ci où dort son mari.

Avant d'être initiée au christianisme, Mygdonia demande à sa nourrice, Narcia, de lui apporter les choses dont on aura besoin pour le rituel:

(Chapitre 121)

G	S
Et Mygdonia disait: 'Viens participer avec moi à la vie éternelle, afin que je reçoive de toi une nourriture parfaite. Je suis une femme libre, prends et m'apporte donc du pain et un mélange d'eau.'	Elle lui disait: 'Viens participer avec moi à la vie éternelle et je recevrai de toi une éducation parfaite. Je suis une femme libre. Prends donc en secret un pain et m'apporte un mélange de vin.'
Et la nourrice disait: 'J'apporterai beaucoup de pains et au lieu d'eau des litres de vin et je satisferai votre désir.'	Narcia lui disait: 'Moi, je vous apporterai du pain en abondance et beaucoup de litres de vin et j'accomplirai votre volonté.'

---

34. Ainsi Hennecke et Schneemelcher: *New Testament apocrypha* 470 et Vogel: Anaphores eucharistiques 406.

Mais elle disait à sa nourrice:

'De litres je n'en ai pas besoin,
ni de beaucoup de pains.
Apporte uniquement ceci:
un mélange d'eau,
un (seul) pain
et de l'huile.'

Mygdonia disait à Narcia, sa nourrice:
'Beaucoup de litres ne me sont pas utiles.
Apporte-moi
un mélange dans une coupe
et un seul pain entier
et un peu d'huile,
au besoin prise d'une lampe.'

Suivent alors dans les deux versions une onction prébaptismale avec de l'huile, versée sur la tête de Mygdonia, et le baptême (avec de l'eau) de celle-ci. Après quoi a lieu une célébration eucharistique.

G	S
Et après qu'elle avait été baptisée	Et après qu'elle était montée
et qu'elle s'était vêtue,	et s'était vêtue,
il rompit le pain	il apporta et rompit l'eucharistie
et ayant pris la coupe avec l'eau,	et prit la coupe
il la fit participer	et il fit participer Mygdonia
au corps du Christ	à la table du Christ
et à la coupe du Fils de Dieu,	et à la coupe du Fils de Dieu.
en disant:	Et il lui disait:
'Vous avez reçu votre sceau,	'Vous avez reçu le sceau
créez pour vous-mêmes	et vous avez obtenu
la vie éternelle.'	la vie en éternité.'
Et en ce moment fut entendue	Et fut entendue
une voix d'en haut,	une voix venant du ciel
disant:	qui disait:
'Oui, Amen.'	'Oui. Amen. Amen.'

Les deux versions concordent pour l'essentiel. Dans leurs grandes lignes elles présupposent le même déroulement de la célébration eucharistique. Celle-ci comporte d'abord la fraction et la distribution du pain eucharistique – précédée, sans aucun doute, par une 'bénédiction', entendons une prière d'invocation qui n'est pas expressément mentionnée, mais est certainement sous-entendue – et ensuite la 'participation' à la coupe.

L'intérêt principal de ce passage réside dans la mention de ce dernier élément, la coupe. Jusqu'à présent il avait été uniquement question du pain (béni, rompu et distribué). Ce passage montre pourtant à l'évidence que dans la célébration eucharistique des Actes de Thomas la coupe aussi a joué un rôle (encore que, force est de l'admettre, assez subordonné).

Reste pourtant à savoir qu'est ce qui se trouve dans la coupe. Est-ce uniquement de l'eau (peut-être mélangée avec quelques gouttes de vin?) comme le veut la version grecque? Ou est-ce qu'elle contient du vin (mélangée d'eau), conformément à ce qu'on peut lire dans le texte syriaque?

A notre avis il n'y a pas de doute que ce soit à nouveau la version grecque qui, sur ce point aussi, est la plus proche de la rédaction primitive (en syriaque). De fait, l'absence de toute allusion au vin trahit une attitude encratite – hostile non seulement à la sexualité et au mariage, mais aussi au vin –, qui cadre parfaitement avec la teneur originelle des Actes de Thomas. L'élimination de ce trait encratite, d'autre part, qu'il faut dans cette hypothèse attribuer à l'auteur du texte syriaque, s'expliquerait aisément par la tendance évidente de ce dernier à éliminer de l'original syriaque (perdu) certains vestiges d''hérésie'. A quoi nous voulons ajouter que cette hypothèse sera largement appuyée par le passage suivant des Actes de Thomas que nous allons examiner maintenant.

2.4. La bénédiction du pain
A la fin du dixième acte est décrite une autre initiation, à savoir celle du général Siphor et de sa femme et de sa fille qui s'achève, comme il fallait s'y attendre, par une célébration eucharistique.

(Chapitre 133)

G	S
Et après qu'ils avaient été baptisés et s'étaient vêtus, il (Thomas) mit le pain sur la table	Et après qu'ils avaient été baptisés et s'étaient vêtus, il apporta du pain et du vin et les mit sur la table et il commença
et le bénit par ces mots: 'Pain de vie par lequel ceux qui en mangent, demeurent immortels; pain qui rassasie par sa bénédiction les âmes affamées; c'est toi qui a été jugé digne de recevoir le don pour obtenir ainsi pour nous la rémission des péchés et afin que ceux qui te mangent, deviennent immortels. Nous appelons sur toi le nom de la mère, de l'ineffable mystère des puissances et des forces cachées. Nous invoquons sur toi le nom de Jésus.'	à les bénir par ces mots: 'Pain de vie par lequel ceux qui en mangeront, ne mourront pas; pain qui remplit les âmes affamées de sa bénédiction. Tu as été jugé digne de recevoir le don et de faire obtenir la rémission des péchés, de telle sorte que ceux qui te mangent, ne mourront pas. Nous invoquons sur toi le nom du Père. Nous invoquons sur toi le nom du Fils. Nous invoquons sur toi le nom de l'Esprit; nom sublime qui pour tous est caché.'
Et il dit: 'Que la force de la bénédiction vienne et demeure en ce pain, pour que toutes les âmes qui en prendront, soient lavées de leur péchés.'	Et il dit: 'Que la force de la bénédiction et de l'action de grâces vienne et demeure sur ce pain afin que toutes les âmes qui en prendront, soient renouvelées et que leurs péchés soient pardonnés.'

66

Et après avoir rompu le pain,	Et il le rompit
il le donna à Siphor,	et le donna à Siphor
à sa femme et à sa fille.	et à sa femme et à sa fille.

En comparant les deux versions on constate assez vite un certain nombre de divergences entre le texte syriaque et la traduction grecque. D'abord, à la différence du texte syriaque, la traduction grecque ne fait pas mention du vin. Deuxièmement, au lieu d'invoquer les noms de la mère et de Jésus, comme le fait la recension grecque, le texte syriaque s'adresse aux noms des trois personnes de la Trinité. A noter enfin la présence du mot 'action de grâces' dans la version syriaque, mot qui fait défaut dans le texte grec.

Au risque de nous répéter, nous constatons que c'est à nouveau la version grecque qui transmet le texte le plus primitif. Quant au vin, mentionné dans le texte syriaque, celui-ci y est certainement ajouté: la preuve convaincante en est fournie par le manuscrit Sinai 30, le plus ancien manuscrit renfermant le texte syriaque des Actes de Thomas – malheuresement très lacuneux, mais ayant conservé le texte du chapitre 133 –: il concorde ici avec la version grecque.[35] Cela montre à l'évidence le caractère secondaire de la mention du vin dans le texte syriaque (révisé) de ce chapitre (comme d'ailleurs aussi dans celui du chapitre 121 examiné et discuté ci-dessus!). Que l'énumération des trois personnes de la Trinité n'ait pas figuré dans la version primitive, paraît presque aller de soi, étant donné la préoccupation d'orthodoxie si caractéristique de l'auteur du texte syriaque révisé. Pareillement, l'allusion à l'action de grâces a l'air d'un ajout secondaire, vu que cet élément ne joue aucun rôle dans la célébration eucharistique des Actes de Thomas.

Quant aux parties communes aux deux recensions qui constituent le noyau le plus ancien de ce passage, il faut reconnaître qu'elles n'apportent pas grand-chose de nouveau. L'intéressant est d'autre part qu'elles montrent une fois de plus d'une façon très claire comment se déroule la célébration eucharistique et en quoi consiste la signification essentielle de ce rituel. Il s'ensuit notamment que le but de cette célébration est de faire participer les fidèles qui y assistent, à la force du nom divin (de Jésus ou, ce qui semble revenir au même, de l'Esprit) qui a été de façon solennelle et instante invoquée sur le pain de l'eucharistie et qui permet d'obtenir la rémission des péchés, de conduire une vie chrétienne et de vaincre la mort, de devenir immortels.

2.5. La dernière eucharistie

Dans le dixième acte (chapitres 150-158) la fin de la vie de Thomas approche. Il a été jeté en prison par le roi Mazdai qui est enragé depuis que sa femme, Tertia, a été gagnée au message, pour lui désastreux, de l'apôtre et s'est décidée à la continence sexuelle. Bientôt Thomas subira le martyre. Avant de mourir l'apôtre sort encore une dernière fois de la prison – à nouveau de façon miraculeuse et laissant perplexes ses geôliers qui le considèrent comme un

---

35. Cf. KLIJN: *The Acts* 288.

magicien (cf. chapitre 162) – pour aller baptiser avec de l'huile et de l'eau les convertis qui n'ont pas encore été initiés et qui sont tous des parents très proches du roi: Tertia, la femme du roi; Vizan, le fils du roi et Manashar, la femme de celui-ci. Cette initiation se termine, bien entendu, par une célébration eucharistique, la dernière de Thomas, à laquelle, en dehors des nouveaux baptisés, participent aussi la très fidèle Mygdonia et sa nourrice Narcia, ainsi que le général Siphor, sa femme et sa fille.

(Chapitre 158)

G	S
Et après qu'ils étaient montés,	Et après qu'ils avaient été baptisés et étaient montés,
il prit du pain et une coupe et les bénit, en disant:	il apporta du pain et une coupe mélangée et les bénit par ces mots:
'Nous mangeons ton corps saint qui fut crucifié pour nous et nous buvons ton sang versé pour notre salut. Que par ton corps nous obtenions le salut et par ton sang la rémission des péchés. Qu'à cause du fiel que tu as bu, soit enlevé de nous le fiel du diable.	'Nous mangeons ton corps saint qui fut crucifié pour nous et nous buvons ton sang vivifiant qui fut versé pour nous. Que par ton corps nous obtenions la vie et par ton sang la rémission des péchés. Qu'à cause du fiel que tu as bu, soit enlevé de nous le fiel de notre ennemi.
Qu'à cause de vinaigre que tu as bu pour nous, soit fortifiée notre faiblesse. Qu'à cause de la salive que tu as reçue,	Qu'à cause de vinaigre que tu as bu pour nous, soit fortifiée notre faiblesse. Et que par la salive que Tu as reçue à cause de nous,
nous recevions la rosée de ta bonté. Et que par le roseau dont on T'a frappé pour nous, nous recevions la maison parfaite.	nous recevions la vie parfaite.
Et parce que tu as reçu pour nous la couronne d'épines, que nous qui T'aimons, nous portions la couronne qui ne se fane pas. Et qu'à cause du linge dont Tu as été enveloppé,	Et parce que Tu as reçu à cause de nous la couronne d'épines, que nous recevions de Toi la couronne qui ne se fane pas. Et parce que Tu as été enveloppé à cause de nous d'un linge,
nous soyons ceints de ta force invincible.	que nous soyons ceints de ta force puissante qui ne peut pas être vaincue.

68

Et qu'à cause du sépulcre neuf
et de ton ensevelissement

nous recevions le renouvellement
de l'esprit et de l'âme.
Et parce que Tu es ressuscité
et es revenu à la vie,
que nous revenions à la vie
et vivions
et nous tenions debout
devant Toi au jugement juste.'

Et il rompit l'eucharistie
et la donna à Vizan
et à Tertia et à Manashar
et à la femme et à la fille
de Siphor, en disant:
'Que cette eucharistie vous serve
au salut et à la joie
et à la santé
de vos âmes!'
Et ils dirent: 'Amen.'
Et une voix fut entendue qui
disait:
'Amen.

Ne craignez pas, mais croyez
seulement.'

Et parce que Tu as été
enseveli dans un sépulcre neuf
à cause de notre mortalité,
que nous recevions la communion
avec Toi au ciel.
Et comme Tu es ressuscité,

que nous ressuscitions nous
(aussi)
et nous tenions debout
devant Toi au jugement de la
vérité.'
Et il rompit l'eucharistie
et la donna à Vizan
et à Tertia
et à la femme et à la fille
de Siphor, en disant:
'Que cette eucharistie vous serve
à la vie et à la joie
et à la santé et à la guérison
de vos âmes et vos corps!'
Et ils dirent: 'Amen.'
Et une voix fut entendue qui
disait:
'Amen.'
Et lorsqu'ils entendirent cette
voix, ils tombèrent la face
(contre terre). Et encore fut
entendue la voix qui disait:
'Ne craignez pas, mais croyez
seulement.'

Il n'y a pas lieu de s'attarder aux divergences qu'il y a de ci de là entre les deux versions. Celles-ci ne regardent que des détails qui sont à négliger et en tout cas n'ont guère trait au déroulement ou au caractère du rituel de l'eucharistie.

En ce qui concerne les parties communes aux deux recensions, le seul élément vraiment nouveau y est constitué par la bénédiction intéressante et, faut-il ajouter, quelque peu étonnante qui précède la fraction du pain. En effet, la forme et le contenu de cette prière diffèrent totalement de ceux des 'bénédictions' rencontrées aux passages examinés ci-dessus. Cette fois-ci on n'a pas affaire à une invocation des noms de Jésus et de l'Esprit, mais à une série de demandes adressées au Christ, à Jésus, dont le trait le plus frappant est qu'y sont énumérés un certain nombre de détails très concrets tirés du récit de la Passion du Seigneur, à partir des humiliations jusqu'à la résurrection.

Comment expliquer l'apparition si soudaine d'un élément de l'eucharistie jusqu'ici entièrement absent (au point de susciter notre étonnement)? Est-ce que nous nous trouvons ici face à un tout autre type de célébration eucharistique, reflétant peut-être une tradition liturgique différente? A vrai dire, pour expliquer les traits propres à cette 'bénédiction' il n'est nullement nécessaire de supposer l'existence d'une tradition liturgique différente. Ces traits s'expliquent parfaitement par la place que la célébration eucharistique du chapitre 158 prend dans l'ensemble de la narration des Actes de Thomas. Cette célébration se situe tout juste avant la mort de l'apôtre qui bientôt sera tué par les soldats du roi Mazdai (chapitres 159-168): dans les Actes, Thomas est représenté comme le frère jumeau de Jésus, voire comme une espèce d''alter Jésus';[36] sa vie est modelée sur celle de son Frère jumeau. Rien d'étonnant donc que, juste avant sa propre 'passion', pendant sa dernière eucharistie qui est à comparer avec la dernière cène, Thomas fasse mémoire de la passion de Jésus.

Au reste, du point de vue de la forme et même de celui du contenu, cette prière ne s'écarte guère moins des prières eucharistiques classiques que les invocations des chapitres 50 et 133. Y manquent par exemple des éléments caractéristiques tels que l'action de grâces, la louange adressée à Dieu, l'invocation de l'Esprit (et cela à la différence des invocations étudiées ci-dessus). A la vérité, plutôt qu'avec les anaphores de l'église ancienne, cette prière présente des parallèles avec un certain nombre de textes pascals (syriaques) qui se caractérisent par une attention particulière à des détails du récit de la passion du Christ, tels que nous en rencontrons ici.[37]

2.6. Conclusion

Les cinq descriptions de l'eucharistie dans les Actes de Thomas, que nous venons d'examiner et de commenter, présentent entre elles un certain nombre de différences et chacune possède ses accents propres. Néanmoins, elles concordent sur les points essentiels, ce qui signifie d'après nous qu'au moins dans leur rédaction primitive – qu'il est difficile de reconstruire avec une certitude absolue, mais qui en tout cas a été mieux préservée par la traduction grecque – elles sous-entendent au fond les mêmes rites. Tâchons donc de reconstituer le déroulement de ces rites en synthétisant les éléments rencontrés dans les versions 'primitives' des passages que nous avons étudiés ci-dessus.

Dans ses grandes lignes la célébration de l'eucharistie selon les Actes de Thomas se déroule comme suit:

a. D'abord est apportée et préparée une table (chapitre 49). On y met du pain (chapitres 49 et 133) ainsi qu'une coupe avec de l'eau (probablement mélangée avec quelques gouttes de vin; cf. chapitres 121 et 158). Du chapitre

36. Cf. PUECH: *En quête de la gnose* 2, 212-216, 222-224; H. DRIJVERS: Die Legende des Alexius und der Typus des Gottesmannes im syrischen Christentum, dans *Typus, Symbol, Allegorie bei den östlichen Vätern und ihren Parallelen im Mittelalter* (= Eichstätter Beiträge 4) (Regensburg 1982) 187-217, pp. 193-195.
37. Cf. surtout EPHREM: *Hymnes sur la crucifixion* 5 et 8 (E. BECK: *Des heiligen Ephraem des Syrers Paschahymnen (De azymis, De crucifixione, De resurrectione)* (= Corpus scriptorum Christianorum orientalium 248-249) (Louvain 1964); cf. pour une traduction française: G. ROUWHORST: *Les hymnes pascales d'Ephrem de Nisibe* (= Supplements to Vigiliae christianae 7, 1-2) (Leiden 1989) tome 2. Voir également les sermons (pseudo-) éphrémiens pour la semaine sainte VI et VII (E. BECK: *Ephraem Syrus. Sermones in hebdomadam sanctam* (= Corpus scriptorum Christianorum orientalium 412-413) (Louvain 1979).

49 on peut déduire que cette tâche est accomplie par un diacre.

b. Une fois que les dons eucharistiques ont été mis sur la table, Thomas, qui remplit la fonction de 'presbytre' ou d''évêque', prononce une longue bénédiction sur le pain (et également sur la coupe qui joue pourtant un rôle nettement subordonné). Le texte de cette 'bénédiction' varie considérablement selon les descriptions. A deux reprises (chapitres 50 et 133), on rencontre une longue invocation du nom de Jésus (qui paraît être identifié à celui de l'Esprit et encore à l'Esprit lui-même): elle frappe par son caractère insistant et sa parenté avec certaines prières de conjuration 'païennes'. La bénédiction du chapitre 158 respire une atmosphère tout à fait différente: elle n'a pas la forme d'une invocation et comporte un élément entièrement absent des deux autres 'bénédictions', à savoir une énumération d'un grand nombre de détails du récit de la passion.

c. La 'bénédiction' du pain (et de la coupe) est suivie de sa fraction: celle-ci revient dans toutes les descriptions de la célébration eucharistique et doit dès lors constituer un des points culminants du rituel (encore que rien ne soit dit sur sa signification précise). A remarquer en outre que dans chapitre 50, avant d'être rompu, le pain eucharistique est d'abord marqué du signe de la croix.

d. Quant à la communion qui conclut la célébration eucharistique, on peut signaler qu'à côté de la manducation du pain eucharistique – parfois simplement désigné comme l''eucharistie' –, les Actes de Thomas connaissent aussi une participation à la coupe. Force est cependant de constater que celle-ci ne joue qu'un rôle très mince.

Ensuite, dans tous les passages, la 'communion' est accompagnée d'une brève prière prononcée par Thomas. L'intéressant de ces courtes prières est qu'elles indiquent très bien en quoi consiste la signification de la participation au pain eucharistique et à la coupe d'après les Actes de Thomas: par l'eucharistie les fidèles obtiennent surtout deux choses, d'une part la rémission des péchés (cf. chapitres 29, 50 et 133) et d'autre part la vie éternelle (chapitre 121). Les mêmes effets sont d'ailleurs attribués à la communion par l''invocation' du chapitre 133 et par la 'bénédiction' du chapitre 158.

e. Il n'est pas à exclure que la version grecque du chapitre 50 fasse allusion à l'existence d'une *agape* distincte de la manducation du pain eucharistique et de la participation à la coupe. Il faut pourtant en même temps constater que, si la célébration eucharistique a comporté une telle *agape*, celle-ci ne peut avoir occupé qu'une place très subordonnée, étant donné qu'elle n'est mentionnée qu'une seule fois. En effet, toutes les descriptions montrent à l'évidence que, dans la célébration eucharistique des Actes de Thomas, tout tourne autour de la communion avec le Christ et l'Esprit par l'intermédiaire du pain qui a été béni et sur lequel a été invoqué le nom divin. Ce pain donne la force pour surmonter les ennemis principaux de l'humanité, Satan qui est à l'origine du péché – celui-ci a pour l'auteur (le rédacteur) des Actes de Thomas une forte connotation sexuelle – et la Mort. Le repas en tant que tel a été relégué au second rang.

3. VESTIGES D'UNE TRADITION LITURGIQUE

Ayant reconstitué, dans la mesure du possible, le déroulement de la célébration eucharistique selon la version primitive des Actes de Thomas, on en reste sans aucun doute avec plusieurs questions qu'une célébration à première vue aussi singulière ne peut pas manquer de soulever. Cependant, la question qui s'impose le plus est certainement celle de la tradition liturgique dont cette célébration se fait l'écho. Est-ce que celle-ci reflète une tradition rituelle particulière et, dans l'affirmative, quelle est cette tradition?

A vrai dire, nous ne sommes pas les premiers à poser cette question. Elle a déjà occupé la plupart des savants qui ont étudié les Actes de Thomas. Voyons donc d'abord quelles sont les solutions apportées par ces savants. A quelle tradition liturgique ont-ils proposé de rattacher la célébration eucharistique telle qu'elle apparaît dans les Actes de Thomas?

3.1. Une célébration hétérodoxe?

En prenant connaissance des publications (assez rares) des derniers cents ans sur les passages eucharistiques des Actes de Thomas, on constatera assez vite que la plupart des auteurs qui s'en sont occupés, sont restés tributaires de l'opinion séculaire d'après laquelle les Actes de Thomas sont un écrit 'hérétique'. En effet, les célébrations eucharistiques décrites dans ces passages ont fait l'objet d'hypothèses assez divergentes, mais ces hypothèses ont ceci de commun qu'elles montrent une forte tendance à tenir ces célébrations pour des rituels 'hétérodoxes' (notamment gnostiques[38] et parfois aussi manichéens[39]).

Cette thèse du caractère hétérodoxe des célébrations eucharistiques des Actes de Thomas semble être – ou, du moins, avoir été – presque communément acceptée. Néanmoins on peut se demander si elle est vraiment fondée. Est-ce que les arguments qu'on allègue pour prouver ce caractère hétérodoxe sont si probants? A vrai dire, il me paraît que tel n'est pas le cas et je veux expliquer pourquoi.

De fait, en lisant les auteurs qui défendent cette thèse, on constate assez vite qu'ils se basent essentiellement sur deux arguments. D'une part, ils s'appuient sur la présence d'un certain nombre de motifs et d'idées dans les 'épiclèses' – notamment dans celle du chapitre 50 – qu'on trouve également dans les systèmes mythologiques (théologiques) de certains mouvements 'hétérodoxes' (gnosticisme, manichéisme etc.). En second lieu, on croit pouvoir tirer un argument de l'absence d'allusions au vin.

Or, à y regarder de plus près, aucun de ces deux arguments invoqués ne se révèle vraiment concluant. Quant aux épiclèses, il est vrai que certains motifs, titres divins etc. qu'on y rencontre, interviennent aussi dans des systèmes

---

38. Ainsi surtout Lipsius: *Die apokryphen Apostelgeschichten* 338-343; Bornkamm: The Acts 437-438.
39. Ainsi Bousset: Manichäisches in den Thomasakten 6-11, qui considère (la plupart des) passages eucharistiques des Actes de Thomas comme des interpolations manichéennes.

gnostiques, manichéens etc., mais ce n'est pas dire qu'ils sont connus uniquement de ces systèmes. Il n'est aucunement impossible qu'ils aient été également répandus en dehors de ceux-ci, dans ce qu'on appelle parfois la 'grande église'. Ensuite, en ce qui concerne l'absence du vin, on sait qu'il y a eu des mouvements 'hétérodoxes' qui ont consciemment célébré l''eucharistie' sans vin.[40] Seulement, la question est de savoir si cet usage était exclusivement connu de ces mouvements. Est-ce qu'ailleurs on utilisait toujours du vin pour l'eucharistie et, même si c'était le cas, avec combien d'eau était-il mêlé? La pratique liturgique dont témoignent les Actes de Thomas était-elle effectivement si singulière dans l'église ancienne? Ce n'est pas sûr du tout.

3.2. Les Actes de Thomas et la célébration de l'eucharistie dans le christianisme syriaque primitif

Aux objections que nous venons de soulever contre la thèse du caractère hétérodoxe des célébrations eucharistiques des Actes de Thomas, on peut ajouter une autre qui est encore plus pertinente. En effet, on peut opposer aux adhérents de cette thèse qu'en général ceux-ci passent entièrement sous silence un certain nombre de données très relevantes fournies par des sources syriaques qui viennent d'un milieu très apparenté à celui des Actes de Thomas et qui en outre datent à peu près de la même époque, mais qui en différent en ceci que leur orthodoxie n'a jamais été mise en doute. Je pense ici surtout aux oeuvres d'Ephrem qui parle assez souvent de l'eucharistie et qui, en outre, a consacré à ce sujet quelques très belles hymnes.[41] En plus, je veux mentionner ici la fameuse anaphore d'Addai et Mari dont le noyau primitif remonte, selon toute vraisemblance, au quatrième sinon au troisième siècle.[42]

Or, quand on compare ces sources syriaques anciennes avec les passages eucharistiques des Actes de Thomas, on constate bientôt quelques points communs très frappants.

---

40. Cf. Vogel: Anaphores eucharistiques préconstantiniennes 409-410; Kretschmar: Abendmahl 74-75.
41. Voir surtout les Hymnes sur la foi 10 et 40 (E. Beck: *Ephraem des Syrers Hymnen De Fide* (= Corpus scriptorum Christianorum orientalium 154-155) (Louvain 1967) (traduction française de l'hymne 10: F. Graffin: L'eucharistie chez saint Ephrem, dans *Parole de l'Orient* 4 (1973) 93-121, pp. 117-119). Voir pour d'autres passages et leur interprétation: E. Beck: Die Eucharistie bei Ephraem, dans *Oriens Christianus* 38 (1954) 41-67; Graffin: L'Eucharistie chez saint Ephrem; P. Yousif: *L'eucharistie chez saint Ephrem de Nisibe* (= Orientalia Christiana analecta 224) (Roma 1984).
42. Voir pour une édition critique du texte syriaque: W. Macomber: The oldest known text of the Anaphora of the apostles Addai and Mari, dans *Orientalia Christiana periodica* 32 (1966) 335-371. Des nombreux articles consacrés à cette prière eucharistique nous voulons mentionner: W. Macomber: The Maronite and Chaldean form of the Anaphora of the Apostles, dans *Orientalia Christiana periodica* 37 (1971) 55-84; W. Macomber: The ancient form of the Anaphora of the Apostles, dans *East of Byzantium: Syria and Armenia in the formative period (Dumbarton Oaks Symposium 1980)* (Washington D.C. 1982) 73-88; H. Wegman: Pleidooi voor een tekst. De anaphora van de apostelen Addai en Mari, dans *Bijdragen* 40 (1979) 15-43; A. Verheul: La prière eucharistique d'Addai et Mari, dans *Questions liturgiques* 61 (1980) 19-27. Cf. aussi Rouwhorst: Bénédiction, action de grâces, supplication 231-239.

a. Plusieurs sources syriaques anciennes attestent l'existence d'une espèce d'épiclèse eucharistique. On peut d'abord signaler que, selon toute probabilité, l'épiclèse de l'anaphore d'Addai et Mari fait partie du noyau primitif de ce texte, ce qui signifie qu'elle remonte au quatrième sinon au troisième siècle.[43] Ce qui n'est guère moins intéressant, c'est que pour Ephrem la communion au Corps et au Sang du Christ signifie tout d'abord qu'on est rempli du feu de l'Esprit qui habite dans le pain (et le vin),[44] ce qui suppose évidemment l'existence d'une épiclèse eucharistique qui, en outre, doit avoir constitué pour le diacre de Nisibe un des points culminants de la prière eucharistique.

b. En lisant certains passages d'Ephrem où il s'agit de l'eucharistie, on a l'impression que, dans l'église à laquelle il a appartenu, la fraction et la distribution du pain occupaient une place particulièrement importante, tandis que le vin paraît jouer un rôle subordonné.[45]

Ces points communs entre les Actes de Thomas et les autres sources syriaques mentionnées sont très frappants. Ces dernières sources ont avec les Actes de Thomas ceci de commun qu'elles considèrent comme les points culminants de la célébration eucharistique: a) l'invocation de l'Esprit et b) la fraction et la distribution du pain eucharistique sur lequel a été invoqué l'Esprit. Il paraît évident que l'existence de ces points de ressemblance entre les Actes de Thomas et d'autres sources syriaques telles que les oeuvres d'Ephrem et l'anaphore d'Addai et Mari, fait apparaître sous un jour éclairant et neuf la question de la tradition liturgique sous-entendue par le premier de ces écrits. En effet, on se demande pourquoi il est encore nécessaire d'associer l'eucharistie des Actes de Thomas au gnosticisme ou au manichéisme. N'est-il pas plus naturel de supposer que les caractéristiques les plus saillantes de cette célébration, notamment l'accent qui y est mis sur l'invocation du nom, de l'Esprit, et sur la fraction et la distribution du pain, aient été empruntées à la tradition liturgique des églises syriaques du troisième siècle? Telle est en tout cas la solution que nous aimons à proposer. Précisons encore que, pour nous, il ne s'agit pas de nier la présence de certains traits dans les célébrations eucharistiques des Actes de Thomas qui font une impression quelque peu hétérodoxe, comme par exemple l'absence presque entière d'allusions au vin. Cependant, il nous semble que ces traits s'expliquent facilement par le fait que, dans le christianisme syriaque primitif (d'Edesse), la séparation de l'orthodoxie et de l'hétérodoxie était moins prononcée, ce qui sera parfois reflété dans la façon de célébrer la liturgie. Et cela, nous paraît-il, est autre chose qu'attribuer à la célébration eucharistique des Actes de Thomas un caractère 'hétérodoxe'!

---

43. C'est du moins ce que j'ai essayé de montrer dans mon article cité dans la note précédente. Cette opinion est partagée entre autres par VERHEUL: La prière eucharistique.

44. Cf. YOUSIF: L'eucharistie chez saint Ephrem 256-257.

45. Cf. ROUWHORST: Les hymnes pascales 1, 90-91.

4. UN DERNIER PROBLÈME

Une fois que nous avons réussi à retracer la tradition liturgique dont les descriptions de l'eucharistie dans les Actes de Thomas se font l'écho, tous les problèmes suscités par ces descriptions n'ont pas encore été résolus. La tradition liturgique du christianisme syriaque primitif à laquelle, à notre avis, la célébration eucharistique selon les Actes de Thomas doit se rattacher, peut fournir une explication de plusieurs traits, à première vue étonnants, de cette célébration. Il y a pourtant d'autres particularités qui font toujours mystère.

Un des traits les plus étonnants de la célébration eucharistique en question qui ne s'explique pas si facilement par une influence de la tradition liturgique ou rituelle des églises syriaques, est l'absence de toute référence à l'action de grâces ou à la louange. Ce trait semble aller de pair avec un accent très fort mis sur l'invocation de l'Esprit, l'épiclèse, qui fait l'impression d'avoir entièrement pris le dessus sur l'action de grâces et la louange. En effet, l'absence de ces deux derniers éléments ne s'accorde pas du tout avec l'anaphore d'Addai et Mari, texte qui doit avoir été utilisé par une partie des églises syriaques: celle-ci renferme entre autres des prières de louange et d'action de grâces très développées et très belles dont le contenu théologique a été soumis à une analyse détaillée par Herman Wegman.[46]

Comment expliquer cet écart entre, d'une part, la célébration eucharistique des Actes de Thomas et, d'autre part, la fameuse anaphore d'Addai et Mari qui doit avoir fait autorité dans le christianisme syriaque et à laquelle il faut au moins reconnaître une certaine représentativité? Faut-il en conclure que malgré leur parenté avec des sources syriaques plus ou moins contemporaines, les descriptions de l'eucharistie rencontrées dans les Actes de Thomas reflètent une tradition singulière, différente de celle des églises syriaques, une tradition (hétérodoxe?) qui, contrairement à l'anaphore d'Addai et Mari, n'aurait attribué aucune importance ni à la louange, ni à l'action de grâces? Bien qu'une telle explication ne soit jamais entièrement à exclure (on sait trop peu de choses des traditions liturgiques des églises syriaques des troisième et quatrième siècles pour pouvoir exclure avec certitude n'importe quelle possibilité!), nous proposons une solution qui nous paraît plus probable. Cette solution est basée d'une part sur le caractère littéraire des Actes de Thomas et d'autre part – à nouveau – sur des données tirées de quelques sources syriaques qui ont trait à la célébration de l'eucharistie, non au déroulement rituel 'objectif' de celle-ci, mais à la façon dont elle était vécue.

a) Quant au caractère des Actes de Thomas, force est de constater que dans la recherche sur les rites qui y sont décrits, on a eu tendance à trop facilement oublier qu'il ne s'agit pas d'un document à proprement parler liturgique. Nous avons affaire à une narration, un ensemble de récits qui renferment un certain nombre de scènes liturgiques, sans pour autant avoir le but de donner une description aussi détaillée et précise que possible des rites dont il est question. En

46. Cf. WEGMAN: Pleidooi voor een tekst.

effet, il paraît hors de doute que l'auteur ou le rédacteur s'est basé sur des rites qui existaient dans son église, sur une tradition liturgique, mais il faut en même temps se rendre compte que, parfois il se sera probablement permis quelque liberté par rapport à cette tradition rituelle. N'est-il, par exemple, pas vraisemblable que cet auteur ou rédacteur fasse seulement mention de ce que sont, d'après lui, les points culminants des célébrations décrites, tout en omettant certains éléments qui, à ses yeux, prennent une place plus ou moins subordonnée?

b) Non moins important pour une interprétation exacte des passages eucharistiques des Actes de Thomas, est le fait que l'attention exclusive prêtée à l'épiclèse n'est guère l'apanage des Actes de Thomas, mais a des parallèles dans d'autres sources syriaques qui parlent de la célébration eucharistique. Il est vrai que, comme nous l'avons constaté, on trouve de longues prières d'action de grâces et de louange dans l'anaphore d'Addai et Mari, mais en même temps il faut avouer que, contre toute attente, ces éléments ne jouent (presque) aucun rôle dans certaines sources qui ne donnent pas un texte complet d'une prière eucharistique, mais qui font seulement allusion aux parties considérées comme les points culminants de cette prière. Instructif à cet égard est surtout l'oeuvre d'Ephrem qui parle très amplement de la présence de l'Esprit dans le pain et le vin (et qui renvoie donc indirectement à l'épiclèse), mais qui, en parlant de l'eucharistie, ne fait (presque) jamais allusion à la louange ou à l'action de grâces!

Ces données nous amènent à formuler deux hypothèses. Premièrement, il nous paraît très vraisemblable qu'il faut mettre l'absence de la louange et de l'action de grâces dans les descriptions de l'eucharistie telles qu'elles sont décrites dans les Actes de Thomas, non au compte de la tradition rituelle – au sens des rites 'objectifs' – avec laquelle l'auteur de cet ouvrage doit avoir été familier, mais au compte de cet auteur (ou de ce rédacteur) lui-mème. En second lieu, il nous semble que la prédilection pour l'épiclèse n'a pas été l'apanage de cet auteur, mais qu'au moins jusqu'à un certain point elle a été propre au christianisme syriaque primitif.[47]

5. CONCLUSION

Arrivé à la fin de cette contribution, nous avons le regret de constater qu'au fond nous avons très peu contribué à réaliser le but que les rédacteurs de ces mélanges offerts à Herman Wegman se sont fixés: aider à obtenir une meil-

---

47. A remarquer à ce sujet que l'épiclèse appartient à un type de prière qui, au cours de l'histoire de la liturgie, deviendra de plus en plus 'populaire', à savoir la prière de la bénédiction prononcée sur des objets, des personnes etc. et que ce type de prière semble avoir pris de plus en plus le pas sur la forme plus classique dans laquelle l'accent était plutôt mis sur l'action de grâces, la louange etc. (cf. D. POWER: Het zegenen van voorwerpen, dans *Concilium* 21 (1985) no. 2, 27-40, cité d'après l'édition néerlandaise). La prédilection des Actes de Thomas et du christianisme syriaque primitif pour l'épiclèse eucharistique semble donc s'inscrire dans un cadre historique plus vaste!

leure compréhension de la liturgie telle qu'elle a été vécue par le 'peuple'. En effet, à première vue, les seuls représentants du 'peuple' que nous avons rencontrés étaient des chrétiens fort lettrés et formés dans la théologie, tels que l'auteur (ou le rédacteur) des Actes de Thomas et quelques auteurs de textes liturgiques et théologiques syriaques.

Néanmoins, par l'intermédiaire de ces représentants au premier regard douteux, notre attention a été appelée sur un fait qui ne semble pas être trop éloigné du but que les rédacteurs de ce livre se sont fixés et qui, en outre, ne manquera pas de surprendre maint liturgiste et théologien. En effet, si notre interprétation des Actes de Thomas est exacte, cet écrit montre que, déjà au troisième siècle, il y avait un décalage entre la liturgie telle qu'elle fut célébrée, en l'occurence le texte de la prière eucharistique, et l'expérience des fidèles présents qui l'ont entendu prononcer. Tandis que cette prière doit avoir fait un large part à l'action de grâces et à la louange, pour au moins une partie du 'peuple' chrétien, ces éléments semblent avoir pris une place très surbordonnée. Tout indique que l'attention de beaucoup de chrétiens qui assistaient à la célébration eucharistique, était davantage attirée par l'invocation du nom divin, l'invocation de l'Esprit sur les dons eucharistiques.

Acclamations in the eucharistic prayer

MARC SCHNEIDERS

The eucharistic prayer is a prayer said by the man who presides at the celebration. This is true from the very first moment we have any conclusive evidence.[1] During nearly two thousand years of Christian liturgy the role of the people seems to have been reduced largely to listening or at most, from the time people were provided with Mass books, to silently joining in with the president in the very heart of the eucharistic celebration.

It is not the purpose of this contribution to show how this did come about, neither to defend or criticise the theological background of this traditional role pattern. I would like to point out here, how acclamations have served the people in their participation in the liturgy during the eucharistic prayer. I do not however try to 'escape' from theology completely. After a historical survey (paragraph 2) I will attempt a historical-theological explanation of the specific role pattern that underlies the use of acclamations in the eucharistic prayer (paragraph 4), based upon a grouping of the many acclamations in 4 classes (paragraph 3). But first I have to explain what I mean by 'acclamation'.

I. 'ACCLAMATIONS'

An acclamation is a short utterance, a kind of answer said or exclaimed, sometimes spontaneously, by a group, normally by all. With an acclamation those responding show that they agree with what has been said or done, or, less narrowly put, they show their involvement.[2] Since an acclamation is not an individual utterance, the words are usually traditional. Acclamations are not specifically Christian, not even exclusively religious.[3]

In the Christian liturgy we find many acclamations. *Amen, Kyrie eleison, Gloria tibi Domine, Deo gratias, Agios o Theos*, to mention just a few. Many

---

1. JUSTIN: *Apologia* 65, 3 (Anton HÄNGGI and Irmgard PAHL: *Prex eucharistica* (= Spicilegium Friburgense 12) (Fribourg 1968) 68). Henceforth I will refer to this collection of eucharistic prayers as *Prex eucharistica*. If the eucharistic prayer, as most scholars nowadays assume, developed from the Jewish *berakha*, then we could consider the role pattern a Jewish inheritance.
2. This definition is based upon G. VOLLEBREGT: Acclamatie, in *Liturgisch woordenboek* 1 (Roermond-Maaseik 1958-1962) 33-35.
3. See the survey in Th. KLAUSER: Akklamation, in *Reallexikon für Antike und Christentum* 1 (Stuttgart 1950) 216-233.

of these acclamations have been the object of important studies.[4] The acclamations in the eucharistic prayer and the role they imply for the people saying them are however somewhat neglected by liturgists.

I will use 'acclamation' in a rather wide sense, including those elements of the eucharistic prayer which are said or sung by the people, which can perhaps not properly be said to acclaim or applaud the prayer of the president and which could perhaps better be called 'responses'. In the third paragraph of this contribution, however, I will try to draw some distinctions, based on the function of the different acclamations.

2. HISTORICAL SURVEY: FROM ST. JUSTIN UNTIL POPE PAUL VI AND A LITTLE BEYOND

2.1. Early Church

The New Testament does not yield much information on the character and content of the prayer used at the Eucharist. About the use of acclamations in the celebrations we can only speculate. Scholars have postulated a liturgical setting for exclamations like *maranatha*, but certainty about their exact use at the Eucharist cannot be reached.[5]

The *Didache*, which gives prayers that are probably connected with the Eucharist,[6] is the first text that offers information for our survey. The prayer of thanksgiving after the meal in chapter 10 ends:

Elthetô charis kai pareltheô ho kosmos houtos. Amèn. Hôsanna tôi oikôi Dauid. Ei tis hagios estin erchesthô; ei tis ouk esti, metanoeitô. Maranatha. Amèn.[7]
May grace come and may this world pass. Amen. Hosanna to the house of David. When somebody is holy, let him come. When somebody is not holy let him do penitence. Maranatha. Amen.

As we do not find any indication where the prayer of the president of the celebration ends, it is not possible to say definitely which parts of this text are acclamations. The twofold *Amen* seems a likely candidate. 'Hosanna to the house of David' is in my view also an acclamation. But we have no

4. See KLAUSER: Akklamation; Reinhard DEICHGRÄBER and Stuart George HALL: Formeln, Liturgische II, in *Theologische Realenzyklopädie* 11 (Berlin-New York 1983) 256-265 and Hans-Cristoph SCHMIDT-LAUBER: Formeln, Liturgische III, in *Theologische Realenzyklopädie* 11, 265-271. For the opening dialogue of the *anaphora* see the articles by Fr. Robert TAFT in *Orientalia christiana periodica* 49 (1983) 340-365; 52 (1986) 299-324; 54 (1988) 47-77 and 55 (1989) 63-74.
5. Cf. Herbert GOLTZEN: Acclamatio anamneseos. Die Gemeinde-Anamnese des eucharistischen Hochgebetes, in *Jahrbuch für Liturgik und Hymnologie* 19 (1975) 187-195, p. 187; DEICHGRÄBER and HALL: Formeln 257.
6. On the discussions about the character of the eucharistic prayers in chapters 9 and 10 of the *Didache* see Georg KRETSCHMAR: Abendmahlsfeier I, in *Theologische Realenzyklopädie* 1 (Berlin 1977) 229-278, p. 232 and Allan BOULEY: *From freedom to formula. The evolution of the eucharistic prayer from oral improvisation to written texts* (The Catholic University of America studies in Christian antiquity 21) (Washington D.C. 1981) 91-97.
7. *Didache* 10, 6 (*Prex eucharistica* 68).

proof.[8] St. Justin's description of the Eucharist in chapter 65 of his Apology is much more clear. When the eucharistic prayer has ended, Justin says:

pas ho parôn laos epeuphèmei legôn: Amèn.[9]
all the people present applaud saying: Amen.

And he proceeds explaining what *Amen* means.

Justin seems to attach quite some importance to the acclamation *Amen*, for he mentions it again in his description in chapter 67.[10] *Amen* remained the acclamation to conclude the eucharistic prayer throughout the history of the liturgy.

The *Traditio apostolica* provides us with the first full text of a eucharistic prayer.[11] It presents the first instance of the introductory dialogue to this prayer, another element which is, with minor variations,[12] from this time onwards omnipresent.

[Episcopus] dicat gratias agens: Dominus uobiscum.
Et omnes dicant: Et cum spiritu tuo.
Sursum corda.
Habemus ad dominum.
Gratias agamus domino.
Dignum et justum est.[13]

Absent in Justin and the *Traditio apostolica* is a third element which could be styled 'acclamation', that is found in nearly all later eucharistic prayers: the *Sanctus*.[14] Opinions on the moment at which this acclamation was introduced in the eucharistic prayer and on the reasons for the introduction vary.[15] Apart from the two authorities already mentioned, a few others contribute evidence to the absence of the *Sanctus* in the early period.[16] From the fourth and certainly in the fifth century we find the *Sanctus* everywhere.[17] There are no

8. The three *Amen*'s printed between [] in the prayer of *Didache* ch. 9 in *Prex eucharistica* 66 are conjectural additions, which have no manuscript support.
9. *Apology* 65, 3 (*Prex eucharistica* 70).
10. *Apology* 67, 5 (*Prex eucharistica* 70). Cf. also 65, 5, where, taking up his explanation interrupted by the explanation of *Amen* in 65, 4, Justin repeats not only the thanksgiving of the president, but also the acclamation of the people.
11. Some of the apocryphal acts of the apostles also contain prayers connected with the Eucharist. Some of these prayers may be older than the *Traditio apostolica*. Since I have not found an acclamation in any of these texts, it is not necessary to discuss this question here. Cf. the contribution of Gerard Rouwhorst to this volume.
12. Cf. e.g. *Prex eucharistica* 219, 320, 375, 410.
13. *Traditio apostolica* 4 (Bernard BOTTE: *La tradition apostolique de Saint Hippolyte* (Liturgiewissenschaftliche Quellen und Forschungen 39) (Münster 1989⁵) 10-12). I have cited the text of the Latin version. The other versions indicate more clearly which parts are to be said by the people.
14. The *Sanctus* is called an *acclamatio* in the introduction to the new Roman missal, paragraph 55b. Perhaps it would be better to see the *Sanctus* as a development from the acclamation (cf. SCHMIDT-LAUBER: Formeln 266).
15. Cf. KRETSCHMAR: Abendmahlsfeier 243-245.
16. Cf. H.A.J. WEGMAN: Pleidooi voor een tekst: de anaphora van de apostelen Addai en Mari, in *Bijdragen. Tijdschrift voor filosofie en theologie* 40 (1979) 15-43, pp. 25-27.
17. KRETSCHMAR: Abendmahlsfeier 244.

indications, as far as I know, that the *Sanctus* was not from its introduction into the eucharistic prayer a part intended for the whole people.[18]

Apart from these three parts intended for the people, the introductory dialogue, the *Sanctus* and the final *Amen*, which are found everywhere, there are other acclamations used only in parts of the Church. To these we may now turn, for they form the object of this contribution.

2.2. Anaphorae in the Syrian, Byzantine and Armenian Churches

Among the *anaphorae* to be considered in this paragraph, that of St. John Chrysostom takes prime place, since it is the one most used throughout history. The acclamations in this *anaphora*, apart from the 'universal' dialogue, *Sanctus* and *Amen*, are limited to two: the institution narrative is concluded by an *Amen* of the people; following the *anamnesis* the people say:

Se humnoumen se eulogoumen soi eucharistoumen Kurie kai deometha sou ho Theos hèmôn.[19]
We praise You, we bless You, we give You thanks, Lord, and we pray You, our God.

The *anaphora* of St. Basil has only the acclamation just cited.[20] This anamnetic acclamation is of Antiochene origin. It is found in many 'Antiochene' *anaphorae*, but is absent in those of James, Mark and Cyril.[21] Jerusalem and Egypt are therefore not very likely candidates for its introduction.

The *anaphora* of James the brother of the Lord presents us with two acclamations which we will see in many other texts. It has a double *Amen* after the consecration of each of the elements and an anamnetic acclamation, which differs from the Antiochene formula we just saw. This acclamation is recently introduced in the Roman Catholic and other western liturgies. In the *anaphora* of James it follows a version of the institution narrative which is longer than present day western texts, but which was current in the West and still is in the East.[22] After the words over the chalice, concluded, as I said, by the *Amen* of the people, it proceeds:

18. Cf. e.g. the *anaphora* in the *Constitutiones apostolorum* VIII, 12, 27 (*Prex eucharistica* 90): *kai pas ho laos hama eipatô: hagios, hagios, hagios...*: 'and let the whole people say together: Holy, holy, holy...'; Theodore of Mopsuestia, *Catechesis mystagogica VI*: 'He [the priest] makes then mention [...] of the Seraphim, who offer that praise which the blessed Isaiah learned in a Divine vision and committed to writing, and which all of us in the congregation sing in a loud voice, as if we were also singing that which the invisible natures sing: 'Holy [...]' (A. Mingana: *Commentary of Theodore of Mopsuestia on the Lord's prayer and on the sacraments of baptism and the Eucharist* (= Woodbrooke studies 6) (Cambridge 1933) 100, cf. 101); the *immolatio* for the *dies passionis sancti Iohannis Baptistae* in the *Missale Gothicum* (Cunibert Mohlberg: *Missale Gothicum* (= Rerum ecclesiasticarum documenta, Fontes 5) (Roma 1961) 96): *Et cum his caelestibus supernisque uirtutibus fidelis populi sinphonia misceatur* [...] *dicentes: sanctus, sanctus, sanctus.*
19. *Prex eucharistica* 226.
20. *Prex eucharistica* 236.
21. See below paragraph 2.3. The Antiochene acclamation is also absent from the Maronite *anaphora* ascribed to St. Peter, for which see the end of this paragraph.
22. Cf. Fritz Hamm: *Die liturgischen Einsetzungsberichte im Sinne vergleichender Liturgieforschung untersucht* (= Liturgiegeschichtliche Quellen und Forschungen 23) (Münster 1928) 90-92 and note 133 below.

Do this in remembrance of me. For as often as you will eat this bread and drink this cup, you announce the death of the Son of man and you proclaim his resurrection, until He comes.

And the deacons answer: 'We believe, we proclaim.' And the people:

Ton thanaton sou, Kurie, kataggellomen kai tèn anastasin sou homologoumen.[23]
Your death, Lord, we announce and your resurrection we proclaim.

The oldest text in which this acclamation is found, is the *papyrus* fragment from Dêr-Balyzeh.[24] It is found in many but not all other Egyptian texts.[25] As we also find it in Syriac texts,[26] this acclamation probably has its origin in the Church of Jerusalem, to which we owe the *anaphora* of James.[27]

There are more acclamations in St. James's *anaphora*. At the end of the *anamnesis*, which concludes with a prayer not to look upon our sins, the priest says:

Ho gar laos sou kai hè ekklèsia sou hiketeuei se.
Ho laos: Eleèson hèmas, Kurie, ho Theos, ho Patèr, ho pantokratôr.[28]
Because your people and your Church beg You.
The people: Have mercy on us, Lord, God, Father, Almighty.

This acclamation also seems to be of Jerusalem origin.[29]

During the following *epiklesis* the people respond twice with *Amen* to the prayer for the 'change' of the elements.[30]

Just before the final doxology there is a last acclamation:

Anes, aphes, sunchôrèson, ho Theos, ta paraptômata hèmôn, ta hekousia, ta akousia, ta en gnôsei, ta en agnoiai.[31]

---

23. *Prex eucharistica* 248.
24. Cf. paragraph 2.3.
25. It is absent from the *anaphora* of Mark. See below paragraph 2.3.
26. In the *anaphorae* of the twelve apostles and the Syriac James.
27. Cf. André TARBY: *La prière eucharistique de l'église de Jérusalem* (= Théologie historique 17) (Paris 1972) 26. It is remarkable how many *anaphorae* have both anamnetic acclamations, the Antiochene and the Jerusalem ones: the *anaphora* of the twelve apostles, the Syriac James and the Egyptian Basil and Gregory. The last two were imported into Egypt; they are generally considered to belong to the Antiochene type. We may presume that the Jerusalem acclamation, which was known in Egypt at the time when the Dêr-Balyzeh papyrus was written, was added to these two *anaphorae* in Egypt.
28. *Prex eucharistica* 248.
29. It is found in the Syriac James and the Syriac *anaphora* of the twelve apostles combined with the Antiochene anamnetic acclamation into a responsory. In the Armenian *anaphora* of Athanasius this acclamation is included in a longer hymnic text. It was also adopted in Egypt in the *anaphora* of Cyril. These texts are cited below in due course. See further TARBY: *Prière eucharistique* 150, note 44.
30. *Prex eucharistica* 250. Another *Amen* at the end of the *epiklesis* is said by the clerics only (*Prex eucharistica* 250). This and another acclamation which only the clerics say (*Prex eucharistica* 257) may have originally been said by all. The second of these is introduced by a text said aloud by the priest, the first follows silent prayer.
31. *Prex eucharistica* 260.

Let go, take away, forgive, O God, our offenses, those we did willingly, those we did unwillingly, those we know of, those we do not know.

In the *anaphora duodecim apostolorum*, a Syriac text closely related to the *anaphora* of St. John Chrysostom, we find a longer version of the anamnetic acclamation of the *anaphora* of James after the 'extended' institution narrative:

Do this in remembrance of Me. For as often as you will eat this bread and drink this cup, you announce my death and you proclaim my resurrection, until I come.[32]

People: Your death, Lord, we commemorate, your resurrection we proclaim and your second coming we expect. Mercy and indulgence we ask You and we beg for forgiveness of sins. May your mercy be ever upon us.[33]

The same text has two acclamations, one of them being the Antiochene anamnetic acclamation, during the *anamnesis*. These constitute a little responsory for priest and people.

Priest: ...for your Church and your flock pray to You and through You and with You to your Father, saying: Have mercy on me.

People: Have mercy on us, God Father almighty, have mercy on us.

Priest: We too, Lord, give thanks and proclaim You before all and because of everything.

People: We praise You, we bless You, we give You thanks, Lord, and we pray You, our God, be gracious, O Good One, and have mercy on us.[34]

After the *epiklesis* which follows, there is an *Amen*. During the intercessions we find an acclamation very similar to the one we saw just before the doxology in the *anaphora* of James.[35] Apparently the people are also expected to say the final doxology.[36]

The Syriac *anaphora* of James, which is a translation of a forerunner of the Greek *anaphora* of James as we now have it, made in the sixth or seventh century,[37] contains all the acclamations found in the twelve apostles text as well as some others: the double *Amen* after the consecration of each of the elements,

---

32. Note that, unlike James's, this *anaphora* puts the call to remember (the introduction to the acclamation) not in the third person, but in the first ('my death', 'my resurrection, until I come'). This is the way in which it is put in all other *anaphorae* which have the Jerusalem acclamation, except in the Maronite *anaphora* of Peter. The only Western rite which has an acclamation at the end of the institution narrative, the Mozarabic liturgy, has the extension in the third person: ...*mortem Domini adnuntiabitis, donec ueniat, in claritatem e celis* (Mario FÉROTIN: *Le Liber ordinum en usage dans l'église wisigothique et mozarabe* (= Monumenta ecclesiae liturgica 5) (Paris 1904) 238; José JANINI: *Liber missarum de Toledo y libros místicos* 1 (= Instituto de Estudios Visigotico-Mozarabes de Toledo, serie liturgica, fuentes 3) (Toledo 1982) 548).

May we assume, that the first person was changed into the third in an attempt to come closer to the biblical text?

33. *Prex eucharistica* 266.
34. *Prex eucharistica* 267.
35. *Prex eucharistica* 268.
36. *Prex eucharistica* 268 only gives the first two words: 'As it was.'
37. Cf. TARBY: *Prière eucharistique* 33. The Syriac translation is ascribed to James of Edessa, who died in A.D. 708 (KRETSCHMAR: Abendmahlsfeier 253).

also found in the Greek James, preceded in both instances by an *Amen* of the priest;[38] three *Amen*'s during the *epiklesis*, again each time preceded by an *Amen* said by the priest;[39] more *Amen*'s during the intercessions, after each of the prayers for the clergy, for the faithful, for the kings, for the saints and for the deceased bishops; the prayer for the other deceased is acclaimed with: 'Let go, take away', which the priest takes up, continuing: 'Let go, take away, forgive...'[40]

Other Western Syrian *anaphorae*[41] largely conform to the *anaphora* of James in Syriac as regards acclamations. They do not offer anything not found in the Syriac texts we just saw, except for triple *Kyrie eleison* one or a few times in the *epiklesis*.[42]

The Armenian *anaphora* of Athanasius of Alexandria is the only one still in use in the Armenian Church.[43] It has the double *Amen* during the institution narrative.[44] Part of the *anamnesis* is sung by the choir or said by the clerks.[45] This might originally have been an acclamation for all.[46] In any case it includes the Antiochene anamnetic acclamation:

And the Priest, slightly raising the Gifts, shall offer them to the Father and then he shall place them on the holy Table saying, aloud: And thine of thine own unto thee we offer from all and for all.
The Clerks: In all things blessed art thou, O Lord.
We bless thee, we praise thee;
We give thanks to thee;
We pray unto thee, O Lord our God.[47]

Following the *anamnesis* there is an introductory dialogue with an acclamatory text. This must originally have been said by the people. Nowadays only the clerks take this role.[48]

The Priest, aloud: + Peace unto all.
The Clerks: And with thy spirit.

---

38. *Prex eucharistica* 270.
39. *Prex eucharistica* 271-272.
40. *Prex eucharistica* 272-275.
41. *Prex eucharistica* 276-314. The Maronite *anaphora sanctae Romanae ecclesiae* is not considered here. It is a text made from the *canon Romanus* and the Syriac *anaphora* of the apostles in the eighteenth century (*Prex eucharistica* 315). It is interesting however to note that some of the acclamations are reserved for the *minister*, presumably in imitation of Roman *praxis*.
42. *Prex eucharistica* 283, 291 etc.
43. *Prex eucharistica* 319.
44. *Prex eucharistica* 322.
45. The translations I have at my disposal differ in this respect. *Prex eucharistica* 322 has: *Chorus canit. Divine liturgy of the Armenian Apostolic Orthodox Church.* Translated by Tiran NERSOYAN (London 1984⁵) 77 reads: 'The Clerks'.
46. It is thus indicated in other Armenian *anaphorae*: *Prex eucharistica* 329, 335.
47. *Divine liturgy* 77.
48. Cf. *Prex eucharistica* 323, where the texts are introduced with 'P.' for *populus* with the text cited from a present day Armenian missal.

84

The Deacon: Let us bow down to God.[49]
The Clerks: Before thee, O Lord.
Son of God, who art sacrificed to the Father for reconciliation, bread of life distributed amongst us, through the shedding of thy holy blood, we beseech thee, have mercy on thy flock saved by thy blood.[50]

Properly speaking this text is not an acclamation; like the *Sanctus* it may be a development from the acclamation.
At the end of the *epiklesis* we find another long 'acclamation':

The Clerks: Spirit of God, who descending from heaven dost accomplish through us the mystery of Him who is glorified with thee, by the shedding of his blood, we beseech thee, grant rest to the souls of those of us who have fallen asleep.[51]

During the intercessions the people answer 'Be mindful, Lord, and have mercy' after the prayer of each of the catagories.[52]

Peculiar is the acclamation: 'Glory to your resurrection/nativity/apparition', which is added, just after the apostles, doctors etc. are invoked, on these three feasts and of which there is also a variant form for days of saints.[53]

After the prayer for the departed in a second series of intercessions follows the acclamation: 'From all and for all'.[54]

Other Armenian *anaphora* show no significant differences.[55]

It may seem a bit strange, that I present the acclamations in the *anaphorae* of the Eastern Syrians at the end of this paragraph. Are these not among the most 'primitive'? Apart from the problems surrounding the reconstruction of an 'original' text of these Syriac *anaphorae*,[56] which makes it difficult to use the evidence of these texts, there is in fact only one acclamation in the *anaphorae* of the Nestorians which has to be noticed here: *Amen*. We find it at the end of the institution narrative or *anamnesis*[57] and in one text once during the intercessions.[58] In the *anaphorae* of the Malabar and Maronite churches there is something more. The *anaphora* of Addai and Mari as it is used in the Syro-Malabar Church has a text for the people, which looks like the *Orate fratres* of the Roman liturgy. It is a response to an apology of the priest which is part of the *post-sanctus*.[59] This cannot be but a late intrusion into the text.

49. *Prex eucharistica* 323 translates: *Deum adoremus*.
50. *Divine liturgy* 79.
51. *Divine liturgy* 81. Although the intercessions follow, we can not consider this acclamation as a 'bridge' between *epiklesis* and intercession, for the prayers for the departed do not follow immediately, but are preceded by those for peace and fair weather.
52. *Divine liturgy* 81-85.
53. *Divine liturgy* 83; *Prex eucharistica* 324.
54. *Divine liturgy* 87.
55. *Prex eucharistica* 327-346. Some Armenian *anaphorae* have fewer acclamations than that of Athanasius.
56. Cf. WEGMAN: Pleidooi 15-19.
57. *Prex eucharistica* 384, 390, cf. 377.
58. *Prex eucharistica* 393.
59. *Prex eucharistica* 407.

The Syro-Malabar *anaphora* also has the *Amen* after the consecration of each of the elements and at the end of the *anamnesis*.[60]

The *anaphora* ascribed to St. Peter in use in the Maronite Church has only the Jerusalem acclamation 'Your death, O Lord...' following the institution narrative.[61]

With the possible exception of the last text, none of these Eastern Syrian *anaphorae* yield important data for a history of the acclamations in the eucharistic prayer.

2.3. Anaphorae in the Egyptian and Ethiopian Churches

When we turn to the Egyptian Church, we come upon texts with much more and different acclamations. In the *anaphora* of St. Mark the number is still limited. According to this text the people are expected to say *Amen* after the consecration of the bread and again after the consecration of the wine.[62] In the same text there is another *Amen* after the consecratory *epiklesis*[63] and a quite long doxology at the end, introduced by *ho laos*, and thus clearly intended for all present:

Hôsper èn kai estin kai estai eis genean kai genean kai eis tous sumpantas aiônas tôn aiônôn. amèn.[64]
Like it was and is and will be from generation to generation and in all ages of ages. Amen.

The problem is of course to ascertain the date of introduction of these texts. It is quite clear that the double *Amen* in the institution narrative is absent from the two fragmentary sixth and seventh-century *papyri* that are related to the *anaphora* of St. Mark.[65] It must have been introduced sometime between the centuries mentioned and the twelfth, when we find it in the *codex Rossanensis*.[66] Or perhaps little words like *Amen* were not included in the written text, because they were not said by the priest? It may even have taken more time before the acclamations were fixed, than it took to come to established formulas for the eucharistic prayer. The people may still have been acclaiming spontaneously (even if with traditional words) at moments which they thought appropriate, at a time when the priest was already using a written prayer. Of course we have no trace in the texts to substantiate this supposition. It would

---

60. *Prex eucharistica* 407-408.
61. *Prex eucharistica* 413.
62. *Prex eucharistica* 112.
63. *Prex eucharistica* 114. Cf. the *Amen*, however without an explicit indication that it is to be said by all, after the *epiklesis* in the related fragmentary papyrus Manchester, John Rylands University Library, no. 465 (*Prex eucharistica* 122).
64. *Prex eucharistica* 114. The same doxology is found already in the *Euchologion* of bishop Serapion of Thmuis from the fourth century. The way in which it is introduced there, by a prayer for the people, may suggest that even that early it was said by all. We also find it in the Ethiopian *Anaphora sanctorum patrum nostrorum apostolorum* (*Prex eucharistica* 149).
65. See *Prex eucharistica* 120, 126.
66. Cf. *Prex eucharistica* 101.

account for the many differences in the acclamations, which we find in the texts. But we cannot be sure about it.

Neither can we be sure about the evidence offered in the *papyrus* of Dêr-Balyzeh. This does contain the words of the anamnetic acclamation 'Your death we announce':

ton thanaton sou k[ataggell]omen
tèn anastasin [sou homologoum]en
kai deometha t[...][67]
Your death we announce,
your resurrection we proclaim
and we pray...[68]

Unfortunately it is uncertain who is supposed to say these words here: priest or people. Since later texts always give the formula as an acclamation for the people the assumption that this was already so in the community which used this sixth-century text is perhaps not too rash. It is, however, in my view also possible that the formula is part of the *anamnesis* said by the priest; the *papyrus* is too fragmentary to draw conclusions.[69]

What we can be sure about is the growth of the number of times *Amen* had to be said in the Egyptian Church during the eucharistic prayer in the course of time. For the Coptic *anaphora* of St. Cyril of Alexandria, which is based on that of Mark, contains, apart from the double *Amen* in the institution narrative already found in the *anaphora* of St. Mark, six more *Amen*'s in this part of the prayer. That is a total of four at the consecration of each element![70] The acclamations in the *anaphora* of Cyril are not restricted to the institution narrative. We also find *Amen* three times in the first *epiklesis*, without indication, however, that the people have to say these *Amen*'s. Then there is a 'We believe' said by all, just before the priest pronounces the words 'He took bread in his holy hands...'[71] And in this eucharistic prayer we also find the Jerusalem anamnetic acclamation 'We announce your death, O Lord, and we proclaim your holy resurrection and ascension'.[72]

---

67. *Prex eucharistica* 127.
68. 'And we pray' is absent from most versions of the Jerusalem acclamation. We do find it in the Syriac *anaphorae* of James and of the twelve apostles (text cited in paragraph 2.2.). It is possible that the acclamation reached Egypt from Syria, with which contacts were intimate after the rise of the Monophysite church. Both Syriac texts have, however, an inserted 'and your second coming we expect', which is absent from the Dêr-Balyzeh *papyrus*.
69. Of course the Dêr-Balyzeh *papyrus* may reflect a usage older than that of the time in which it was written. The statement that the acclamation was already in use in the third century (thus GOLTZEN: Acclamatio 188, following the date proposed by Joachim BECKMANN: *Quellen zur Geschichte des christlichen Gottesdienstes* (Gütersloh 1956) 8) I cannot acclaim. Cf. Dom Bernard CAPELLE cited in Robert J. LEDOGAR: *Acknowledgement. Praise-verbs in the early Greek anaphora* (Roma 1968) 34, note 13.
70. *Prex eucharistica* 136-137.
71. *Prex eucharistica* 136. In the Ethiopian *Anaphora sanctorum patrum nostrorum apostolorum* there is a similar acclamation. Just after the priest has said 'and He took bread in his holy and blessed and immaculate hands', the people say: 'We believe. This is true. We believe.' (*Prex eucharistica* 148).
72. *Prex eucharistica* 137.

At the conclusion of the *anamnesis*, which ends with the expectation of the second coming, the people are expected to say:

'According to your mercy, O Lord, and not according to our sins.' And again, after the following prayer for forgiveness: 'Have mercy on us, Lord, almighty Father.' This is said two times by priest and people in a kind of little responsory.[73]

Near the end of the *anaphora*, within the second *epiklesis* all have again to respond *Amen* four times. A doxology is also said by the people.[74]

As is the case with the *anaphora* of Mark, we cannot be certain about the time of introduction of these acclamations, for an older sixth-century fragment from the Coptic Church does not yet contain the indicated acclamations.[75]

It is clear however from the text of two *anaphorae* of the Antiochene type which were adopted in the Egyptian Church that the growth of the number of acclamations is not restricted to Coptic texts. The single surviving complete manuscript of the Egyptian *anaphora* of Basil in Greek contains the following acclamations, which we have also seen in the Coptic *anaphora* of Cyril. The first is:

Kata to eleos sou kurie kai mè kata tas hamartias hèmôn.[76]
According to your mercy, Lord, and not according to our sins.

This acclamation we find at a place which differs from that in the text ascribed to Cyril. In that going under Basil's name it precedes the institution narrative. As we will see, it is also found in the *anaphora* ascribed to Gregory of Nazianzen; it is a typical Egyptian acclamation. Basil also has the 'We believe' and many *Amen*'s which are found only in Egyptian texts, although the number of times the institution narrative is interrupted by *Amen* is limited here to six.[77] The whole narrative is concluded with a threefold *Amen* and an extended version of the Jerusalem acclamation:

Ton thanaton sou kurie kataggellomen kai tèn hagian anastasin sou kai analèpsin homologoumen.[78]
We announce your death, O Lord, and we proclaim your holy resurrection and ascension.

Basil also has in common with Cyril the *Amen*'s in the *epiklesis*. Basil adds a triple *Kyrie eleison* after the last of these *Amen*'s. The doxology is here, as in Cyril, said by the people.[79]

---

73. *Prex eucharistica* 138.
74. *Prex eucharistica* 139. The doxology for the people is followed by one said by the priest only.
75. *Prex eucharistica* 140. This is a fragment of the first *epiklesis* and the institution narrative only. We may assume however that the other parts did not contain the many acclamations either.
76. *Prex eucharistica* 350.
77. *Prex eucharistica* 350-351. In the *anaphora* of Basil, unlike in that of Cyril, the words at the bread are not separated from those at the chalice nor 'As often as you eat...' from the words at the chalice by an *Amen*.
78. *Prex eucharistica* 352.
79. *Prex eucharistica* 356.

The Egyptian *anaphora* of Basil also has acclamations not found in the Coptic Cyril. The first of these was already in the 'Antiochene' text on which it is based.[80] It follows the *anamnesis*:

Se ainoumen, se eulogoumen, soi eucharistoumen kurie kai deometha sou ho theos hèmôn.[81]
We praise You, we bless You, we give You thanks, Lord, and we pray You, our God.

During the intercessions there is a responsory for priest and people, with the acclamations 'Have mercy on us, Lord, Father, Almighty' and *Kyrie eleison*. The last acclamation is repeated once a little further on.[82]

The other *anaphora* of the Antiochene type adopted in Egypt is the remarkable text ascribed to Gregory of Nazianzen.[83] This *anaphora* is directed to Christ not to the Father. The text is full of *Kyrie eleison*'s. This acclamation is found no less than 12 times: 3 times during the long *post-Sanctus*; once at the end of the *epiklesis* and 8 times during the intercessions! Other acclamations in this *anaphora* we are already familiar with from the Egyptian Basil: 'According to your mercy...' just before the institution narrative; 'We believe' after the first words of the narrative, but not the related *Amen*'s; the anamnetic 'Your death...' preceded by a threefold *Amen*; 'We praise You...' at the end of the *anamnesis*; the *Amen*'s in the *epiklesis*.[84] Special to the *anaphora* of Gregory is an extended *Kyrie eleison* halfway the intercessions:

Eleèson hèmas ho theos ho sôtèr hèmôn.[85]
Have mercy on us, God, our Saviour.

The Ethiopian *Anaphora sanctorum patrum nostrorum apostolorum* contains a number of acclamations we have not seen hitherto.[86] After the *Sanctus* the priest says a few lines which may be looked upon as an embolism:

Truly the holiness of your glory fills heavens and the earth, through our Lord and God and Saviour Jesus Christ. Your holy Son came, who was born from the Virgin, to fulfil your will, and to make You a people.[87]

Is it a coincidence that the long text which the people are to say, follows upon 'to make You a people'?[88]

---

80. Cf. note 27.
81. *Prex eucharistica* 352.
82. *Prex eucharistica* 354.
83. Edition, German translation and commentary: Albert GERHARDS: *Die griechische Gregorios-anaphora* (= Liturgiewissenschaftliche Quellen und Forschungen 65) (Münster 1984). Text also in *Prex eucharistica* 358-373.
84. GERHARDS: *Gregoriosanaphora* 32-36.
85. GERHARDS: *Gregoriosanaphora* 40-41. This is said three times and repeated three times by the priest.
86. Other Ethiopian *anaphorae* usually have the same acclamations as the one considered here. Some however have fewer acclamations. Cf. *Prex eucharistica* 150-203.
87. *Prex eucharistica* 147.
88. Cf. note 64 above.

Remember us, Lord, in your kingdom.
Remember us, Lord, our master.
Remember us, Lord, in your kingdom,
as You remembered the criminal
who was on your right,
when You were hanging on the wood of the holy Cross.[89]

In the same *anaphora* we also find an extended version of the *Amen* after the consecration of the bread and after that of the wine. The Ethiopian acclamation is here:

Amen. Amen. Amen. We believe and profess.
We praise You, O our Lord and our God.
We believe this is truly your body/blood.[90]

The anamnetic acclamation after the institution narrative is an expanded version of the Jerusalem acclamation:

We announce your death, O Lord, and your holy resurrection. We believe in your ascension and your second coming. We praise You and worship You. We ask You and pray You, O our Lord and our God.[91]

The *Amen* after the consecratory *epiklesis* is also expanded. It reads:

Amen. O Lord, have mercy. O Lord, spare us. O Lord, forgive us.[92]

2.4. The West

A survey of the history of acclamations in the eucharistic prayer in the West can be much shorter than it's counterpart for the East. Recent innovations in many churches make up, however, for this lack of material from the past.

The Roman liturgy did not know any acclamation in the *canon* other than those which we saw in paragraph 2.1: the introductory dialogue, the *Sanctus* and the final *Amen*.[93] Other western texts which do have extra acclamations are few. We have only one text of the Gallican institution narrative.[94] This does not give any indication that an acclamation was said. Neither do the texts we still possess for the *post-Sanctus* and the *post-mysterium* parts indicate any acclamation.

---

89. *Prex eucharistica* 147. According to another tradition the text ends: 'According to your mercy, Lord, and not according to our trespasses.'
90. *Prex eucharistica* 148.
91. *Prex eucharistica* 148. Or could this text be considered as a combination of both anamnetic acclamations, the Jerusalem and Antiochene formulas?
92. *Prex eucharistica* 148.
93. The attempt to introduce the practice of having the people say the *Amen* after the final clauses *per Christum Dominum nostrum* at the end of every part of the *canon* in the Neo-Gallican missal of Meaux (1709) proved abortive. Therefore it need not be discussed here.
94. Alban DOLD and Leo EIZENHÖFER: *Das irische Palimpsestsakramentar in Clm 14429 der Staatsbibliothek München* (= Texte und Arbeiten 53-54) (Beuron 1964) 15-16. Cf. also GOLTZEN: Acclamatio 190.

The Mozarabic liturgy on the other hand did (and still does) have acclamations in the eucharistic prayer, in the institution narrative. The evidence is scanty. Only two manuscript texts of the institution narrative survive,[95] to which may be added the printed texts of the *Missale mixtum*.[96] The manuscripts are not older than the tenth century.[97] One of the manuscript texts indicates an *Amen* after the words over the bread and an *Amen* after those over the chalice. At the end of the extended command to do this in remembrance of the Lord, which the Spanish liturgy shares with the Gallican[98] and Eastern liturgies, there is a *Sic credimus, Domine Iesu*. This acclamation is found in both manuscripts.[99]

In the printed editions of the *Missale mixtum* which I have been able to consult, these three acclamations are either reduced to one *Amen* at the end of the extended command[100] or to three times *Amen*, the *Sic credimus* etc. being replaced by an *Amen*.[101] The changes may be due to the use of the words of institution from the Roman canon, instead of the ancient Mozarabic version.[102] In the absence of a study of the development of the institution narrative in the Mozarabic liturgy,[103] it seems safest to take the version found in the most ancient witness as evidence for the Mozarabic practice in the earlier period, when this liturgy was still widely used.[104]

The number and extent of acclamations in the medieval western liturgy may be called meagre without qualification. Apart from Spain the people's role in the West has been very small. This situation has changed considerably since the Second Vatican Council ordered the liturgy to be reformed. The *Missale Romanum* of 1970 prescribes an acclamation of the anamnetic type after the institution narrative. The first text is the Jerusalem acclamation:

95. *Prex eucharistica* 494. The manuscripts are the *Liber ordinum* of San Millán (no. 391 in Klaus GAMBER: *Codices latini liturgici antiquiores* (Spicilegii Friburgensis subsidia 1) (Fribourg 1968²)) and Ms. 35.6 in the Cathedral Library of Toledo (GAMBER: *Codices* no. 313). The texts of these two manuscripts are printed in FÉROTIN: *Le Liber ordinum* 238. The text of the second one is also printed in JANINI: *Liber missarum* 1, 547-548.

96. The printed texts of the Mozarabic missal show some differences, especially as regards the acclamations. I have not been able to consult the original edition, printed in 1500 A.D. I have used the edition of Lesley (Alexander LESLEY: *Missale mixtum secundum regulam beati Isidori dictum Mozarabes* (Romae 1755) and that of Lorenzano, according to the reprint of the *ordo missae* in JANINI: *Liber missarum* 1, 553-579.

97. Cf. GAMBER: *Codices* nos. 313 and 391.

98. Cf. DOLD and EIZENHÖFER: *Palimpsestsakramentar* 16 and George F. WARNER: *The Stowe missal* 2 (= Henry Bradshaw Society 32) (London 1915) 13.

99. JANINI: *Liber missarum* 1, 547-548; FÉROTIN: *Liber ordinum* 238.

100. LESLEY: *Missale* 5 and 229.

101. Thus the edition of Lorenzano (JANINI: *Liber missarum* 1, 573). This edition is still used in the cathedral of Toledo (JANINI: *Liber missarum* 1, 554).

102. These words from the Roman *canon* are printed in the lower margin in the two editions I consulted.

103. Are there perhaps more manuscripts which have the text of the institution narrative somewhere inserted in a mass, like the *Liber ordinum*, or written in the margin, as Toledo 35.6?

104. The Mozarabic practice of reciting the creed immediately after the eucharistic prayer hardly qualifies as an acclamation *in* the eucharistic prayer. I do not agree with GOLTZEN: Acclamatio 190, who thought that the creed here represents 'die Akklamation des Volkes auf das Mysterium der Heilsgegenwart'.

Mortem tuam annuntiamus, Domine,
et tuam resurrectionem confitemur, donec venias.

There are two[105] alternative texts:

Quotiescumque manducamus panem hunc
et calicem bibimus,
mortem tuam annuntiamus, Domine, donec venias.

Salvator mundi, salva nos,
qui per crucem et resurrectionem tuam liberasti nos.[106]

One of these acclamations must be used in any of the four eucharistic prayers and in most of the eucharistic prayers which have been approved for certain countries or for special groups and occasions. The prayers for Masses with children however contain other and, which is quite remarkable, many more acclamations.[107]

Although I have no indication that these eucharistic prayers are widely used, they should be considered here, since they deviate in many respects from the traditional use of acclamations.[108]

The first of the prayers for Masses with children contains the following acclamations:

During the preface two texts taken from the *Sanctus*:

Pleni sunt caeli et terra gloria tua. Hosanna in excelsis.

and:

Benedictus qui venit in nomine Domini. Hosanna in excelsis.

The *Sanctus* is reduced to:

Sanctus, sanctus, sanctus, Domine Deus Sabaoth. Hosanna in excelsis.

There is no acclamation after the institution narrative. Instead we find after the *anamnesis*:

Christus pro nobis mortuus est, Christus resurrexit. Te expectamus, Domine Iesu.[109]

The second eucharistic prayer for Masses with children abounds with acclamations. During the preface we find four times:

105. In the Irish version of the new Roman missal there are three alternatives. To the two which are found in the Latin text has been added: *Mo Thiarna agus mo Dhia* ('My Lord and my God') (*An leabhar aifrinn Rómhánach... Leagan Gaeilge* (Maynooth 1984) 193). I am not aware of any other translation in which this has also been done.
106. *Missale Romanum cum lectionibus ex decreto Sacrosancti Oecumenici Concilii Vaticani II instauratum, auctoritate Pauli PP. VI promulgatum*, editio iuxta typicam alteram 1 (Civ. Vaticana 1977) 791.
107. There are three *preces eucharisticae pro missis cum pueris*. I have used the texts in Enrico MAZZA: *Le odierne preghiere eucharistiche* 2 (= Liturgia e vita) (Bologna 1984) 52-68.
108. I only present the Latin version here. There are small differences in the Italian translation.
109. MAZZA: *Preghiere* 52-56.

92

Gloria tibi, qui nos homines amas.

After the *Sanctus* the priest continues with a prayer which looks remarkably like the Gallican *post-Sanctus*.[110] This is followed by a repetition of the second part of the *Sanctus*:

Benedictus qui venit in nomine Domini. Hosanna in excelsis.

After the consecration of the bread the people say:

Iesus Christus pro nobis traditus.

This acclamation accompanies the elevation of the Host. The same text is said by all after the words *in remissionem peccatorum* of the consecration of the wine, which are thus separated from *Hoc facite in meam commemorationem*![111] In this and the two other eucharistic prayers for Masses with children *Hoc facite* follows an inserted *Deinde dixit ad eos*. There is no acclamation at the end of the institution narrative. After the *anamnesis* the people say:

Gloria et laus Deo nostro.

or:

Te laudamus, te benedicimus, tibi gratias agimus.[112]

During the intercessions all have to respond three times:

Unum corpus sint ad gloriam tuam.[113]

The third text for Masses with children is more sober with acclamations. We find here three times during the intercessions:

Te Deum, qui bonus es, laudamus; tibi gratias agimus.[114]

The anamnetic acclamation introduced in the Roman liturgy from the *anaphora* of James and related texts, has inspired reformers of the eucharistic liturgy of many non-Catholic Churches. To provide a complete and detailed survey of all different texts is of course impossible. It would make this survey, long enough already, too long for inclusion in this volume. Most of the new liturgies of Anglican and Reformed communities are moreover not available to me. I give those which I have seen.[115]

---

110. As in the Gallican *post-Sanctus* the *vere sanctus* is applied to Jesus Christ, not, as it is in the second eucharistic prayer of the Roman missal of 1970, to the Father.
111. Is the omission of a rubric to show the chalice after the consecration to the people in the Latin text an accident? The Italian translation, which is printed in MAZZA: *Preghiere* on opposite pages (here page 59), indicates that the priest should show the chalice to the people during the acclamation, i.e. before all the words of the Lord are said...
112. This seems to be based on the Antiochene acclamation.
113. MAZZA: *Preghiere* 56-60.
114. MAZZA: *Preghiere* 66.
115. It seemed convenient and pragmatical to exclude from treatment here acclamations in Dutch prayers. For a nineteenth-century attempt to introduce the anamnetic acclamation in the German Lutheran Church, the *Wirkung* of this attempt and a few more examples of this acclamation in non-Catholic Churches, see GOLTZEN: Acclamatio 190-192. For Anglican liturgies see R.C.D. JASPER and Paul F. BRADSHAW: *A companion to The alternative service book* (London 1986) 223-224.

The alternatieve service book approved and published in 1980 for use in the Church of England has different forms for the Eucharist. Only the eucharistic prayers in 'Holy Communion A' have an acclamation. It resembles the anamnetic acclamation we have seen in the *anaphora* of James and the new Roman liturgy. In the four eucharistic prayers of 'Holy Communion A' follows after the institution narrative this acclamation:

Christ has died:
Christ is risen:
Christ will come again.[116]

The Anglican Church of Canada produced a new service book in 1985. In the first of the eucharistic prayers in this book the English acclamation has been included, but another one is given as an alternative. This alternative is introduced with these words of the celebrant: 'Therefore we proclaim our hope.' The first one has the more 'Roman' introduction: 'Therefore we proclaim the mystery of faith', while in the English book the acclamation follows immediately after the words of the Lord.[117]

The alternative acclamation in the Canadian Church is:

Dying you destroyed our death,
rising you restored our life.
Lord Jesus, come in glory.[118]

The second eucharistic prayer in the Canadian service book has no acclamation apart from the initial dialogue, the *Sanctus* and the final *Amen*. The third prayer does contain a text said by the people which looks like an acclamation, but can also be regarded as part of the prayer said by all. For after the institution narrative the celebrant does not call upon the people to proclaim, but says:

Therefore, Father, according to his command,
All: we remember his death,
we proclaim his resurrection,
we await his coming glory;
Celebrant: and we offer our sacrifice [...][119]

The punctuation of this text, which is taken exactly from the book, indicates that the compilers regarded the 'acclamation' here as a part of the prayer of the celebrant, said by all.

The fourth Canadian text has a repeated:

116. *The alternative service book 1980. Services authorized for use in the Church of England...* (Cambridge 1980) 132, 134, 137, 141. The first eucharistic prayer of 'Holy Communion A' has an additional acclamation at the end of the prayer: 'Blessing and honour and glory and power be yours for ever and ever. Amen.' (*Alternative service book* 132).
117. *The book of alternative services of the Anglican Church of Canada* (Toronto 1985) 195; *Alternative service book* 132, 134, 137, 141.
118. *Book of alternative services* 195. Cf. JASPER and BRADSHAW: *Companion* 223.
119. *Book of alternative services* 199.

Glory to you for ever and ever.

It is said four times during the preface, immediately following the institution narrative, after the *epiklesis* and as a final doxology.[120] The fifth prayer resembles the fourth in that it contains the same acclamation. In this prayer it is said once during the preface, once during the *post-Sanctus*, after the institution narrative, after the *epiklesis* and as a final doxology.[121]

The sixth and last Canadian eucharistic prayer has again another acclamation. At the end of the *anamnesis* the people respond:

We praise you, we bless you,
we give thanks to you,
and we pray to you, Lord our God.[122]

This is the Antiochene acclamation, taken from the *anaphorae* of Chrysostom and Basil. It is also included in the two eucharistic prayers in the alternative service 'in the language of the Book of Common Prayer 1962', in which however God is addressed with 'Thee' instead of 'You'.[123]

3. TYPES

After this long survey it seems expedient to attempt a short classification of the many acclamations into a few types, as a preliminary to the analysis of the way in which acclamations function in the eucharistic prayer. In this paragraph I disregard the more 'anomalous' acclamations, about which something has already been said at the proper places in the survey.

In defining and distinguishing the types I discern, the length of the acclamation is not given much importance. The development, which we saw, of a simple *Amen* during the institution narrative into a long profession of belief in the Ethiopian liturgy is interesting, but it does not alter the function of the acclamation or the role of the people who say this acclamation.

I distinguish four types of acclamations. First we may deal with what I would call 'interjections'. To this type belong texts like 'According to your mercy' etc. in the Egyptian *anaphorae* of Basil, Gregory and Cyril. This type is usually integrated in the text in a far from harmonious way. These acclamations can easily be left out without harm to the structure of the prayer. Their insertion quite often results in an interruption of the prayer. A second type consists of the many *Amen*'s and acclamations which developed from *Amen*. I would also put in this class the Mozarabic *Sic credimus, Domine Iesu*.[124] Acclamations of the *Amen*-type, like the interjections, are often not really integrated into the text of the eucharistic prayer. They can usually be removed

---

120. *Book of alternative services* 201-203.
121. *Book of alternative services* 204-206.
122. *Book of alternative services* 209.
123. *Book of alternative services* 242, 244.
124. Cf. note 139.

without doing any harm to the text. They can also be multiplied, as we have seen in the survey above: from one *Amen* at the end of the institution narrative to eight *Amen*'s spread through the text in the *anaphora* of Cyril. The acclamations in this class differ from those of the interjection-type by their more narrow connection with the words said by the priest, which they acclaim or ratify.

A third type I call 'responses'. This class consists of acclamations, most often found at the intercessions, which call upon the Lord to grant that which the priest has just asked. The initial dialogue also belongs to this class. Acclamations of the response-type can often also be qualified as either *Amen*-type, interjection-type or as an anamnetic acclamation. The purpose of this separate class of responses is to draw attention to the different way in which the acclamations which belong in this class function.

A fourth and last type consists of the so-called 'anamnetic acclamations'.[125] Of these there are two, which I have labelled the 'Jerusalem' and 'Antiochene' acclamation. The first one follows the institution narrative, the other the *anamnesis*. The text of the Jerusalem acclamation is traditionally:

Your death, Lord, we announce,
and your resurrection we proclaim.[126]

And that of the Antiochene:

We praise You, we bless You,
we give You thanks, Lord,
and we pray You, our God.

These two acclamations differ profoundly, not only in origin, wording and location in the prayer, but most of all in the way in which they function. This, however, is an aspect which may best be treated in the theological evalua-tion.[127]

4. EVALUATION

The acclamations which are of the interjection-type or of the *Amen*-type do not require a profound evaluation. Their function and the corresponding role of the people are clear. Some acclamations of the interjection-type are indeed interjections, emphasizing an important moment in the prayer, at which it

125. For the origin of this expression see GOLTZEN: Acclamatio 192.
126. The expectation of the second coming is absent from this text in the *anaphorae* of James, of Cyril and in the Egyptian Basil and Gregory. GOLTZEN gives much attention to the expecta-tion of the second coming in his analysis (GOLTZEN: Acclamatio, passim). If this theme was really that ancient and so important, why is it only present in the text preceding the acclama-tion (cf. note 133 below) and was it not included in all versions of the acclamation?
127. The *Sanctus* does not fit in any of the four groups. It does not seem useful to me, to define a fifth, say 'hymnic', type for this one text and the texts sung after the *anamnesis* and after the *epiklesis* in the Armenian *anaphora* of Athanasius. These texts are not acclamations *stricto sensu*. Cf. note 14.

seems appropriate to ask for mercy or indulgence. Other acclamations of these two types and especially those of the *Amen*-type, 'acclaim'. They are a repetition in advance at different more or less important moments of the final *Amen* which Justin gave such weight. These acclamations are a kind of applause. With these the people show they 'agree' with what the priest is saying and doing.

Acclamations of the third class, those of the response-type, can imply a more involved role of the people. People and priest can have an equal part in these, as may be seen e.g. in the Syriac *anaphora* of the twelve apostles:

Priest: [...] for your Church and your flock pray to You and through You and with You to your Father, saying: Have mercy on me.
People: Have mercy on us, God Father almighty, have mercy on us.
Priest: We too, Lord, give thanks and proclaim You before all and because of everything.
People: We praise You, we bless You, we give You thanks, Lord, and we pray You, our God, be gracious, O Good One, and have mercy on us.[128]

Acclamations of the response-type sometimes follow upon a mentioning of the people in the words the priest speaks.[129] The people are thus implicitly invited to participate in the prayer.

The two anamnetic acclamations are the most interesting to determine the role of the people. They are much older than most, if not all other acclamations we have seen in paragraph 2, with the exception of course of the initial dialogue, the *Sanctus* and the final *Amen*. The Antiochene formula we find in any case from the fourth century onwards.[130] It occurs in the *anaphorae* of Chrystostom and Basil, in the Egyptian Basil and Gregory, and as part of the 'responsory' just cited from the Syriac *anaphorae* of the twelve apostles and of James and in the Armenian text ascribed to Athanasius. In the recent eucharistic prayers we have seen, it occurs only in the second eucharistic prayer for Masses with children as an alternative text and in three of the eucharistic prayers included in the service book of the Canadian Anglican Church.

There is not much variety in the text. Nearly all *anaphorae* have three verbs in the first person plural expressing praise and thanks, followed by something like 'we pray to You'.

The role of the people is not difficult to determine. This acclamation is a kind of 'summary' of the whole eucharistic prayer. It follows the fulfillment of the Lord's command to do this to remember Him, the *anamnesis*. The people acclaim and ratify the *anamnesis* and the complete prayer by the priest, which the acclamation summarizes.

128. *Prex eucharistica* 267.
129. Cf. in paragraph 2.2 above St. James's *anaphora* after the *anamnesis*, in paragraph 2.3 above the Ethiopian text after the *post-Sanctus* and note 64 above.
130. Cf. LEDOGAR: *Acknowledgement* 32: 'From the quasi-universality of this acclamation in the ancient witnesses of the Byzantine, Armenian and Syrian liturgies, one must conclude at the very least, that it represents a very ancient tradition of the Antioch patriarchate.'

The other, the Jerusalem acclamation which follows upon the institution narrative is probably as old as the one we just considered. We find it in the *anaphorae* of James, in the Egyptian Basil and Gregory, in the *anaphora* of Cyril, in the Syriac *anaphorae* of the twelve apostles and of James, in the text ascribed to St. Peter used in the Maronite church. The papyrus of Dêr-Balyzeh also contains it, but does not indicate that the people say it.[131] The Dêr-Balyzeh papyrus is from the sixth or seventh century. The acclamation was already in the text of the *anaphora* of James from which the Syriac James was made in the sixth or seventh century.[132]

This acclamation has been recently introduced in many western liturgies, as has been shown above. The text of this acclamation is quite uniform. The main differences consist of the addition of the ascension or the expectation of the second coming to the 'facts' remembered.

As to the role of the people which this text suggests, I would like to attempt an interpretation which starts from the roles played by priest and people. Looking at what happens as a 'play' we see the priest repeating what the Lord has done at the Last Supper. The last words 'Do this to remember Me', in the ancient texts enlarged with an extension based upon Paul's first letter to the Corinthians,[133] are followed by an *anamnesis* of the people. The *anamnesis* said by the priest can be seen as an embolism to the people's *anamnesis*.[134] The people therefore are the subject of the *anamnesis*. The anamnetic acclamation is much more than, indeed something very different from acclamations like *Amen*. The people fulfil the command of the Lord. The priest's part is to invite or command it to do so, *in persona Christi* so to speak.

This role pattern becomes even more clear when we take into account the

131. Cf. note 67.
132. See note 37.
133. This text developed from a simple 'As often as you eat this bread and drink this chalice, you announce my death and keep my memory' in the Dêr-Balyzeh text (*Prex eucharistica* 126). 'Until I come' is added in all other texts. The proclaiming (Greek: *homologein*) of the resurrection is a later addition. It is found in the *anaphorae* of the twelve apostles, of Cyril, of James, of Peter and in the Egyptian Gregory and Basil. The Egyptian texts ascribed to Basil and Gregory add to this the ascension. The 'and keep my memory' in the Dêr-Balyzeh papyrus (if this is the correct reconstruction of the text: cf. GOLTZEN: Acclamatio 188), which does not have the words 'Do this in memory of Me', was dropped in later texts, except in Cyril, which takes the 'Do this in memory of Me' with the words at the chalice, separating it from the following text by an *Amen*. All other texts, except the Maronite Peter, have the command beginning: 'Do this in memory of Me.'
134. GOLTZEN: Acclamatio 188 stated: 'Die Anamnesis, die in der heilswirksamen Proklamation des Opfertodes des Kyrios in der Handlung der Eucharistie besteht, wird von der Gemeinde aufgenommen mit ihrer Akklamation, die den in ihre Mitte "kommenden" Herrn begrüßt.' (Cf. also 189: 'Mit dieser Akklamation schließt sie sich mit dem priesterlichen Vorbeter zusammen und übt damit das Priestertum aller Gläubigen aus'). If GOLTZEN is right, the institution narrative would be the real *anamnesis*. Quite apart from such questions as to at what precise moment (and how) the Lord comes amongst us during the Eucharist, I prefer to see the acclamation as the true *anamnesis* and the institution narrative as the call to perform it. If GOLTZEN is right, the anamnetic acclamation is nothing more than an extended *Amen* (cf. GOLTZEN: Acclamatio 194: '[...] ratifiziert [...]').

direction of the acclamation. The priest repeats the words of the Lord in the first person: 'Do this in memory of Me.' The people's acclamation is quite logically directed to Jesus Christ, not to the Father.[135] The Father may be the person who is spoken to in the *anaphora*. The 'play' of the institution narrative and anamnetic acclamation requires that this pattern is interrupted.[136]

The scholar whom this contribution seeks to honour, has argued that the institution narrative was not 'originally' a part of the eucharistic prayer, but was later 'inserted' in a prayer which in structure and content resembled the *birkat-ha-mazon*.[137] Upon this hypothesis I would like to build another one. Was there perhaps in Jerusalem at the time when the eucharistic prayer was still without institution narrative a separate ritual, which took place before the *eucharistia*, consisting of the narrative and the acclamation, and was this little ritual, narrative and acclamation, later on inserted as a whole in the eucharistic prayer? I am afraid we will never have any evidence to substantiate this hypothesis. I present it here, just in case it might throw some light on texts I have not read, with the sole purpose which every hypothesis should have: to aid attempts towards an understanding of the material.

The introduction of the anamnetic acclamation *Mortem tuam annuntiamus*, perhaps first said (or sung?) in the Church of Jerusalem, in the Roman liturgy and in many other western eucharistic prayers[138] is a good example how elements from the tradition can be 'revived' and used in giving

135. Of course there are many acclamations in the liturgy which are directed to Christ. In most acclamations in the celebration of the Eucharist Christ is the one spoken to: *Kyrie eleison*, the main part of the *Gloria in excelsis*, the *Agnus Dei*. These texts are however not part of a larger unit directed to the Father. And even if the *Sanctus* is directed to Christ, as it certainly was in the Gallican liturgy, in this 'acclamation', the *Sanctus*, He is not directly addressed in the second person.

136. Cf. also GERHARDS: *Gregoriosanaphora* 228-230. Those modern anamnetic acclamations in which Christ is not addressed, which are fashioned in the third person, like *Iesus Christus pro nobis traditus* in the second eucharistic prayer for Masses with children, the English 'Christ has died' or the Dutch translation of the Roman acclamation *Quotiescumque* (*Als wij dan eten van dit brood en drinken uit deze beker, verkondigen wij de dood des Heren, totdat Hij komt*: 'When we eat from this bread and drink from this cup, we proclaim the death of the Lord, until He comes.') have lost a vital element of the 'play'. They no longer show the typical role pattern this acclamation can give to the celebration. The *anaphorae* of James and Peter have also lost part of the role pattern, for they have the extended command which precedes the acclamation not in the first, but in the third person (*Prex eucharistica* 248: 'until He comes'; 413; 'until the great day of his coming'). Cf. note 32.

137. H. WEGMAN: Généalogie hypothétique de la prière eucharistique, in *Questions liturgiques* 61 (1980) 263-278, esp. 273-274.

138. I do not know why the extension of the command to 'do this in memory of Me', which in one form or another (cf. note 133) precedes the acclamation in tradition, was not also introduced with the acclamation. The *mysterium fidei* is a weak replacement and when it is translated as a call to proclaim the mystery of faith, as it is in the Dutch version of the Roman missal (*Verkondigen wij het mysterie van ons geloof*: 'Les us proclaim the mystery of our faith'), or in the first Canadian Anglican eucharistic prayer, it obscures the role play of priest and people. When the deacon says the *mysterium fidei* (cf. GOLTZEN: Acclamatio 193) the matter is somewhat different.

shape to the rediscovered role of the people in the very heart of the eucharistic celebration, the *anaphora*. The reformers of the Roman liturgy have made a happy choice in chosing this particular eastern acclamation from the *anaphora* of James.[139] That other attempts with other acclamations seem less succesful,[140] may be due to the absence of a clear role pattern of priest and people in those texts, which give the impression that those acclamations are introduced merely to let the people also 'have a share' in the eucharistic prayer.

139. They could have chosen the Antiochene acclamation or the single ancient western text we know of, that from the Mozarabic rite: *Sic credimus, Domine Iesu*. This is however not a 'strong' acclamation. The aspects of 'memory' and 'proclamation' are not clearly present.
140. I do consider the following anamnetic acclamations not very 'lucky' compositions: *Salvator mundi* (Roman missal 1970), *Iesus Christus pro nobis traditus* (Second eucharistic prayer for Masses with children), 'Glory to you for ever and ever' (Canadian Anglican 4th and 5th eucharistic prayers). The acclamation after the *anamnesis* in the first prayer for Masses with children is out of place, if my analysis of the role pattern is correct.

A sign of resurrection on Good Friday.
The role of the people in the Good Friday liturgy until c. 1000 A.D. and the meaning of the Cross[1]

LOUIS VAN TONGEREN

In a personally coloured, evaluative article from 1985 H. Wegman, the laureate of this contribution, expressed a slight disappointment and dissatisfaction with the development of the western liturgy, which stalled and stagnated in the course of the ninth century.[2] Despite smaller regional or local variations the outlines of western liturgy are fixed ever since. The keynote for this liturgy conceived by monks and bishops was not formed by the community of the faithful, but by the men (!) in the sanctuary. As this monastic or cathedral liturgy quite soon condensed and consolidated into a uniform unchangeable liturgy, form and content disagreed with the religious experience of the community. After all, the liturgy did not come from the faithful and, moreover, the religious experience of the community developed in contrast to the liturgy which did not. The same liturgy was listened to, looked at, and experienced in a different way, time after time. As the current research of the history of liturgy aims through the study of the sources, for a major part, at the description and interpretation of the development of this official liturgy, an evaluation of this kind implies at the same time a critical view at the way in which this branch of the study of liturgy is being studied. At the same time, however, Wegman's article contains an important aspect of a new program. The criticism implies a new direction of research with the religious experience of the community as the focal point. 'I have to place myself in the nave and put my ear to the ground and be all eyes',[3] and doing this the scholar will have to imagine himself in the circumstances and the living world in the various periods of history. Since the publication of the article Wegman took this line of approach as a starting-point in several lectures and publications.[4]

---

1. This contribution was translated by Karin van Tongeren-Kemme.
2. H. WEGMAN: De 'komaf' van het liturgisch gedenken. Anamnese gespiegeld aan menselijk ervaren, in *Tijdschrift voor theologie* 25 (1985) 163-175. See also H. WEGMAN: De la pesanteur de la liturgie catholique romaine, in *Praxis juridique et religion* 4 (1987) 168-175.
3. WEGMAN: De 'komaf' 169.
4. H. WEGMAN: Bidprentjes als liturgische bron. De mentaliteitsgeschiedenis, in *Jaarboek voor liturgie-onderzoek* 2 (1986) 22-31; H. WEGMAN: Dit is uw opgang [...] De liturgie van de Palmzondag, in *Jaarboek voor liturgie-onderzoek* 3 (1987) 1-40; H. WEGMAN: De Romeinse euchologie in de Quadragesima. Verandering van paradigma?, in *Jaarboek voor liturgie-onderzoek* 4 (1988) 5-40; H. WEGMAN: De heimelike passie, in *Jaarboek voor liturgie-onderzoek* 5 (1989) 353-361; H. WEGMAN: De gebeden van de paastijd in het missaal van 1970.

More or less in line, this contribution on the Good Friday liturgy has also the experience of the people as the focal point. Therefore no review will be given of historical development, and no euchological or hymnal texts and scriptural readings will be analysed or evaluated. The history of Good Friday is in general and in detail described sufficiently.[5] I will describe briefly the most important sources which mark the development of the Good Friday liturgy until halfway through the Middle Ages and I will, as it where, reread them with a view to the role and the position of the people. For that, I will first direct my attention to the liturgy of Jerusalem the way in which it is described by Egeria (1), for the rest I will restrict myself to the sources which form the basis for the later western 'Roman' Good Friday liturgy, in which the *Pontificale Romano-Germanicum* will be the last point of reference (2). In second instance, the study of the information from these sources about the position of the people will be concentrated on the two rites that are the most characteristic for the Good Friday liturgy: the veneration of the Cross and the Communion (3). By examining the function of the Cross in the religious imagery of the people the liturgical facts about the rite of the Cross will be placed in a broader context in order to determine more accurately what was the meaning of the Cross for the people in the period under consideration. Finally, the most important elements will be reviewed by way of a conclusion (4).

1. THE FIRST CENTURIES

1.1. From fast day to day with its own liturgy
An important characteristic of the early Christian *Pascha* is the thematic unity of passion, death and resurrection of the Lord. Although the memorial of only the passion and death is mentioned too, and although it is possible to make further distinctions because in the various traditions people put their own accents, this was the central theme in the only Easter service which was held in the night from 14 to 15 Nisan (Quartodecimans) or on the Sunday thereafter.[6] There were still no other days related to Easter which had developed a liturgical form of their own. But there was a period of fasting preceding Easter

Tekstanalyse in het kader van liturgie als verbeelding van geloof, in *Tijdschrift voor theologie* 28 (1988) 349-370; H. WEGMAN: De Eerste Dag na twaalf jaren, in *Kosmos en oekumene* 23 (1989) 102-109.

5. For a general review of the development of Good Friday see B. CAPELLE: Le vendredi saint, in *La maison-Dieu* no. 37 (1954) 93-117; B. CAPELLE: L'office du vendredi saint, in *La maison-Dieu* no. 41 (1955) 73-83; G. RÖMER: Die Liturgie des Karfreitags, in *Zeitschrift für katholische Theologie* 77 (1955) 39-93; H.A.P. SCHMIDT: *Hebdomada sancta* 2 (Roma 1957) 778-808; P. JOUNEL: Le vendredi saint 2. La tradition de l'église, in *La maison-Dieu* no. 67 (1961) 199-212; H. AUF DER MAUR: *Feiern im Rhythmus der Zeit* 1. *Herrenfeste in Woche und Jahr* (= Gottesdienst der Kirche. Handbuch der Liturgiewissenschaft 5) (Regensburg 1983) 76-79, 107-113, 136-137.

6. See the introduction to the collection of Easter texts in R. CANTALAMESSA: *Ostern in der alten Kirche* (= Traditio Christiana 4) (Bern 1981); AUF DER MAUR: *Feiern* 65-70; Th.J. TALLEY: *The origins of the liturgical year* (New York 1986) 5-6.

which could last one, two or more days.[7] Where the *Pascha* was established on the Sunday, strict fasting was accentuated especially on the preceding Friday and Saturday. The mourning over the passion and death of Jesus dominated these days and according to St. Mark 2, 20 people were fasting during the days the groom was taken away.[8] The strict fasting on Friday and Saturday must have made an impression on the faithful. After all, these days were very different from other days and fasting must have been felt physically. People could not back out of this because, according to Tertullian, it was a general and public obligation, which was expressed by omitting the kiss of peace.[9] During lengthy periods of fast people were allowed to eat bread, salt and water, but on the Friday and Saturday preceding Easter it was not allowed to eat anything at all.[10] Only pregnant women and sick people were allowed to reduce the fasting to one day (the Saturday), confining themselves to bread and water.[11]

Although the Saturday had been marked as the most important fast day, the Friday participated also in the fasting in preparation for Easter at an early stage.[12] Because of the strict fasting the Friday before Easter must have had a certain 'impact' on the faithful quite soon. Liturgically however, this day did not develop any form in the early Church. This did not happen until the end of the fourth century. Then the single Easter service was extended to a service of three days, the *Triduum sacrum*, and the whole week before Easter was beginning to be marked and characterized as a special week. Here lies the beginning of 'the proces of the historicizing of the mystery of Easter',[13] when passion, death and resurrection are celebrated as separate phases of the one mystery at the point of time (and in Jerusalem also at the place) at which the historical events took place according to the passion narratives. Within this historicizing of Easter, also the Friday developed a liturgy of its own. This is clear from writings of Ambrose, Augustine, Chrysostom, Innocent I and Leo I, among others.[14] However, a complete description of the liturgy on the Friday before Easter is not given by them. Their information is concerned almost exclusively with the choice of the Scripture readings. That is why we cannot picture the way the people participated in this service. But we can do so on the basis of Egeria's account of her pilgrimage from c. 380 A.D. It is the oldest document containing a complete and detailed description of the liturgy the way it had been celebrated during the Holy Week in Jerusalem at the end of the fourth century.

7. See for example TALLEY: *Origins* 27-31.
8. See TERTULLIAN: *De ieiunio* 2, 2.
9. TERTULLIAN: *De oratione* 18, 7.
10. *Didascalia apostolorum* 5, 18.
11. *Apostolic tradition* 33.
12. Apart from this, each Friday was designated very early as a fast day besides the Wednesday, specifically contrasted to the Monday and Thursday fasts of the Jews (*Didache* 8, 1); see for example TALLEY: *Origins* 28.
13. CANTALAMESSA: *Ostern* XXV.
14. See for example AUF DER MAUR: *Feiern* 76-77.

1.2. The liturgy in Jerusalem according to Egeria's diary

It appears from the description by Egeria that many people took part in the very intensive numerous liturgical services during Holy Week. Especially the last three days people wandered around almost the whole day and also several hours of the evening and the night, praying, singing and listening, in Jerusalem as well as in the near vicinity, from one historical spot of the last days of Jesus' life to the other. To the modern reader this must seem to be a physical task which can hardly be fulfilled. In the night from Thursday to Friday there is a succession of meetings,[15] attended by a mass of people, old and young, rich and poor, and even small children (36, 3: *maiores atque minores, divites, pauperes*; 36, 2: *usque ad minimus infans*). Fatigued because of the vigils through the night and weakend because of daily fasting, people only walked very slowly (36, 2: *lente et lente*) from one place to the other. Physically people had to put in great efforts, but also inwardly people were very touched and moved. Because of the historicizing celebration people experienced the last days of Jesus' life and gave free play to their emotions. When on Gethsemane the account of Jesus' arrest was read, everybody was groaning, lamenting and weeping in such a way that people could almost hear it in the city (36, 3: *tantus rugitus et mugitus totius populi est cum fletu, ut forsitan porro ad civitatem gemitus populi omnis auditus sit*). After the exhausting journey during nighttime which lasted until sunrise on Friday, the people were encouraged by the bishop after which everybody was allowed to go home and take a moment's rest.

However, on Friday morning people met again early to attend two meetings which lasted until late in the evening. On the second hour (8.00 h) everybody was present to venerate the salutary Cross (36, 5: *sanctum lignum crucis[...] ad salutem sibi unusquisque nostrum credens profuturum*) in the small chapel 'behind the Cross' (*post Crucem*) which is situated between Golgotha and the basilica (the Martyrium).[16] There, the bishop was seated and a table with the wood of the Cross and the title, was put before him, surrounded by deacons. One by one the faithful (including the catechumens whom Egeria mentions explicitly) passed this table to venerate the Cross. Approaching the table, people bowed, then they touched the Cross and the title first with their forehead and then with their eyes and finally they kissed the Cross. After this veneration of the Cross they approached the deacon who held out for veneration the ring of Solomon and the horn with which the kings were anointed. After this they left the chapel through a door other than the one through which they had entered. In this passage Egeria also describes a story that was going around in which it was told that once upon a time someone had bitten in

---

15. The descriptions of the meetings on Good Friday and on the previous night are to be found in EGERIA: *Itinerarium* 35-37 (P. MARAVAL: *Egérie. Journal de voyage (Itinéraire)* (= Sources chrétiennes 296) (Paris 1982) 280-291; J. WILKINSON: *Egeria's travels to the Holy Land* (Jerusalem-Warminster 1981²) 135-138).
16. For the geographical locations of the different places see especially Ch. COÜASNON: *The Church of the Holy Sepulchre in Jerusalem* (London 1974).

the Cross and had stolen a piece of it during the veneration of the Cross. Therefore the deacons who were positioned round the Cross functioned as guards and during the veneration of the Cross it was forbidden to everybody to touch the Cross with the hands, probably because they feared another theft. Apparently people were so attracted by the Cross, that they wanted to have a piece of this salutary wood. The relic of the Cross had such a special meaning to the faithful, that they had to be protected from themselves.[17] This veneration of the Cross ceremony started on the second hour (8.00 h) and lasted until the sixth hour (12.00 h). However, it is not certain that everybody was actually present during the whole period which lasted four hours. After all, the ritual took place in the small chapel *post Crucem*, too small for the many people. Moreover, in the description by Egeria, the ritual somewhat comes across as a private affair, especially in comparison with the other meetings which have a strong collective character (37, 3: *omnis populus transit unus et unus*). It only refers to the way the Cross was exhibited and the way it was venerated by each individual. Nothing is said about reading, praying or singing collectively. After they had left the chapel through the door other than the one through which they had entered, they probably went home or they just gathered in the *atrium*, the courtyard 'before the Cross' (*ante Crucem*),[18] where the second meeting would start on the sixth hour (12.00 h). So, when they had venerated the Cross there was a moment's rest until noon.

The afternoon meeting which lasted until the ninth hour (15.00 h) was crowded. The *atrium*, which Egeria described as being very large, could not open its doors anymore because there were so many people (37, 4: *valde grandem* [...] *ita ut nec aperiri possit*). As long as three hours, passages were being read from the prophets, the psalms, the epistles and the gospels which relate to the passion and the death of the Lord, either as a prediction or as a fulfilment.[19] Prayers and hymns alternated with these lectures. Just as in the preceding night people were very moved when they heard how much the Lord had suffered. At three o'clock in the afternoon (15.00 h) the passage from the Gospel according to St. John was read in which it is told that Jesus gives up the spirit and dies. This concluded the meeting.[20] Directly after this meeting they gathered in the *Martyrium*, from where they went to the *Anastasis* where the account of the burial was read.[21] A blessing of catechumens and faithful

---

17. Gregory of Tours (+ 594) also describes hard-handed action against those who approached the Cross too closely during the veneration of the Cross, according to MARAVAL: *Egérie* 286 note 1.
18. This is the walled open space, which, on two opposite sides, is bounded by the *Martyrium* basilica and the *Anastasis*. The chapel *post Crucem* is situated in one of the corners of this *atrium*. Possibly the door through which one had left this chapel after the veneration of the Cross gave access to this *atrium*.
19. An accurate indication of the various readings and psalms is given by the fifth-century *Armenian lectionary* 43 (A. RENOUX: *Le codex arménien Jérusalem 121 2. Edition comparée du texte et de deux autres manuscrits* (= Patrologia Orientalis 36, 2) (Turnhout 1971) 281-293).
20. St. John 19, 16-37; *Armenian lectionary* 43 (RENOUX: *Codex arménien* 293).
21. St. Matthew 27, 57-61; *Armenian lectionary* 43bis (RENOUX: *Codex arménien* 293-295).

concluded the last Friday meeting. For those who wanted it was possible to keep a vigil through the night. But because it was known, as Egeria describes, that everyone probably was too tired, this vigil was optional. Only the ones who wanted to and were capable took part: some of them the whole night (especially the clergy, the strong and the youngsters), others only a part of the night. Obviously, against Egeria's expectations, there were many people (37, 9: *maxima autem turba pervigilant*).

Several times the role and the position of the people are described very clearly by Egeria. First of all, the number of services in Jerusalem, especially in the last days before Easter – also on the Friday – is striking, and the intensity of participation in these services.

Subsequently, the many ways in which so many people were interested in the services to such a large extent. Faithful people of every age and with different social backgrounds took part together. From Egeria's description it is not very clear how the several liturgical roles and tasks were divided on Good Friday. A few times the bishop and the deacons are mentioned, but their role is not a dominant one. Hymns were sung, but we do not know which, how and by whom. Was there some sort of *schola* which lead the singing and did the people answer with antiphons? There were many lessons from the Scriptures, but Egeria does not specify by whom they were read. Although also the manifold moments of prayer are mentioned in a neutral way most of the time (*fit oratio, interpositae orationes fiunt, dicitur oratio*), the description of the services through the night from Thursday until Friday shows that the prayers were said by the bishop (35, 4: *orationes* [...] *quas dicet episcopus*). So apparently there were several functions, but the Jerusalem liturgy does not make a clerical impression. Here, the liturgy is characterized by communality.

A last element which deserves attention is the rite of the veneration of the Cross on Friday morning. Ritually this ceremony is hardly developed, and in comparison with the other services of the Holy Week, which have a strong communal character, the veneration of the Cross makes a more individual impression. The Cross is not shown to the people, as it does happen during the *Encaenia*, the festival for the dedication of the *Martyrium* on September 13 and 14.[22] It is not sung of collectively and there is no service with lessons and prayers. The Cross is venerated by everyone on his own. Maybe it happened like this because there was a lack of space, but perhaps the special position of the veneration of the Cross can also be explained by the fact that there is no scriptural basis as there is for the other services in the Holy Week. The historicizing service of Easter, during which people in chronological order commemorate and experience again the historical events from the last days of Jesus' life at the historical sites, matches the indications which are given by the passion narratives with regard to this.[23] However, there is no question of a

---

22. See EGERIA: *Itinerarium* 48-49 (MARAVAL: *Egérie* 316-319); *Armenian lectionary* 67-68 (RENOUX: *Codex arménien* 361-363).

23. In this context Egeria regularly talks about readings, prayers and hymns which are chosen *apti diei et loco*. For some meetings you might add *apti horae*, as in the service on Friday

veneration of the Cross in the passion narratives. Here we are talking about a ritual not founded upon Scripture, which probably was included especially because Jerusalem was in the possession of a relic of the true Cross. So, the veneration of the Cross does not belong to the historicizing elements of the Good Friday liturgy.

2. ROME AND THE WESTERN TRADITION DEPENDENT UPON ROME (700-1000)

Until the end of the seventh century the Good Friday liturgy in Rome consisted only of a liturgy of the word with the scriptural readings and solemn orations. The *Gelasianum vetus* is the first to have a ritual for Good Friday extended with a veneration of the Cross and with a Communion rite for the presbyteral liturgy in the titular churches.[24] For the papal liturgy this extension is given for the first time by *Ordo Romanus* XXIII, from the first half of the eighth century,[25] while the *Hadrianum* only has a liturgy of the word similar to the ancient Roman custom.[26] Besides the already mentioned texts, the *Gelasianum vetus* and *Ordo Romanus* XXIII, there are still other sources which give us information about the way in which Good Friday was celebrated since the eighth century. I will not discuss them all. There are too many of them, and besides, it is not necessary. After all, some of the sources are so closely related that they hardly show any variation, or they expressly refer to a monastic environment or they do not give any new information which is relevant to determine the position of the people. Therefore I will concentrate especially on the *Gelasianum vetus*, the *Ordines Romani* XXIII, XXIV and XXXI, and on the *Pontificale Romano-Germanicum*. The structure of the service is not always the same because the sources do not always contain the same elements and because the separate elements are sorted in different ways. The most important elements which we can distinguish are: the entrance in the church (in *Ordo Romanus* XXIII preceded by a procession), the liturgy of the word, the veneration of the Cross and the Communion.

With regard to the liturgy of the word, which exists of prayers, readings, responses and the solemn orations (though not the same and not arranged the same way everywhere), the role of the people on Good Friday does not seem to

afternoon, when St. John 19, 30 is read on the ninth hour (15.00 h), for the reading on the burial (St. Matthew 27, 57-60) at the *Anastasis* in the evening, and also the optional wake at night that seems to correspond with St. Matthew 27, 61 in which it is told that Mary Magdalene and the other Mary had seated themselves opposite the grave after the burial was over.

24. A. CHAVASSE: *Le sacramentaire gélasien (Vaticanus Reginensis 316); sacramentaire presbytérale en usage dans les titres romains au VIIe siècle* (= Bibliothèque de théologie IV) (Tournai 1958) 96 dates this ritual before the end of the seventh century.

25. Dating according to M. ANDRIEU: *Les Ordines Romani du haut Moyen Age* 3 (= Spicilegium sacrum Lovaniense 24) (Louvain 1951) 266; CHAVASSE: *Sacramentaire gélasien* 96, however, dates this *Ordo* just before the end of the seventh century.

26. The *Hadrianum* only gives the solemn orations: nos. 338-355. See J. DESHUSSES: *Le sacramentaire grégorien. Ses principales formes d'après les plus anciens manuscrits* 1 (= Spicilegium Friburgense 16) (Fribourg 1971) 176-180.

be specifically different from other services. Here, the people only had a small share. During the readings from Scripture the people performed the role of listener and during the hymns they probably sang the response. However, we do not know anything about the capacity and quality of the singing by the people in the eighth and ninth centuries. The structure of the prayers assumes some activity from the people, an inner involvement in the contents and an approving acclamation. After the summoning call *oremus* the deacon encourages the people to kneel: *flectamus genua* (in an open space without kneeler). The following silence is intended for private prayer by everyone. In the case of the solemn orations it is already directed by the intention indicated by the priest just before. After this the deacon asks the people to rise again (*levate*), after which the priest formulates a concluding prayer which is terminated by a collective *Amen*. It is a pity that we do not know what the people were praying during these moments of silence. Only the intentions and the presidential prayers remain, because these were written down in the liturgical books.

2.1. Ordo Romanus XXIII[27]

Preceding the liturgy of the word, the entrance took place – according to the oldest sources in silence – from the sacristy to the altar (*Gelasianum vetus, Ordines Romani* XXIV, XXVII, XXVIII). The papal liturgy however, as described in *Ordo Romanus* XXIII, began with an elaborate procession from Saint John Lateran to the Church of the Holy Cross. In this procession a relic of the Cross was carried by the deacon in a precious decorated box. During the procession Psalm 118 (119: *Beati immaculati*) was chanted, probably with the antiphon 'Behold the wood of the Cross on which hung the salvation of the world' (*Ecce lignum*).[28]

Nothing is said about participation of the people in this procession, but should it be excluded? Maybe the people were lined up along the route and maybe they joined in after the procession with the relic had passed, or maybe they gathered in the stational Church of the Cross awaiting the arrival of the pope and his retinue as it was the case at the papal stational liturgy in *Ordo Romanus* I?[29] The sources do not give a definite answer about this. After entering the Jerusalem Church, as the Church of the Holy Cross is also named, the box containing the relic was placed on the altar after which it was opened by the pope. Then the pope prostrated before the altar and thus before the Cross, and prayed. Hereafter he was the first person to venerate the Cross with a kiss, in hierarchical order followed by the bishops, the priests, the

27. ANDRIEU: *Ordines Romani* 3, 270-272.
28. According to Regan (P. REGAN: Veneration of the Cross, in *Worship* 52 (1978) 2-13, p. 4) because the antiphon, although not mentioned explicitly in *Ordo Romanus* XXIII, is included with Psalm 118 in three manuscripts of the ancient Roman antiphonary. Cf. R.-J. HESBERT: *Antiphonale missarum sextuplex* (Bruxelles 1935) 97.
29. See J.P. KIRSCH: *Die Stationskirchen des Missale Romanum* (= Ecclesia orans 19) (Freiburg 1926) 1 (34)-48.

deacons and the subdeacons. In the meantime the liturgy of the word had already started immediately after the veneration of the Cross by the pope. To give the people the opportunity to venerate the relic of the Cross, it was moved first *super arcellam ad rugas* (*Ordo Romanus* XXIII, 15). This movable fence or *ruga* expressed the demarcation between the nave and the sanctuary or *presbyterium*, which is not accessible for the people. The Roman liturgy knew a strong hierarchical separation between the clergy and the faithful.[30] The faithful were allowed only to approach this fence, that is to say, half of them: *feminae ibi non introeunt* (*Ordo Romanus* XXIII, 16). After the men had venerated the Cross first, the relic was moved again to another place where the women were allowed to venerate the Cross.[31]

As a conclusion of the service the people had the possibility to communicate. The pope and the deacons explicitly did not. *Ordo Romanus* XXIII only describes briefly what possibilities there are to communicate, but does not describe a Communion rite. In the Church of the Holy Cross people could consume the bread which was kept from the service on Holy Thursday, but you could also go to one of the other churches in Rome or to one of the *tituli* to receive Communion (in both kinds).

2.2. Gelasianum vetus[32]

In the other churches of Rome services were being held at about the same time.[33] In some respects, however, the Good Friday liturgy in the titular churches was different from the papal liturgy. The *Gelasianum vetus* does not include a procession. The Cross (a relic?) was already placed on the altar without any ceremony before the liturgy began. Whereas in the papal liturgy the rite of the veneration of the Cross started before and continued during the service of the word, in titular churches it was quite different. When after the liturgy of the word the consecrated bread and wine, left over from Holy Thursday, were being put on the altar, the priest venerated and kissed the Cross before the altar. Then the Lord's prayer and the embolism were recited

---

30. S. DE BLAAUW: *Cultus et decor. Liturgie en architectuur in laatantiek en middeleeuws Rome. Basilica Salvatoris, Sanctae Mariae, Sancti Petri* (Delft 1987) 28-30.
31. Already in the early Christian church-buildings it was common that men and women were separated. The men stood on the right and the women on the left, probably according to a hierarchical principal, viz. that right was given priority to left and consequently men to women. See DE BLAAUW: *Cultus et decor* 32.
32. *Gelasianum vetus* 395-418 in L.C. MOHLBERG: *Liber sacramentorum Romanae aeclesiae ordinis anni circuli* (= Rerum ecclesiasticarum documenta, Fontes 4) (Roma 1960) 64-67.
33. The *Gelasianum vetus* records 15.00 h as the starting time for the service in the titular churches. According to *Ordo Romanus* XXIII people gather at 14.00 h in the Lateran basilica for the procession, so it seems likely that the service in the Holy Cross also began on 15.00 h. For that matter, this point of time does not seem to have been chosen at random. According to Auf der Maur the reasons for this are that all liturgical actions on fast days do not begin before the ninth hour and that the ninth hour is the dying hour of the Lord (St. Matthew 27, 46): AUF DER MAUR: *Feiern* 108. Besides, the papal liturgy should have ended earlier in order that the people could arrive in time for the Communion rite at one of the *tituli*.

after which everybody venerated the Cross and communicated.[34]

Because of the preparation for the Communion (Lord's prayer and embolism), the veneration of the Cross by the people is clearly separated from the veneration of the Cross by the priest. Did they find it more practical to combine the veneration of the Cross with the Communion in one 'movement' for the people, so that they only had to come forward once?

2.3. Ordo Romanus XXIV[35]

Several decades later, however, also in Rome both rites are clearly separated, according to *Ordo Romanus* XXIV from about the middle of the eighth century. Moreover, the Good Friday liturgy then has seen several alterations. The liturgy of the word, in which participated every priest, the entire clergy and the people, is moved to the third hour (9.00 h) and takes place in one of the churches in the city. This means that not all the faithful will have been participating in this, but representatives of the several *tituli*, in conformity with the stational practice. In the evening then, during vespers (*ad vesperum*), the veneration of the Cross and the Communion rite took place in the separate titular churches. But again, also here, first the liturgy of the word was held. This is also a reason to presume that not all the faithful had attended the service in the morning. After the liturgy of the word the Cross was held by two acolytes at some distance from the altar and it was venerated in hierarchical order by clergy and people. Furthermore, the veneration of the Cross was now being accompanied by a hymn for the first time. They sung Psalm 118 (119) and the antiphon *Ecce lignum crucis in quo salus mundi pependit*, which was mentioned earlier in *ordo Romanus* XXIII for the procession of the papal liturgy. According to Regan this antiphon calls attention to the wood of the Cross in a quite litteral sense – whether it be sung in procession, or during the veneration or during the exposition (as we will see later) – because the text is composed of phrases strongly reminiscent of various accounts of the finding of the true Cross. The people are thereby made to participate in the original discovery of the Cross, and therefore the rite which is accompanied by these words requires a relic of the true Cross.[36] However, it may be doubted whether the people were that familiar with these various accounts of the finding of the Cross that they were recognized in the antiphon, and besides, we do not know if all the *tituli* were in the possession of a relic of the Cross.

After this veneration of the Cross by clergy and people the Communion rite

---

34. Jungmann suggests the existence of different practices with regard to the people's participation in the Lord's prayer. In the old Gallican liturgy it was said by the whole people but in the other western liturgies only by the celebrating priest. In Rome, however, only the last line should have been said by the people since the seventh century: J.A. JUNGMANN: *Missarum sollemnia. Eine genetische Erklärung der römischen Messe* 2 (Wien 1952³) 355-359. The *Gelasianum vetus* does not describe how the people venerated the Cross, but in accordance with the other sources we may presume that they also kissed the Cross.

35. ANDRIEU: *Ordines Romani* 3, 291-294.

36. REGAN: Veneration 6.

began with the Lord's prayer and the embolism. But, because they only kept the bread from the Eucharist of Holy Thursday for the Communion, first the wine was consecrated, and this was done by the rite of the *immixtio*, which is the mixing of consecrated bread with unconsecrated wine. This was done without any words. Then everybody communicated in silence, which concluded the service.

This Good Friday liturgy of *Ordo Romanus* XXIV is to be found again almost literally in the *Ordines Romani* XXVII and XXVIII and it was therefore also introduced in the Frankish territory around 800.

2.4. Ordo Romanus XXXI[37]

Ordo Romanus XXXI, dating from the ninth century, shows a further separation between the Cross and Communion rites of the priest and the people and it also shows that the rite of the veneration of the Cross of the people is further extended. When bread and unconsecrated wine had been put on the altar after the intercessory prayers, only the pontifex venerated the Cross on the altar, after which he broke into the Lord's prayer, performed the *commixtio* rite in silence and communicated alone. When the service seemed to have ended for the bishop, a more extensive Cross- and Communion rite took place for the people. The veiled Cross was placed behind the altar. From here it was carried by two acolytes in front of the altar in three stages. During the three standstills two cantors bowed before the Cross and sung *Hagios ho Theos*, after which the choir sung *Sanctus Deus*. After the third time the bishop unveiled the Cross and sung *Ecce lignum crucis*. During the singing of Psalm 118 with the same antiphon the Cross was venerated by the clergy and the people after it had been brought to another place (*Ordo Romanus* XXXI, 48: *ut deportetur ad locum destinatum adorationis*). Then everybody communicated, while the *Pange lingua* was being sung with the antiphon *Crux fidelis*.

2.5. The Pontificale Romano-Germanicum[38]

The *Pontificale Romano-Germanicum*, which was composed in Mainz about the middle of the tenth century, provides two services for Good Friday as in *Ordo Romanus* XXIV. On the fifth hour (11.00 h) the liturgy of the word was held in one of the churches in the city, after which the same liturgy of the word was repeated in separate churches in the afternoon on the ninth hour. Contiguously the veneration of the Cross and the Communion rite took place *ad versperum*. Of these two rites the veneration of the Cross in particular has undergone some expansion in the *Pontificale Romano-Germanicum* in comparison with the *ordines* which were described above. Especially the number of hymns has increased, and the veneration of the Cross, moreover, is accompanied by a threefold prayer: people kneel three times and each time a prayer

37. ANDRIEU: *Ordines Romani* 3, 496-498.
38. C. VOGEL and R. ELZE: *Le pontifical romano-germanique du dixième siècle* 2 (= Studi e Testi 227) (Città del Vaticano 1963) 86-93.

is said. After the Cross has been venerated by everyone, it is brought back to its place and the Communion rite begins. This rite consists of bringing the consecrated bread and the unconsecrated wine, the Lord's prayer and the embolism, and the consecration of the wine by means of the *immixtio* in silence. As a conclusion of the service everybody communicates in silence.

The composition of the service in the *Pontificale Romano-Germanicum* shows a structure in which the veneration of the Cross and the Communion are two clearly distinguishable rites, and in which the participation of clergy and people in these two rites is fully integrated. First both groups venerate the Cross after which they both communicate.

3. THE PEOPLE AND THE MEANING OF THE CROSS

From the description of the Good Friday liturgy, the way it has developed until the middle of the tenth century, it appears that the role and the position of the people is most obvious with regard to the veneration of the Cross and the Communion rite. This is why I will go into these a little further. By making an attempt to discover what has been the experience of the faithful with regard to the Cross in the Good Friday liturgy, I will try to place the factual information about the Cross in a wider early medieval context.

3.1. Veneration of the Cross

The veneration of the Cross has its origin in Jerusalem, but the western liturgy for Good Friday has its roots in Rome (*Gelasianum vetus* and *Ordo Romanus* XXIII). The Gallican liturgy is not familiar with this, and although the Mozarabic liturgy did know the veneration of the Cross on Good Friday about 700 A.D., it took it straight from Jerusalem and not via Rome; and moreover, the Mozarabic rite did not have so much influence on the western liturgy as Rome did.[39] In the Frankish territory the rite of the Cross was introduced from Rome only later. The *Ordines Romani* XVI and XVII only know a liturgy of the word and a Communion rite without a veneration of the Cross. Besides the example of the eastern liturgies, which is accepted generally in relation to the introduction of the veneration of the Cross on Good Friday in Rome at the end of the seventh or early in the eighth century in the time of one of the eastern popes,[40] possibly also the spread of relics of the Cross has been influential. Initially the presence of a Cross relic was perhaps an important condition. Jerusalem was in the possession of a relic of the Cross and Rome possessed even several Cross relics around 700.[41]

---

39. M. FEROTIN: *Liber ordinum* (= Monumenta ecclesiae liturgica 5) (Paris 1904) 193ff. SCHMIDT: *Hebdomada sancta* 2, 791; H.A.P. SCHMIDT: Goede Vrijdag, in *Liturgisch woordenboek* 1 (Roermond 1958-1962) 888-889.

40. See for example SCHMIDT: *Hebdomada sancta* 2, 791; SCHMIDT: Goede Vrijdag 889; AUF DER MAUR: *Feiern* 109-110.

41. Especially in the *Liber Pontificalis* the presence of a Cross relic in Rome is mentioned several times. This does not mean of course that it concerns a different relic each time. Constantine

The papel liturgy in *Ordo Romanus* XXIII seems to be focussed on the Cross relic. This relic is the heart of the procession and this is emphasized by the antiphon *Ecce lignum (!) crucis*. Anyway, the whole service is dominated by the Cross ritual. The veneration of the Cross is the principal part and in the mean time the liturgy of the word begins at a certain moment. Although it is most likely that not every titular church possessed a relic of the Cross, also in the service of the *Gelasianum vetus* the Cross was highlighted, but less predominant than in the papal liturgy. Already at the beginning of the service the Cross is placed on the altar; this is the focal point and it fixes the attention. Together with the Communion rite the veneration of the Cross takes place at the end. The Cross frames the service, as it where. That originally a relic of the Cross was probably desirable for the Good Friday liturgy, but soon after considered unnecessary, is made clear by Amalarius of Metz (c. 775-852/3). Apparently there were several opinions on this subject in his time. People venerated Cross relics, but also crosses which had no relic. Amalarius himself did not think it necessary to have a relic in order to venerate the Cross.[42]

In the liturgy of the titular churches, as described in the *Gelasianum vetus* and in *Ordo Romanus* XXIV, the rite of the Cross is sober in contrast to that in the papal liturgy. However, as from *Ordo Romanus* XXXI the veneration rite by the people is extended, while the veneration by the celebrant stays sober. In *Ordo Romanus* XXXI the service actually has been completed at the moment the people and the remaining clergy are going to participate. The pontifex has, in a simple way, venerated the Cross, performed the Communion rite in silence and communicated, before the solemn veneration of the Cross by the people begins. Here, the service by the priest is not integrated in the service by the people. These popular extension and embellishment of the

should have placed a Cross relic in the Sessorian basilica, which he had built and which became the later *S. Croce in Hierusalem* (L. DUCHESNE: *Le liber pontificalis. Texte, introduction et commentaire* 1 (Paris 1886) 179). However, according to Krautheimer this donation must not be dated in the days of Constantine the Great, but in the days of his son Constantius (R. KRAUTHEIMER: *Corpus basilicarum Christianarum Romae. Le basiliche Cristiane antiche di Roma (sec. IV-IX)* 1 (Città del Vaticano 1937) 167 and 192). In the middle of the fifth century, in 454, pope Leo the Great confirms – in a letter to Juvenal, bishop of Jerusalem – the reception of a relic of the Cross which the bishop had sent him (*Epistola* 139; J.-P. MIGNE: *Patrologia Latina* 54 (Paris 1881) 1101-1110, c. 1108). Somewhat later Hilary (461-468) placed a Cross relic in one of the three oratories of the Lateran baptistery (DUCHESNE: *Liber pontificalis* 1, 242). Then Symmachus (498-516) placed a Cross relic in one of the oratories, which he had built around the baptistery of the St. Peter (DUCHESNE: *Liber pontificalis* 1, 261), and at the end of the seventh century pope Sergius found a black silver box containing a Cross relic in the sacristy of the St. Peter (DUCHESNE: *Liber pontificalis* 1, 374). See H. GRISAR: *Die römische Kapelle Sancta sanctorum und ihr Schatz. Meine Entdeckungen und Studien in der Palastkapelle der mittelalterlichen Päpste* (Freiburg 1908) esp. 58-100; DE BLAAUW: *Cultus et decor* 96. For that matter, also the veneration of the Cross in the Mozarabic rite was emphatically connected with the Cross relic. See FEROTIN: *Liber Ordinum*, 193ff.

42. AMALARIUS OF METZ: *Liber officialis* 1, 14, 10 (I.M. HANSSENS: *Amalarii episcopi opera liturgica omnia* 2 (= Studi e Testi 139) (Città del Vaticano 1949) 102).

veneration of the Cross are part of the Frankish dramatization tendencies that had their influence on the styling of the liturgy in the course of the eighth century.[43] In the tenth-century *Pontificale Romano-Germanicum* this tendency continues, although the parts of priest and people are no longer isolated as they are in, especially, *Ordo Romanus* XXXI. Also the priest takes part in the dramatization, which was not the case previously. The people have taken the priest along with them.

3.2. The Communion rite

Originally the western liturgies did not have a Communion rite on Good Friday. On Good Friday and Holy Saturday people had to fast and so there was no Eucharist. The first sources which record the Communion rite are Roman: the *Gelasianum vetus* and *Ordo Romanus* XXIII. It is the general view that this rite is of eastern origin.[44] Probably this rite was introduced in the titular churches because of the big Greek colony in Rome in the seventh century. These Greeks wanted in Rome what they were accustomed to originally. It is most likely that the Latins soon adopted this custom and thus it became common practice in the *tituli*. The papal liturgy held on to the old tradition without the Communion rite. Only the people were allowed to communicate but only in one kind. People had to go to one of the *tituli* if they wanted to communicate in both kinds (bread and wine). It is therefore probably that the Communion rite was adopted in the Roman liturgy at the instigation of the Greek faithful in the first place, after which it became something for all people. Apparently the Communion rite was primarily a popular element in Rome.

In the Frankish territory this custom was first introduced by the monastic *Ordo Romanus* XVI,[45] and we find it back there in all sources. Evidently this fitted in with the Frankish national character in contrast to the Mozarabic, the Gallican and the Milanese. These peoples were not familiar with this custom. As far as ritual is concerned, the Communion underwent a less extensive development than the veneration of the Cross did. In the *Gelasianum vetus* the primitive archetype can be seen: the people made use of bread and wine both consecrated on Holy Thursday.[46] Since *Ordo Romanus* XXIV there is only question of reserved consecrated bread, while the wine is consecrated by means of *immixtio* or *commixtio*. Anyway, it is a rather sober rite: bread and

---

43. RÖMER: Die Liturgie des Karfreitags 73-75. Although *Ordo Romanus* XXIV can still be called sober, nevertheless Römer also sees in *Ordo Romanus* XXIV, 29-30 the first influences of this Frankish dramatization.

44. See for example M. ANDRIEU: *Immixtio et consecratio. La consécration par contact dans les documents liturgiques du Moyen Age* (Paris 1924) 20ff.; CHAVASSE: *Sacramentaire gélasien* 90, 92-93; JOUNEL: Le vendredi saint 209; H.B. MEYER: *Eucharistie. Geschichte, Theologie, Pastoral* (= Gottesdienst der Kirche. Handbuch der Liturgiewissenschaft 4) (Regensburg 1989) 150-151, 553-554.

45. ANDRIEU: *Ordines Romani* 3, 139.

46. ANDRIEU: *Ordines Romani* 3, 139.

wine are put on the altar (sometimes already during the veneration of the Cross), then the Lord's prayer is said followed by the embolism *Libera nos*, after which the wine is consecrated by means of the *immixtio* and everybody communicates; originally in silence. Only *Ordo Romanus* XXXI mentions the *Pange lingua* during the Communion.

According to Becker this so-called *liturgia praesanctificatorum* quite soon developed itself in the perception of the people more and more into the direction of a real Mass.[47] On the basis of the sources here discussed it seems to me that this is not the case until the end of the first millennium.

3.3. The meaning of the Cross

For lack of source material that gives insight in the reception of the liturgy by the people, it is difficult to retrieve the meaning of the veneration of the Cross on Good Friday for the faithful during the period we are dealing with here. A way to get some insight, nevertheless, is to indicate by means of a short characteristic how the Cross functioned in the religious imagery of the people in this period. The experience and the meaning of the Cross are not the same in Jerusalem c. 400 A.D., in Rome around 700 and in the Frankish-Germanic territory during the eighth, ninth and tenth centuries. Therefore one characteristic is not sufficient; we have to make some distinctions.

Although the Cross is often raised in the early Christian literature and iconography, it is impossible to derive from these a general description of the meaning of the Cross for the people at the time of Egeria's stay in Jerusalem.[48] It is uncertain to what extent these writings and iconographical expressions corresponded with the imagery of the people. Did they influence the experience of the people? Have they been affected by the people's imagery? Or did they perhaps correspond more or less with each other, so that they can be looked upon as a reliable reproduction of the meaning and function of the Cross in everyday life? In literature the early Christian Cross is multi-interpreted and thematically connected with various motives. On the basis of this diversity we can formulate some coordinating significations.[49] Predominant seems to be that people never have regarded the Cross as a mere reference to the historical crucifixion of Jesus; they have always interpreted it also as a sign which refers to Jesus' resurrection. This historical Cross is the foundation of the Cross as a sign of salvation. And further, the Cross as a sign of salvation

---

47. H.-J. BECKER: Kommunion am Karfreitag? Gedanken zum Entwurf der Liturgie der heiligen Woche, in *Bibel und Liturgie* (1970) 16-19, p. 16.
48. See for example H. RAHNER: *Symbole der Kirche. Die Ekklesiologie der Väter* (Salzburg 1964) 241-564; G.Q. REIJNERS: *The terminology of the Holy Cross in early Christian literature as based upon Old Testament typology* (Nijmegen 1965); Croix et crucifix, in F. CABROL and H. LECLERCQ (eds.): *Dictionnaire d'archéologie chrétienne et de liturgie* 3, 2 (Paris 1948) 3045-3131; Kreuz, in J. HÖFER and K. RAHNER (eds.): *Lexikon für Theologie und Kirche* 6 (Freiburg 1961² = 1986ʳ) 605-617; E. DINKLER and E. DINKLER-VON SCHUBERT: Kreuz, in E. KIRSCHBAUM (ed.): *Lexikon der christlichen Ikonographie* 2 (Roma 1970) 562-590.
49. See for example DINKLER and DINKLER-VON SCHUBERT: Kreuz 563-569.

can have several meanings. It may refer to the victory on the Cross; as a defence against evil the Cross may get a magical meaning (especially the relic worn as an amulet); and as a sign of hope it may refer to the end of the world. In short, the Cross can be interpreted soteriological, apotropeic and eschatological.

In order to answer the question concerning the meaning of the Cross in the religious imagery of the people in the West, I take Delaruelle as my guide.[50] Delaruelle does not focus on literary (liturgical) sources, but on the Cross and the crucifix as an object. In his research on the meaning of the Cross in popular religion Delaruelle makes a dinstinction between an élite culture and a popular culture, existing side by side. This distinction manifested itself in the first half of the Middle Ages in a duality in spirituality, doctrine and art. The art of the élite culture in the ecclesiastical, monastic and aristocratic *milieus* was modelled on already existing forms and religious feelings. The faith in redemption of the previous centuries was continued herein. On the other hand, there was no such continuance in the popular culture, and the religious sensitivity of the people, moreover, did not undergo any influence of the élite. Superstition and new interpretations on Christianity made its entry through the people.[51]

The élite embroidered on the tradition of the faith in redemption and understood the Cross especially as a sign of victory.[52] The rich iconographical portrayal of this theme shows that this tradition had settled in Rome too.[53] Further research will have to show whether this signification of the Cross was a reproduction of the spirituality and theology of merely the ecclesiastic élite in Rome or that the Roman people subscribed to these views too.

According to Delaruelle people in the Frankish territory were practically not aware of the meaning and the position of the Cross in the mystery of redemption in the Merovingian period. The meaning of the Cross was especially apotropeic; it did not have an exclusive Christian meaning yet. In the Carolingian period this apotropeic character is maintained, it is true, but a new meaning is added clearly: crosses are signs of triumph, *croix glorieuses*.[54] This victory character is already present in the Cross hymns written by Venantius Fortunatus in Poitiers in 569; in these it prevails over the apotropeic character of the Cross. In the Good Friday liturgy Fortunatus' hymn *Pange lingua*, however,

50. E. DELARUELLE: Le crucifix dans la piété populaire et dans l'art, du VIe au XIe siècle, in E. DELARUELLE: *La piété populaire au Moyen Age* (Torino 1975) 27-42. See also J. LECLERCQ: La dévotion médiévale envers le crucifié, in *La maison-Dieu* no. 75 (1963) 119-132.

51. DELARUELLE: Crucifix 27-28.

52. Cf. F. VAN DER MEER: *Christus' oudste gewaad. Over de oorspronkelijkheid van de oudchristelijke kunst* (Baarn 1989ʳ) 181-186.

53. See the plates as mentioned in VAN DER MEER: *Christus' oudste gewaad* 181-186. One of the most expressive representations of the Cross as trophy (*tropaion*) is to be found on a Roman *sarcophagus* from the middle of the fourth century; see F. VAN DER MEER and Chr. MOHRMANN: *Atlas van de oudchristelijke wereld* (Amsterdam 1961ʳ) plates 466-467 and also plates 468-471.

54. DELARUELLE: Crucifix 29-32.

was introduced only in the ninth-century Frankish *Ordo Romanus* XXXI. So this would endorse Delaruelle's thesis. Through the introduction and the dissemination of the Good Friday liturgy in the Frankish and Germanic territory in the course of the eighth and ninth centuries people venerated the Cross especially as a sign of victory. In the liturgical texts the Cross is not associated with the passion or with the historic Jesus.[55] And the crucifixes at the end of the Carolingian period show that the crowd did know any other Crucified than the one they knew from procession crosses, border crosses, sermons or hymns: 'The almighty Son, victor of sin, death, greed and the devil, who makes a liturgical sacrifice on the Cross, the truly real pontifical Mass which he conducts on his throne in the highest, eyes opened, surrounded by his ministrants, already sharing the glory of his resurrection and tasting the first fruits of the goodness which He shares with the faithful who come to witness this sight of peace.'[56] The Cross was the tool of the victory and not yet the passion instrument which it would become later in the Middle Ages. 'The stress during the first thousand years fell upon the victory which God had won in the Cross, a victory which overcame the devil's hold upon men, opened all mankind to the action of God's grace, and established Christ's lordship over the world.'[57] The big majority of the people did not have any religious imagery yet on which they could base a picture of Christ and his execution. The crucifixion scene was depicted only rarely[58] and when it was, it was done inconspicuously. Also the preaching and reading from the Scripture formed no breeding ground for a more sensitive impression of the content of the Gospel.[59]

4. CONCLUSION

Looking back on the sources of the Good Friday liturgy, which were studied here mainly from the viewpoint of the role of the people, I will review some main points by way of a conclusion.

In the Jerusalem liturgy, as Egeria described it, the accent lies on the remembrance of Jesus' passion and death, in such a strong way that people experience this again, as it were. This interpretation and experience is mainly inspired by the historicizing set-up of the services. People gather early in the afternoon and read from Scripture that which relates to the passion and death of the Lord. This happens exactly within the span of Jesus' conviction and crucifixion – according to the chronology of St. John on approximately the sixth hour (St. John 19, 14) – and the moment of his death on the ninth hour

---

55. DELARUELLE: Crucifix 32.
56. DELARUELLE: Crucifix 36.
57. C. MORRIS: *The discovery of the individual, 1050-1200* (New York 1972) 139.
58. The oldest representations of a somewhat historical conceived crucifixion date from the fifth and sixth centuries. Iconographically the *passio Christi*, however, is still an exception to the rule in this period. See VAN DER MEER and MOHRMANN: *Atlas* plates 475-478.
59. DELARUELLE: Crucifix 36-37.

(St. Matthew 27, 45-50; St. Mark 15, 34).[60] On Friday morning the commemoration of passion and death is preceded by a Cross rite, which distinguishes itself by its individual character in a, for the rest, very strongly communal organised liturgy of the Holy Week. Because of this the veneration of the Cross has a less historicizing character than the reading service in the afternoon, which seems to be the highlight in the remembrance of the passion and death of the Lord on Good Friday in Jerusalem.

Looking for the specific role and position of the people in the Good Friday liturgy especially two moments prove to be of importance in the developing western (Roman) liturgy: the veneration of the Cross and the Communion. After all, the information about the preceding liturgy of the word gives no cause to assume that the role of the people on Good Friday was different from the one during a regular Eucharist. Although it is possible to distinguish for the period studied several different models with regard to the way in which the veneration of the Cross and the Communion are in proportion and the way in which the priest (and the clergy) and the people participate,[61] at least in *Ordo Romanus* XXIV and in the *Pontificale Romano-Germanicum* the participation of priest and people are integrated. The *Pontificale Romano-Germanicum* shows also that the priest has a share in the increasing dramatization, which in *Ordo Romanus* XXXI still is restricted to the people's part.

The Communion rite on Good Friday – traditionally a non-liturgical day, which is a day without Eucharist – seems to have made its entry on instigation of the people. Initially this rite was introduced by the Greek colonists in Rome, then adopted by the papal liturgy and subsequently accepted as a permanent element in the Frankish and the Roman liturgy. So the people laid the foundation of the introduction of this rite in the Western liturgy.

The veneration of the Cross, which in Jerusalem as well as initially also in Rome was strongly concentrated on the relic of the Cross, functioned in the afternoon service since its introduction in Rome. It kept this position, also when the Good Friday liturgy was split up into two services. According to the model of the stational liturgy a liturgy of the word may precede in one of the churches in the city in the morning. However, this service was not meant for all but especially for the clergy and representatives of the various churches in the city. The people gather in their own church for the afternoon service at the ninth hour.[62] So in the West the Cross (relic) has always been connected to Jesus' dying hour in contrast to Jerusalem. Judging from the oldest text, which, since the papal liturgy, probably is connected with the veneration of the Cross, the devotion was not determined by passion and death, but much more by what Jesus brought about by his passion and death: salvation and

---

60. St. Mark 15, 25 mentions the third hour as being the point of time of the crucifixion.
61. See AUF DER MAUR: *Feiern* 108.
62. *Ordo Romanus* XXIII gives the eighth hour as being the starting time. This earlier point of time can be explained because of the foregoing procession. In this way the service in the Church of the Holy Cross could still begin about the ninth hour.

redemption: *Ecce lignum crucis in quo salus mundi pependit.* When the Good Friday liturgy is adopted in the Frankish territory, this image fits in with the Cross devotion which is developing there.[63] The Roman period is the period of public prayer in which devotion was not yet privatized.[64] The people gather round the Cross of their Saviour and Redeemer. The Cross is not explicitly the sign of Jesus' passion and death but more of his resurrection, and thus it refers beyond Good Friday already to Easter.

63. Although in this contribution no detailed analysis of texts is intended, it should not be left unmentioned that the Cross is connected emphatically with the resurrection in the antiphon *Crucem tuam adoramus, Domine, et sanctam resurrectionem tuam laudamus et glorificamus*. This antiphon is probably of Egyptian origin and introduced in the Frankish territory via the Byzantine liturgy (A. BAUMSTARK: Der Orient und die Gesänge der Adoratio crucis, in *Jahrbuch für Liturgiewissenschaft* 2 (1922) 1-17). The text is mentioned for the first time by Amalarius in his *Liber officialis* 1, 14, 8 (HANSSENS: *Amalarii episcopi* 2, 101) and returns in the antiphonaries of Compiègne and Senlis (HESBERT: *Antiphonale missarum sextuplex* 97), and in the *Pontificale Romano-Germanicum* (VOGEL and ELZE: *Pontifical* 2, 92).
64. DELARUELLE: Crucifix 37-38.

The solitary celebration of the supreme pontiff. The Lateran basilica as the new temple in the medieval liturgy of Maundy Thursday[1]

SIBLE DE BLAAUW

'Into the second tabernacle went the high priest alone once every year, not without blood, which he offered for himself, and for the errors of the people.'[2] It is this verse from the Letter to the Hebrews that is cited again and again in the liturgical books describing the papal liturgy of Maundy Thursday in the *Basilica Salvatoris* in Rome during the twelfth and thirteenth centuries. The biblical quotation refers to a curious liturgical and topographical configuration that was typical for the ancient bishop's church of Rome, where the station traditionally took place on this day with a papal celebration.

The most complete account of the ceremonial is that presented in the Pontifical of the Roman curia of the thirteenth century. From its first recension under the pontificate of Innocent III (1198-1216) the Pontifical contained an *Ordo in cena domini* that incorporated various older elements.[3] We follow this source for a first presentation of the ritual.[4]

1. I want to thank the Netherlands Organization for Scientific Research (NWO) for its financial support and Dr. Ingo Herklotz, University of Konstanz (BRD), for sharing with me his knowledge on the history of the Lateran. The English text of this contribution was corrected by Peter Mason.
2. Hebrews 8, 7.
3. The same rubrics are to be found with minor variants in the so-called Ordinal of the papal court, originating in the liturgical reforms of Innocent III: S.J.P. van Dijk: *The ordinal of the papal court from Innocent III to Boniface VIII and related documents* (= Spicilegium Friburgense 22) (Fribourg 1975) 231-240. For a general historical view of the liturgy of Maundy Thursday see: H.A.J. Wegman: Witte Donderdag, in *Liturgisch Woordenboek* 2 (Roermond 1968) 2923-2929.
4. *Pontificale Romanum saec. XIII* xlii, in M. Andrieu: *Le pontifical romain au Moyen Age* 2 (= Studi e testi 87) (Città del Vaticano 1940) 459-461:
   15. *Verumtamen scire nos convenit quod si fuerit pontifex Laterani, decantato Credo [...], et antequam intret ad sacrificandum, a diaconibus et subdiaconibus levatur mensa de altari, palliis desuper complicatis, et cum reverentia et omni devotione ab eisdem reportatur in capella sancti Pancratii iuxta claustrum canonicorum, quia ibi est locus conservationis, et cum omni cautela usque in diem sabbati custoditur.*
   16. *Deinde pontifex venit ad altare, accipiens ampullam vitream, que intus se continet quoddam vasculum aureum, et in illo vasculo est lapis preciosus concavus et in illa concavitate lapidis est sanguis preciosus Christi <qui dicitur miraculose de quadam ymagine Christi percussa fluxisse> diligenter inclusus, qui annualiter extrahitur et reponitur ibi in concavitate arche. Et tunc levatur a pontifice et ostenditur, ut tota turba populi valeat cum timore et reverentia et omni devotione eum videre. Postea traditur custodienda priori et canonicis eiusdem ecclesie usque in diem sabbati.*
   17. *Tunc pontifex ad sacrificandum intrat solus infra arcam, ut significetur quod in veteri testamento scriptum est quia solus pontifex intrabat semel in anno in Sancta Sanctorum, tamen cruce et linteamine <ac duabus candelabris cum faculis accensis> superpositis, episcopo vel <presbitero> cardinali cum capellano sacerdote ministrante sibi.*

120

The service starts at about three o'clock in the afternoon in the papal sacristy of the Lateran basilica with the preparation of the oils to be consecrated during the Mass. The ordinary procession of the cardinals, the pope and the assistants proceeds from this sacristy in the narthex of the basilica toward the high altar. There Mass is celebrated according to the usual rubrics of papal liturgy, with a few characteristic complications. The first is the inclusion of the two rites of consecration of the oils. That of the oil of the sick takes place after the *Sanctus*, that of the chrism and oil of the catechumens between the Communion of the pope and the people. But it is the second set of ceremonies which concerns us here. After the Creed, the assisting cardinals remove the table (*mensa*) of the altar. They bring it to St. Pancras' chapel, the sacristy and oratory of the canons near the cloister, where it will remain until Holy Saturday. Then the pope approaches the altar. From the cavity of the altar block he takes a reliquary containing some blood of Christ and shows this to the people. Then the pope celebrates the Eucharist alone on the hollow altar, which bears an altar cloth, a cross and two candlesticks: 'that means what is written in the Old Testament, that the pontifex alone once a year entered the Holy of Holies'. After the Canon the pope takes Communion by himself at the altar, drinking the consecrated wine directly from the chalice, without using the reed.

Contrary to the consecration of the oils, the ceremony with the *mensa*, the blood relic and the hollow altar is specific to the Lateran: if, for some reason, the papal Mass is not held in the *Basilica Salvatoris* but, for example, in St. Peter's, then the ceremony is omitted, whereas the consecration of the oils is carried out regulary.

This essay is intended to shed some more light on the history, meaning and liturgical performance of this rite, that demonstrates a unique tie between the papacy and the Lateran basilica.[5]

---

18. Confecto itaque sacrifio, pontifex solus *communicat super altare* sine ministris, *et non cum calamo, sed cum calice tantum se confirmat* illo die et sexta feria et ponit illam quartam partem in calice. Postquam autem communicaverit, *ponit calicem super altare* <ex latere sinistro> *et patenam iuxta eum cum corpore domini* reservato, quia sexta feria de ipso sacrificio resumit *et cooperitur utrumque sindone* unda. [add. in marg.:] *Et portetur honorifice ad sacristiam cano-nicorum* <in tabernaculo> *per iuniorem episcopum cardinalem.*
N.B. The sections 15, 16 and 17 are entirely new in the *Pontificale Romanum saec. XIII.* The fragments printed in Roman type in section 18 are also new, whereas the rest is taken from the Roman Pontifical of the twelfth century.
5. Making use of two important recent publications on the theme: J.M. POWELL: Honorius III's 'Sermo in dedicatione ecclesie Lateranensis' and the historical-liturgical traditions of the Lateran, in *Archivum historiae pontificiae* 21 (1983) 195-209; I. HERKLOTZ: Der mittelalter-liche Fassadenportikus der Lateranbasilika und seine Mosaiken. Kunst und Propaganda am Ende des 12. Jahrhunderts, in *Römisches Jahrbuch der Bibliotheca Hertziana* 25 (1989) 25-95. I also refer to the treatment of the subject in my doctoral thesis, which is worked out here with new data and insights: S. DE BLAAUW: *Cultus et decor. Liturgie en architectuur in laatantiek en middeleeuws Rome. Basilica Salvatoris, Sanctae Mariae, Sancti Petri* (Delft 1987) esp. 114-119 and 143-144.

I. THE LITURGICAL ELEMENTS

The specific ritual elements of the stational celebration on Maundy Thursday are: the transfer of the *mensa*, the display of the blood relic and the exclusiveness of the celebration. We shall analyze them in succession.

The actions involving the *mensa* of the high altar during the papal Mass on Maundy Thursday are mentioned for the first time by Bonizo, the bishop of Sutri who died in 1095, in his *Liber de vita christiana*. He situates the moment of the removal of the table after the Canon of the Mass, but before the consecration of the chrism.[6] The slab is carried back to the high altar during the *Alleluia* in the Mass of Holy Saturday. The second source is some fifty years later: the ordinal of the Lateran chapter, composed by prior Bernardus between 1139 and 1145. The rubrics describe the transfer of the altar *mensa*, in accordance with the later Pontifical, before the offertory. The cardinal priests and deacons remove the table and prepare the hollow altar that is left for the Eucharist.[7] After Mass the altar is sealed and continues to be guarded by the Lateran canons until Holy Saturday. The *mensa* is said to remain in St. Pancras' chapel on a wooden structure until Holy Saturday. Then it is reinstalled on the high altar during the pause between the baptismal ceremony and the Mass.[8] Hence Bonizo and Bernardus agree on the actual removal and reinstallation, called by Bonizo the *violatio mensae* and the *reconciliatio* respectively, whereas Bernardus is speaking of the *elevatio mensae*. However, the two authors disagree about the timing of the acts, also implying a difference in the purpose of the removal: according to Bonizo the pope consecrates chrism and oil of exorcism on the hollow altar, while according to Bernardus he celebrates the mystery of the Eucharist on it. The later sources confirm Bernardus' version of the rite.[9]

Is Bonizo really our first witness for the removal of the *mensa* and the subsequent celebration on the hollow altar? One intriguing source is much older and points in the same direction. It is a Roman *Ordo* for Maundy Thursday

6. E. PERELS: BONIZO SUTRINENSIS: *Liber de vita christiana* IV 98 (Berlin 1930) 165: *Quod in cena Domini post dominici corporis et sanguinis celebratam comemorationem a sacerdotibus violatur, mensaque sublata in ipso altaris concavo usque hodie oleum exorcizatum et crismale ab ipso papa benedicitur.*

7. L. FISCHER: *Bernhardi cardinalis et Lateranensis ecclesiae prioris Ordo officiorum* (München 1919) 50-51: [...] *maioris altaris mensa cum omnibus suis vestibus a presbyteris cardinalibus et diaconis curie ex toto auferri debet ac ita archa preparari, ut ipse domnus papa in figura illius summi pontificis [manibus] ad sacrificandum ingrediatur secundum apostoli dictum: In secundo tabernaculo semel in anno solus pontifex introibat non sine sanguine, quem offeret pro sua et populi ignorantia. Que tabula deportatur ab eisdem cardinalibus cum magna reverentia in ecclesiam sancti Pancratii ac ponitur super ligneum instrumentum ad hoc opus factum et usque in sabbatum sanctum sic permanebit.*

8. FISCHER: *Bernhardi Lateranensis* 64.

9. The term *violatur* recurs in the *Ordo* of Albinus, written in 1189: *Ordo Romanus Albini* 24, in P. FABRE and L. DUCHESNE: *Le Liber censuum de l'église romaine* 1-2 (Paris 1910-1952) 2, 129.

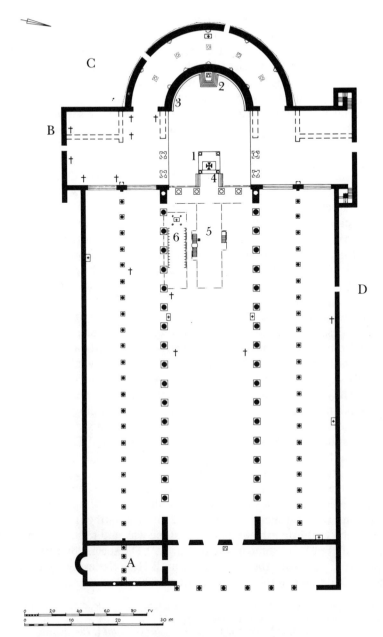

Fig. 1. Rome, Lateran basilica. Reconstructed plan as of c. 1200.
1. High altar.   2. Papal cathedra.   3. Cardinals' subsellia.   4. Confessio/crypt.
5. Main choir.   6. Canons' choir.
A. Papal sacristy/St. Thomas' chapel.   B. Cloister.   C. St. Pancras' chapel/sacristy
of the canons.   D. Entrance to the papal palace.

123

dating from the seventh century and containing the striking note: *et altare est cavum*.[10] It is missing in the other early medieval *ordines* for Maundy Thursday, that were obviously not intended to pass on all local Roman details to their Frankish public. The moment at which the cavity of the altar is mentioned conforms to the high medieval sources, Bonizo excepted: just before the offertory. Consequently we might infer that the Lateran high altar already played a special role in the Maundy Thursday liturgy in the seventh century, and that its distinctive feature was the fact that it was visibly hollow during the celebration of the Eucharist.

The display of the blood relic seems to be a relatively recent feature. Its first source is Censius, who composed a revised edition of Albinus' *Ordo Romanus* in 1192.[11] The relevant phrase is an intentional supplement to Albinus' rubric of three years before on the removal of the *mensa*: as soon as the altar is opened, the pope removes two *ampullae* containing blood and water of the Lord from the interior of the altar. Yet the act does not appear to be a complete innovation, for Censius mentions it in a self-evident way, without referring to a demonstration. On the other hand, the fact that Bernardus, who was well informed on Lateran matters, says nothing about the handling of the relics, indicates the non-existence of the rite in the first half of the twelfth century. The rite appears to have been given a pronounced shape just after 1200, when the Pontifical describes it in clear terms in a special entry. The pontiff removes a glass cruet from the altar containing a golden receptacle. In the receptacle is a hollow stone with some blood of Christ. The reliquary is only taken out on this day and is displayed by the pope to the people. After that it is preserved by the canons until Holy Saturday and replaced at the same time as the *mensa*.[12]

The data point to an intensification of the cult of the holy blood in the Lateran around 1200.[13] The two *ampullae* with water and blood are mentioned as already existing in the altar in the late eleventh century.[14] They are repeatedly reported as belonging to the precious contents of the high altar during the twelfth and thirteenth centuries. Around 1200, however, there seems to have been some change in the method of preservation: whereas Cencius still mentions the two receptacles, the curial Pontifical presents a detailed description of one reliquary with a stone. The versions of this text dating from later in the thirteenth century add that the blood in the stone was said to have been miraculously transferred from some image of Christ.[15] The special preservation of the reliquary together with the altar *mensa* until Holy Saturday again is witnessed for the first time in the Pontifical after 1200.

10. *Ordo feria V* 2, in A. CHAVASSE: A Rome, le Jeudi-Saint, au VIIe siècle, d'après un vieil ordo, in *Revue d'histoire écclésiastique* 50 (1955) 21-35, p. 24.
11. *Ordo Romanus Cencii* 24, in FABRE and DUCHESNE: *Liber censuum* 1, 294-295.
12. *Pontificale Romanum saec. XIII* xliv 28, in ANDRIEU: *Pontifical* 2, 478.
13. Cf. the general development in R. GRÉGOIRE: Sang, in *Dictionnaire de spiritualité* 14 (Paris 1988) 319-333.
14. *Descriptio Lateranensis ecclesiae*, in R. VALENTINI and G. ZUCCHETTI: *Codice topografico della città di Roma* 1-4 (Roma 1940-1953) 3, 319-373, p. 337.
15. Cf. note 85 below.

The papal celebration on Holy Thursday had an exclusive character on two different levels. First of all there was the general reservation of the high altar in a patriarchal basilica for the pope. Only the pope and his strict substitutes, the seven cardinal bishops, had the right to celebrate at the high altar of the Lateran basilica.[16] Bernardus indeed stipulates that, if the pope for some reason were unable to lead the stational service in the Lateran on Maundy Thursday, a cardinal bishop could conduct the liturgy as prescribed for the pope, the consecration of the oils and the removal of the *mensa* included.[17] If the cardinal bishops were absent too, the canons celebrated Mass at the chapter altar and neither the consecration of the oils nor the removal of the *mensa* could take place. Hence the ritual at the high altar was a typically papal celebration, the cardinal bishop acting as a full representative of the pope.

A second feature of exclusiveness is the liturgical solo performance of the pope. As the papal *Ordo* of Benedict Canonicus, contemporaneous with Bernardus' Lateran ordinal, puts it: 'the pontiff alone enters the altar for the offering'.[18] The details are given by his successor Albinus: contrary to the usual procedure of the stational Mass, in which the pope takes Communion at his seat, assisted and surrounded by the cardinals, today the supreme pontiff does so alone, standing at the altar. The assisting cardinal deacons serve him, but receive Holy Communion only after the consecration of the chrism, at the same time as the other clergy and the congregation.[19] The unusual Communion service on this day had a long tradition, as the solitary Communion of the pontiff appears already in the directories of the seventh and eighth centuries.[20] However, at that time it took place at the pontifical *cathedra*, so that the location at the altar seems to be a development of the high Middle Ages.

The rubrics concerning the exclusiveness prevailed in principle for every place where the pope was to celebrate on Maundy Thursday. Bernardus, however, describes the solitary celebration as a direct effect of the removal of the *mensa*, thus associating a general characteristic of papal liturgy on this feast with a local feature of the Lateran.

Clearly, this exclusively papal and solitary character of the celebration elicited a metaphorical association with the temple liturgy of the old covenant. The comparison is expressed for the first time by Bernardus. The image re-

---

16. *Descriptio*, VALENTINI and ZUCCHETTI: *Codice* 344.
17. FISCHER: *Bernhardi Lateranensis* 52.
18. *Ordo Romanus Benedicti* 40, FABRE and DUCHESNE: *Liber censuum* 2, 150-151: *Offerenda non dicitur, sed solus pontifex intrat ad altare ad sacrificium.*
19. *Ordo Romanus Albini* 24, FABRE and DUCHESNE: *Liber censuum* 2, 129-130; *Ordo Romanus Cencii* 24, FABRE and DUCHESNE: *Liber censuum* 1, 295.
20. *Ordo feria V* 9, CHAVASSE: Vieil ordo 26: *Et pontifex tacite signat calicem cum oblata sanctificata, nemine respondente*; *Ordo feria V* 19, CHAVASSE: Vieil ordo 28 [after consecration of the oils]: *Communicante clero omnique populo* [...]. *Ordo Romanus XXIII*, 7, in ANDRIEU: *Les ordines romani du haut Moyen-Age* 3 (= Spicilegium sacrum Lovaniense 24) (Leuven 1951) 269-270: *Et, cum tota oblatio fracta fuerit, communicat solus apostolicus* [...]. *Ordo Romanus XXXB* 16/24, ANDRIEU: *Ordines Romani* 3, 469-470: *Deinde communicat pontifex tantum* [...]; *Deinde communicat cunctus clerus seu et populi.*

appears in a sermon for Maundy Thursday by Innocent III and extensively in a homily by his successor Honorius III (1216-1227).[21] It was introduced into the Pontifical of the Curia at the same time, as mentioned earlier.

2. THE HISTORICAL AND ARCHAEOLOGICAL ELEMENTS

The liturgy described is inextricably bound up with the Lateran basilica. The archeological and historical factors of the site that appear to have contributed to the form and meaning of the ritual may be categorized as: the relics of the Old Testament, the wooden altar and the table of the last supper. Our main source in discussing them is the *Descriptio sanctuarii Lateranensis ecclesiae*, written shortly before 1100 and revised and re-edited several times during the next centuries. The tract is a product of the renewed importance of the Lateran basilica during the investiture conflict and presents a proud enumeration of its historical, liturgical and devotional qualities.[22]

The relics of the old covenant play a prominent role in the *Descriptio*. They are presented as the main cult objects of the Jewish temple that were supposed to have been taken to Rome by Titus and Vespasian after the destruction of Jerusalem in 70 A.D. According to the author's informants the ark of the covenant was located inside the high altar of the basilica, and the altar was just a case for the ark.[23] The ark was supposed to contain many relics, including various implements of the temple: seven candlesticks from the holy place, the tables of the law, the rod of Moses and the budding rod of Aaron.[24]

However, there were clear doubts as to the exact disposition of the relics, so that the twelfth-century editors of the *Descriptio* changed the original wording of the text: the ark with the candlesticks, the tables and the rods was said to be inside or below the high altar, the latter indication perhaps referring to the *confessio* or crypt.[25] No more topographical clarity appears until after 1200, in

---

21. See notes 83 and 87 below.
22. DE BLAAUW: *Cultus et decor* 101-102, with further references.
23. *Descriptio*, VALENTINI and ZUCCHETTI: *Codice* 3, 336 (Biblioteca Apostolica Vaticana, Reg. lat. 712, f. 87): [*In ecclesia est*] *archa federis Domini, vel, ut aiunt, archa est interius*, et altare ad mensuram longitudinis et altitudinis arcae conditum est exterius (in Roman type: marginal gloss by the same hand).
24. *Descriptio*, VALENTINI and ZUCCHETTI: *Codice* 3, 337 (Biblioteca Apostolica Vaticana, Reg. lat. 712, f. 87): *In altari vero* [...] *est tale sanctuarium: septem candelabra que fuerunt in priori tabernaculo. Unde Paulus dicit: 'Tabernaculum primum factum', et cetera. Est ibi etiam virga Aaron que fronduerat et tabule testamenti et virga Moysi qua percussit bis silicem, et fluxerunt aque.* The tables of the decalogue were placed within the ark in the tabernacle (Exodus 25, 16); in front of it were put, in the course of time, the pot of manna (Exodus 16, 34) and Aaron's rod (Numbers 17, 4-10). Hence the Lateran relics were directly related to the ark, apart from the seven candlesticks and the rod of Moses: the first might be the result of a contamination with the seven *candelabra* donated to the Lateran by Constantine according to the *Liber pontificalis* 34 c. 11 (cf. HERKLOTZ: Fassadenportikus 75 note 161), the second of a similar proces with Aaron's staff.
25. *Descriptio*, VALENTINI and ZUCCHETTI: *Codice* 3, 336: *ara principalis est arca foederis Domini, vel, ut aiunt, arca est inferius, et altare ad mensuram longitudinis, latitudinis et alti-*

a chapter on the Roman basilicas in the *Speculum ecclesiae* of Giraldus Cambrensis (1223). It states that the temple objects were kept in the crypt below the high altar.[26] The fact that the crypt is mentioned explicitly for the first time, and the remark that it was furnished with bronze plating, suggest that the author had witnessed the result of a relatively recent resumption of the location below the high altar.

In the meantime the alleged range of the temple treasure expanded. A history of the popes and the *Graphia aureae urbis*, both from the middle of the twelfth century, asserted that it consisted not only of the objects already known from the *Descriptio* but of much more appurtenances of the temple service, such as the golden jar of manna, the table of the shewbread, the golden censer and the incense altar.[27] Though the twelfth-century authors of the *Descriptio* merely mentioned these objects in a quotation from the Letter to the Hebrews, the complete list was soon definitely projected onto the alleged collection in the Lateran. The resulting extended catalogue is cited repeatedly in the thirteenth century, from Giraldus to a mosaic inscription dating from late in the century, and in various later sources.[28]

None of the authors gives the impression of having seen the famous spoils in person. The first edition of the *Descriptio* made do with an apologetic 'as they say', and it was just this vague description that seems to have been the source for all later authorities. Giraldus too, who was well informed on the location, bases his enumeration of the relics merely on literary tradition. Even the polemics on the authenticity of the temple loot in the Lateran are conducted with purely literary means, whereas the material objects themselves are never brought into action. Severe doubts regarding the tradition must indeed have existed for quite a long time: already the first version of the *Descriptio* con-

tudinis arcae conditum est superius. If *inferius* indeed referred to the crypt, it would cause confusion with the tradition of the images of Constantine that were said to be kept underneath the high altar: *Descriptio*, VALENTINI and ZUCCHETTI: *Codice* 3, 338.

26. GIRALDUS CAMBRENSIS: *Speculum ecclesiae* IV iii, in J.S. BREWER: *Giraldi Cambrensis opera* 4 (= Rerum Britannicarum Medii Aevi scriptores [Rolls series] 21, 4) (London 1873) 273: *Haec omnia inferius sub principali et patriarchali altari in cripta laminis aereis munita, cum ipso toto tabernaculo, quod [ad] baptismum beati Constantini beata Helena Romam devexit, recondita manent.*

27. A history of the popes, in FABRE and DUCHESNE: *Liber censuum* 2, 166-167: [*Constantinus*] *posuit ibi archam Testamenti quam Thitus asportaverat de Jerusalem et multa milia Judeorum et candelabrum aureum cum VII infusoriis lucernis; in qua archa sunt hec: ani aurei, mures aurei, tabule Testamenti, virga Aaron, manna, panes ordeacei, urna aurea, vestis inconsutilis et arundo, et vestimentum sancti Johannis Baptiste et forcipes unde tonsus fuit sanctus Johannes Evangelista.* Cf. *Graphia aureae urbis*, in VALENTINI and ZUCCHETTI: *Codice* 3, 83-84. On the confusion between the menorah and the 7 *candelabra* of Constantine's donation: cf. note 24 above. On the golden emerods and mice (1 Samuel 6, 4-5, 8), unique in the History of the popes and the *Graphia*, see FABRE and DUCHESNE: *Liber censuum* 2, 170 note 4. The mention of New Testament and saint's relics in the ark must be the result of a contamination between the tradition of the ark and the catalogue of relics inside the wooden altar; see notes 35 and 36 below. Cf. HERKLOTZ: Fassadenportikus 62 note 97, 76.

28. Inscription edited by Ph. LAUER: *Le palais de Latran. Étude historique et archéologique* (Paris 1911) 294-295. The extended catalogue also in DURANDUS: *Rationale* I ii.

tained defensive sections against the adversaries of the Lateran temple relics. Their argument was mainly based on biblical grounds: Jeremiah the prophet was supposed to have hidden the ark and the other implements of Solomon's temple in an unknown cave when the Jewish people was driven out into the Babylonian captivity.[29] In the new version of the *Descriptio* written between 1159 and 1181, the plea in favour of the temple relics is strongly reinforced and extended.[30]

The second element with a liturgical significance is the wooden altar, said to have been the portable altar of St. Peter and the first papal martyrs. The earliest mention of this tradition is Bonizo's *De vita*, late in the eleventh century. The author attempts to account for the fact that the high altar of the Lateran basilica was not made of stone, as in other churches, but of wood.[31] Bonizo's explanation is that it was the portable wooden altar used by the pre-Constantinian popes who had had to celebrate Mass in different houses and in the catacombs. When Pope Silvester consecrated the Lateran basilica, he installed the ancient altar in the new church and out of respect for the prince of the apostles, who was said to have celebrated at this altar himself, it was prescribed that all other churches should erect stone altars: the altar of the Lateran was to remain unique.

The statement that the Lateran high altar was made of wood and was relatively small in size is repeated in the various versions of the *Descriptio*,[32] but no mention is made in this text of its being the altar of the first bishops of Rome. This argument does not reappear until the first decades of the thirteenth century: in the sermon by Honorius III and the *Speculum ecclesiae* by

---

29. 2 Maccabees 2, 4-6. On the controversy and the respective arguments cf. HERKLOTZ: Fassadenportikus 76-77.

30. Johannes Diaconus, the redactor, announces the theme already in his prologue: *Descriptio*, VALENTINI and ZUCCHETTI: *Codice* 3, 327; the new chapter itself: VALENTINI and ZUCCHETTI: *Codice* 3, 339-341, with the title: *Ratio circa eos, qui opponunt de absconsione tabernaculi et arcae, vel altaris incensi.* A contemporary defensive argument with a commonsensical 'either/or' explanation in A. BONAVENTURA: NICOLAUS MANIACUTIUS: *De sacra imagine SS. Salvatoris in Palatio Lateranensi tractatus* (Roma 1709) 16-17, a text dating from about 1145: *Tunc arca, et tabulae, candelabrum, et tubae, atque alia vasa templi Romam delata sunt, seu illa utique, quae Jeremias occultasse in secundo Machabeorum libro legitur, seu alia post restaurationem templi a Patribus sequentibus condita, quod evidenter apparet in arcu triumphali [...].* (With thanks to Dr. Gerhard Wolf, Rome, who drew my attention to this text and that cited in note 61 below.)

31. PERELS: BONIZO: *De vita* IV 98, 164-165: *In Lateranensi vero prima ecclesia altare non erexit lapideum, set stabilivit ligneum [...]. [...] missam celebrabant super altare ligneum in modum arce concavum, habens in quattuor angulis circulos, in quibus vectes immittebantur, quibus a sacerdotibus portabatur, ubicumque Romanus episcopus latitabat [...] Quod ob reverentiam apostolorum principis, qui super altare hoc dominicum dicitur celebrasse sacramentum, et sanctorum suorum predecessorum martyrum, licet decreto firmasset, ut nullum deinceps altare esset nisi lapideum, hoc tamen in dominicum et patriarchale stabilivit altare, ut nullus super illud nisi Romanus papa audeat celebrare.*

32. VALENTINI and ZUCCHETTI: *Codice* 3, 337 (late eleventh cent.): *In altari vero, quod parvum est et ligneum de argento coopertum est tale sanctuarium [...];* (twelfth cent.): *In altari vero, quod superius est ligneum de argento coopertum, atque sub eo inferius, est tale sanctuarium.*

Giraldus, both unmistakably relying on Bonizo.[33] The mosaic inscription concurs with Giraldus:[34] the two seem to have had a common source that combined the tradition of the *Descriptio* with new, more accurate observations.

The *mensa Domini*, the table of the last supper, appears for the first time in the earliest edition of the *Descriptio*. It is mentioned together with the five barley loaves and the two fishes of the feeding of the five thousand (St. John 6).[35] These relics are said to be united with the temple spoils in one collection of *sanctuaria* inside or below the high altar. Besides the *mensa* and the loaves, the New Testament relics were said to include the towel that had been used by Christ in drying the feet of his disciples before the last supper, two *ampullae* with Christ's blood, and many other relics of Christ, Mary and of the two patron saints of the Lateran basilica, St. John the Baptist and St. John the Apostle. Giraldus Cambrensis again makes a clear distinction between the temple treasure in the crypt underneath the altar and the relics of the New Testament, among them the *mensa Domini*, in the wooden altar itself.[36] The table is constantly mentioned without any emphasis, embedded in a long catalogue of relics. That has changed towards the end of the thirteenth century, when the mosaic inscription presents the *mensa Domini* at the head of the relic list, immediately after the wooden altar. The identity as well as the location of the table of the Lord are specified for the first time: it is 'the table at which Christ ate with his disciples on the day of the Supper' and it covers the wooden altar of the early popes.[37]

The actual history of the three relevant elements can be followed easily from the report of the great fire that ravaged the basilica in May 1308. On that occasion the clerics, eager to save what could be saved, had to dismantle the venerated altar. Their finds are well documented.[38] First they removed the altar cloths and the *mensa Domini*. After breaking the iron bonds of the altar block they found many other sacred objects, that were also carried to safety and registered. They encountered several of the objects enumerated in the earlier catalogues, including the loaves of the feeding of the five thousand, the towel used to dry the apostles' feet and the *ampullae* with Christ's blood, all kept in one coffer. The ark of the covenant was found and saved too, but

---

33. Honorius, in POWELL: Honorius' III 'Sermo' 206; GIRALDUS: *Speculum* IV, 1, in BREWER: *Giraldi Cambrensis opera* 4, 269; see notes 68 and 69 below.

34. LAUER: *Palais* 294: [...] *consistit in primis hoc altare ligneo quod sancti Dei pontifices et martires ab apostolorum tempore habuerunt, in quo per criptas et diversa latibula missas celebrabant.*

35. VALENTINI and ZUCCHETTI: *Codice* 3, 337: [...] *De quinque panibus ordeaciis et duobus piscibus. Item mensa Domini* [...]. Cf. the oldest version in Reg. lat. 712, f. 87: *De quinque panibus ordeaceis et duobus panibus. de mensa domini.*

36. GIRALDUS: *Speculum* IV iv, in BREWER: *Giraldi Cambrensis opera* 4, 275: *In principali vero altari ligneo, argento cooperto, hujusmodi Novi Testamenti sanctuaria manent* [...].

37. LAUER: *Palais* 294: *Super quo desuper [altare ligneo] est mensa domini, in quo christus cenavit cum discipulis in die coene.*

38. *Lateranensis basilice combustio tempore Clementis V rythmo descripta,* edited by LAUER: *Palais* 245-250.

nothing is said about any of the other temple implements. Finally, the wooden altar itself could be saved. The pope immediately decided on the restoration of the basilica and the altar disposition, below and above floor level: the wooden altar 'at which the apostle Peter celebrated' had to be reinstalled, its relics included, 'where and as it was before'.[39]

The wooden altar seems indeed to have been replaced on its original site during the restorations and afterwards incorporated in the gothic altar of Urban V in 1369.[40] There is still a wooden chest inside the present marble high altar of the Lateran basilica. It consists of a mantle encasing a box of considerable antiquity, measuring approximately 1.35 m in length, 1 m in width and 1 m in height. It has obviously been preserved carefully and consciously during the ages and may without much hesitation be identified with the wooden altar of the basilica, mentioned from the eleventh century onward.[41]

The table of the last supper and the ark of the covenant were not replaced after 1308, but were kept in St. Thomas' chapel, the former papal sacristy near the narthex. They are mentioned there by all late medieval pilgrim's guides.[42] The ark was exposed on the altar of St. John the Baptist, whereas the table 'on which Christ ate with his apostles before his passion' was placed upon the ark. There were also the rods of Moses and Aaron. Some of the late medieval catalogues repeat the older sources in enumerating the other temple objects, like the tables of the law. In some cases they also suggest that they were still kept inside or below the high altar, always blindly relying on older texts.[43] Nevertheless the real situation in the later Middle Ages is crystal clear.

39. Clement V to cardinal Jacopo Colonna, 11-8-1308, CLEMENS V: *Regestum* [...] *cura et studio monachorum ordinis sancti Benedicti* 1-8 (Rome 1885-1888, Index Paris 1957) 5, 367-368, no. 3591: [...] *nam celeberrimas ipsas reliquias necnon archam seu altare ligneum, in quo beatus Petrus apostolorum princeps celebrasse recolitur, per devotorum manus intrepidas ignis flammis eripuit, illesa custodivit* [...]. [...] *proponimus, quod celeberrimum prefatum altare ligneum per manus nostras illic, ubi et prout fuerat, cum memoratis reliquiis collocetur.*

40. L. DUCHESNE and C. VOGEL: *Le Liber pontificalis. Texte, introduction et commentaire* and *Additions et corrections* 1-3 (Paris 1886-1957 = Paris 1981ʳ) 2, 494: [...] *fabricatoque tabernaculo seu ciborio super altare ligneo quod in medio lateranensis ecclesie situatum est.*

41. The investigations of the altar, in connection with its renewal around 1850, are reported by F. MARTINUCCI: *Intorno le reparazioni eseguite all'altare papale Lateranense e suo tabernaculo breve commentario* (Roma 1854) 22-23 and analyzed by J. BRAUN: *Der christliche Altar in seiner geschichtlichen Entwicklung* 1 (München 1924) 57-62. The results conform to the data in Archivio Segreto Vaticano, S.C. Visita Apostolica 98 no. 4 [acts of the visitation by Cardinal Lorenzo Brancati di Lauria on 21-10-1693]: [...] *adest Altare, quod dicitur illud in quo S. Petrus sacrificium Misse celebrabat, ex ligno veluti cupressino, in cuius medio est Crux more antiquo exculpta.* Cf. note 90 below.

42. One of the first sources is a text dating from the last three decades of the fourteenth century, edited by LAUER: *Palais* 408: *In sacristia ejusdem ecclesie* [...] *est archa federis Domini sive archa testamenti* [...] *Hec est illa archa quam Judei tenebant in secreta Sancta Sanctorum* [...] *Et hanc archam adhuc Judei hodie veniunt ad videndum et valde venerantur. Supra praedictam archam federis est postea mensa Domini, in qua cenavit cum apostolis suis ante suam passionem et supra mensam ipsam positum est corpus Domini seu Eucharistia. Et etiam ibi Virga Moysi* [...] *cui virge summi pontifices addiderunt caput in modum crocee episcopalis* [...].

43. E.g. *Tabula magna* (early sixteenth century), in LAUER: *Palais* 297, 298.

Only three of the alleged temple spoils existed as material objects in the Lateran basilica: the ark and the two rods. All the others were purely literary projections and had probably always been so.

Whereas the ark and the rods enjoyed a more or less intensive veneration in the chapel near the entrance, the doubts about the identity of the temple relics did not fade. Cardinal Francesco Mendoza y Bobadilla (1508-1566) used the same arguments as the medieval adversaries to deny their authenticity: the ark, he claimed, had been hidden by Jeremiah and was never discovered again, so that the second temple did not possess any ark.[44]

As a result of his pastoral visit in 1592, pope Clement VIII made a proposal to transfer all the relics from St. Thomas' chapel to a more decent place. The project is interesting because of its retrospective character: the table of the last supper was to be inserted in the high altar, where it had once been, and the other relics were to be accommodated in the crypt underneath.[45] Though the pope appears to have had a genuine interest in the *mensa*, not even this part of his proposal was realized. It was only in 1647, when the ancient chapel of St. Thomas was demolished, that the *mensa* and the temple relics were removed and transferred to the deambulatory of the basilica's apse. Since then the temple relics and the *mensa* were exposed separately. Below the ark stood a glass-covered box in which the two rods could be admired.[46] As for the temple relics, this rearrangement meant a last revival of their significance. Cardinal Cesare Rasponi (1615-1675), historian of the basilica, installed cult lamps in front of them[47] and Famiano Nardini († 1661) wrote a defence of their Jerusalem origins.[48] Nevertheless, they were not to survive the age of Englightenment. When pope Benedict XIV observed the relics in the deambulatory on the occasion of his pastoral visit to the Lateran in May 1745, he decided that the so-called ark of the covenant and the alleged rods of Moses and Aaron

44. Cited in a manuscript *De oratorio S. Thomae apostoli in Laterano*, Archivio Capitolare Lateranense A7 (unnumbered pages; second half seventeenth century?). Doubts on the authenticity of the ark also in *Relazione dello stato* [...] (c. 1645), in LAUER: *Palais* 591.

45. Visitation acts 1592, Archivio Segreto Vaticano, Arm. VII vol. 3, f. 9v-10: *Sacrae reliquiae in Sacello S. Thomae repositae* [...] *in aliud Ecclesiae locum magis congruum eisque conservandis accomodatum transferantur. Quae vero nullum alicuius Sancti certum nomen retinent in altari confessionis sub maiori altari recondantur, et cum eisdem sacris reliquiis idem confessionis altare (postquam fuerit decenter instauratum) consecretur in honorem S. Silvestri Papae* [...] *Sacram mensam ligneam super quam D. N. Jesus Christus* [...] *ultimam coenam cum suis Discipulis fecit, e Sacello S. Thomae, ubi nunc asservatur, transferri, et in maiori altari, ubi antiquitus erat collocata, reponi et adaptari mandavit.*

46. On the transfer to the deambulatory: ms. as note 44. On the new arrangement, Visitation acts 1693, as note 41: *In alio proximo cubiculo servatur Arca, que dicitur Foederis, et subtus in Capsula oblonga vitro cooperta, due virge, quarum altera Moyses, altera Aaronis fuisse dicuntur. Sed hec omnia Apocripha censeo, eo quod Arca a Hyeremia abscondita fuit in Crypta Montis Nobbe* [= Nebo], *et amplius non reperta.* Cf. note 90 below.

47. *Stato della SS. Chiesa papale Lateranense nell'Anno MDCCXXIII* (Roma 1723) 123.

48. A. NIBBY: F. NARDINI: *Roma antica* 1-4 (Roma 1818-1820) 1, 279-281. Nardini believed that the ark had been remade for the Temple of Herodus, see note 73 below.

were to be removed and no longer exhibited.[49] The canons do not seem to have been surprised by the papal order. The authenticity of the *mensa*, on the other hand, was beyond all doubt and the table of the last supper is still venerated in the Lateran today.

When we confront the evidence, the wooden altar clearly emerges as having the firmest tradition. Its continous existence as the high altar of the Lateran basilica can not only be demonstrated from the eleventh century onwards, but its history can also be traced further back. When Pope Leo III had the Lateran high altar covered with silver panels in 804, the redactor of the *Liber pontificalis* employs the word *renovabit*, a term that is unique in the context of an altar commission.[50] It suggests that the preservation of the existing altar was of primary concern. This observation may be connected with the state of affairs at the moment of the foundation of the basilica by the emperor Constantine. According to the donation list in the *vita* of Silvester in the *Liber pontificalis*, the Lateran basilica was the only church for which an altar was not included in the donation programma: an indication that the bishop's church had an older altar.[51] Though the later wooden altar may not have been materially identical with the altar of Silvester's times, specific formal characteristics will have conveyed the continuity of its history. At the time of the *Descriptio* the altar does not appear to have had a very different aspect from that of the time of Leo III and probably also of Silvester: a wooden chest, covered with silver panels. Afterwards, under Urban V at the latest, it received a marble casing.

The tradition of the temple relics is less soundly documented. Its accuracy depends upon the history of the destruction of Jerusalem by Titus and Vespasian, but the only objects materially present in the Lateran, the ark and the rods, did not exist at all in the second temple that was plundered by the Romans. The holy of holies of the Herodian temple was practically empty.[52] The relief on the arch of Titus of the triumphal procession in which the temple spoils are carried as trophies does not depict the ark, as the medieval defenders

49. Acts of the visitation by Benedict XIV, Archivio Segreto Vaticano, S.C. Visita Apostolica 98 no. 3 and 5, *Relatio* [1-5-1745]: *Deinde Sanctissimus ad Capellam ascessit in qua asservatur insignis et veneranda Tabula in qua Misericors Dominus in suprema nocte coene cum Apostolis recumbens sanctissimum instituit sacramentum. Eodem in loco esse dicitur Archa Foederis, in qua Moyses Tabulas Divinae legis recondidit. Ibidem Virga quae dicitur eiusdem Moysis et baculus qui Aaronis asseritur manent, quae omnia Sanctissimus visitavit et aliquid pro his decernendum ad sequentem diem suspendit [...]. Decreta* [2-5-1745]: *In visitatione Sacrarum Reliquiarum hexterna die peracta* [...] *Tabula coene Domini Nostri in suo loco solitaque veneratione permaneat; amoveantur vero ea, quae asseruntur Archa Foederis, Virga Moysis et Baculus Aaronis, et amplius non ostendantur.*
50. DUCHESNE and VOGEL: *Liber pontificalis* 98 c. 51. Cf. DE BLAAUW: *Cultus et decor* 82.
51. DUCHESNE and VOGEL: *Liber pontificalis* 34 c. 9-11. Cf. DE BLAAUW: *Cultus et decor* 54, with further references.
52. The old ark was not contained in the second temple and there is no evidence that any new one was made. Cf. K. HOHEISEL: Kerube im Zweiten Tempel und die Anfänge der Kabbala, in Ernst DASSMANN and Klaus THRAEDE (eds.): *Vivarium. Festschrift Theodor Klauser zum 90. Geburtstag* (= Jahrbuch für Antike und Christentum, Ergänzungsband 11) (Münster 1984) 175-187, with reference to the sources.

Fig. 2. Rome, Arch of Titus. Relief showing the triumphal procession with the spoils of Jerusalem: the silver trumpets, the table of the shewbread and the menorah (last decades of the first century A.D.).

of the Lateran relics asserted again and again, but the golden table of the shewbread, besides the golden lampstand or menorah and the silver trumpets.[53] The iconographical details correspond fairly closely to the historiographical account by Flavius Josephus.[54] According to the sources, the precious loot was lodged in the *Templum pacis* in the new forum of Vespasian, but had disappeared from Rome in all probability by the time of the sackings of the fifth century.[55] The story that the emperor Constantine donated it to the Lateran basilica therefore had its origins in the medieval rumours about the fate of the famous spoils.

3. THE NEW TEMPLE

Despite the doubts regarding the historical veracity of the temple spoils, every visitor to the Lateran basilica in the high Middle Ages would have noticed that this church wanted to be seen as the direct successor of the temple of Jerusalem. When entering through the new narthex, erected in the late twelfth century, the visitor would see among the mosaic panels of the frieze a series of scenes from the Jewish war and the capture of Jerusalem by the Romans, which were apparently intended to demonstrate one of the major grounds for the greatness of the basilica.[56] Once inside the church the visitor would be impressed by the huge bronze columns of the pergola in front of the high altar and would be told that they were spoils from the temple of Solomon. At the back in the curve of the apse shimmered an inscription celebrating the basilica as the new Sinai, from which the law proceeds. Finally there were the rumours about the revered holy relics of Israel kept below the high altar: they were not visible, but their fame was widely disseminated by all written and oral guides of the basilica.

An attempt to trace the origins of the concept of the Lateran basilica as the direct heir of the old convenant can begin with the inscription in the apse of the basilica, attributed to Sergius III (904-911) in commemoration of his restoration campaign: *Aula Dei haec similis Synai sacra iura ferenti* [...] *lex hinc exivit mentes quae ducit ab imis.* ('This house of God is like Sinai, the bearer of the holy law [...] from here proceeded the law which moves the spirits from the depths.')[57] An association of such a general import has no value as evidence, but one wonders whether this statement could refer to

---

53. M. PFANNER: *Der Titusbogen* (Mainz 1983) 72-74.
54. FLAVIUS JOSEPHUS: *Bellum Judaicum* VII 148-151.
55. HERKLOTZ: Fassadenportikus 75-76, with further references.
56. HERKLOTZ: Fassadenportikus esp. 73-80.
57. The source for the inscription is an appendix to the *Descriptio* in two sixteenth century manuscripts (C. VOGEL: La descriptio ecclesiae lateranensis du diacre Jean. Histoire du texte manuscrit, in *Mélanges en l'honneur de Monseigneur Michel Andrieu* (Revue des sciences religieuses, hors série) (Strasbourg 1956) 457-476, p. 471 no. LXVI), see J.B. DE ROSSI: *Inscriptiones Christianae urbis Romae* 1-2 (Roma 1857-1888) 2, 306. Cf. HERKLOTZ: Fassadenportikus 74-75, with complete translation. The sources do not prove De Rossi's attribution to Sergius III, but merely indicate a date between the ninth and thirteenth centuries.

concrete remnants of the old convenant in the basilica, in particular in the *confessio* of the high altar. This relic chamber was arranged in 844 by pope Sergius II, but there is no reference to its sacred contents in the report of the foundation.[58] On the other hand, relics of the Old Testament were reported to be kept in the Lateran palace chapel: a stone of Mount Sion, where the temple had stood, and of Mount Sinai, where the law was given.[59] Moreover, the idea of a Christian church building as a new, perfect temple of Jerusalem was well known since the Carolingian age.[60]

The first reference to an object from Jerusalem, retrieved by Titus and Vespasian and ending up in the Lateran, is a document of 1029 which mentions the icon of Christ, painted by angels and venerated in the chapel of the Lateran palace.[61] Some 75 years later the story of the temple spoils appears in the first edition of the *Descriptio*. It does not seem to be a recent tradition then in view of the polemics already going on and the hesitations of the author in identifiying the location of the relics. He was acquainted with the story of the temple spoils and obviously wanted to give it a prominent place in his treatise. He therefore glossed over the established tradition of the wooden altar as the altar of the pre-Constantinian popes and suggested that the peculiar form of the Lateran high altar could be explained by its identity with the ark of the covenant, at least in its inner substance. The possibilities for linguistic and allegorical associations and confusions were ready to hand: the wooden altar had the appearance of a chest, just like the ark of the covenant, and for all objects of this basic form medieval Latin employed the term *arca*.[62] The meaning of *arca* shifted from box containing relics via tomb of a martyr to altar, whereas allegorical comparisons were drawn between the incorruptible timber of the ark of the covenant and the incorruptible body of Christ.[63]

At the same time Bonizo of Sutri wrote a contribution on the Lateran high altar in which the tradition of the temple relics was significantly ignored. Nevertheless, without lapsing into in the confusion of the *Descriptio*, he describes the wooden altar of the early popes in terms that seem to be directly taken from the description of the ark, the shewbread table and the sacrificial

58. DUCHESNE and VOGEL: *Liber pontificalis* 104 c. 19: *Ubi etiam confessionem mirificam, Christo cooperante, construxit, et argenteis tabulis auroque perfusis fulgide compsit; quam propriis manibus consecrans reliquias posuit.* Cf. DE BLAAUW: *Cultus et decor* 82-83.
59. *Descriptio*, VALENTINI and ZUCCHETTI: *Codice* 3, 358 (text from the first edition).
60. P. BLOCH: Seven-branched candelabra in Christian churches, in *Journal of Jewish art* 1 (1974) 44-49, p. 46.
61. Document of 1029 in G.M. SORESINI: *De imagine SS.mi Salvatoris in basilica ad Sancta Sanctorum custodita* (Roma 1675) 53-56.
62. *Mittellateinisches Wörterbuch* 1 (München 1967) 872-873.
63. HRABANUS MAURUS: *Allegoriae in universam sacram scripturam*, in J.-P. MIGNE: *Patrologia Latina* 112 (Paris 1852) 864. A summary of the associations relating the ark in M.Q. SMITH: Anagni: An example of medieval typological decoration, in *Papers of the British School at Rome* 33 (1965) 1-47, p. 33-36. See esp. the interesting association between the ark of the covenant and the altar of Christ by abbot Suger of St. Denis († 1151) in E. PANOFSKY: *Abbot Suger on the abbey church of St.-Denis and its art treasures* (Princeton 1979²) 74-75.

altar in the book of Exodus.[64] The wooden altar looked 'like a hollow ark' and had four rings at the corners into which staves could be inserted, so that it could be borne by the priests.

The twelfth century revisors of the *Descriptio* again disregard the tradition of the altar of the first popes, but are still more reluctant to accept the equivalence of ark and altar than their predecessor.[65] In the meantime non-Lateran authorities rarely speak about the temple treasure,[66] which may well be considered remarkable at a time when the temple tradition was playing a dominant role in the 'self-representation' of the Lateran basilica. Benjamin of Tudela, a Spanish Jew who visited the basilica between 1165 and 1168 and was highly interested in Jewish antiquities, was apparently not convinced of the real existence of the temple implements. All the same, he mentions the bronze columns, 'taken from the temple, the handiwork of king Solomon, each column being engraved "Solomon the son of David"' and claims to have heard of 'a cave where Titus the son of Vespasianus stored the temple vessels which he brought from Jerusalem'.[67]

A balanced synthesis of the traditions is achieved by pope Honorius III in his sermon for the feast of the dedication of the Lateran basilica on November 9, written somewhere between c. 1200 and 1220. The sermon, edited and commented by James Powell in 1983, draws many elements from Bonizo, with the main difference that it gives explicit expression to the parallel between the Lateran wooden altar and the portable furniture of the Jewish cult.[68] His elaborated statement bears the features of a compromise between the old tradition of the altar of the first popes and the emergence of the item of the temple relics in the twelfth century. The pope agrees with Bonizo and the liturgical sources

---

64. Exodus 25, 10-30; 27, 1-8.
65. The last authority tending to equate the altar with the ark is the author of the History of the popes, in FABRE and DUCHESNE: *Liber censuum* 2, 166-167: *Posuit ibi archam Testamenti* [...] *Super quam posuit tiburium* [...].
66. An exception is PETRUS COMESTOR († 1178): *Historia scholastica*, Liber Exodi XLVI, in J.-P. MIGNE: *Patrologia Latina* 198 (Paris 1855) 1170: *Quod apparet in altari Lateranensi, infra quod dicitur esse arca.*
67. M.N. ADLER: *The itinerary of Benjamin of Tudela* (New York 1907 = [1975]ʳ) 7. Contemporaneously the History of the popes, in FABRE and DUCHESNE: *Liber censuum* 2, 167, speaks of Roman origins (temple of Jupiter) of the columns. The 'Jewish' explanation became the dominant one, cf. e.g. the mosaic inscription, LAUER: *Palais* 294.
68. Honorius III, in POWELL, Honorius' III 'Sermo' 206-207: [...] *sancti martires super altare istud ligneum in modum arce concavum, quod vectibus inmissis in circulos in quatuor angulis a sacerdotibus portabatur* [...], *missarum sollempnia celebrant. Sanctus vero Silvester in dicta Lateranensi ecclesia* [...] *illud altare ligneum stabilivit in formam et similitudinem altaris Abrahe quo iussus est a Domino filium immolare, cuius ligna crucem passionis Domini figurabant, et etiam in similitudine illius altaris in quo thimiama sempiternum coram Domino urebatur* [...], *necnon et in similitudine mense Christi qua fuit sub Dominica cena sumpta, cuius res in eodem existens materiales lapides superat universos, et in formam et similitudinem crucis Christi cuius res et sacramentum in materiali altari assidue presentatur, in quo pontifex gratie per legis pontificem figuratus, pontificis glorie in terris vicarius constitutus, quod idem in mensa docuit et in ara crucis seipsum offerens adimplevit, iugi sacrificio representat.*

in not mentioning the controversial relics themselves, but he stresses the typological continuity between the altars of the Old Testament and that of the early popes. Thus the wooden altar of the Lateran incorporated the altars of the old covenant through its material appearance, but only in a symbolic sense. This need not have been a merely personal solution of pope Honorius, for it is found at the same time in the treatise of Giraldus.[69]

Honorius' approach reflects an effort to put an end to the confusion about the temple relics and their relationship with the Lateran high altar as appearing in the *Descriptio*.[70] His view means in practice a denial of the importance of the actual temple relics. The fact that the pope does not refer to the objects at all in the course of his detailed account can hardly be fortuitous.[71] Nor can there be anything fortuitous in the fact that it is precisely the ark – the central object in the Lateran tradition – which is conspicuously absent from the series of symbolic comparisons with the Old Testament cult.

A rearrangement of the altar disposition seems to have taken place more or less at the same time as the papal statement, with the result that the so-called temple spoils could be situated in the crypt below the high altar and the altar itself was entirely free to be recognized as the portable altar of the time of the persecutions. The fact that Giraldus supposed that the crypt contained only particles of the ark,[72] whereas a century later a complete chest-like object was saved from the fire and displayed in St. Thomas' chapel, might indicate that the ark was a thirteenth century fabrication. The producers knew exactly to which typological characteristics their artefact had to correspond: the wooden chest removed by Benedict XIV showed traces of a metal revetment and bronze rings at the corners.[73]

69. The relationship between Honorius and Giraldus is obscure. A common source is conceivable. GIRALDUS: *Speculum* IV 1, in BREWER: *Giraldi Cambrensis opera* 4, 269, draws the following passage from PERELS: BONIZO: *De vita* IV 98, 165 and adds the words printed in Roman type that are not found in Honorius' sermon: [...] *altare ligneum scilicet in modum arcae concavum, habens in quatuor angulos circulos in quibus vectes immitebantur, quibus,* more quondam arcae foederis per desertum portatae, *a sacerdotibus tantum deferrebatur ubicumque Romanus pontifex latitabat* [...].

70. It will be clear that I disagree with BRAUN: *Altar* 1, 60-61 and POWELL: Honorius' III 'Sermo' 203-204, that the tradition of the portable altar of the early popes was a relatively recent development. On the contrary, I have tried to demonstrate that it was older than that of the temple relics and that the popes never openly supported the tradition of the temple treasure.

71. For a similar conclusion see HERKLOTZ: Fassadenportikus 77.

72. GIRALDUS: *Speculum* IV 3, in BREWER: *Giraldi Cambrensis opera* 4, 274: *Contrarietas vero de arca sic solvi potest, ut aliqua scilicet ipsius pars cum contentis ejusdem tabulis, scilicet, urna aurea, et virga Aaron quae fronduerat, ad honorem ecclesiae suae Romam postea nutu divino sit translata.*

73. NIBBY: NARDINI: *Roma antica* 279-280: [...] *lamine, che la coprivano, come dice la Scrittura; delle quali vi ho scorti io minutissimi residui sotto alcune teste di bollettine, che ancor vi durano.* NIBBY: NARDINI: *Roma antica* 281: *Mi ricordo avere osservato i quattro anelli, ch'ella ha per le stanghe vicino agli Angeli, essere non d'oro, come si legge ne l'Esodo, ma di Bronzo* [...], *segno della minore spesa, e magnificenza, con cui Zorobabele rifè ogni cosa* [...]. Nardini's conclusion, NIBBY: NARDINI: *Roma antica* 280: *Io nondimeno osservata bene quest'Arca alla descritta nell'Esodo somigliante, non so immaginarlami cosa fabbricata in Roma ad altro uso, nè ardisco pronunciarla opera vanamente fatta per finzione.*

The efforts to specify the physical presence of the temple relics in the basilica may have constituted a last vain attempt to counteract the decrease in their prominence during the thirteenth century. Other relics, such as the table of the last supper, came to the fore. The pre-eminent position was secured by the relics of the heads of the apostles Peter and Paul, formerly preserved in the Lateran palace chapel but elevated to the new canopy of the high altar in 1370. With these symbols of the apostolic succession in the centre of its cult, the basilica was well armed in the struggle with St. Peter's.[74] The Sinai inscription disappeared from the apse during the restoration of 1291, the temple relics were not reinstalled in the sanctuary after the fire of 1308, and the crypt under the altar remained obscure.

All the same, the fame of the Lateran basilica as the temple of the new covenant had never depended on the authenticity of the temple relics. It is even tempting to assume that the idea of the Christian Church in general and, derived from it, of the Lateran basilica, 'head and crown of all churches',[75] in particular, as the new temple, combined with the typological parallel between the wooden altar of the Lateran and the portable furniture of the Jewish temple and, finally, the possible existence of particles of the holy places of the old law in the *confessio* of Sergius II, formed the matrix from which the tradition of the temple relics emerged.[76] The liturgy of Maundy Thursday may have been a crucial element in this chain of associations.

4. THE HIGH PRIEST OF THE NEW COVENANT

The *altare est cavum* in the seventh-century *Ordo* for Maundy Thursday points directly to the *elevatio mensae* of the high medieval sources, as Chavasse, editor of the ancient *Ordo*, already suspected.[77] The intention may now be clear. The stational Mass in the Lateran basilica on the afternoon of Maundy Thursday was celebrated by the pope on the altar of his predecessors, that had to be prepared intentionally by removing the upper slab of the existing altar construction. The fact that is was precisely – and perhaps exclusively – the commemoration of the *natale* of the Eucharist which had to be performed by the chief priest of the city on the eucharistic table used by his predecessors seems to stress the special character of the priesthood of the pope.[78] The setting may be recognized as a stage towards a deliberate liturgical expression of the apostolic succession.

74. Cf. HERKLOTZ: Fassadenportikus 84-87.
75. *Constitutum Constantini* 13 (eighth century): H. FUHRMANN: *Das Constitutum Constantini* (= Fontes iuris Germanici antiqui in usum scholarum separatim editi 10) (= Monumenta Germaniae historica) (Hannover 1968) 84-85.
76. Cf. HERKLOTZ: Fassadenportikus 79.
77. CHAVASSE: Vieil ordo 24 note 4.
78. On the concept of the pope as the new Melchisedech, 'king and priest', see P.E. SCHRAMM: Das Alte und das Neue Testament in der Staatslehre und Staatssymbolik des Mittelalters, in *Kaiser, Könige und Päpste. Gesammelte Aufsätze zur Geschichte des Mittelalters* 4, 1 (Stuttgart 1970) 123-140.

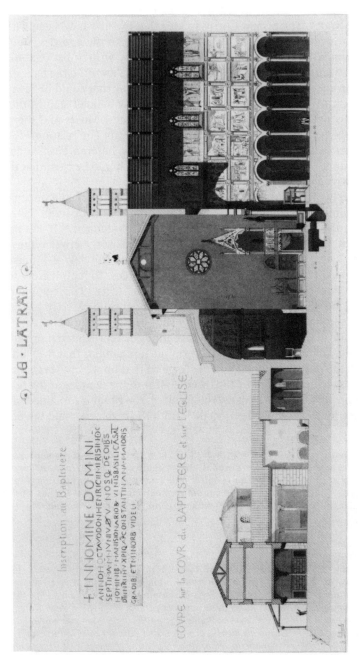

Fig. 3. Rome, Lateran basilica. Reconstructed section by G. Rohault de Fleury (1877) with the high altar canopy of 1369 and the crypt. (The reconstruction of the nave arcades has been shown to be incorrect.)

139

The Old Testament-inspired imagery of the liturgy of Maundy Thursday has early roots. The primal Christian idea that the new law began with the last supper, when Christ offered his body and blood to the apostles, finds a pregnant formulation in Amalarius' *Liber officialis*, written between 820 and c. 833: 'On Maundy Thursday Christ ends the Old Law'.[79] In the light of the special celebration of the pope on this day at an altar that could be regarded as a monument of the apostolic succession, it is only a small step to the link between this notion and that of the pope as the new Moses and the new high priest, which had a long ecclesiastical history too.[80] The relationship of cause and effect between this concept and that of the Lateran basilica as the new temple cannot be established any further, but it should be clear that they share the same roots.

Bonizo highlights the factor of the apostolic tradition: the pope celebrates at the unique wooden altar used by his predecessors back to St. Peter; but he describes the altar in terms taken from the Old Testament.[81] It was only in the course of the twelfth century that the comparison between the pope on Maundy Thursday and the Jewish high priest on the day of atonement was given a pronounced form in the liturgical sources, though merely in a comment on the rubrics and not in euchological texts. The compilers of the liturgical books always avoid the temptation to refer directly to the controversial temple relics present at the very spot of the ceremony.

The final interpretation of the ritual cannot be represented more adequately than in paraphrasing Honorius' III sermon. It maintains that the wooden altar at which the pope celebrated had the form of that on which Abraham was prepared to sacrifice his son, of the incense altar in the temple, of the table of the last supper and of the wooden Cross itself.[82] The ritual is explained in terms of prefigurations in the Old Testament.[83] Both the high priest and the pope make

79. AMALARIUS SYMPHOSIUS: *Liber officialis* I xii 51, in J.M. HANSSENS: *Amalarii episcopi opera liturgica omnia* 2 (Città del Vaticano 1949) (= Studi e testi 139) 88: *Ipsa die finitur lex veteris testamenti* [...] and 52: *Christus in quinta feria veteri legi finem dat, peccata absolvit.* Cf. H. DOUTEIL: JOHANNES BELETH: *Summa de ecclesiasticis officiis* (= Corpus Christianorum. Continuatio mediaevalis 41-41A) (Turnhout 1976) 95b: [...] *quia novum testamentum tunc incepit et vetus terminatum fuit.*
80. HERKLOTZ: Fassadenportikus 74-75.
81. See note 31 above.
82. See note 68 above.
83. Honorius' main sources are: Leviticus 16 and Hebrews 9. His text, POWELL: Honorius' III 'Sermo' 207-208, reads: *Hec quidem aperte prefigurata fuerunt in veteri testamento, nam sicut noster pontifex non semper intrat sanctuarium, sed semel tantum ad hoc sacrum misterium peragendum, sic pontifex legis intrabat. Unde in Levitico dixit Dominus Moysi: Loquere ad Aaron fratrem tuum ne ingrediatur omni tempore sanctuarium ut non moriatur, sed mense septimo decimo die mensis, et sicut noster pontifex solus intrans sacrificans pro se et tota Dei ecclesia et populo universo, sic legis pontifex faciebat.* [...] *Et sicut alias in sacrificio communicant cum nostro pontifice fratres sui, tunc autem ipse sacrificium offerens solus sumit, sic in lege fiebat. Unde Paulus ad Hebreos: In priori tabernaculo semper introibant sacerdotes sacrificiorum officia consumantes. In secundo autem semel in anno solus pontifex non sine sanguine quem offert pro sua et populi ignorantia. Et sicut iste evangelii*

the offering alone, for themselves and for the entire people. In the old dispensation the priests had the right to enter the first tabernacle, but the high priest alone went into the second, once a year: thus the pope normally takes Communion together with the cardinals, but on this day he does so alone. As the first testament was not dedicated without the blood that Moses had sprinkled on the law book and the people, so the pope showed the quickening blood of Christ to the congregation. Therefore the day on which Christ offered his own blood to his apostles to drink is the end of the old law and the beginning of the new. Hence our real pontiff is Christ, who in offering his own blood entered the unmade tabernacle once and alone. He alone can open the kingdom of heaven.

Honorius in fact presents a fusion of the concepts of the apostolic succession and of the prefiguration in the Old Testament. The high priest entered the sanctuary and sprinkled blood on the gold plate that covered the ark: an atonement for the transgressions and sins of the people, but at the same time a reminder of the sealing of the covenant by Moses. The pope standing before the inner core of the Lateran high altar repeated the offering of Christ and commemorated the sealing of the new covenant by Christ's blood. He did so on the eucharistic table of his predecessors, covered by a plate that was believed to be the table of the last supper. Christ is said to be the real pontiff, but this particular liturgical scenery shows the pope in the clearest liturgical forms as his direct vicar. After the ending of the Mosaic law, the pope embodies the fact that the cult of the temple has become superfluous. The Lateran basilica, as the chief papal church, was the new temple and the high altar was its sanctuary.

The role of the blood relic in the ceremony may not only have referred to Christ's offering and its prefiguration in the Old Testament, but may also have stressed the guilt of the Jews for Christ's death and the consequent justice of the destruction of the old temple.[84] The addition in the thirteenth century Pontifical that the blood relic in the Lateran high altar derived from a bleeding image of Christ can be linked with a story told by Giraldus Cambrensis in the late twelfth century. It tells of some Jews who struck an image of Christ painted above the door to a chapel in the Lateran palace with a stone. Immediately blood poured from the forehead of the painted Christ in 'an abundant flow'. The one who had thrown the stone died at once in a frenzy and the other Jews fled out of fear and horror. The blood was taken up and

---

iam finito mandato ad accendenda corda fidelium et expianda peccata vivificum Christi sanguinem causa humane salutis aspersum cuncto populo circumstanti manifeste demonstrat, sic ille ad expianda peccata populum sanguine aspergebat. [...] Verus autem pontifex noster est Christus, qui per proprium sanguinem introivit tabernaculum non manufactum semel et solus. [...] Ipse aspergit sanguine populum, quia presentem ecclesiam proprii sanguinis aspersione reddit a suarum culparum contagiis expiatam. Et vere solus tabernaculum introivit [...].

84. On the long tradition of this idea in Christian thought: H.A.J. WEGMAN: De liturgie van Palmzondag, in *Jaarboek voor liturgie-onderzoek* 3 (1987) 1-40, pp. 25-26.

brought health to many, whereas 'many of the Jews who heard about this incident were converted to the faith'.[85]

The origin of the *mensa Domini* as a relic may have been a spontaneous effect of the manipulations with the wooden altar on Maundy Thursday. The celebration on the portable altar of the first popes would receive a special dimension if the slab of this altar, visible after the removal of the upper *mensa*, were identical with the table at which the Lord instituted the sacrament of the Eucharist. Whereas the altar itself connected the papal celebrant with Peter, the table linked him directly with Christ: the celebrant was the successor of Peter and the vicar of Christ. Thus the growing importance of the *mensa Domini* provides a perfect illustration of the ideology of the papacy in the thirteenth century.

Unlike the solitary function of the Jewish high priest, who stayed in one room all alone, hidden behind curtains and heavy clouds of incense, the Roman pontiff fulfilled his highest liturgical role in full view of all and in the presence of his clerical colleagues and the people. Indeed, prior Bernardus of the Lateran chapter observes that on this day many faithful, coming 'from different parts of the world', attended the papal service in the basilica.[86] In general the sanctuaries of Roman churches in the high Middle Ages were as open as they had probably been in early Christian times. There were no high choir screens or curtains hiding the officiants from the view of the congregation. On Maundy Thursday moreover, there was an aspect of deliberate public presentation.

According to the *Ordines*, the pope always delivered a sermon on this day which, as Bernardus stresses, was intended for the people. One text of a sermon held on Maundy Thursday, by Innocent III, is known from preserved manuscripts: it draws the comparison with the entering of the high priest in the holy of holies.[87] The sermon of Honorius, though intended for another feast, gives a striking impression of how the complicated liturgical action of Maundy Thursday might be explained to the faithful. Honorius himself testifies that he had spoken his sermons in the vernacular.[88]

The removal of the *mensa* was visible for everyone in the nave. The celebrant himself stood on the apse side of the free-standing altar, his face turned to the congregation. Of course the inner space of the altar with the wooden

85. GIRALDUS CAMBRENSIS: *Gemma ecclesiastica* I 31, in J.S. BREWER: *Giraldi Cambrensis opera* 2 (= Rerum Britannicarum Medii Aevi scriptores 21, 2) (London 1862) 103; translation in John J. HAGEN: GIRALDUS CAMBRENSIS: *The jewel of the Church* (= Davis medieval texts and studies 2) (Leiden 1979) 79-80.

86. FISCHER: *Bernhardi Lateranensis* 50: *Sciendum quoque est, quod, dum domnus papa in hac die populo, qui ex diversis mundi partibus in hanc ecclesiam convenerit, sermonem facit* [...].

87. INNOCENTIUS III: *Sermones*, in J.-P. MIGNE: *Patrologia Latina* 217 (Paris 1855) 399-400, *In coena domini: Quarum alteram Romanus pontifex repraesentat, in eo quod hodie remota tabula Lateranensis altaris, intra ipsum altare conficit eucharistiam: illud in hoc facto commemorans, quod pontifex summus in lege semel in anno in Sancta sanctorum cum sanguine introivit.*

88. POWELL: Honorius' III 'Sermo' 197.

chest and the *mensa Domini* could not be discerned from the nave. As if in response to this disadvantage, the second half of the twelfth century saw the introduction of the exhibition of the blood 'to the entire people' as Honorius stresses, or, with even more emphasis in the Pontifical: 'so that the entire crowd may see it with fear and reverence and with full piety'. It is the age of the introduction of the elevation of the Host.

Whereas the faithful played no active role in the rite surrounding the consecration of the oils, as they had done in the past, they could participate actively in the Communion. Cardinal Cencius, who later became Pope Honorius III, suggests in his *Ordo* that it was precisely in the papal Mass of Maundy Thursday that the people's Communion occupied a pronounced place. This is the only occasion on which he describes the administration of the Communion to the faithful: it is conducted by the pope himself, standing in front of the high altar.[89] If this was indeed a unique event, it would strikingly emphasise the way in which the liturgical framework of the solitary celebration at the wooden altar was directed toward the public.

Thus all those standing in the nave could see the high priest of the new covenant with their own eyes as he performed his most exclusive liturgical function. All those present could see the opening of the altar, the elevation of the blood relics and the solitary position of the pope during the canon and his Communion. Many will also have heard the pope's explanation of the actions. It remains doubtful to what extent they all grasped the full purport of the typological imagery of the ritual. But their understanding of it must have been powerfully reinforced by the notion that it was above the physical remains of the cult of the old covenant that the pope was celebrating.[90]

89. *Ordo Romanus Cencii* 24, FABRE and DUCHESNE: *Liber censuum* 1, 295: *Postquam vero dixerit Pax Domini sit semper vobiscum, communicat solus pontifex ante altare, et diaconus confirmat eum cum calice illa tantummodo die.* [Consecration of the chrism] *Quibus expletis, pontifex ablutis manibus venit ante altare et communicat populum ordine suo et servat de sancta in crastinum in corporale.*

90. As this contribution was already in the press, J. FREIBERG: *The Lateran and Clement VIII* (Dissertation New York University 1988) (Ann Arbor 1989) was brought to my attention. Freiberg's study provides interesting information from unknown sources concerning the central objects op this paper. The most relevant additions to the foregoing are some measurements, which I will summarize in converted values. The measurements of the outer chest of the wooden altar are reported by Fiorvante Martinelli in a manuscript dating from about 1658 (FREIBERG: *Lateran* 547-549): $153 \times 121 \times 108$ cm (corresponding fairly well with those mentioned by BRAUN: *Altar* 1, 57). The ark of the covenant, examined by Martinelli together with Borromini, had smaller proportions: $108 \times 60 \times 91$ cm (the measurements prescribed in Exodus 25, 10 are: c. $170 \times 100 \times 100$ cm). The *mensa Domini* was seen by an English author before it was transferred to the Sacrament Altar in the 1860's: the fragment of cedar wood measured 107×51 cm (FREIBERG: *Lateran* 467 n. 94). Martinelli (FREIBERG: *Lateran* 547-549) believed the *mensa Domini* to be the portable altar of the pre-Constantinian popes and the wooden chest the original Lateran altar of pope Silvester. He had obvious doubts about the identity of the ark. The rods of Aaron and Moses are described as iron staffs, decorated with rings of wood and ivory and with a globe of crystal or gold at the top as well as below.

The medieval city as a holy place

PETER RAEDTS

For a long time historians thought that the growth of medieval cities had been a spontaneous, organic process. It was not until the Renaissance, or so the argument went, that popes and princes started to think of cities as objects of planning, and began to hire architects to redraw the map of their capitals to change them into a more fitting place for them to live in. It was the sixteenth century which saw the first designs for vast squares in front of glorious, new churches and for broad avenues leading up to magnificent palaces. In the Middle Ages people did not have a concept of the city itself as a work of architecture. When they built, they just changed and added bits and pieces, which, almost miraculously, in the end turned out to form a coherent and esthetically pleasing whole. The romantic origins of this idea are too obvious to need further discussion.

This view came under attack when, forty years ago, the German art historian Bandmann pointed out that medieval builders seldom built to please the eye but, in the first place, to convey a message, to express meaning.[1] Moreover, the message which the architect tried to express in a building was usually not his own. Most of the time he acted under strict orders of his patrons, who took every care that the commissioned building expressed only what they wanted it to express and nothing else.[2] That medieval architecture was significant and not esthetic architecture and that the patron was more important than the artist, was a first attack on the romantic notion of medieval art. But there was more to follow. Wolfgang Braunfels proved, at the same time, that the medieval city as a whole was not a haphazard collection of buildings, but must be approached as a more or less successful result of careful planning. He showed that not only individual buildings were carriers of an idea but that the sum total of all buildings within the whole of a city was the expression of a very definite idea of the city and its purpose in the life of men.[3]

Braunfels maintained that the idea of the city as an ideal form of social life

---

1. G. BANDMANN: *Mittelalterliche Architektur als Bedeutungsträger* (Berlin 1951) 11.
2. BANDMANN: *Mittelalterliche Architektur* 7-9.
3. W. BRAUNFELS: *Mittelalterliche Stadtbaukunst in der Toskana* (Berlin 1959²) 12: *Denn wie immer die Stadt als ein Werk der Jahrhunderte sich de facto gebildet hat, die Vorstellung sah in ihr zu jedem Zeitpunkt ein einheitlich errichtetes, hochaufragendes Bauwerk, in dessen planvoller Gestaltung sich ein hoher und idealer Gedanke spiegelt. [...] Die Geschichte der Stadtbaukunst ist die Geschichte unserer guten Vorsätze, die nie ganz verwirklicht wurden.* See also: 43, 50, 136.

was older than the ideas of empire or Church.[4] It certainly survived the fall of the Roman empire and coalesced with the idea of the Church in the notion of the *civitas Dei*, which could be and was applied to both. The inhabitants of a city, the citizens, were seen as bearers of a special vocation. Hrabanus Maurus argued that citizens are called to live together, so that life will be safer and more decorous.[5] Communal life was just as important in a city as it was in a monastery, even although it was true that monastic rules tended to remain unchanged, whereas the statutes of most cities were constantly adapted to meet new requirements. It was from that claim that medieval cities deducted the right to be free from the interference of princes and to organize their own forms of government.[6] In other words, in the Middle Ages the city was widely seen as an ideal form of social life, willed by God, just like the Church or the empire, and as such it was a terrestrial image of the heavenly Jerusalem, the city of God. And this was also the idea which inspired most medieval building legislation, according to Braunfels. In cities such as Utrecht, Bamberg and Paderborn, architectural crosses of five or more churches were designed to serve as a visible token of the city's holiness. Even liturgical functions served to give voice to this conviction. In Siena the bishop and the people went to the Porta Salaria on Palm Sunday to greet Christ, entering the city riding on an ass, and they accompanied Him to the cathedral, where Mass was celebrated.[7] Recently the Lorenzetti frescoes in the Palazzo Publico of Siena, representing good and bad government, have also been interpreted as images of Jerusalem and Babylon.[8]

The discovery that medieval cities were the expression of an idea also led to a revaluation of a literary genre, that so far had been thought of as rather uninformative and boring, the *laudes civitatis* or *urbium*.[9] Local historians eager to discover the topography of their beloved hometown in the past, had been studying these songs of praise since a long time, but the results had been disappointing. Apparently the medieval poets were not interested in exact

---

4. Braunfels: *Mittelalterliche Stadtbaukunst* 18.
5. Hrabanus Maurus: *De universo*, in J.-P. Migne: *Patrologia Latina* 111 (Paris 1852) 451: *Cives vocati, quod in unum coeuntes vivant, ut vita communis et ornatior fiat et tutior.*
6. Braunfels: *Mittelalterliche Stadtbaukunst* 22, 36-37, 44, 135.
7. Braunfels: *Mittelalterliche Stadtbaukunst* 85; see also: 22, 50, 135.
8. Uta Feldges-Henning: The pictorial programme of the Sala della pace. A new interpretation, in *Journal of the Warburg and Courtauld Institute* 35 (1972) 145-162, pp. 160-162.
9. The most important contributions to this theme are Paul Gerhard Schmidt: Mittelalterliches und humanistisches Städtelob, in: August Buck (ed.): *Die Rezeption der Antike* (= Wolfenbütteler Abhandlungen zur Renaissanceforschung 1) (Hamburg 1981) 119-128; C.J. Classen: *Die Stadt im Spiegel der Descriptiones und Laudes urbium in der antiken und mittelalterlichen Literatur bis zum Ende des zwölften Jahrhunderts* (= Beiträge zur Altertumswissenschaft 2) (Hildesheim etc. 1980); Chiara Frugoni: *Una lontana città. Sentimenti e immagini nel medioevo* (Torino 1983); Gerhard Theuerkauf: Accipe Germania pingentia carmina terram, in *Archiv für Kulturgeschichte* 65 (1983) 89-116; Hartmut Kugler: *Die Vorstellung der Stadt in der Literatur des deutschen Mittelalters* (München 1986); Alfred Haverkamp: 'Heilige Städte' im hohen Mittelalter, in: Frantisek Graus (ed.): *Mentalitäten im Mittelalter* (= Vorträge und Forschungen 35) (Sigmaringen 1987) 119-156.

descriptions of churches, public buildings and streets, but more given to wild flights of the imagination. Moreover, historians of literature noticed that most of these hymns were highly conventional and that the medieval preference for following standard procedures was nowhere as marked as in the *laudes urbium*. Most of the songs proved to be full of well-known *topoi*, such as the *locus amoenus* tradition, taken straight from classical literature.[10] The general conclusion was that the *laudes* were negligible as a historical source. A few years ago this conclusion was questioned by Kugler. He denied that topography or *topoi*-research could bring out the value of the *laudes urbium*. Resuming Braunfels' main theme he claimed that the medieval city must be seen as an effort to realise a high ideal and that the *laudes urbium* contained the poetic articulation of that ideal. Uninformative as these *encomia* may be about real cities, yet they do tell us a great deal about the dreams of medieval people about their cities, and as such they are a most valuable source to the history of mentalities.[11]

Just like Braunfels Kugler is convinced that the notion of the city as a reflection of the heavenly Jerusalem formed the heart of these songs about the form and quality of urban life.[12] Three *topoi* form, in his opinion, a link between the praised city and its heavenly counterpart. First of all the city is usually depicted as a place where many people can live together in peace. And as the very word 'Jerusalem' means: vision of peace, according to medieval exegetes, peace is what makes cities participate in the glories of the heavenly city. Secondly, cities are renowned for the quality of their communal life; each citizen and each group of citizens fits into the whole like the living stones which together form the new Zion. Finally, cities were also praised as places of hard work. That could be fitted into the biblical tradition which holds that the new Jerusalem is not just coming from on high, but that it has to be built up by the good works of the faithful.[13]

It all sounds rather far-fetched. In my opinion the connection between these three *topoi* and the concept of the heavenly Jerusalem is a theory which needs corroboration by at least some explicit references in the texts themselves. And it is here that disappointment sets in. When I started looking at some poems in praise of cities, the number of references to the heavenly Jerusalem proved to be very small, even when taking quite a wide semantic field. Kugler himself comes up with not more than two examples. The first is a hymn on Bamberg, written by Gerhard of Seeon between 1012 and 1014, which praises the city for taking part in Jerusalem's glory (*Haec Iebusaice partem capit inclita doxae*).[14]

---

10. For a systematic comparison of the *topoi* in classical and medieval *laudes* see CLASSEN: *Stadt im Spiegel*, passim. His conclusions are not fundamentally different from the short remarks of Ernst Robert CURTIUS: *Europäische Literatur und lateinisches Mittelalter* (Bern 1954²) 166.

11. KUGLER: *Vorstellung der Stadt* 5, 8-10, 37.

12. KUGLER: *Vorstellung der Stadt* 81.

13. KUGLER: *Vorstellung der Stadt* 116-121.

14. KUGLER: *Vorstellung der Stadt* 154; full text of the hymn in Karl STRECKER: *Poetae Latini Medii Aevi 5. Die Ottonenzeit* (= Monumenta Germaniae historica) (Berlin 1937-1939) 397-98.

The second is a letter, written by Enea Silvio Piccolomini (later Pope Pius II) in 1438, in which he described Basel as the centre of the world because of the Council in progress there at the time. The argument is that Basel is seen here as another Jerusalem, the real centre of the world.[15]

The text of the letter does not justify the conclusion that Piccolomini is alluding to Jerusalem. It seems more likely that in the heat of the battle between pope and Council Piccolomini contrasts Basel, the new centre, with Rome, which has now lost its claim to be *caput mundi*. It is clear from other sources, e.g. monumental sources, that medieval cities were built to reflect the image of the heavenly Jerusalem.[16] Ceremonial royal entries were also an occasion to celebrate the city as another Zion.[17] I myself found an example of a comparison with Jerusalem in a hymn on Padua, written about 1440 by Michel Savonarola: *Et cum menia, urbis nostre magnum decus, diligenti cura animo revolvo, ea gloriosa vetuste Hierusalem videre me sentio, [...] Nullam quippe usque modo urbem, preter Hierusalem et Patavium, sic triplici meniorum ordine cingi legisse me memini.*[18] The question is whether the poet is referring to the heavenly Jerusalem or simply comparing the qualities of two cities on earth. The latter seems to be the case. Except for this one example I did not find any clear reference to the heavenly Jerusalem in the *laudes urbium* which I examined. That is not to say that medieval poets did not praise the city as a holy place. But, on the whole, they seem to have chosen a different manner to do so. A city's holiness seems to depend on three points: its centrality, its saints and monasteries, and on the life of its citizens. Let me say something about each of them.[19]

A common feature of the *laudes urbium* is that the beloved city is pictured as if it were in the centre of the world. In an anonymous life of St. Bavo (written c. 1020) Ghent is situated in the centre of Flanders: [...] *certus cognoscere possis/Urbibus hic cunctis caput esse prioribus annis.*[20]

Regensburg is situated in the middle between Lower Austria and the Upper Rhine valley.[21] But the finest example is probably Heinric van Veldeke's description of Maastricht, a city which lies:

In eynen dall scoen ende liecht,
Effen ende wael gedaen
Daer twee water tsamen gaen,

15. KUGLER: *Vorstellung der Stadt* 195-199.
16. HAVERKAMP: 'Heilige Städte' 126-134, 137-139.
17. Gordon KIPLING: The idea of the civic triumph. Drama, liturgy, and the royal entry in the Low countries, in *Dutch Crossing* no. 22 (1984) 60-83, pp. 64-67.
18. A. SEGARIZZI: MICHAEL SAVONAROLA: *Libellus de magnificis ornamentis regie civitatis Padue*, in *Raccolta degli storici Italiani del 500 al 1500* 24, 15 (Città di Castello 1902) 51.
19. A very long, though by no means exhaustive, list of city *encomia* and descriptions is given by KUGLER: *Vorstellung der Stadt* 235-74.
20. *Carmen de Sancto Bavone*, in STRECKER: *Poetae Latini Medii Aevi* 5, 248.
21. *Translatio S. Dionysii Areopagitae*, ed. R. KÖPKE, in *Scriptores* [*in folio*] 11 (= Monumenta Germaniae historica) (Hannover 1854) 352.

Eyn groot ende eyn cleyne,
Dats die Jeker ende die mase.
Beide te korne ende te grase
Es die stadt wale gheleghen
[...]
Aen eynre ghemeynre straten
Van Inghelant in ongheren
Voer Colne ende voer tongheren
Ende also dies ghelijck
Van Sassen in vrancrijck.[22]

In the poem Maastricht's geographical location is perfectly balanced: situated between a big and a small river, in a valley in which both wheat and grass can be grown, on the crossroads between England and Cologne, between Saxony and France. Such a central city is a perfect setting for the great deeds of St. Servais.

But not always should centrality be understood too geographically. Another way to praise the city's central position was to point out that it had a good share in all the delights this world had to offer, that it was a *locus amoenus*. When Cassiodorus described Como around 535, he emphasized that Como was so well situated *ut ad solas delicias instituta esse videatur*. On the one side it had the fertile Ligurian plain, on the other a beautiful lake that abounded with fish. In the background were the snowy mountain summits, and on the fruitful slopes vineyards produced a delicious wine.[23] Cassiodorus' description obeyed all the rules of classical rhetoric for the *encomia* of cities, laid down by a certain Menandros in the third century A.D.[24] And on this point medieval poets strictly followed these ancient rules. When Gozwin of Mainz wanted to praise the glories of Liège around 1060, he compared the city with a hen sitting on its chicken. He praised the hills that surrounded the town, the river Meuse which gave plenty of fish and was the source of a lively trade, the gardens in the suburbs and the temperate climate.[25] The region of Paderborn is praised as a land of milk and honey because it lies in the middle of forests, in which cattle can be grazed and honey can be collected by bees.[26] Adam of Bremen calls Wollin in Pomerania the largest city in Europe, and exalts it as the central point where all the many different peoples which inhabit the continent, 'both Greek and barbarian', meet.[27]

22. G.A. VAN ES: *Sint Servaes legende in dutschen dichtede dit Heynrijck die van Veldeke was geboren, naar het Leidse handschrift uitgegeven* (Antwerpen etc. 1950) 48, lines 958-965, 972-976.

23. CASSIODORUS: *Variae* 14, 2-3, in Th. MOMMSEN: *Cassiodori senatoris Variae* (= Auctores antiquissimi 12) (= Monumenta Germaniae historica) (Berlin 1894) 343.

24. E. FENSTER: *Laudes Constantinopolitanae* (= Miscellanea Byzantina Monacensia 9) (München 1968) 5-6 (about Menandros), 9 (rules to bring out the centrality of the praised city).

25. GOZWIN OF MAINZ: *Epistola ad Valcherum*, in J.-P. MIGNE: *Patrologia Latina* 143 (Paris 1882) 886-908, cc. 888-889.

26. *Translatio S. Liborii*, ed. G. WAITZ, in *Scriptores* [*in folio*] 4 (= Monumenta Germaniae historica) (Hannover 1841) 150.

27. ADAM OF BREMEN: *Gesta Hammaburgensis ecclesiae pontificum* II, 22, in W. TRILLMICH: *Quellen des 9. und 11. Jahrhunderts zur Geschichte der Hamburgischen Kirche und des Reiches* (= Freiherr vom Stein Gedächtnis Ausgabe. Ausgewählte Quellen zur deutschen Geschichte des Mittelalters 11) (Darmstadt 1978⁵) 252-253.

It was, of course, not easy in Western Europe to exalt a city as the centre of the world, as there existed one holy city which was recognized as the real centre by all, and that was Rome. Some poets were apparently well aware of that. The writer of the life of a ninth-century bishop of Naples, St. Athanasius, royally admitted in his praise of Naples that, although the city was in the noblest region of Europe and was founded by Aeneas, son of Anchises and Venus, it nevertheless took second place after Rome.[28] William FitzStephen, biographer of St. Thomas Becket, is less modest in his praises of London. He assures his readers that the city of London was founded by Brutus, a descendant of the survivors of the siege of Troy, long before Rome was founded by Romulus and Remus.[29] It is very characteristic of medieval writers – and we shall come across it again – to use the argument of antiquity to create a pecking order. Royal families loved to proclaim their descent from ancient heroes or biblical figures. The fact that cities did the same shows that they felt on an equal footing with princes. So both space and time are used to put the city in the very centre of things, to show it as the navel of the world, a first, but important feature of any holy place.

Yet in another hymn on London, dating from the same time, a decidedly more secular note creeps in: *Par la vent la marchandise/de tutes les teres qui sunt/U marcheant cristien vunt.*[30] London is here nothing more than the trading centre of the world, the words of the poem contain no reference to a spiritual ideal. It is the sort of secularity which one expects not before the Renaissance. When Leonardo Bruni praises Florence for its central position at the beginning of the Quattrocento, he makes it look like a political statement about the relation of Florence to the *contado*. The city is in the middle, surrounded by smaller towns, just as the moon is by stars. Inbetween are castles, to which the peasant population can take refuge in time of war, an arrangement which makes for the utmost happiness of all.[31] Florence's central position is not seen by Bruni as a gift of nature, let alone of God, but as the result of sensible decisions made by the city fathers, who themselves create the political conditions in which civic virtues can flourish.

But in this as in so many other things Italy was far ahead of Northern Europe. At the same time that Leonardo Bruni sang the praises of Florence as a civic centre, an anonymous writer gave voice to his love for holy Cologne in the most rapturous tones: *Gaude et letare urbs beata felix Agrippina sanctaque*

28. *Vita S. Athanasii episcopi Neapolitani*, in L.A. MURATORI: *Rerum Italicarum scriptores* 2, 2 (Mediolani 1726) 1051.
29. WILLIAM FITZSTEPHEN: *Vita s. Thomae Cantuariensis archiepiscopi et martyris*, in J. Craige ROBERTSON: *Materials for the history of Thomas Becket* 3 (= Rerum Britannicarum Medii Aevi scriptores [Rolls series] 67) (London 1877) 8: *Urbe Roma, secundum chronicorum fidem, satis antiquior est. Ab eisdem quippe patribus Trojanis haec prius a Bruto condita est, quam illa a Remo et Romulo; unde et adhuc antiquis eisdem utuntur legibus, communibus institutis.*
30. B.H. WIND: *Les fragments du roman de Tristan* (Leiden 1950) 140.
31. LEONARDO BRUNI: *Laudatio Florentinae urbis*, in H. BARON: *From Petrarch to Leonardo Bruni* (Chicago-London 1968) 240.

Colonia [...] *Gloriosa facta sunt in te civitas Dei, civitas mirabilis.*[32] From this city the sun of justice, rays of prudence, love of peace rise. Cologne surpasses every other city in the world in power, wealth, and above all holiness, because after the city had given birth to Christianity, it always remained inviolate.[33] The metaphor is a bit contrived, but it is obvious that the writer is relating the city's sanctity to that of the Virgin Mary of whom the liturgy sings: *Post partum Virgo inviolata permansisti.*

The signs of Cologne's holiness were manifold, but most outstanding was its countless number of churches and monasteries, filled with the relics of martyrs and other saints. Among them St. Peter's cathedral took pride of place, because it contained the gold shrine of the three Magi, the relics of St. Felix, St. Nabor and St. Gregory, St. Peter's stick, the head of St. Sylvester and many others. The most interesting relic may well have been preserved in the Benedictine church of Gross St. Martin; it was the finger with which St. John the Baptist had pointed out Christ. All in all Cologne contained eleven collegiate churches, twenty five monastic churches, twenty parish churches, and over a hundred chapels. And if that summing-up has not convinced the reader, he is encouraged to think of the name 'Colonia', which means *colens omnia*, 'worshipping everything', i.e. to say everything that contributes to the glory of God, the honour of men and the benefit of the community.[34] This fulsome hymn in praise of Cologne is typical; churches, saints and relics figure largely in all *laudes urbium*. The writer of the life of St. Athanasius is an interesting exception to this general tendency. He refuses to describe the buildings and churches of Naples, first of all because he thinks that it is better to see them than to write about them, and also because it is not the buildings which are important but the prayers uttered in them. They keep the city safe and sound.[35]

Some cities took special pride in the fact that their conversion to christianity went back to apostolic times. To be able to trace back the roots of the faith to the preaching of the apostles, to the oldest time of Christianity, constituted, of course, a very strong claim to holiness. Again Naples is an obvious example, because, in fact, there had been a Christian community in the city since apostolic times. But later on this historical fact was wrapped in legend and by the time of Bishop Athanasius in the ninth century it was generally thought that Naples had received the faith from St. Aspren, who was allegedly

---

32. *Laudes Coloniae* in J.F. BOEHMER: *Fontes rerum Germanicarum* 4 (Stuttgart 1868) 463.
33. *Laudes Coloniae* 464: *Si eciam de tua potencia magna quis dubitaret, aspiciat ad te et consideret, qualiter tu civitas regia post tue christiane religionis partum inviolata semper permansisti.* [...] *Postquam enim fidem suscepisti, civitas prenobilis, recidiva non fuisti sed in fide stabilis, propter quod exaltata es et nomen habere meruisti in sigilli tui circumferencia: Sancta Colonia sancte romane ecclesie fidelis filia.* Note that the second sentence (*exaltata es, nomen habere meruisti*) contains a reference to Philippians 2, 9.
34. *Laudes Coloniae* 465-469; 465 (the cathedral), 467 (the Baptist's finger), 468-469 (the name 'Colonia').
35. *Vita S. Athanasii* 1053.

ordained a bishop by St. Peter himself.[36] The claims of other cities were even more spurious. Metz claimed to be converted by St. Clement, a former Roman consul and also a disciple of St. Peter. In the *Gesta episcoporum Mettensium* it is told that he came to Metz in the fifth year of the reign of Claudius, was bishop for twenty five years and died under Vespasian.[37]

The most renowned disciple of the apostles was, of course, St. Dionysius the Areopagite, who was converted by St. Paul in Athens. Medieval legend had it that, later in life, feeling the need to preach the faith, he came to Gaul, and finally suffered martyrdom in Paris on the hill of Montmartre during the reign of Domitian. The legend, fully formulated for the first time by Hilduin, abbot of St. Denis around 830, was based on the identification of the disciple of Paul with a certain Dionysius, first bishop of Paris around 250 and with the anonymous writer of a number of very influential spiritual treatises in Greek around 500.[38] There can be no doubt that this amalgam of fact and fiction must be counted among the most successful of these fabrications, because it not only established Paris as the holy centre and the apostolic source of Christianity in France, but it also provided the Kings of France, who from Carolingian times on were buried in the abbey of St. Denis, with an almost apostolic authority. It is a unique example of a legend in which the claims to holiness of a city and of a royal family supported each other instead of contradicting each other.

Churches and saints, relics and apostolic foundation may have been quite important to establish a city's holiness, but they were empty shells without the living faith of the people who inhabited these holy places. Many poets stress this point. In most *laudes*, and not only the oldest, it is the clergy which is marked for special praise. Anselm of Mainz, in his life of archbishop Adelbert II of Mainz, written about 1140, praises the city of Reims, for its priests: they obey the rule of the Fathers, are full of justice, look after the poor in their flock, and keep to their vows of celibacy.[39] The poet Hugo of Orléans, with perhaps more than a hint of mockery in his voice, also praises Reims, because its schoolmasters waste no time on Plato, Socrates or Priscian, but go straight to the prophets and the sacraments:

Non de falsis argumentis,
Sed de Christi sacramentis.
Non hic artes Marciani,

---

36. *Vita S. Athanasii* 1053.
37. *Gesta episcoporum Mettensium*, ed. G. Waitz, in *Scriptores* [*in folio*] 10 (= Monumenta Germaniae historica) (Hannover 1852) 534-535.
38. Hilduinus: *Passio Sanctissimi Dionysii*, in J.-P. Migne: *Patrologia Latina* 106 (Paris 1864) 23-50.
39. Anselm of Mainz: *Vita Adelberti II Moguntini*, in Ph. Jaffé: *Bibliotheca rerum Germanicarum* 3 (Berlin 1866) 576: *Hic alit et clerum cunctarum copia rerum,/legibus ornatum, quas sanxit regula patrum,/iusticia plenum, pascentem vulgus egenum,/virginei moris vel casti signa pudoris/integra servantem.*

Neque partes Prisciani,
Non hic vana poetarum,
Sed archana prophetarum,
[...]
Non est scola vanitatis,
Sed doctrina veritatis;
Ibi nomen non Socratis,
Sed eterne trinitatis;
Non hic Plato vel Thimeus,
Hic auditur unus Deus;
Nichil est hic nisi sanctum.[40]

The poem shows, and it returns in many other *laudes*, that clergymen and schoolmasters were seen as belonging to the same category: the school belonged to the sacred universe of the Church; if you praised the virtues of one, you included the other. Medieval cities were proud of their schools and liked them to be praised as yet another token of holiness. When Guido of Bazoches wrote a letter to one of his noble pupils to urge him to return to Paris, he exalted the city both for the fact that the seven sisters, the liberal arts, had made it their permanent home, and that it was the source of the three rivers which irrigated the mind. i.e. to say, the historical, allegorical and moral understanding of Scripture.[41]

But what about the ordinary people who lived in the city, the laity? Did they contribute to a city's fame as a holy place? For Italy the answer can be in no doubt. From the early Middle Ages on the life of all the citizens together was seen as an integral part of a city's claim to holiness. That was true for Naples, as we saw, and it is true for Milan, the subject of a hymn written around 740. After the poet has summed up the many saints who are buried in Milan and who defend it ceaselessly in its many battles, he goes on to praise the inhabitants, because they clothe the naked and give plenty of food to the poor and the stranger.[42] In other words their life is in keeping with and, indeed, enhances Milan's reputation as a holy place. What happens when citizens fail to comply with God's commandments, can be seen in an elegy on the fall of Aquileia. This city, once so proud and full of glorious churches, is now a ruin and a swamp, inhabited only by frogs and vipers, because of the sins of its people: *Ob illorum pertinacem fraudem et maliciam/ibi colubres et ranae degent in lacunulis:/sicut deo sunt extorres, sic terreno agmine.*[43] The message from Italy is clear: the city's continued well-being is not only the result of the protection of the saints, and not only the responsibility of the clergy, it is a

40. K. LANGOSCH: *Hymnen und Vagantenlieder* (Darmstadt 1961³) 150.
41. H. ADOLFSSON: *Liber epistolarum Guidonis de Basochis* (= Studia Latina Stockholmiensia 18) (Stockholm 1969) 15.
42. *Versum de Mediolano ciuitate*, in E. DÜMMLER: *Poetae Latini Medii Aevi 1. Poetae Latini aevi Carolini 1* (= Monumenta Germaniae historica) (Berlin 1881) 26.
43. *Versus de Aquileia* in E. DÜMMLER: *Poetae Latini Medii Aevi 2. Poetae Latini aevi Carolini 2* (= Monumenta Germaniae historica) (Berlin 1884) 152.

burden shared by all citizens. The civic tradition never died in this part of Europe.

In the North we must wait much longer before similar themes appear in the *laudes urbium*. One of the earliest indications that life in the city could also be seen as a holy vocation on the other side of the Alps, comes from Germany. Nicholas of Bibera, writer of a hymn in praise of Erfurt around 1280, ended his poem with an original interpretation of Christ's advice to his disciples to remain in the city until the coming of the Holy Ghost (St. Luke 24, 49). He saw it as a clear statement that Christ preferred cities to the country.[44] Curiously enough, the hymn on Cologne, which we discussed earlier on, is another example. Fulsome as the *Laudes Coloniae* may be about the city's ecclesiastical glories, the summing-up of them is preceded by a passage about the holy life of its citizens, clearly showing the writer's pride in his city's freedom: *Civitas libera* [...] *Quod in te est, tui et tuorum filiorum est.* In Cologne one finds good counsel, mutual benevolence, harmony. Its people are devote, benign, peaceful, gentle, humble, sobre, kind, pious, meek, prudent, chaste, beautiful and modest.[45] The writer does make his point but he cannot be called very specific.

If we compare these inarticulate outpourings with Piccolomini's precise description, dating from about the same time, of the virtues of the citizens of Basel, the difference is telling. Piccolomini observes that Basel is not girded with mighty walls, because its citizens are convinced that concord is the real defense of a city. And then he continues with a survey of Basel's constitution, the corner stone of its unity. The city used to be subjected, he says, to the authority of its bishop, but now it is free, although it recognizes the Emperor as its king. He discusses in detail the position of the *burghomaster*, the large council and the small council, the contribution of the guilds (*zumphta*) and he pays special attention to the impartiality of the judges, who neither accept money nor listen to the pleas of mighty friends of the accused. And if necessary they are not afraid to use torture. Finally he says something about Christian life in Basel: the citizens love the faith, respect the clergy, they go to Mass on Sundays and many even on weekdays, and they venerate a large number of saints.[46] Piccolomini knows how a civil society functions and what

---

44. Th. FISCHER: NICOLAI DE BIBERA OCCULTI ERFORDENSIS: *Carmen satiricum*, in *Geschichtsquellen der Provinz Sachsen 1. Erfurter Denkmäler* (Halle 1870) 107-108: *Ecce bonum vere probo quod sit in urbe manere./Quando triumphator mortis nosterque creator/Vellet adire polos et discipulos quasi solos/Consolaretur, dixisse tamen perhibetur/Ore loquens blando: scitis quod ad aethera scando/Ut, quia speratis, promissa patris capiatis./Vos autem lete, si vultis, in urbe sedete,/Donec uti mirtus flagrans altissima virtus/Ignis in ardore vos concremet absque dolore./[...]Ex hiis colligitur et pro certo quasi scitur,/Quod si scivisset, ubi commodius statuisset/Vulgus apostolicum, sibi non servum sed amicum,/Non tam sincere iussisset in urbe sedere./Inde tenere volo, quod ab urbe recedere nolo.*

45. *Laudes Coloniae* 464-465 (quote on 464).

46. ENEA SILVIO PICCOLOMINI: Letter to Cardinal Giulano de Cesarini, July 1434, in R. WACKERNAGEL: *Concilium Basiliense. Studien und Quellen zur Geschichte des Concils von Basel 5* (Basel 1904) 370-372. This letter is different from the one mentioned earlier.

laws and rules are necessary to maintain peace and concord. It is the knowledge of an Italian, used to centuries of uninterrupted civic life. Holiness and peace were not only gifts of God, but the result of constant effort on the part of man, which is an interesting point of view for a future pope.

It is often assumed that in the Middle Ages holiness was something that was inextricably bound up with priests and monks, that ordinary people were at the receiving end of long lines of communication and could only share in the gifts of heaven through the mediation of the ordained clergy. I hope to have shown in this contribution that this is not entirely true. From the early Middle Ages on a constant tradition asserted that city communities could radiate holiness just as much as monastic communities. It is also true, on the other hand, that in the North of Europe such holiness was largely seen as the result of the amazing concentration of saints, relics and churches, which was possible only in a city. Italy, however, preserved the more ancient ideal that an organized community of ordinary lay people, living together in peace and concord, was, in fact, just as much a sign of God's presence in the world as a professional religious establishment. And it was probably from these cities *ultra montes* that Northern Europe learnt to appreciate civic life as a way to God.

Herman Wegman has always been concerned to show that the Church's life consists of much more than the enactment of arcane rites by a privileged élite.He might recognize some of his ideals in this ninth-century evocation of Christian life in, of all places, the city of Naples:

Here the clergy and the laity worship God, praying together in Greek and Latin, and together they perform the offices. Here the poor do not extort money by going round disguised as pilgrims, but they receive everything which they might possibly want, in the place where they live; in this city the rich, following the Lord's commandment, are more likely to go around looking for poor Lazaruses to give them plenty of money, than that the poor rob the rich of their wealth.[47]

47. *Vita S. Athanasii* 1054.

The role of the people in the liturgy according to the synodal statutes of the ancient dioceses of Cambrai, Liège and Utrecht (c. 1300-c. 1500)[1]

CHARLES CASPERS

1. INTRODUCTION

In the past decades the importance of synodal statutes as a source for Church and religious history was underlined in many studies. This interest is due to two things, which corroborate each other. The first is the increasing interest in subjects from religious history like 'popular religion', which we see especially after 1970; the second is that new editions of sources and repertories made the synodal statutes better accessible.[2]

Naturally the revaluation of the old statutes has resulted in studies which are mainly relying on these sources. Usually these studies deal with one of the many subjects about which the statutes give information, such as: legislation in relation to marriage, pastoral theology, trade, tithe, costumes.[3] Occasionally a scholar deals with almost every subject for which the synodal statutes provide information, as Paul Adam did in his book on parochial life in fourteenth-century France.[4] The subject of this contribution is, more or less, similar to one of those aspects which Adam has dealt with under the heading: *L'organisation de la vie religieuse. Devoirs des fidèles.*[5]

---

1. This contribution was translated by Karin van Tongeren-Kemme.
2. Important editions are e.g. F.M. POWICKE and C.R. CHENEY: *Councils and synods with other documents relating to the English Church* 2. *1205-1313* (Oxford 1964) 2 vols.; Odette PONTAL: *Les statuts synodaux français du XIIIe siècle* 1. *Les statuts de Paris et le synodal de l'Ouest* (Paris 1971) and 2. *Les statuts de 1230 à 1260* (Paris 1983); Joseph AVRIL: *Les statuts synodaux français du XIIIe siècle* 3. *Les statuts synodaux angevins de la seconde moitié du XIIIe siècle* (Paris 1988). A useful repertory is André ARTONNE, Louis GUIZARD and Odette PONTAL: *Répertoire des statuts synodaux des diocèses de l'ancienne France du XIIIe à la fin du XVIIIe siècle* (Paris 1969²).
3. See e.g.: E. DIEBOLD: L'application en France du canon 51 du IVe concile de Latran d'après les anciens statuts synodaux, in *L'année canonique* 2 (1953) 187-195; Cécile PIVETEAU: *La pratique matrimoniale en France d'après les statuts synodaux (du Concile de Trente à la Révolution)* (Paris 1957); Raymonde FOREVILLE: Les statuts synodaux et le renouveau pastorale du XIIIe siècle dans le Midi de la France, in *Cahiers de Fanjeaux* 6 (1971) 119-150; B. JACQUELINE: Les foires et marchés dans les statuts synodaux des diocèses normands, in *Revue historique de droit français et étranger* 53 (1975) 268-277; Ch. RENARDY: Synodes, juridiction de la paix et cessions de dîmes aux églises (XIe-XIVe siècles), in *Moyen Age* 31 (1975) 245-264; Georg RETZLAFF: Die äussere Erscheinung des Geistlichen im Alltag. Eine Untersuchung zur Frage des 'habitus clericalis' im Spiegel synodaler Entscheidungen von 398 bis 1565, in *Internationale kirchliche Zeitschrift* 69 (1979) 46-57, 88-115, 129-208.
4. Paul ADAM: *La vie paroissiale en France au XIVe siècle* (= Histoire et sociologie de l'église 3) (Paris 1964).
5. ADAM: *Vie paroissiale* 100-112.

The history of the synodal statutes begins in the sixth century, when bishops began to feel the need to maintain through synods contacts with their priests, who often lived far away. In the Carolingian era the synods were held frequently. Their main goal was to give instructions to the priests for their discharge of office and moral life. The late medieval synods had the same objective. The written instructions of these synods are called the synodal statutes. During the tenth and the eleventh centuries the synods were of rare occurrence in contrast with the so-called provincial councils. However, just after the Gregorian reform the diocesan synods began to flourish again. An enormous religious activity was going on in the Western Church in the twelfth and the thirteenth centuries. Because of this the number of priests increased steadily and the Church authorities had to provide better pastoral schooling for the clergy.[6] This responsibility, together with a fundamental theological reflection on the administration of the sacraments in such a way that we can speak of a *révolution pastorale*, was taken up by the Fourth Lateran Council (1215).[7] This Council determined that diocesan synods had to gather once or twice a year and contribute – more than they had done before – to the education of the clergy. The diocesan synods had to pass on relevant decrees of general councils and important papal resolutions (which we find for a large part in the *Corpus iuris canonici*) to the local clergy and through them also to the laity in the diocese.[8] Later on the resolutions of 1215 were supplemented by a regulation of the Council of Basle (1431-1443): the synodal and provincial statutes had to be read out at every synod.[9]

During the fourteenth and fifteenth centuries, the period which will be considered in this contribution, the synods became more and more occupied with matters of Church-politics, especially disputes between the ecclesiastical and the secular courts of law. The education of the clergy in pastoral care and the administration of the sacraments fell behind.[10] The periodicity of the synods declined, despite the council regulations mentioned before. This is why no continuous series of yearly statutes has been preserved in any medieval diocese, including Cambrai, Liège and Utrecht. On the contrary, the number of years in which no statutes were formulated, is generally a multitude of that in which it has been done. The resolutions of the Council of Trent (1545-1563)

6. Joseph AVRIL: L'évolution du synode diocésain, principalement dans la France du Nord, du Xe au XIIe siècle, in Peter LINEHAN: *Proceedings of the Seventh International Congress of Medieval Canon Law, Cambridge, 23-27 July 1984* (= Monumenta iuris canonici, series C, subsidia 8) (Città del Vaticano 1988) 305-325; Odette PONTAL: *Les statuts synodaux* (= Typologie des sources du Moyen Age occidental 11) (Turnhout 1975) 18-19 and 39.

7. FOREVILLE: Renouveau pastoral 120.

8. See Charles-Joseph HEFELE: *Histoire des conciles d'après les documents originaux* 5, 2 (Paris 1913²) 1334-1335 (the sixth canon of the Fourth Lateran Council).

9. R. NAZ: Synode, in *Dictionnaire de droit canonique* 7 (Paris 1965) 1134-1140, c. 1136.

10. PONTAL: *Statuts synodaux* 50-51; cf. A.L. MAYER: Der Wandel des Kirchenbildes in der abendländischen Kulturgeschichte, in *Liturgie und Mönchtum* 17 (1955) 50-64 and Willibald M. PLÖCHL: *Geschichte des Kirchenrechts* 2. *Das Kirchenrecht der abendländischen Christenheit 1055 bis 1517* (Wien-München 1962) 144-145.

again caused a revival of the synods as a means to carry through the Tridentine reforms.[11] But these reforms also ensured that many of the tasks which originally were performed by the synods were taken over by other Church institutions.

Because many subjects could be brought up at the synods, their statutes vary quite often as a consequence. Some important characteristics of late medieval synodal statutes may be given here:[12]

- The statutes had force of law. The bishop or his *vicarius* laid down the text of the statutes during the synod. Those who were present had to guarantee that the statutes would be observed immediately.
- Although the statutes are canonical writings, they are important for practical theology, especially because they contain regulations on the administration of the sacraments.
- In his decisions, the bishop made a compromise between general Church doctrine and local morals and circumstances in his diocese. The statutes became more and more a vade-mecum for the parish clergy, because these practical measures were something in between *rituale* and catechism. In every presbytery a copy of the synodal statutes of the diocese to which it belonged had to be kept.
- The foregoing characteristics are the more important when one considers that there were no seminaries nor any other form of structured pastoral education. The statutes were the only handguide for canon law which the parish clergy had.

During the *révolution pastorale* many bishops began to feel the need to arrange the synodal statutes within manageable codifications in order to help their subordinates. Besides the old regulations, which sometimes date back to the Carolingian era, the eleventh and twelfth-century decrees of provincial councils and the twelfth-century statutes of the Cistercians have had a great influence on the contents of the synodal statutes.[13] The model for a codification of synodal statutes was provided by the Eudes de Sully, bishop of Paris (1196-1208), in the early part of the thirteenth century. His statutes were largely adopted by the Fourth Lateran Council (1215). They were the foundation for nearly all synodal codifications after this Council.[14]

Despite their being tributary to the Parisian statutes, the thirteenth-century statutes of other dioceses, the distant as well as the nearby dioceses, have something that is vital and original. The statutes of Eudes underwent great or

11. See note 9 above.
12. PONTAL: *Statuts synodaux* 31-32.
13. PONTAL: *Statuts synodaux* 40.
14. PONTAL: *Les statuts synodaux français du XIIIe siècle* 1, lxxvii; and recently Joseph AVRIL: Naissance et évolution des législations synodales dans les diocèses du Nord et de l'Ouest de la France (1200-1250), in *Zeitschrift der Savigny-Stiftung für Rechtsgeschichte* 103 Kanonistische Abteilung 72 (1986) 152-249, pp. 163-167.

small alterations in every diocese. Precisely those *moderationes* and *additiones* show how much attention the bishops paid to the religious life of the ordinary people.[15]

In the period with which we are concerned here the statutes lost their originality more and more. Just like the synods of which they are the record, they show increasingly less of the development of Church life within a diocese and seem to have got bogged down in regulations of a Church-political nature.[16]

In what follows I will first give a survey of the participation of the laity in public worship in the later Middle Ages. The following aspects will be dealt with successively: public holy days, the sacraments (with the exception of ordination) and religious education. I will use 'participation' in the sense in which it is used in the synodal statutes of medieval dioceses, including those of Cambrai, Liège and Utrecht: the intended (minimal and generally present) devotion. The real participation, in all its wealth and variety, is not considered in this contribution; to get a picture of these, additional sources would have to come in.[17]

My second main objective is to give an answer to two questions: What kind of changes can be noticed in the intended participation of the laity according to the statutes between 1300-1500? And: What differences can be observed in the contents of the statutes of the three most extended dioceses of the Netherlands, Cambrai, Liège and Utrecht, with other dioceses and among these three? Only working to find an answer to these questions, it is possible to give an evaluation and to arrive at conclusions. It is especially essential to deal with the second question in order to find out if there was ever question of situations or endeavours concerning the role of the people that were specific to the Netherlands.

In case the statutes make clear that 'the history of the one diocese is the same as that of the other', the results presented in this contribution would be rather irrelevant. Beforehand, it may be said that the synodal statutes of the ancient dioceses of the Low Countries indeed harmonize in broad outline with for instance those of French dioceses. In the survey which follows I will regularly refer to the ancient Parisian statutes of Eudes de Sully and to Paul Adam's *conspectus* of parochial life in fourteenth-century France, which I mentioned earlier, which is based especially on synodal statutes. It may look as if the relevance of this contribution is marginal, and in a way it is. But the 'margins' are interesting enough to offer this sequel to the reader.

---

15. Pontal: *Statuts synodaux* 32; cf. Joseph Avril: Les 'Precepta synodalia' de Roger de Cambrai, in *Bulletin of medieval canon law* 2 (1972) 7-15, pp. 9-10.
16. Cf. note 10 above.
17. Cf. Henri Platelle: Les origines, le Moyen Age, in Pierre Pierrard (ed.): *Histoire des diocèses de Cambrai et Lille* (Paris 1978) 9-93, p. 54; J. Laenen: *Kerkelijk en godsdienstig Brabant vanaf het begin der IVe tot in de XVIe eeuw of voorgeschiedenis van het aartsbisdom Mechelen* 2 (Antwerpen 1936) 167.

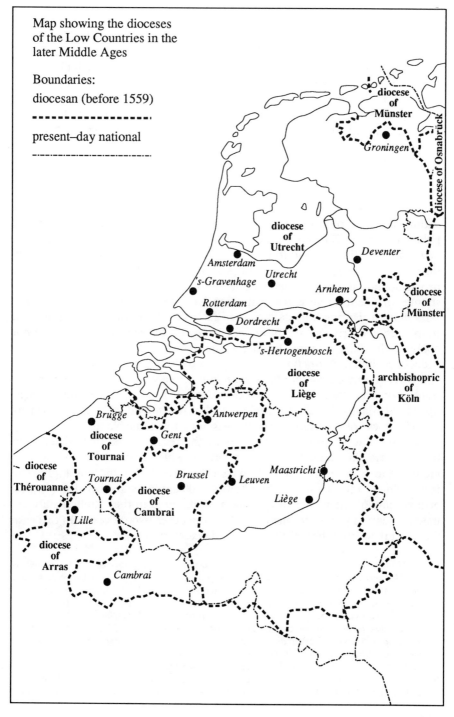

Map showing the dioceses
of the Low Countries in the
later Middle Ages

Boundaries:

diocesan (before 1559)

▪▪▪▪▪▪▪▪▪▪▪▪▪▪▪▪▪▪▪▪▪

present–day national

▪▪▪▪▪▪▪▪▪▪▪▪▪▪▪▪▪▪▪▪▪

diocese
of
Münster

Groningen

diocese of Osnabrück

diocese
of
Utrecht

Deventer

Amsterdam

Utrecht

'␣s-Gravenhage

Arnhem

diocese
of
Münster

Rotterdam

Dordrecht

'␣s-Hertogenbosch

diocese
of
Liège

archbishopric
of
Köln

Brugge

Antwerpen

diocese
of
Tournai

Gent

diocese
of
Thérouanne

Tournai

Brussel

Leuven

Maastricht

diocese
of
Cambrai

Liège

Lille

diocese
of
Arras

Cambrai

2. SURVEY

First I have to say something about the order in which the synodal statutes are treated. I start with those of Cambrai; Liège and Utrecht follow. The reason for this is the interdependance of these statutes. They are all directly or indirectly tributary to the ancient statutes of Eudes de Sully. Moreover, the statutes of Cambrai and Liège are strongly influenced by older Cambrai statutes from the thirteenth century. In their turn the statutes of Liège have influenced the statutes of Utrecht directly or through decisions made by Church-meetings in Cologne.

Whenever the contents of the late medieval statutes of the three dioceses are mentioned in this contribution I will usually refer to the most recent edition.[18]

2.1. Sundays and public holy days
During the period we deal with, one of the main tasks for every Christian within the Western Church was to 'keep holy' the numerous Sundays and public holy days. The synodal statutes of every diocese are very explicit about how this sanctification had to be expressed. They are all in the negative: each time that they enumerate the holy days of obligation, they also decree that the people are not allowed manual labour (*opus servile*) during those days. In the statutes of Cambrai an extra distinction is made between *festa maiora* and *festa minora*. During holy days of the first grade the faithful are not allowed 'to plough and drive a cart' (*arare et carrucare*), but this prohibition did not apply to the *festa minora*. From the statutes of Liège and Utrecht can be deduced a similar distinction. Unlike those of Cambrai the statutes of Liège and Utrecht only enumerate the *festa maiora*. Regarding the *festa minora* the statutes of Liège remark that the celebration of other, not specifically mentioned holy days is left to the religious zeal of the individual layman. The person who does not celebrate one of these is not going to be blamed.[19]

For easy comparison I give the lists of the feasts of the three dioceses in tabular form, in which * indicates a day on which manual labour was forbidden, and + a *festum minus* to which this prohibition did not apply. The feasts added to the list in Cambrai before 1500 are indicated between ( ). The orthography of the names of the days is that found in the Cambrai statutes, unless a feast is proper to one or both of the other two dioceses. In this case they are taken from the statutes of these dioceses.[20]

18. For Cambrai E. REUSENS: Statuta antiquissima dioecesis Cameracensis ad fidem codicis Mechliniensis, in *Analectes pour servir à l'histoire ecclésiastique de la Belgique* 2e section *Série des cartulaires et des documents étendus* 6 (1903) i-xii, 1-116; for Liège E. SCHOOLMEESTERS: *Les statuts synodaux de Jean de Flandre, évêque de Liège, 16 février 1288* (Liège 1908); for Utrecht J.G.C. JOOSTING and S. MULLER: *Bronnen voor de geschiedenis der kerkelijke rechtspraak in het bisdom Utrecht in de Middeleeuwen* 5, 4de afdeeling *Provinciale en synodale statuten* (= Werken der Vereeniging tot Uitgaaf der Bronnen van het Oud-Vaderlandsche Recht, tweede reeks 16) ('s-Gravenhage 1914).
19. SCHOOLMEESTERS: *Statuts synodaux de Jean de Flandre* 45-46.
20. Cambrai: *Statuta synodalia Cameracensia*, Tilburg Theological Faculty ms. 15.1 [contains a codification of 1307 (ff. 1ʳ-28ʳ) and later *additiones*] ff. 16ʳ-16ᵛ and 29ᵛ; REUSENS: Statuta

	Cambrai 1307	Liège 1288	Utrecht 1346
Every Sunday	*	*	*
Parasceve	*	-	-
Pascha	*	*	*
Feria secunda in Pascha	*	*	*
Feria tertia in Pascha	+	*	*
Feria quarta in Pascha	+	*	*
Ascensio Domini	*	*	*
Penthecostes	*	*	*
Feria secunda in Penthecostes	*	*	*
Feria tertia in Penthecostes	+	*	*
Feria quarta in Penthecostes	+	*	*
Dies sanctissimi sacramentis altaris	*	*	*
Dies trinitatis[21]	*	*	*
January			
1 Circumcisio Domini	*	*	*
6 Epiphania Domini	*	*	*
14 Poncianus	-	-	*
21 Agneta	-	-	*
25 Conversio S. Pauli	+	*	*
February			
2 Purificacio B. Marie	*	*	*
22 Cathedra S. Petri	+	*	*
24 Mathias	+	*	*
March			
17 Gheertrudis	-	-	*
25 Annunciacio	*	*	*
April			
25 Marcus	+	-	-
May			
1 Philippus et Jacobus	*	*	*
3 Invencio S. Crucis	*	*	*
12 Pancracius	-	-	*

antiquissima 38-40; Liège: SCHOOLMEESTERS: *Statuts synodaux de Jean de Flandre* 45-46; Utrecht: JOOSTING and MULLER: *Bronnen* 113-114 (1346), 116 (1347), 120 (1347), 156-157 (1525); cf. Bonaventura KRUITWAGEN: Studiemateriaal (Heiligen geografie) voor den middeleeuwschen kalender van het bisdom Utrecht, in Bonaventura KRUITWAGEN: *Laat-middeleeuwsche paleografica, paleotypica, liturgica, kalendalia, grammaticalia* ('s-Gravenhage 1942) 153-224, pp. 176-183. For a complete synopsis of the calendars of Arras, Tournai, Cambrai, Köln (Cologne), Liège, Münster, Reims, Thérouanne, Trier (Trèves) and Utrecht, see I. STRUBBE and L. VOET: *De chronologie van de Middeleeuwen en de moderne tijden in de Nederlanden* (Antwerpen-Amsterdam 1960) 155-197.

21. In Liège and Utrecht the feast of the Trinity was celebrated on the same Sunday as in Cologne: the second Sunday after Pentecost. In Cambrai, however, it was celebrated on the first Sunday after Pentecost. Cf. Pl. LEFÈVRE: Un problème de chronologie liégeoise au XIIIe siècle. La date primitive de la Fête-Dieu, in *Revue d'histoire ecclésiastique* 42 (1947) 417-422; Pl. LEFÈVRE: *L'ordinaire de la collégiale autrefois cathédrale de Tongres, d'après un ms. du XVe siècle* 2. Le sanctoral (= Spicilegium sacrum Lovaniense 35) (Louvain 1968) 572-573 (Particularités de la célébration de la fête de la Trinité à Liège au XVe siècle).

161

13	*Servacius*	-	-	*
June				
5	*Bonifacius*	-	-	*
12	*Odulphus*	-	-	*
24	*Nativitas B. Ioannis*			
	Baptiste	*	*	*
25	*Translacio Lebuini*	-	-	*
29	*Passio Petri et Pauli*	*	*	*
July				
2	*Visitacio B. Marie*	(*)	-	-[22]
4	*Translacio Martini*	-	-	*
22	*Magdalena*	*	*	*
25	*Jacobus et*			
	Christophorus	*	*	*
August				
1	*Petrus ad vincula*	+	*	*
10	*Laurencius*	*	*	*
15	*Assumpcio B. Marie*	*	*	*
24	*Bartholomeus*	*	*	*
29	*Decollacio Iohannis*			
	Baptiste	+	-	*
September				
8	*Nativitas B. Marie*	*	*	*
14	*Exaltacio S. Crucis*	*	-	*
17	*Lambertus*	-	*	*
21	*Matheus*	*	*	*
22	*Mauricius*	-	-	*
29	*Michael*	*	*	*
October				
1	*Remigius*	-	-	*
9	*Dionysius*	-	*	*
10	*Victor*	-	-	*
18	*Lucas*	+	-	*
28	*Simon et Juda*	*	*	*
November				
1	*Dies omnium sanctorum*	*	*	*
2	*Commemoracio animarum*	-	-	*
3	*Hubertus*	-	*	-
7	*Willibrordus*	-	-	*
11	*Martinus*	*	*	*
12	*Lebuinus*	-	-	*
25	*Catharina*	(*)	*	*
30	*Andreas*	*	*	*
December				
6	*Nicolas*	*	*	*
8	*Dies conceptionis*			
	B. Marie Virginis	(*)	-	*
14	*Nicasius et socii*	+	-	-

22. Later added to the list in Utrecht.

21	Thomas	*	*	*
25	Nativitas Domini	*	*	*
26	Stephanus	*	*	*
27	Johannes evangelista	*	*	*
28	Dies SS. innocentium	+	*	*
	Dies patroni ecclesie	*	*	*
	Dies dedicacionis ecclesie	*	*	*

The total numbers for the three dioceses are revealing: Cambrai had, apart from the Sundays, only 34 to 37 holy days on which manual labour was forbidden, Liège had 44 and Utrecht no less than 62![23]

2.2. Baptism

From the special attention given to lay baptism in the statutes of the three dioceses (as in those of the neighbouring dioceses and in the ancient statutes of Paris), it is clear that this sacrament was to be administered as soon as possible after birth. In this way the risk that the new born baby should miss eternal salvation when passing away was made minimal.[24]

In Cambrai the priests had to teach the men and women in their parishes the baptismal formula in the vernacular. In case an emergency would occur they would be able to baptize a child: *P. ou N. Je te baptize au nom du père et du fil et du saint esprit amen*, and water was to be poured three times over the baby's head. When the child received lay baptism from the father or mother, the married couple did not have the duty or right to end the relationship because of the affinity which was the result of the baptism performed. The fourteenth-century statutes of most dioceses, also of those of the Low Countries, decreed that women who died in childbirth were not to be denied a Church funeral because *poenam non debemus ei vertere in culpam*. This regulation is absent in the ancient Parisian statutes, but occurs already in the statutes of Cambrai from the early thirteenth century. An important task is preserved for the godmothers and the godfathers. Four people, two men and two women for every child, was the maximum allowed in Cambrai. But the parents could enlarge this number to eight by chosing secular priests as extra godfathers. The godfathers and godmothers had to teach the growing child the *Pater noster* (*oratio dominica*), the *Credo* the way it was said in Sunday's Mass, and the *Ave Maria*.[25]

---

23. We arrive at these numbers when we distract from the total number of feast days those which fall upon a Sunday. If we take into account that approximately one seventh of the saints' days will also fall upon a Sunday we get the following numbers: Cambrai 30 to 33; Liège 39; Utrecht 54 to 55.

24. ADAM: *Vie paroissiale* 104; PONTAL: *Statuts synodaux* 54-56.

25. *Statuta synodalia Cameracensia* ff. 1ᵛ-2ʳ and 33ʳ; REUSENS: Statuta antiquissima 2-5; PONTAL: *Les statuts synodaux français du XIIIe siècle* 1, 54-59; P.C. BOEREN: Les plus anciens statuts du diocèse de Cambrai (XIIIe siècle), in *Revue de droit canonique* 3 (1953) 1-32, 131-172, 377-415; 4 (1954) 131-158, esp. 3 (1953) 133 (c. 1240).

Concerning the godparents the statutes of Liège differ from those of Cambrai; as in the regulations of Eudes de Sully, there is a maximum of three godparents for each child. In the statutes of Liège and Lisieux this is specified: for a boy one godmother and two godfathers, for a girl one godfather and two godmothers. In the diocese of Liège parents and godparents both have the task to teach the children the *Pater noster*, *Credo in Deum* and *Ave Maria* and to guide them on the right path of life ([...] *et exhortentur eos sepe pie et juste vivere*).[26] In the statutes of Utrecht of A.D. 1293 the same is stated about the number (three) of godparents as in the statutes of Eudes. In 1310 it is specified the way it had been done in Liège more than 22 years earlier. It is curious that here we find no mention of catechetical tasks for the godparents, the more since the statutes of Utrecht pay more attention to catechesis than it receives in the statutes of Cambrai and Liège.[27]

2.3. Confirmation

The synodal statutes of the Western Church show very differing opinions about the time at which the sacrament of confirmation ought to be administered. In the statutes of Eudes the parents are advised not to wait after baptism until the bishop comes. Eudes wants them to bring their children to him as quickly as possible for the administration of confirmation, as soon as they have heard where he abides. He also points out to the parents that they can still change the name of their child at confirmation.[28]

The statutes of Cambrai of 1307 and those of Liège of 1288, following the thirteenth-century Cambrai statutes, have very different views on this sacrament. According to these the priests have to encourage their parishioners to bring all children from seven years onwards to the bishop. The children must of course have been baptized and not have received confirmation yet. Beforehand the child's hair must be cut so that the forehead is clear and a bandage has to be wrapped around his head. Those who bring the children before the bishop should be sure that they had not received confirmation already. Three days after the administration of the sacrament the parents have to bring the children to the parish church, where the priest washes their foreheads and solemnly burns the bandages. There is an addition in later Cambrai statutes, which reads that the parents must prepare the children for this sacrament; the young people have to learn by heart the *Pater noster*, *Ave Maria* and *Credo*, and they have to say these texts twice a day, in the morning and in the evening.[29]

26. PONTAL: *Les statuts synodaux français du XIIIe siècle* 1, 56; SCHOOLMEESTERS: *Statuts synodaux de Jean de Flandre* 4-5; ADAM: *Vie paroissiale* 104.
27. PONTAL: *Les statuts synodaux français du XIIIe siècle* 1, 56; JOOSTING and MULLER: *Bronnen* 61, 73-74. For catechesis see paragraph 2.8 of this contribution.
28. PONTAL: *Les statuts synodaux français du XIIIe siècle* 1, 56.
29. *Statuta synodalia Cameracensia* fol. 2vo (1307) and 33vo; REUSENS: Statuta antiquissima 5-6; BOEREN: Plus anciens statuts (1953) 134 (c. 1240); cf. Bruno KLEINHEYER: *Sakramentliche Feiern* 1. *Die Feiern der Eingliederung in die Kirche* (= Gottesdienst der Kirche. Handbuch der Liturgiewissenschaft 7, 1) (Regensburg 1989) 205-209, p. 209.

The statutes of Liège have other additions. Children who are already capable to sin (*doli capaces*), for instance because they are older than twelve years of age, have to go to their parish priest for confession before they can receive confirmation. Another addition says that the children learn that the bishop may change their name at confirmation. Moreover, the priests of the diocese of Liège have to warn their parishioners that among those who are directly involved in the administration of this sacrament, a spiritual relationship (affinity) will arise, comparable to the one which comes into being at baptism between godparents and the baptized child. Later on this relationship might impede marriage and could invalidate a solemnized marriage.[30]

The statutes of Utrecht of 1310 are brief and archaic concerning confirmation: 'the priests have to inform their parishioners that at confirmation, which is – after Baptism – administered by the bishop on the forehead of the children, a kind of relationship may arise like at baptism, which not only may be an impediment to marriage but even may invalidate a solemnized marriage'. Also in the following centuries confirmation would be administered soon after baptism in the diocese of Utrecht.[31]

2.4. Confession

As regards confession the statutes of Cambrai, Liège and Utrecht are all built on those of Eudes.[32] In these model statutes it is determined, among other things, that the priests have to encourage their parishioners not to commit any mortal sin again, so that God will relieve the sinner's heart. When a priest finds out that a person coming to confession does not have good intentions, he is allowed neither to give the absolution nor a penance but only exhortations.[33] The confessor must attune the penance to the character of the sinner and to the nature of the sin. That the privacy of the sinner is taken into account in the statutes is clear from the heavy penalties a priest may incur if he violates the seal of confession. In later statutes of the three large dioceses of the Netherlands, especially in those of Liège, the circumstances in which the sin was committed are taken into account more than Eudes did. Moreover, it is dilated upon that the nature of the penance must be in agreement with the sin: abstinence for unchastity, meditations and prayers for spiritual sins and restitution for theft.[34] In the statutes of each diocese complete lists are given of sins which are so grave that they must be confessed to the bishop or his representative. In the Utrecht statutes from 1293 it is even determined that the priests have to tell to the church-goers in the vernacular which sins fall under

---

30. SCHOOLMEESTERS: *Statuts synodaux de Jean de Flandre* 5-7.
31. JOOSTING and MULLER: *Bronnen* 74; cf. J. WENNER: Geistliche Verwandtschaft, in *Lexikon für Theologie und Kirche* 4 (Freiburg 1960 = 1986ʳ) 628.
32. PONTAL: *Les statuts synodaux français du XIIIe siècle* 1, 62-64.
33. It is interesting to note that the statutes of Cambrai (1308) even require *contritio*: *Statuta synodalia Cameracensia* f. 28ʳ; REUSENS: Statuta antiquissima 5, additio.
34. REUSENS: Statuta antiquissima 4-5, 6-8; SCHOOLMEESTERS: *Statuts synodaux de Jean de Flandre* 7-14.

this category of 'reserved' sins.[35] In contrast with nearly all synodal statutes of the fourteenth and fifteenth centuries the statutes of Eudes lack regulations about the obligatory yearly confession and therefore of course also about the time of the year when this has to be done. The Fourth Lateran Council, which was held some years after Eudes had drawn up his statutes, gave much attention to the yearly confession and the related paschal Communion.[36] In the French dioceses people generally had to confess *ab anno discretionis* (in Bourges the age of eight years and in Avignon the age of fourteen).[37]

In Cambrai everybody older than fourteen has to go to confession at least once a year in Lent. The same is true for Liège, but there the period was limited to the weeks from the feast of *Purificatio beate Marie* to Palm Sunday.[38] In the statutes of Utrecht there are neither explicit references about confession before Easter, nor is any age mentioned. Still, it can be taken for granted that the situation was not really different from that of Cambrai and Liège; had not the Fourth Lateran Council decreed that everyone had to confess his sins every year and receive Communion *in Pascha*? It is for certain that in Utrecht they strongly believed in an obligatory and yearly confession. In a statute from 1310 the clergy is dictated to keep an account of the parishioners which are not at least once a year coming to confession.[39]

2.5. Eucharist

In relation to 'the sacrament of all sacraments' there are not many regulations in which something about the participation of the laity is visible. Naturally, the obligatory yearly Communion is mentioned – an important subject during the Fourth Lateran Council, as was already said in the last paragraph – which is not yet to be found in the statutes of Eudes.[40] In the Cambrai statutes it was assumed that everybody received Holy Communion at Easter, but also on other high days many communicants were expected. As soon as children possessed the *discretio fidei* (at the age of approximately ten years) they were allowed to receive Communion in this diocese.[41]

In the diocesis of Liège the situation was not any different. The faithful were assumed to receive Communion not only at Easter but also on other high

35. JOOSTING and MULLER: *Bronnen* 67.
36. HEFELE: *Histoire des conciles* 5, 2, 1349-1351 (canon 21).
37. ADAM: *Vie paroissiale* 107.
38. REUSENS: Statuta antiquissima 4; SCHOOLMEESTERS: *Statuts synodaux de Jean de Flandre* 11.
39. JOOSTING and MULLER: *Bronnen* 76.
40. See note 36 above.
41. *Statuta synodalia Cameracensia* ff. 5ʳ-8ʳ (*De eucharistia*), f. 7ʳ: *Pueri autem non communi-centur, nisi antequam fidei discretionem habere dignoscuntur ut circiter circa decimum annum.* [...] *Inhibemus ne aliquis sacerdos bis in die missam celebrare presumat, nisi in magna necessitate et urgenti, videlicet in diebus pasche, penthecostis, omnium sanctorum, quibus solet copiosa multitudo fidelium communicari*; REUSENS: Statuta antiquissima 10-16, pp. 14-15. Cf. Peter BROWE: *Die Pflichtkommunion im Mittelalter* (Münster i. W. 1940) 129-184.

days.[42] In the statutes of some French dioceses Christmas and Corpus Christi are also mentioned as suitable days to communicate.[43]

About the people's conduct during Mass we can only deduce something from a casual remark. Indirectly it becomes clear from Cambrai statutes that it must have been a very important moment for the faithful to look at the Elevated Host.[44] For the rest all activities during Mass seem to have been reserved to the clergy. The laity and especially the women (sometimes more clearly referred to as Beguines) are not allowed to approach the altar or to assist during worship.[45]

However, one part of the chapter on the Eucharist in the statutes of the dioceses of Cambrai and Liège gives the laity a notable and active role, viz. to assist the priest in bringing the *viaticum* to a sick person. In the statutes of Eudes this role is a rather modest one: the people are to be warned that when the *Corpus Domini* (*viaticum*) is carried past them, they have to kneel at once before their Lord and Creator and join their hands in prayer until the *viaticum* has passed.[46]

In the Cambrai statutes a lot is added to this, in imitation of the thirteenth-century statutes of Guiard de Laon, bishop of Cambrai from 1238 until 1248. Before the priest brings the *viaticum* to someone ill, he has to ring the bell, so that the faithful may come to the church; subsequently they all have to accompany the priest to the sick person and back to the church again. Meanwhile they must pray for the patient. While the sick person receives Communion, the faithful wait outside. On his way back to the church, the priest, again, has to carry a consecrated host, *ne populus in redeundo nihil adoret*. The faithful who do not accompany this 'small procession' but see it pass, have to kneel, beat themselves on the chest and pray with bent head and

---

42. SCHOOLMEESTERS: *Statuts synodaux de Jean de Flandre* 14-21 (*De sacramento*), p. 20: *Pueri autem non communicentur antequam discretionem fidei dinoscantur habere ut circiter decennium. Item, precipimus ut in die Pasche et ceteris sollempnitatibus quibus fideles communicantur, tot hostie consecrentur, ut non oporteat frangi formas quando fideles communicantur.*

43. ADAM: *Vie paroissiale* 110.

44. REUSENS: Statuta antiquissima 12; this is a repetition of an older statute (c. 1240): BOEREN: Plus anciens statuts (1953) 141 (*Sacerdos non elevet hostiam ad videndum populo, nisi postquam dixerit haec verba: hoc est enim corpus meum. Et tunc pulsetur magna campana tribus vicibus ex una parte, ut fideles qui audierint, ubicumque fuerint adorent*); cf. PONTAL: *Les statuts synodaux français du XIIIe siècle* 1, 82; cf. H. WEGMAN: De witte hostie, in R.E.V. STUIP and C. VELLEKOOP (eds.): *Licht en donker in de Middeleeuwen* (= Utrechtse bijdragen tot de mediëvistiek 9) (Utrecht 1989) 107-120.

45. REUSENS: Statuta antiquissima 89 (1325) with an interesting note: *On lit en marge: 'Contrarium communiter fit in hospitali Herentalensi et in beginagio ibidem, ubi communiter vel hospitalisse vel beghine ministrant altari'*. Cf. W. HARTMANN: Neue Texte zur bischöflichen Reformgesetzgebung aus den Jahren 829/831. Vier Diözesansynoden Halitgars von Cambrai, in *Deutsches Archiv für Erforschung des Mittelalters* 55 (1979) 368-394, p. 384. For Beguines see Andrea POLONY: Synodale Gesetzgebung in der Kirchenprovinz Mainz, dargestellt an der Beginenfrage, in *Rottenburger Jahrbuch für Kirchengeschichte* 5 (1986) 33-51.

46. PONTAL: *Les statuts synodaux français du XIIIe siècle* 1, 58-60.

joined hands; horsemen have to dismount, 'so that they can worship Him, who descended from heaven for them'. Also the sick person is given attention to. He ought to have confessed already during an earlier visit of the priest. If he is not capable to eat the *viaticum* because he has to throw up all the time, he does not necessarily have to communicate; he may believe safely that he has communicated spiritually. Before the priest gives the Communion to the sick person, he asks him whether he believes that in the Host is present the body of Christ who was born of the Virgin, suffered upon the Cross and was raised on the third day. Only after he confessed his faith the sick person will receive Communion.[47]

The statutes of Liège contain (in altered order) the same regulations which date back to Guiard de Laon. But they do add that the faithful who accompany the priest on his way to the sick person and back to the church again may earn an indulgence of five days.[48]

The Utrecht statutes on the *viaticum* are very short and meagre in contrast with those of Cambrai and Liège in this respect. In Utrecht the priests only have to remind the people that when somebody falls ill, he quickly has to send for a priest in order that the sick person may confess and receive the sacraments.[49] Usually other Western European statutes say more about the *viaticum* than the Utrecht statutes but (seldom or) never as much as those of Cambrai and Liège do.[50]

2.6. Marriage

The statutes of the three dioceses contain several regulations on marriage, partly in imitation of the statutes of Eudes and the regulations of the Fourth Lateran Council. Much accent was put on the three announcements (the 'banns') that were to precede the actual marriage and on the many impediments to marriage.[51] Every diocese had its peculiarities concerning this sacrament, as in Utrecht, where a regulation stated that you were not allowed to marry from the first Sunday of Advent until the octave of Epiphany, from *Septuagesima* until the octave of Easter and from the Sunday preceding Ascension day until Trinity Sunday.[52] Probably the late medieval statutes show most development in the chapters which deal with marriage. However, in this contribution it is not necessary to go into this matter any further, be-

---

47. REUSENS: Statuta antiquissima 13-14 (1307); BOEREN: Plus anciens statuts (1953) 143-144.
48. SCHOOLMEESTERS: *Statuts synodaux de Jean de Flandre* 19.
49. JOOSTING and MULLER: *Bronnen* 62 (1293) and 82 (1310).
50. ADAM: *Vie paroissiale* 110; cf. Peter BROWE: Die Sterbekommunion im Altertum und Mittelalter, in *Zeitschrift für katholische Theologie* 60 (1936) 1-54, 211-240; Joseph AVRIL: La pastorale des malades et des mourants aux XIIe et XIIIe siècles, in Herman BRAET and Werner VERBEKE (eds.): *Death in the middle ages* (= Mediaevalia Lovaniensia, series 1, studia 9) (Louvain 1983) 88-106.
51. ADAM: *Vie paroissiale* 111-112; PONTAL: *Les statuts synodaux français du XIIIe siècle* 1, 66-68; REUSENS: Statuta antiquissima 16-20; SCHOOLMEESTERS: *Statuts synodaux de Jean de Flandre* 28-31.
52. JOOSTING and MULLER: *Bronnen* 91-92 (1310).

cause all these regulations refer to matters of canonical law rather than to worship.[53]

2.7. Extreme unction

In the statutes of Eudes it is decreed that priests have to administer extreme unction to the poor and to the rich, the young and the old, with appropriate respect. It is stated emphatically that the faithful do not have to pay for the administration of this sacrament. The priests have to inform the people that extreme unction can be repeated as soon as another situation of danger of life occurs, from the age of fourteen onwards.[54]

The Cambrai regulations are more detailed. The sense-organs, through which the sick person (from the age of fourteen or older) has sinned, and which are to be anointed, are enumerated: the eyes, the ears, the nose, the mouth, the hands and the feet (and later also the breast). The less well off are not allowed to refuse this sacrament out of a false feeling of shame on the poor excuse that they do not have enough candles or linen. The threefold value of this sacrament was summarized in the following verse:

Ungor in extremis ut fiat gratia maior.
Et mortis [read morbus] levior.
Et mea culpa minor.

The sick person had to confess before receiving extreme unction. Therefore it was administered when the priest brought the *viaticum* or during his previous visit to the sick person.[55]

Although the regulations of Liège are somewhat shorter than those of Cambrai, the contents are similar.[56] These regulations are missing in the Utrecht statutes, but they do discuss the question from what age the faithful ought to receive extreme unction. The answer to this question was: [...] *quod doli capax vel pubertati proximus potest inungi, ex quo peccare potest.* Also in this case, it is likely that the age of fourteen is meant or possibly a somewhat younger age when by *doli capax* is understood the age of twelve, as it was in Liège.[57]

---

53. For literature see DIEBOLD: L'application, and PIVETEAU: *La pratique matrimoniale,* cited in note 2 above; P. BANGE and A.G. WEILER: De problematiek van het clandestiene huwelijk in het middeleeuwse bisdom Utrecht, in D.E.H. DE BOER and J.W. MARSILJE (eds.): *De Nederlanden in de late Middeleeuwen* (Utrecht 1987) 393-409; A.G. WEILER: De ontwikkeling van de middeleeuwse kerkelijke rechtspraak in het bisdom Utrecht inzake excommunicatie belopen vanwege clandestiene huwelijken, tot aan het Concilie van Trente, in *Archief voor de geschiedenis van de Katholieke Kerk in Nederland* 29 (1987) 149-165.
54. PONTAL: *Les statuts synodaux français du XIIIe siècle* 1, 68-70.
55. *Statuta synodalia Cameracensia* ff. 9ʳ-10ʳ (*De extrema unctione*); REUSENS: Statuta antiquissima 21-22.
56. SCHOOLMEESTERS: *Statuts synodaux de Jean de Flandre* 23-24.
57. JOOSTING and MULLER: *Bronnen* 117, 121 (1347); SCHOOLMEESTERS: *Statuts synodaux de Jean de Flandre* 6.

2.8. Religious education

Catechesis does not concern the participation of the laity in worship directly, but it may shed some light on the issue as to what extent the people were educated and equipped to understand the prayer of the Church and able to take part in it. In the statutes of Cambrai and Liège catechesis is only very summarily mentioned as being a task for parents and especially for godparents,[58] not, however, for parish priests. From the French statutes, with the exception of those of Carcasonne, we also learn that generally religious instruction was not a task prescribed to priests. Adam presumes that in this the bishops will have depended on the Friars Minor, because they considered them more capable than the 'ordinary' priests to pass on the most important religious instruction to the people.[59]

It is all the more remarkable that precisely the Utrecht statutes deal, relatively speaking, extensively with catechesis, and this already before the fourteenth century, and that they also see a clear task for the priests in religious education. Every Sunday the priests have to explain the *Pater noster* and the *Credo* to their parishioners in such a way that they can understand it and in the vernacular. Every month, or at least three or four times a year, the same is expected for the ten commandments and the seven sacraments. After this regulation the ten commandments are named one by one in the statutes. Then follows an enumeration of the five sacraments which are necessary for everyone, and the two optional sacraments. The first five are necessary because a human being cannot gain salvation when he renounces these wilfully.[60] In later statutes these regulations are repeated almost literally, with a remarkable variant; the tenth commandment now runs: *Diliges proximum tuum sicut te ipsum.*[61]

3. REMARKS

3.1. Important changes between 1300 and 1500

The late medieval synodal statutes of Cambrai and Liège differ fundamentally from the older regulations of Eudes and of the Fourth Lateran Council when they discuss from what age the faithful are allowed to receive certain sacraments. It is Utrecht which follows the old guidelines. In some matters, however, such as the regulations on confession (and marriage), Utrecht shows the

---

58. See for this paragraphs 2.2 and 2.3 above.
59. ADAM: *Vie paroissiale* 90.
60. JOOSTING and MULLER: *Bronnen* 72 (1294); the ten commandments are presented in a shortened version, based literally on Exodus 20: *Non habebis deos alienos. / Non assumes nomen Dei tui in vanum. / Memento ut diem sabbati sanctifices. / Honora patrem tuum et matrem tuam. / Non occides. / Non mechaberis. / Non furtum facies. / Non loqueris contra proximum tuum falsum testimonium. / Non concupisces domum proximi tui nec desiderabis uxorem proximi tui etc.*
61. JOOSTING and MULLER: *Bronnen* 78-79 (1310). The first eight commandments are the same as in 1294; the ninth commandment is: *Non concupisces rem proximi tui.*

same development as the other two; as regards education the Utrecht statutes are developed further. Let us again consider the ages at which people could receive the 'five necessary sacraments', in the order of the course of life, according to the statutes of Cambrai and Liège: baptism, as soon as possible after birth, confirmation from seven years, the Eucharist from the age of ten, confession and extreme unction from fourteen years onwards. Five sacraments in four phases. The meaning of this phasing, which did not exist before the later Middle Ages, can hardly be overestimated. I think that two things can be concluded from it.

First, the administration and the reception of the sacraments was not just something mechanical for the clergy or for the laity. The faithful were only eligible for the sacraments – with the exception of baptism – when they were mentally capable and willing. The terms *doli capax* and *annus discretionis* clearly allude to this, just like the many regulations on confession for adults, for example the rule that no absolution was to be given when the sinner in question did not show sincere remorse. The phasing in the administration of the sacraments and the ever more detailed elaborations in this respect clearly show how much the layman was emancipated in the eyes of the clergy. Every faithful has his own mental development, has his own responsibility; every layman has to be judged differently, according to his temperament and circumstances. These observations imply that the layman's role in the liturgy – although proportionally small – differs essentially from that in the period before c. 1200. His contribution acquires a status which is different from that in the past, because from now on the layman is taken seriously by the Church. The picture of the administration of the sacraments, adapted as it was to the course of life, fits in with the image which we know from the literature on the emancipation of the laity and the increased pastoral solicitude of the Church after the high Middle Ages (the *révolution pastorale*). What is so extraordinary, however, about the facts here discussed, is that they express, hidden in large codifications and many *additiones*, but nevertheless very clearly, the new status of the layman. Possibly better than long tracts on confession and preaching, they illustrate the qualitative change in the participation of the laity in the liturgy, a change which a theologian on the edge of the 21st century has to evaluate positively.

At first sight, such a positive judgement (which I am driving at here) seems to be a contradiction of what has been said about the administration of the sacraments in the introduction of this contribution. In the later Middle Ages this subject was given rather less attention at synods and in statutes, in favour of matters which were formulated disadvantageously for the laity. From the end of the thirteenth century the synodal statutes were full of threats with excommunications and interdicts in order to safeguard the privileges of the clergy. So much that the Dutch Church historian Post remarks in his masterpiece on the history of the Church in the Netherlands in the Middle Ages:

A consultation on the privileges of the clergy and maybe a renunciation of possessions and rights, which were too extensive, should perhaps have been more effective than these punishments which undermined the service of the Church itself. These regulations reveal a spirit hostile to the laity. It is as if the clergy and the laity were opposed to each other as parties.[62]

Still, a clear hostility to (or rather fear for) the laity from the part of the clergy does not have to be in contradiction with the fact that the people were taken seriously by this group in (and outside) the liturgy. On the contrary! From the constant defending of the rights and privileges of the Church against the laity, and the continuous threatening with the *anathema*, it is clear that the clergy became aware that they had to deal with a group of people who became more and more emancipated. To take the faithful seriously and to assist them in obtaining eternal salvation on the one hand and to threaten them, once emancipated, with the *anathema* on the other hand, were in fact two sides of the same coin.

The fact that the regulations which were hostile towards the laity increased in the course of time indicates, moreover, that the social developments went simply too fast for the Church. The growing impotence of the Church to anticipate the changes may be clearly seen when we compare the writings of the popes with which Western Christianity entered the thirteenth with those with whom it began the fourteenth century. The optimism and friendliness of Innocentius III towards the laity contrast sharply with the gloominess and hostility of Bonifatius VIII.[63] The diocesan legislation of this period – on which both popes have had great influence – shows the same change to a negative atmosphere. This depressive mood reached rock bottom in the late fifteenth-century statutes of Henricus de Berghes, bishop of Cambrai (1480-1502), who fought for the preservation of the typical clerical identity. His regulations show a caricature: a clergy without any *élan*; a bishop who quixotically tries to keep the priests of his diocese together. But these priests do not listen to him, their bishop, because they prefer to follow the 'modern' trends set by the laity.[64] Small wonder that the Church authorities of a specific

---

62. R.R. Post: *Kerkgeschiedenis van Nederland in de Middeleeuwen* 1 (Utrecht-Antwerpen 1957) 183-193 (synods of Liège and Utrecht until c. 1340) p. 187. For the synodal statutes of Utrecht see also pp. 253-258 (until c. 1378) and the same author's: *Kerkgeschiedenis van Nederland in de Middeleeuwen* 2 (Utrecht-Antwerpen 1957) 37-38 (until 1529); 273-275 (until 1549) and *Kerkelijke verhoudingen in Nederland vóór de Reformatie van ± 1500 tot ± 1580* (Utrecht-Antwerpen 1954) 18-34.

63. For a characterization of Innocentius' attitude, see e.g. the 27th canon of the Fourth Lateran Council (Hefele: *Histoire des conciles* 5, 2, 1356); for Bonifatius see his bull *Clericis laicos infestos oppido tradit antiquitas* (Ae. L. Richter and Ae. Friedberg: *Corpus Iuris Canonici* 2. *Decretalium collectiones* (Leipzig 1881) 1062-1063). Cf. Post: *Kerkgeschiedenis van Nederland* 1, 187.

64. E.g. *Statuta synodalia Cameracensia*, Tilburg Theological Faculty ms. 15.2 (statutes of Henricus de Berghes, formulated between 1481 and 1500) ff. 76ᵛ-77ʳ (statute of 1495): *Quia multos sacerdotes et clericos abiectis vestibus proprio congruentibus ordini, alias inhonestas et laicis convenientes passim videmus assumere et in publicum deferre taliter que se habere*

diocese seldom realized that the extreme use of the *anathema* was, in itself, conflicting with the salvation-mediating task which the Church had actually laid down for itself.[65] If we review what has been said about this first conclusion, we can maintain the positive judgement on the qualitative change in the participation of the laity, but we must qualify this statement by remarking that the Church can claim no credit for this change; it was rather forced upon this institution by the situation.

A second conclusion which can be drawn from the phasing of the administration of the sacraments has a connection with the first. We just saw that the Church did not consider adults to be children (anymore), but also the reverse was true: they did not consider a child to be a small-scale adult any longer. These are also two sides of one coin, because when adults are looked upon as children, a distinction between these two is less relevant. Only far too often, usually following Ariès, it is maintained that this distinction has never, or hardly ever, existed in the Middle Ages.[66] From the literature we get the impression that it was only after the Council of Trent (1545-1563) that the Roman-Catholic Church, following the churches of the Reformation, began

quod in habitu et in incessu inter eosdem et laycos nulla aut pauca notetur differentia. Nam vestes suas appertas et super spatulas reversas et sine colleriis, Sotularesque largos instar cussinorum. In quibus nulla pedum forma illicitur, Aut illorum loco alia calciamenta inhonesta nimis pantouffles appellata crines longos comatos et desuper bireta reserva, manicas fissas et cornettas sericas non colla eorum sed potius humeros tegentes et in modum circuli cum modo alligatas nequaquam verentur deportare unde magna iam dudum in clero est nata et in dies nascitur derisio et petulantia. For a characterization of Henricus de Berghes, see L. JADIN: Berghes (Henri de), in *Dictionnaire d'histoire et de géographie ecclésiastiques* 8 (Paris 1935) 464-466. For the absurd relation between Henricus and his canons, see Carolus DU PLESSIS D'ARGENTRÉ: *Collectio judiciorum de novis erroribus, qui ab initio duodecimi seculi post Incarnationem Verbi, usque ad annum 1632 in Ecclesia proscripti sunt et notati* 1 (Lutetiae Parisiorum: apud Andream Cailleau 1728) 343-345 (*Imprecationes Capituli Cameracensis factae contra suum Episcopum, et responsiones Parisiensis Facultatis Theologiae ad quaestiones ex eis deductas*); Henri PLATELLE: Crises et nouveaux départs (1313-1529), in Louis TRENARD (ed.): *Histoire de Cambrai* (= Histoire des villes du Nord/Pas-de-Calais 2) (Lille 1982) 89-104, p. 104 and Claude FOURET: Cambrai en folie (XIVe-XVIe siècle), in *Revue du Nord* 69 (1987) no. 274, 483-502, p. 487.

65. In the statutes of Cambrai of 1349 we find a rare example which shows that sometimes the problem was recognized: *Quia pena excommunicationis late sententie, que apponitur in multis statutis synodalibus Cameracensibus, periculosa nimium animabus esse dinoscitur [...] ideo Nos, volentes huiusmodi periculis obviare, dictam penam excommunicationis [late] sententie de dictis statutis detrahimus et ammovemus, statutis ipsis quantum ad alia duraturis.* (REUSENS: Statuta antiquissima 106-107). A similar example I found in the fourteenth century statutes of Barcelona, J.N. HILLGARTH and Giulio SILANO: A compilation of the diocesan synods of Barcelona (1354). Critical edition and analysis, in *Mediaeval studies* 46 (1984) 78-157, pp. 85-86.

66. Philippe ARIÈS: *Centuries of childhood. A social history of family life* (New York 1965) (originally: *L'enfant et la vie familiale sous l'Ancien Régime* (Paris 1960)). Cf. Edward SHORTER: *The making of the modern family* (New York 1975); Lawrence STONE: *The family, sex and marriage in England, 1500-1800* (London 1977); Jean-Louis FLANDRIN: *Families, parenté, maison, sexualité dans l'ancienne société* (Paris 1984); D. ELSCHENBROICH: *Kinder werden nicht geboren. Studien zur Entstehung der Kindheit* (Frankfurt a. M. 1977).

to recognize the different stages of maturation of the faithful. We get such an image when we compare only the regulations of the important councils, for example Lateran IV and Trent, and ignore the fact that general councils normally confirm practices which existed in many places long before. The phasing of the administration of the sacraments was effective, in any case, centuries before 1563![67] Therefore it can be stated that the statutes of Cambrai and Liège (and to a lesser degree those of Utrecht as well), and those of many other dioceses, bring down a central thesis of Ariès. According to this author a child who had reached the age of seven was considered a small adult in Western Europe before 1600. From the moment when he was seven no special status was assigned any longer to a child and he had to come up to the standards which applied to adults.[68] Should the child ever have been considered as a small adult, then the important change in this image dates from (the end of) the thirteenth century. The objection could be made that the Church might have been a trendsetter in this particular development, and that possibly large ranks of society continued to consider the child as a small adult. But this objection can easily be brushed aside. For the statutes also require a contribution from the parents, which would have been possible only when this group had a view on the child which more or less corresponded to that of the Church.

3.2. An important difference between the statutes of the dioceses of the Low Countries and those of other Western European dioceses

The previous survey, and also the present state of research in general, do not allow an overall view on what is specific to the Netherlands as regards the participation of the laity in the liturgy. But one point deserves particular attention here once more: the bringing of the *viaticum* and the active involvement of the faithful in this. As is well known, a new feast had been introduced in Liège in 1246, which later would be extended to the entire Catholic Church: Corpus Christi.[69] The statutes on the *viaticum* make clear that this feast was introduced precisely there, because it fitted in with the religious atmosphere. We can derive from these regulations that the Church leaders in the dioceses of Cambrai and Liège, more than their colleagues elsewhere, tried to encourage the eucharistic piety of the faithful. Furthermore, these statutes support the hypothesis that the processions which were kept ever since the beginning of the fourteenth century with the Sacrament during Corpus Christi

---

67. Richard L. DEMOLEN: Childhood and the sacraments in the sixteenth century, in: *Archiv für Reformationsgeschichte* 66 (1975) 49-71, pp. 56 and 58.
68. DEMOLEN: Childhood 49-50.
69. The most complete work on Corpus Christi with an excellent bibliography still is *Studia eucharistica: DCCi anni a condito festo sanctissimi Corporis Christi*, with a preface by Stephanus AXTERS (Bussum-Antwerpen 1946); for an up to date bibliography see Angelus A. HÄUßLING: Literaturbericht zum Fronleichnamsfest, in *Jahrbuch für Volkskunde* Neue Folge 9 (1986) 228-240 and Angelus A. HÄUßLING: Literaturbericht zum Fronleichnamsfest. Ergänzungen und Nachträge, in *Jahrbuch für Volkskunde* Neue Folge 11 (1988) 243-250.

(or within the octave of this feast) had their precursor in the so-called 'small procession': the priest bringing the viaticum to somebody ill, accompanied by a number of the faithful.[70]

3.3. Internal differences between Cambrai, Liège and Utrecht

From the survey it may be clear that the statutes of Cambrai and Liège correspond well with each another, and that they both sometimes differ considerably from those of Utrecht. Apparently mutual contacts between dioceses were more important than belonging to a particular archbishopric. A first difference between Cambrai and Liège on the one hand and Utrecht on the other is in the regulations on the observance of holy days. It is not surprising that there were differences, because every diocese had a number of its 'own' saints. But the amazing thing about it is the difference in the number of obligatory holy days per diocese. The faithful in the diocese of Utrecht had an average of one working day less per fortnight than the faithful in the diocese of Cambrai.[71] Still, we cannot conclude from this fact only that the northernmost diocese also had a more intensive religious life. On the contrary, many religious authors from the later Middle Ages have pointed out that a surplus of holy days paved the way for a certain inflation through which the pious attention of the faithful weakened.[72] That is why as early as the thirteenth century the bishop of Cambrai, Guiard de Laon, abolished fifteen obligatory holy days in one go, to bring about a purification of religious life.[73] From the many holy days in Utrecht we could draw the conclusion that this diocese lacked a reform-minded bishop like Guiard. Another thing is that holy days, with their ban on physical labour, laid a heavy burden on the economy. Such a fact easily tempts one to see a direct connection between the higher degree of urbanization and the smaller number of *festa maiora* in the Southern Netherlands in comparison with the Northern Netherlands. A statement like this, however, can only be made after a thorough investigation, considering the numerous privileges and special positions which have always existed in the three dioceses.

The second difference between Cambrai and Liège on the one hand and Utrecht on the other had to do with the age from which the faithful received the sacraments. This subject has already been discussed in detail in the previous section. The differences in the way in which in particular confirmation was administered must have been noticed at that time by many people who, after all, were living in neighbouring dioceses. When the Middle Ages are coming to an end no less a person than Erasmus of Rotterdam expresses an unfavourable opinion on the archaic way in which some dioceses still admin-

---

70. Cf. S.J.P. van Dijk and J. Hazelden Walker: *The myth of the aumbry. Notes on medieval reservation practice and eucharistic devotion. With special reference to the findings of Dom Gregory Dix* (London 1957) 79-83.
71. Cf. note 23 above.
72. Post: *Kerkgeschiedenis van Nederland* 2, 58, 293-294.
73. P.C. Boeren: *La vie et les oeuvres de Guiard de Laon, 1170 env.-1248* (La Haye 1956) 66-67.

ister confirmation. The great humanist himself was probably also confirmed at such an early age, that he could not remember the event.[74]

A third difference concerns religious education. The previous remarks give the impression that in Utrecht, with its old-fashioned statutes, the faithful were involved less actively in religious life.The regulations on catechesis, however, which were more differentiated in the northern than in the two southern dioceses, largely take away this impression. In Cambrai and Liège the faithful receive religious instruction as a preparation for the reception of the sacraments. In Utrecht they have it during the Sunday service. In the South the parents and godparents are allotted a more important part of the religious education. In the North the priest has to do more in this field. At first sight the quality of the catechesis in the diocese of Utrecht seems to be the most solid, because it is more differentiated and is taught more often as well. But this impression also seems to be premature: the synodal statutes may have a varied content, but they do not give an indication of everything which happened in the parishes.[75] Therefore we cannot deduce from the sources which are discussed here in which diocese they gave more or better religious instruction; but the fact remains that the parents and godparents in the southern dioceses were structurally more involved in the religious education of their children.[76]

When we review all our remarks again, it seems that the information from the synodal statutes on the participation of the laity in the liturgy, which is presented here, can certainly not be called marginal. The last remarks made clear that there is still more to 'distill' from the statutes about this subject. More research has to be done, and with the aid of other sources in most cases. Besides giving new information, I wanted to illustrate in this contribution how much sources which are not liturgical, but (in this case) canonical, may be relevant for historical liturgy.[77] And I have also tried to work in the opposit direction. Deliberately the term 'historical liturgy' is used here at the end instead of 'liturgical history', to point out that liturgy is not only the object of its own history.[78] May this contribution confirm in the reader the idea that the study of the worship of the past can add substantially to the history of culture and mentality.

74. Franz Jozef KÖTTER: *Die Eucharistielehre in den katholischen Katechismen des 16. Jahrhunderts bis zum Erscheinen des Catechismus Romanus (1566)* (= Reformationsgeschichtliche Studien und Texte 98) (Münster i. W. 1969) 113.
75. Cf. note 55 above.
76. It is a pity that in his studies on catechesis in the Netherlands Troelstra did not pay attention to the different customs in each diocese (A. TROELSTRA: *De toestand der catechese in Nederland gedurende de vóór-reformatorische eeuw* (Groningen 1901) and A. TROELSTRA: *Stof en methode der catechese in Nederland vóór de Reformatie* (Groningen 1903)).
77. Cf. Gabriel LE BRAS: Liturgie et sociologie, in *Mélanges en l'honneur de Monseigneur Michel Andrieu* (= Revue des sciences religieuses, volume hors série) (Strasbourg 1956) 291-304.
78. Cf. S.A. VAN DIJK: Historical liturgy and liturgical history, in *Dominican studies* 2 (1949) 161-182.

Gottesdienst und Gemeinde bei Thomas Müntzer und Martin Luther[1]

JOH. P. BOENDERMAKER

Die Veränderungen im Gottesdienst und vor allem in der Messe waren maßgeblich daran beteiligt, um die Reformation zu einer Volksbewegung zu machen. Natürlich waren diese Entwicklungen im Gottesdienst schon vorbereitet, z.B. im Pronaus und in den Liedern, die man bereits vor der Reformation während der Messe singen konnte. Dennoch müssen die radikalen Veränderungen bei der Konsekration und Kommunion in jener Zeit einen tiefen Eindruck hinterlassen haben. Das Merkwürdige ist, daß Wittenberg hier nicht so wegbereitend war, wie man vielleicht annehmen möchte, sieht man einmal von Karlstadts Versuch im Jahre 1521 ab. Wir werden hierauf noch eingehen.

Bereits seit 1522 gab es an vielen Orten deutschsprachige Messen und dies nicht nur in Sachsen. Man übersetzte aber meist nur die Konsekration ins Deutsche, die dann laut gesprochen oder gesungen wurde. Die Kommunion wurde *sub utraque* gefeiert und man stand nun vor dem Problem, wie man die musikalische Seite neu gestalten sollte.

Bald darauf folgten weitere Schritte: Sehr wichtig wird Straßburg, wo am 16. Februar 1524 (an einem Dienstag!) die erste vollständig in deutscher Sprache gehaltene Messe zelebriert wurde. Diese schnelle Entwicklung ist natürlich auf Martin Bucer zurückzuführen.

An dieser Stelle nun möchte ich auf die Messereform von Thomas Müntzer in Allstedt eingehen, ein wichtiges Kapitel in seiner Biographie, das meistens aber im Schatten seiner anderen Aktivitäten steht. Völlig zu Unrecht, wie wir meinen, denn seine liturgische Arbeit ist nicht nur von hoher Qualität, sodern auch zutiefst in seinem gesamten Glauben und Streben verwurzelt. Das zeigen sowohl seine einleitenden Bemerkungen, als auch der Vollzug der Messe selber. Beide sind uns gut überliefert worden in der Ausgabe von Franz.[2] Eine neuere, ausführlichere Darstellung findet sich bei Koch.[3]

1. MÜNTZER

Wir wollen uns an erster Stelle mit der Rolle des Volkes in Müntzers Messereform beschäftigen. Um diese aber gebührend beurteilen zu können, benötigen

---

1. Übersetzung aus dem Niederländischen von Martin Sander-Gaiser.
2. Günther FRANZ: *Thomas Müntzer: Schriften und Briefe. Kritische Gesamtausgabe* (= Quellen und Forschungen zur Reformationsgeschichte 33) (Gütersloh 1968).
3. Ernst KOCH: Das Sakramentsverständnis Thomas Müntzers, in: Siegfried BRÄUER und Helmar JUNGHANS (Hrsg.): *Der Theologe Thomas Müntzer. Untersuchungen zu seiner Entwicklung und Lehre* (Göttingen 1989) 129-155.

wir zunächst eine Übersicht über Müntzers Gesamtentwurf. Dabei dürfen wir nicht vergessen, daß seine Messereform nur ein Teil seiner gesamten Gottesdienstreform ausmacht. So übersetzte er etwa auch das *officium*, den täglichen Gottesdienst, über den wir ebenfalls später sprechen wollen. Müntzer kam 1523 nach Allstedt und begann Ostern 1523, kurz nach seiner Ankunft mit seinen Reformen. Seine Bemühungen, um die Messe und die täglichen Gottesdienste zu verdeutschen, scheinen einen sehr einfachen Beweggrund gehabt zu haben:

Es wirt sich nicht lenger leiden, das man den Lateinischen worten wil eine kraft zuschreiben, wie die zaubrer thun, und das arme volgk vil ungelarter lassen aus der kirchen gehen dan hyneyn [...][4]

In seiner einleitenden Bemerkung zur Messe sieht man aber auch, daß es ihm jedoch hier noch um viel mehr geht. Er will:

[...] das testament Christi offenbar handeln und deutsch singen und erkleren, uff das die menschen mügen christförmig werden'.[5] Das Sakrament ist für die: 'hungerigen im geist [...] Was sol doch Christus im sacrament bey den menschen thun, do er keine hungerige und lehre sele findet?'[6]

Der verständliche, erfahrbare Text der Liturgie ist auf diese Weise eine Hinleitung zur Kommunion, auf welche die Feier der Messe abzielt.

Dieses 'christförmig' werden, ein wichtiges Thema bei Tauler, ist für Müntzer der Kern des Erlebnisses des Sakramentes. In der Einleitung zur Messe sagt er über die Konsekration, da wo für ihn das Zentrum des Geschehens liegt, daß sie: 'durch die gantze vorsamelte gemein geschicht'.[7]

Es gibt noch immer die Meinung, daß die Einsetzungsworte gemeinsam gesprochen wurden, doch dies trifft den Sachverhalt nicht recht. Das öffentlich in Deutsch singen jener Worte war gewiß nicht neu. Jedoch in Verbindung mit der Kommunion *sub utraque*, ohne die vorhergehende obligatorische Beichte, dazu die völlig in Deutsch gehalten Liturgie, dies alles zusammen war damals sehr radikal.

Doch es fällt auf, wie Müntzer – und hier kommt er merkwürdigerweise in die Nähe Luthers – sich sehr darum sorgt, was die Menschen an Neuem ertragen können. 'Und dis alles doch mit senfftem und gelindem abbrechen' der alten in seinen Augen nutzlosen Zeremonien.[8] So erhält er noch die Elevation, welches ihm etwa Karlstadt noch übel nimmt! Dies ist um so mehr interessant, als hier das Bild von Thomas Müntzer als dem großen, radikalen Messereformer eben nur noch teilweise stimmt. Er ist nur da radikal, wo es seiner Meinung nach notwendig ist, um das Volk zum wahren Sakramenterlebnis zu führen.

---

4. FRANZ: *Müntzer: Schriften* 162.
5. FRANZ: *Müntzer: Schriften* 165.
6. FRANZ: *Müntzer: Schriften* 211-212.
7. FRANZ: *Müntzer: Schriften* 211.
8. FRANZ: *Müntzer: Schriften* 210.

Den Ablauf der Konsekration und Kommunion beschreibt Müntzer sehr genau und alles wird konsequent aus der überlieferten Tradition heraus aufgebaut:

Zum IX. So singet man die form der termung oder des abentessens im tone der prefation, lauts diser wort folgende: 'Einen tag zuvorn, do Jesus wolte leyden, nam er das brot in seine heiligen, wirdigen hende und hub auff seine augen in himmel zur dir, Got, seinem almechtigen vater, sagete dir danck und gesegnete das und brach es und gab es seinen jungern, sagende: "Nemet hin und esset all darvon!" Elevando manu dicit: "Das ist mein leichnam, der vor euch dargegeben wirt." Vertens se minister, accipiens calicem coram vulgo dicit: Desselbigen gleichen, do man gessen hatte, nam er den kelch in seine heiligen, wirdigen hende und sagete dir danck und gsegnete den und gab yn seinen jungern, sagende: "Dis ist der kelch meines blutes, des newen und ewigen testamentes, ein geheim des glaubens, der vor euch und vor viel vorgossen wirt in vortzeyhunge der sunde." Rursus vertens se ad altarem dicit: "So offt und dick yr das thut, solt yr meiner darbey gedencken etc."'

Zum zehenden: Balt nach der elevation singet man im selben thon flux drauff also: 'Darumb last uns alle bitten, wie uns Jesus Christus, der warhafftig son Gottis, hat geleret, sagende: Vater unser, der du bist in himmeln etc.' Und alles volck singet drauff: 'Amen.' Darnach wirt es stille, ein wenig athem zu holen, unter wilcher zeyt der priester der communicanten halben das sacrament teylet und singet: 'Durch alle ewigkeit der ewigkeit.' So antwort das gemein volck: 'Amen.' Der priester wider: 'Der fride des Herrens sey altzeit mit euch.' So antwort das volck: 'Und mit deinem geist.' Bald nach disem, auff das im geheim Gottis der todt und aufferstehung Christi betrachtet werde, dasselbe weitter zu ercleren, singet alles volck das gezeugnis Joannis, des teuffers Christi, zu dreymal: 'O lamb gottes, wilchs du wegnimpst die sunde der welt etc.' Dotzu singt man aus den evangelio Luce XVII: 'Erbarme dich unser!' Und zum letzten: 'Gib uns deinen fride.' Dann Christus ist umb unser sunde willen gestorben und erstanden, auff das er uns wolt rechtfertigen, wilchs er allein thut, und wir mussen sie erleiden. Auff solchen glauben gibt man dann den leuthen das hochwirdigste sacrament unter dem agnus dei, on die beptische heuchlische beicht.[9]

Hier wird deutlich, daß Müntzer alles sehr sachlich aufbaut. Nichts wird dem Geist, der momentanen Inspiration überlassen. Er bleibt, ohne seine Prinzipien zu verraten, absichtlich bei der überlieferten liturgischen Tradition. Er stand ebenfalls vor dem Problem des Konsekrationsgesanges. Hier passte er die Melodie der Präfation an, sodaß der Priester im gleichen Ton weitersingen konnte. Die Noten hierfür schreibt Müntzer vollständig auf.

Beim *hoc est corpus meum* wird corpus mit 'Leichnam' übersetzt, wie Luther dies auch anfänglich tat. Erst später in der Deutschen Messe wird hieraus 'Leib'. Hier finden sich auch die lateinischen Worte: *elevando manu* und in einer Randnotiz: *elevat minister oculos et parat sacrificium!* Das Letztere meint die unmittelbare Vorbereitung der Konsekration, das Erstere eine wirkliche Elevation. Aus den nun folgenden Worten *vertens se minister* wird deutlich, daß die Elevation mit dem Rücken zum Volk gesagt und durchgeführt wurde. Nach den Worten, die über den Kelch gesprochen wurden, wendet sich

---

9. FRANZ: *Müntzer: Schriften* 212.

der Priester wieder zum Altar. Die Handlungsanweisungen sind noch alle in Latein geschrieben, denn sie waren nur für den Priester bestimmt!

Eine Bemerkung zur Haltung des Priesters während der Messe: Es ist wichtig zu wissen, daß dieser, jedenfalls später in Allstedt, sei es mit dem Gesicht oder mit dem Rücken zum Volk, hinter einem Tisch (*mensa*) 'östlich des Altars' stand. Ein großer Eingriff in die Messeordnung, von der wir in einer Visitation 1533 erfahren,[10] der dann auch nach Koch auf Müntzer selber zurückzuführen ist.

Sehr auffällig ist auch das Festhalten an der Elevation der Hostie. Denn wer es wagte dieses Element wegzulassen, der wagte sich an das heran, was für das Volk eigentlich das Zentrum der Messe war. Doch Müntzer wollte, genau wie Luther dem Volk verdeutlichen: Hier wird trotz aller eingreifenden Veränderungen eine Messe zelebriert und nichts anderes!

In den Kelchworten fehlt auch das *mysterium fidei* nicht. Das Vater-unser wird natürlich noch nicht durch das Volk mitgebetet, aber wohl durch ein gemeinsames *Amen* bekräftigt. Danach folgt ein Moment der Stille, wie in der überlieferten Tradition eben nach dem *Libera nos*, wenn der Priester in der Stille weiter betet.

Es gibt eine stattliche Zahl von Antworten, die vom Volk einfach auswendig zu lernen sind. So auch der Friedensgruß, nun also in Deutsch und wichtig als Ersatz für die Absolution, die ja mit der Beichte zusammen weggefallen war. So kann man auch die Betonung des *Agnus Dei* möglicherweise erklären: 'nach solchem Glauben gibt man dann den leuthen das hochwirdigste sacrament!' Daß die Kommunion ausdrücklich im Zeichen des *Agnus Dei* steht, stimmt mit dem überein, was wir vorhin schon erkannt haben: Für Müntzer ist die *conformitas* mit dem leidenden Christus von größter Wichtigkeit. Diese findet ihren Ausdruck in der Messefeier mit dem Höhepunkt der Kommunion in der Gestalt der Menschen, die zu den 'Hungrigen im Geist' gehören.

Die Messe von Thomas Müntzer wurde auch an anderen Orten eingeführt. 1543 wurde sie noch in Braunschweig so gehalten. Wichtig war auch die Einführung in Erfurt, in einer durch Joh. Lang überarbeiteten Version. Hierüber ließ sich Luther in einem Brief an Lang recht positiv aus ('nicht ungefällig'), gleichwohl wir noch sehen werden, daß er über die Verbindung des gregorianischen Gesanges mit der deutschen Sprache noch Zweifel äußerte und natürlich zu jener Zeit (1525) keine positive Meinung über Müntzer hatte.

2. KARLSTADT UND LUTHER

Daß Luther erst so spät eine wirklich deutsche Messe entwickelte, hatte verschiedene Ursachen: Seine Zweifel, ob es sich wohl musikalisch realisieren ließe, oder ob man nicht eine ganz andere Gesangsform entwickeln müßte. Und da gab es noch seine Angst, daß das Wittenberger Beispiel wie ein ehernes Gesetz aufgefaßt werden würde. Das Letztere hielt ihn besonders lange von

---

10. Walter ELLIGER: *Thomas Müntzer. Leben und Werk* (Göttingen 1975) 318.

Versuchen ab. Der Zwickauer Nikolaus Hausmann mußte ihn erst viele Mahle hierzu ermahnen.

Aber es gibt auch eine geschichtliche Ursache: Während Luthers Aufenthaltes auf der Wartburg hatte Karlstadt schon die Gelegenheit ergriffen, um die Messe radikal zu reformieren. Dies alles tat er im Bewußtsein im Sinne Luthers zu handeln. Im Nachhinein geht man davon aus, daß Karlstadt die Schuld dafür trägt, daß auf einmal ein zu großer Zwang die Freiheit des Gewissens belastete. Dies war sicherlich auch Karlstadts Fehler, aber *de facto* nahm er, was die Reformen anging, eine moderate Zwischenstellung ein. Melanchton etwa hatte vielmehr Eile![11] Außerdem gingen die Augustinermönche noch viel weiter: Bei ihnen mußte nicht nur die Elevation, sondern auch die Verehrung der Elemente abgeschafft werden. So etwas forderte Karlstadt nicht. Merkwürdig ist, daß er an einem einzigen Punkt weiter geht als Melanchton und die Augustiner zusammen. Er behauptete, daß *communio sub una* Sünde sei. Dann noch lieber überhaupt keine Kommunion! Allerdings war er weniger ablehnend gegen die private Messe als jene, wenn etwa beabsichtigt wurde, um die Kommunion in beiden Gestalten zu feiern, falls dies in der gemeinschaftlichen Messe noch nicht möglich sein sollte.

Die Messereform war also keine Unternehmung von Karlstadt alleine, sondern es gab wie man sieht doch eine breite Diskussion. Karlstadt meint, daß zuerst über diese Themen gepredigt werden sollte. Melanchton denkt, daß dies bereits hinreichend geschehen ist. Karlstadt fürchtet, nicht zu Unrecht, wie sich später zeigen wird, daß Chaos und Aufruhr in der Bevölkerung entstehen. Darum sollten auch der wittenbergische Hof und der Stadtrat seine Zustimmung geben. Der Kurfürst denkt zunächst nicht daran. Dann aber brechen in der Tat Aufstände aus. Manche Augustinermönche verlassen das Kloster, Studenten demolieren die Stadtkirche und verjagen den Priester vom Altar. Steine werden während der Messe ins Franziskanerkloster geworfen und der Altar wird entfernt! Dies alles geschieht zu Beginn des Jahres 1521. Der Kurfürst reagierte nach seiner Gewohnheit sehr gelassen auf die Ereignisse, aber er verbietet am 19 September jede Veränderung an der Messe.

Dies alles, zusammen mit Aufruhr um ihn herum, muß Karlstadt bewogen haben seine anfänglichen Bedenken fallen zu lassen. Er kündigt zu Neujahr eine 'evangelische' Messe an. Später wird Weihnachten daraus. Nach einem unruhigen Weihnachtsabend, an dem wieder einige Priester bedroht wurden, zelebrierte Karlstadt am Morgen die Messe ohne Priestergewand. Er feierte in lateinischer Sprache und unterließ alles, was nach Meßopfer aussah. Die Konsekration ertönte in Deutsch, es gab keine Elevation und er lud das Volk zur Kommunion in beiderlei Gestalten ein, ohne Beichte, aber guten Mutes:

Ob du gleych nitt hettest gebeycht, Solst du doch frölych inn gütter züversicht, hoffnung, und glauben zügeen, unnd dysses Sacrament empffahen, dann es müss ye war

11. Ronald J. SIDER: *Andreas Bodenstein von Karlstadt. The development of his thought* (= Studies in medieval and Reformation thought 11) (Leiden 1974) 155-156.

seyn, Das der glaub unns allein hailig und gerecht macht.[12]

Es blieb nicht bei diesem einen Mal! Am 1. Januar, am Sonntag danach und an Epiphanias, wurden ebenfalls unter großem Zustrom derartige Messen gehalten. Inzwischen griff Karlstadt auch das Zölibat an und ging selber mit gutem Beispiel voran, indem er den Kurfürsten zu seiner Hochzeit am 19. Januar einlud!

Es wird oft behauptet, daß Karlstadt in dieser Zeit durch die 'Zwickauer Profeten' beeinflusst wurde, die kurz nach Weihnachten in Wittenberg ankamen. Sie betonten die unmittelbare Offenbarung und lehnten die Kindertaufe entschieden ab. Die Wahrheit ist, daß eher Melanchton, als Karlstadt zeitweise ihren Einflüssen unterlag. Karlstadt hatte seine eigenen Ideen!

Der Rat von Wittenberg regelte am 24. Januar die Meßstreitigkeiten, weil es zu viele Meinungsverschiedenheiten gab. Nach der Konsekration in deutscher Sprache, durften die Kommunikanten Brot und Kelch in ihre eigenen Hände nehmen. Alle privaten Messen wurden abgeschafft und die Standbilder wurden aus der Kirche entfernt. Vor allem die letzte Maßnahme schuf ein solches Chaos, daß alle Neuentwicklungen gebremst wurden und der Einfluß von Karlstadt abnahm. Am 2. März 1522 kehrt Luther dann von der Wartburg zurück.

Daß Luther nicht aufgefordert wurde nach Wittenberg zurückzukehren, bestimmt nicht von Seiten der Obrigkeit, wird deutlich an der freimütigen Art und Weise, mit der er seine Rückkehr ankündigt. Der Kurfürst, der ein großer Reliquiensammler war, bekommt von Luther mitgeteilt, daß er in Kürze ein komplettes Kreuz mit Nägeln zugesandt bekäme! In der Tat war die Heimkehr zu seinem Kurfürsten alles andere als (politisch) angenehm. Das ist insofern wichtig, als Luther bei seinen Unternehmungen nicht mehr als Vertreter derjenigen Obrigkeit gesehen werden kann, die lediglich Ruhe und Ordnung wiederherstellen will. In seinen Invocavitpredigten beschwört er die Menge aus der Erneuerung keinen Zwang zu machen und im Namen der Liebe auch mit den 'Schwachen' zu rechnen. Es geht Luther nicht nur um den Glauben, sondern auch um die Liebe:

Also liebe Freunde, das Reich Gottes, das wir sind, steht nicht in der Rede oder in Worten, sondern in der Tätigkeit, das ist in der Tat, in den Werken und in der Übung. Gott will nicht Zuhörer oder Nachreder haben, sodern Nachfolger und über das in dem Glauben durch die Liebe. Daß der Glaube ohne die Liebe ist, ist nicht genugsam, ja ist nicht ein Glaube, sondern ein Schein des Glaubens wie ein angesicht im Spiegel gesehen; ist nicht ein wahrhaftiges Angesicht, sondern nur ein Schein des Angesichts.[13]

Es ging Luther um die Vermeidung jedes Zwanges, der auf's Neue die Gewissen belasten könnte. Wer nicht in der Lage ist die Menschen von innen heraus zu überzeugen, ist dabei seine eigenen Vorschriften, so gut gemeint sie auch sein mögen, zu göttlichen Gesetzen zu erheben. Und das gerade sollte doch überwunden sein. Auch kann jede Ordnung auch wieder zur Unordnung werden.

---

12. SIDER: *Andreas Bodenstein von Karlstadt* 160, Anm. 57.
13. *D. Martin Luthers Werke. Kritische Gesamtausgabe* [Weimarer Ausgabe] 10 III (Weimar 1905) 4.

Karlstadt wird in den Predigten nicht genannt, aber in diversen Briefen läßt Luther sich sehr negativ über ihn aus. Er soll sich vor allem über die Art und Weise geärgert haben, wie er die *communio sub una* für Sünde erklärte. Wenn wir zurücksehen, drehte Luther bestehende Entwicklungen wieder zurück, sogar solche, die schon offiziell bestätigt waren. Die Konsekration wurde wieder in Latein und in aller Stille vollzogen. Die *communio sub utraque* gab es nur, wenn ausdrücklich danach verlangt wurde. Die Beichte wurde wieder eingeführt und man berührte Kelch und Hostie nicht mehr. Was das Latein anging, wußten die meisten doch worum es ging, denn es war nach Luthers Meinung bereits genügend über die Einsetzungsworte gepredigt worden.

Wittenberg war gegenüber anderen Orten ins Hintertreffen geraten. Das blieb so bis 1523, bis der erste echte Vorschlag zu einer Reform der Messe gemacht wird, nachdem wiederholt, vor allem durch Nik. Hausmann aus Zwickau, darauf angedrungen war. Im Ganzen gesehen, ist dies noch keine 'Deutsche Messe', aber es gibt schon einige wesentliche Veränderungen. Daß man sie als eingreifende Veränderungen ansah, wird uns deutlich aus den Stimmen der anderen Parteien.[14] Alles was auch nur nach Opfer roch wurde weggelassen. Luther wollte nur noch die Worte beibehalten, die *pura et sancta sunt.*[15] Die Konsekration wird nur laut gesungen auf die Melodie des Vaterunsers, sodaß jederman es hören konnte. Dennoch räumt Luther auch jetzt noch die Möglichkeit ein, um es auch *silenter vel palam* zu tun. Auch hier wieder: Nichts muß müssen! *In quibus omnibus cavendum, ne legem ex libertate faciamus!*[16] Die Elevation wird ebenfalls beibehalten, aber während des erst jetzt gesungenen *Sanctus* und *Benedictus*:

um der Schwachen willen, die sich vielleicht an so schneller Änderung des fürnehmsten Brauchs in der Messe ärgern möchten.

So lautet es in der deutschen Übersetzung von Speratus. Dasselbe Argument, das wir schon bei Müntzer gefunden haben.

Auf diese Messe (und die spätere Deutsche Messe) sind wir bereits schon in anderen Publikationen eingegangen.[17] Hier soll es nun um die Rolle gehen, die das Volk spielt. Wir sahen bereits, wie Luther auf das einfache Volk Rücksicht nimmt, indem er die Elevation noch beibehält. Das Wesentlichste aber war seine Überzeugung, daß die Feier in der Volkskommunion zum Höhepunkt kommen sollte. Dann aber wurde man gleich mit den Problemen rundum Beichte und Absolution konfrontiert. In der Beschreibung der Messe betont er bereits, daß er aus dem Kanon den Satz *pax domini sit semper vobiscum* entnimmt, *quae est publica quaedam absolutio a peccatis communicantium.*[18] Darum soll dies auch mit dem Gesicht zum Volk hin gesungen werden!

14. *Luthers Werke* [Weimarer Ausgabe] 12 (1891) 199-200.
15. *Luthers Werke* [Weimarer Ausgabe] 12 (1891) 211.
16. *Luthers Werke* [Weimarer Ausgabe] 12 (1891) 214.
17. J.P. BOENDERMAKER: Luthers bemoeienissen met de liturgie, in *Het nodige overbodige. Opgedragen aan W.G. Overbosch ter gelegenheid van zijn 70ste verjaardag* (Kampen 1989) 71-76.
18. *Luthers Werke* [Weimarer Ausgabe] 12 (1891) 213.

Das bedeutet bestimmt nicht, daß nun die Beichte weggefallen ist, obwohl es in der deutschen Übersetzung heißt, daß diese 'nicht gefordert, doch nütz und mit nichten zu verachten' sei. Aber auch das Abendmahl selber wird nicht vom Herrn verlangt, sondern 'einem jeden freigelassen, da er spricht: "Solchs tut, so oft, usw"'. Weder Abendmahl noch Beichte sind heilsnotwendig, sind aber ein Angebot, daß man eifrig annehmen sollte!

Der Zugang zur Kommunion wird wie folgt geregelt: Man muß sich anmelden und sich einmal pro Jahr über sein Glaubensverständnis im Hinblick auf das Abendmahl befragen lassen. Öffentlich begangene Verfehlungen wie Trunkenheit, Spiel, Wucher, Verleumdung oder Ehebruch können den Zugang zur Kommunion verwehren. Wer sich hingegen nur hin und wieder verfehlt, soll nicht weggejagt werden, sondern gerade im Hinblick auf eine Verhaltsänderung durch die Kommunion gestärkt werden. Die Kommunikanten sollen beieinanderstehen und ruhig gesehen werden, sowohl durch diejenigen, die an der Kommunion teilnehmen, als auch durch diejenigen, die dies gerade nicht tun. Denn die Teilnahme an der Kommunion ist eine Angelegenheit des christlichen Bekenntnisses!

Aber auch dies darf kein Gesetz werden, es soll alles in Freiheit und ohne Zwang geschehen, entsprechend 1. Korinther 14, 40: 'Laßt aber alles ehrbar und ordentlich zugehen.' Zum 'Gesetz' ist dies alles auch nicht geworden. Von Luthers Regeln ist nur noch wenig übriggeblieben und vielleicht schon damals nicht viel realisiert worden. Bei der späteren Deutschen Messe hören wir nur noch wenig davon.

Diese Deutsche Messe, jetzt wirklich ganz in deutscher Sprache gehalten, entstand erst 2 Jahre später, im Jahr 1525 und auch nicht als feste 'Form', sondern als gute Möglichkeit.

3. LUTHERS DEUTSCHE MESSE

Für Luthers Ansichten, wie das Volk, die Gemeinde an der Messe teilnehmen könnte, ist seine Einleitung eine wichtige Fundgrube. Es ist merkwürdig, daß er die Gemeinde, das Volk in drei Kategorien unterteilt:

Denn summa, wyr stellen solche ordnunge gar nicht umb der willen, die bereyt Christen sind; denn die bedurffen der dinge keyns, umb wilcher willen man auch nicht lebt, sondern sie leben umb unser willen, die noch nicht Christen sind, das sie uns zu Christen machen; sie haben yhren Gottis dienst ym geyst. Aber umb der willen mus man solche ordnungen haben, die noch Christen sollen werden odder stercker werden. Gleych wie eyn Christen der tauffe, des worts und sacraments nicht darff als eyn Christen, denn er hats schon alles, sondern als eyn sunder. Aller meyst aber geschichts umb der eynfeltigen und des jungen volcks willen, wilchs sol und mus teglich in der schrifft und Gottis wort geubt und erzogen werden [...] umb solcher willen mus man lesen, singen, predigen, schreyben und tichten, und wo es hulfflich und fodderlich dazu were, wolt ich lassen mit allen glocken dazu leutten und mit allen orgeln pfeyffen und alles klingen lassen, was klingen kunde.[19]

19. *Luthers Werke* [Weimarer Ausgabe] 19 (1897) 73.

Man kann diese Einteilung sehr in Frage stellen. Ein wichtiger Hinweis zum Verständnis ist die Tatsache, daß er sich selber zu der zweiten Kategorie zählt. Das ist keine Bescheidenheit, aus Angst vor *superbia*, Hochmut, sondern die erste Kategorie ist eine eschatologische Kategorie: Jetzt noch ist der Mensch immer *iustus*, gerechtfertigt und *peccator*, Sünder zugleich. Der Mensch jetzt lebt im Werden. Es gibt also nur einen graduellen Unterschied, keinen absoluten. Deshalb hofft Luther für die erste und zweite Kategorie auf einen gemeinsamen einfachen Gottesdienst, eine *ecclesiola in ecclesia* (noch nennt er es nicht so), wo man in kleinen Kreisen beieinander kommt und sich vermahnt, nach Matthäus 18, 15 ff. Aber auch hier wird noch nichts konkret, schön wäre es, aber:

[...] wenn man die leute und personen hette [...] Aber ich kan und mag [!] noch nicht eyne solche gemeyne odder versamlunge orden oder anrichten.[20]

Er wollte und konnte nicht und es kam niemals so weit. Zweifellos spielte hier auch Luthers Angst vor unkontrollierbaren 'Grüppchen', in seiner Sprache: 'Rotten und Sekten' eine Rolle. Denn gerade hiermit hatte er genug Elend erlebt. Doch bleibt ihm diese vision vor Augen. Klingt hier vielleicht eine stille Sehnsucht nach seiner Klostergemeinschaft durch, die sich gerade in jenen Tagen auflöste? Über den Gottesdienst im Kloster hatte er noch kurz zuvor (im Perfekt) gesagt:

Denn ym kloster haben wyr Mess gehabt on kasel [Meßgewand], on auff heben [Elevation], schlecht auffs aller eynfeltigst.

Dies sagte er inmitten der hitzigen Diskussion mit den Schwärmern und Karlstadt in seiner Schrift: *Wider die himmlischen Propheten von den Bildern und Sakrament.*[21]

Die Wirklichkeit indes sah anders aus. Weil die Messe, die Liturgie auch ein emotionaler Lernprozeß sein soll, der einem hilft in das Christsein hineinzuwachsen, muß neben der lateinischen Messe von 1523, auch endlich eine Gottesdienstfeier kommen, die dieses Element in sich trägt. In einem einzigen, schönen Satz schreibt er nieder was ihm im Geist vorschwebt. Hat dann die Musik alleine diese Funktion? Das wäre ein Mißverständnis. Kunst und vor allem Musik haben eine eigene dienende Funktion in seiner Vorstellung, was man unschwer an der minutiösen Sorgfalt sehen kann, mit der er, mit Hilfe von u.a. Joh. Walther, die musikalische Seite der Messe entwickelt.

Die Deutsche Messe sollte all dies leisten und weil es nicht die einzige liturgische Möglichkeit war, konnte Luther weit gehen, selbst weiter wie Müntzer 1523! Von außen betrachtet gab es noch nicht so viel Neues zu sehen. Luther läßt auch hier 'die Messegewand, altar, lichter noch bleiben, bis sie alle werden oder uns gefellt zu ändern'. Zum Altar heißt es:

20. *Luthers Werke* [Weimarer Ausgabe] 19 (1897) 75.
21. *Luthers Werke* [Weimarer Ausgabe] 18 (1908) 113.

Aber in der rechten Messe unter eitel Christen [die erste Kategorie?] müsste der Altar nicht so bleiben und der Priester sich immer zum Volck kehren.[22]

Christus hat das nämlich ohne Zweifel auch so getan!

Nach dem *Introitus*-psalm folgt das *Kyrie*, vom *Confiteor* ist nichts zu merken. Nach dem *Collecta*-gebet wird die Epistellesung gesungen mit dem Gesicht zum Volk. Es folgt ein deutsches Lied, wie etwa 'Nun bitten wir den Heiligen Geist'. Dies ist an und für sich nichts Neues, denn dies ist eines der Lieder, die im Mittelalter während der Messe gesungen werden, aber Luther fügt noch Strophen hinzu. Dann kommt das Evangelium *in quinto tono*, bekannt als der *modus laetus*, *delectabilis* oder auch *jubilans*. Luther überarbeitet diese Musik auch für die Einsetzungsworte. Die Predigt geht in diesem Gottesdienst über einen Evangeliumstext. Anstelle des Nicaenum wird durch das Volk das durch Luther 1524 gedichtete 'Wir glauben all an einen Gott' gesungen. Hier wird zum ersten Mal ein Teil des Ordinariums durch ein Lied ersetzt. Auch das *Sanctus* wird ersetzt durch das Lied 'Jesaja, dem Profeten das geschah', wo das 'Heilig' aufgenommen ist in einer großartigen, extatischen Melodie.

Die Präfation ist hinfällig, das ist sicher ein Verlust, aber dennoch verständlich. Luther läßt die letzten Reste des Kanons fallen und setzt an diese Stelle eine Ermunterung zur Kommunion in der Gestalt einer Paraphrasierung des Vater-unsers. Luther erhält den Gebetscharakter und bleibt damit in der Nähe dieses wichtigen Gebetes der Abendmahlsfeier. Außerdem fordert er die Gemeinde zur andächtigen Teilnahme am Sakramentsgeschehen auf:

[...] darynnen uns Christus sein leyb und blut zur vergebung schenckt, ym herzen feste fasset, das yhr gedenckt und danckt der grundlosen liebe, die er uns bewysen hat [...][23]

Luther vermutet, daß es einmal eine derartige Ermahnung gegeben hat, nach der Predigt von der Kanzel herab, und daß daraus später eine öffentliche Beichte geworden ist. Durch diese Anmerkung wird deutlich, daß in dieser Ermahnung, dieser Ermunterung ein Ersatz gesehen wird für die Absolution, die man nicht mehr vor der Kommunion empfangen mußte.

Diese Ermahnung erinnert an spätere Formulierungen, die der Calvinismus, aber auch der süddeutsche und niederländische Lutheranismus entwickelten, eine Mischung aus Katechese und Ermunterung. Bei Luther ist es vor allem der letzte Aspekt der dominiert, auch wenn man ihn nicht ganz vom ersteren loslösen kann. Die Einsetzungsworte (Luther: 'Dermung') folgen unmittelbar. Sie sind nicht mehr aufgenommen im eucharistischen Gebet, wie im heutigen Lutheranismus, der die Kraft der alten eucharistischen Gebete wiederentdeckt hat. Die Elevation wurde ebenfalls von Luther beibehalten.

Direkt hiernach folgt die Kommunion. Luther bietet die Möglichkeit an, um nach den Worten über das Brot, dieses auszuteilen und danach erst die Worte über den Wein zu sprechen und den Kelch zu reichen. Auch dies wurde kein weit verbreiteter Brauch.

22. *Luthers Werke* [Weimarer Ausgabe] 19 (1897) 80.
23. *Luthers Werke* [Weimarer Ausgabe] 19 (1897) 96.

Auffällig ist auch, daß das *Sanctus*-lied als Kommunionsgesang aufgefaßt wird. Dazu bietet Luther als Kommunionsgesang das 'Gott sei gelobet und gebenedeit' an, ein vorreformatorisches Lied, daß aus dem *Lauda Sion* entstanden ist und hier als *Benedictus* verwendet werden kann, obwohl dies nicht ausdrücklich gesagt wird. Das letzte Lied, das er in diesem Zusammenhang nennt ist 'Johann Hussens Lied Jesus Christus unser Heiland' oder das deutsche *Agnus Dei*. Das Gebet nach der Kommunion ist kurz:

Wyr dancken dir, almechtiger herr gott, das du uns durch dise heylsame gabe hast erquicket und bitten deyne barmhertzigkeit, das du uns solchs gedeyhen lassest zu starckem glauben gegen dir und zu brinstiger liebe unter uns allen, umb Jesus Christus unsers herrn willen. Amen.[24]

Dann folgt der aronitische Segen.

Es bleiben ein paar Fragen. Wie lange dauerte die Feier und wie reagierten die Menschen darauf? Es ist jedoch deutlich, daß so viel wie möglich versucht wurde, das ungebildete Volk, das wohl einfache Lieder lernen konnte oder bereits kannte, in den Ablauf des Gottesdienstes zu integrieren, um es zu einer Gemeinde zu machen. Es ist schwierig, dies alles mit den Augen von damals zu beurteilen. In jedem Fall müssen wir uns bewußt machen, das hier für das Gefühl der Menschen keine neue Messeform geschaffen wurde sondern, daß man trotz aller Veränderungen eine Hohe Messe feierte. Es wurde keine 'wittenbergische Liturgie' entworfen, sondern die römische Liturgie wurde weiterentwickelt und angepasst.

Der Einfluß der Deutschen Messe war groß, aber sie wurde nicht zum Allgemeingut. Ganz nach Luthers Absicht, der wahrscheinlich selber verhinderte, daß der damalige Kurfürst die Deutsche Messe für die alleinige Messeform erklärte. Er war nun Nachfolger von Friedrich dem Weisen, der im Jahr 1525 verstarb, und ein eifriger Förderer der Reformation war. Trotzdem: Drei Drucke, die von der Messe in Wittenberg erschienen und auch die sieben anderen Ausgaben im Land zeigen das Interesse hin, das man an dem hatte, was nun endlich auch in Wittenberg entstanden war.

4. DIE TÄGLICHEN GOTTESDIENSTE

Es ist verständlich, daß vor allem die Reform der Messe in der Reformation Aufmerksamkeit erregt hat. Hierüber gibt es auch das meiste historische Material. Für die Reformatoren waren aber die täglichen Stundengottesdienste genau so wichtig. Denn diese boten vielmehr Möglichkeiten, um sich mit der heiligen Schrift vertraut zu machen. Sowohl Müntzer als auch Luther haben darüber ausführlich gesprochen und versucht aus dem, was in den Klöstern und Schulen praktiziert wurde, eine Sache des ganzen Volkes zu machen. Die täglichen Messen wurden abgeschafft, falls nicht die Kommunikanten danach verlangten (Luther noch 1523!) oder gerade ein Feiertag oder ein Tag

24. *Luthers Werke* [Weimarer Ausgabe] 19 (1897) 102.

der Heiligen war. Die Anzahl der Heiligenfeiertage wurde zwar sehr begrenzt, aber Luther behielt noch alle Mariafeiertage bei, weil sie für ihn christologische Feiertage waren. (Wie sehr er Maria weiterhin verehrte, wird u.a. deutlich in seinem Kommentar auf das *Magnificat*.)

Thomas Müntzer überarbeitete die Mette und Vespergottesdienste für das Volk in deutsche, gregorianische Gesänge. Das Meiste wurde durch Schüler (auch Mädchen!) gesungen, aber das Volk sang neben den schon bekannten Hymnen auch liturgische Teile mit.[25] Luther hielt sich hier zurück: Er ließ die Psalmen durch die Schüler in Latein singen, denn diese mußten sowieso perfekt diese Gelehrtensprache erlernen! Die Lesungen wurden zunächst über drei Schüler verteilt und in Latein gelesen. Danach wurde alles noch einmal durch den Vierten in Deutsch verlesen. Es entstanden allgemeine Morgengottesdienste mit Elementen aus dem Katechismus, Epistellesungen, kursorischen Evangelienlesungen. Am Samstag las man in der Vesper aus dem Johannesevangelium. Weitere Gottesdienste für das Volk gab es nicht. Wer mehr wollte, konnte den Feiern der Schüler und Geistlichen beiwohnen. Vielleicht so, wie wir es noch heute in englischen Kathedralen erleben können. Am Sonntag wurde erwartet, daß jederman sich so viel wie möglich beteiligte. Das hieß: Um fünf oder sechs Uhr Metten mit drei Psalmen und der Epistellesung, gefolgt durch die Antiphon und das *Te Deum*. In Stille bat man das Vaterunser, gefolgt durch die *collecta* und das *Benedicamus Domino*. Um acht oder neun Uhr folgte die hohe Messe und am Mittag die Vesper, in der vielfach aus dem Alten Testament gelesen wurde.

In der Mette wurde über die Epistellesung gepredigt, in der Messe über das Tages- oder Feiertagsevangelium. In der Vesper predigte auch Luther selber von 1523-1529 cursorisch über die fünf Bücher Mose!

Es ist bewegend zu sehen, mit welcher Sehnsucht Müntzer und Luther versucht haben die Schrift unter das Volk zu bringen. Sie tun dies in jener liturgischen Form, dem traditionellen *officium*, die schon immer den Rahmen hierzu geboten hat. Dies ist sicher nach anfänglichem Interesse vielen Menschen schlichtweg zu viel geworden. Es konnte nicht so bleiben, denn eine Stadt ist kein Kloster und das Brevier kein Volksbuch. So gesehen ist ein Wunder, wie lange man noch in den Gebieten, wo die Reformation sich durchgesetzt hatte, an Luthers Vorschlägen festhielt.

Wichtig ist, daß die täglichen und sonntäglichen *horae*, neben der Feier von Eucharistie und Kommunion, ihren eigenen Stellenwert hatten. Die von diesem Sakrament abgetrennte Predigtkultur stand niemals zur Diskussion. Es ging um das Volk, die Gemeinde: Um das Lernen mit Herz und Seele, und dies führt in die Nähe der Feier des Gottesdienstes mit Herz und Seele. Katechese wird so zur Liturgie und die Liturgie ist Katechese, Kerygma, Trost. Eigentlich gehören beide Elemente zusammen. In der breiteren ökumenischen Diskussion wird uns gerade dieses Wissen weiterhin mit einander verbinden.

---

25. Hierüber mehr vor allem bei: Karl HONEMEYER: *Thomas Müntzer und Martin Luther. Ihr Ringen um die Musik des Gottesdienstes* (Berlin 1974).

Remarks on the history of congregational singing in the Dutch Reformed Churches

JAN R. LUTH

Calvinists have sung psalms for centuries. Calvin's zeal brought about the Genevan psalter. By 1562 all 150 psalms had been versified by his cooperators. These rhymed psalms were sung in the Genevan liturgy. This big project is not imaginable without the theology which lay behind it. Calvin wanted to give the congregation a substantial part in worship, because in his opinion all members of the congregation have a priestly task. Calvin moreover recognized the force which a hymn can have. Chant is in his opinion not only praise, but also an important element in preaching the Word of God. A spoken text has an influence upon a human being, but the effect is much greater when a melody is added. This prompted Calvin to the *dictum* that the melody is a funnel for the text. Precisely because the influence of singing is very great, you have to monitor what the congregation is singing. For this reason Calvin has separated liturgical from non-liturgical music and thus religious from secular music. Music that sounds in worship should have another style than music outside worship.[1] It is clear that Calvin had very high ideals concerning liturgical music, and at this point the difference between him and Luther is not as great as is often asserted. In Geneva they were used to chant the psalms according to tables. It seems that all 150 psalms were sung in half a year and that each psalm was chanted in its entirety as much as possible. The congregation sang at least fifteen stanzas in a service.[2] In this way Calvin's congregation had an essential part in worship, certainly in the view of his contemporaries.

The Genevan psalter has become part of Dutch Reformed liturgy by the work and influence of Petrus Datheen (c. 1530-1588). Datheen imported the Genevan psalter and translated it into the Dutch language, not because of his esteem for the Genevan melodies, but because he wanted to make stronger the ties with the French Calvinistic Churches. We find his thoughts in the preface to the rhymed psalms of 1567.[3] Datheen's psalter was used by many and became well known in a very short time. In the second half of the sixteenth century some synods declared this rhymed version the only one permitted for use in Church. Thus this psalter got a fixed place in the Netherlands, although there were some regions in the North and East in which the regulations made

---

1. See the prefaces in the Genevan hymnbooks of 1542 and 1543 in P. PIDOUX: *Le psautier Huguenot* 2 (Bâle 1962) 15-17, 20, 21.
2. PIDOUX: *Le psautier* 2, 134, 135.
3. This text is easily accessible in Ph. WACKERNAGEL: *Lieder der niederländischen Reformierten aus der Zeit der Verfolgung im 16. Jahrhundert* (Frankfurt am Main 1867 = Nieuwkoop 1967ʳ) 54.

by synods were duly noted but otherwise ignored.[4]

About the manner in which the rhymed version of the psalms was sung in the time of its origin we do not know very much. But the few data which are available show that singing the Genevan melodies was problematical. Louis Bourgeois, one of the Genevan composers, complained already in 1551 that the congregation was chanting not only slurringly, but moreover the wrong notes![5]

In the Netherlands we see the same kind of problems. We know this because soon after the appearance of Datheen's psalms in 1566 some editions were published in which the notation of the melodies was printed at each stanza (the first known edition thus printed is from 1586) to help the congregation in singing. Moreover we have to point to the detailed instructions for those which had to lead the singing in service. And also the instruction to the organists to play the psalms before and after the service, and the custom to play these melodies at the carillons in the cities have to be understood as pedagogical measures, which had no other purpose than to make the melodies familiar.[6]

From the beginning of the seventeenth century information on the manner of singing is more detailed. Especially a proposal at the National Synod of Dordrecht (1618-1619) concerning the rhymed psalter of Datheen put forward by Patroclus Römeling (a reverend who lived in the provinces of Drenthe and Groningen in the North of the Netherlands and a member of this synod) is an important source for our knowledge of congregational singing during the first decades of the seventeenth century. Römeling's proposal makes clear not only that for most congregations in the Netherlands the Genevan melodies were too difficult and that their number was too great, but also that isometric singing was a general custom.[7] Römeling's information is confirmed by one of his contemporaries, the physicist Isaäck Beeckman, who lived in the South-West of the Netherlands.[8] One can hardly imagine that the isometric way of chanting could arise in a short time. Therefore it is obvious that we may suppose that isometric singing was the normal practice already during the second half of the sixteenth century. Looking at the problems the congregation had with the Genevan psalms we might even ask, whether there had ever been rhythm in congregational singing from the very introduction of Datheen's psalms. This would also explain the fact that in the prefaces to the many metrical psalters published as an alternative for Datheen's psalms from 1581 onwards and espe-

4. J.R. LUTH: 'Daer wert om 't seerste uytgekreten...'. Bijdragen tot een geschiedenis van de gemeentezang in het Nederlandse Gereformeerde Protestantisme ca. 1550-ca. 1850 (Kampen 1986) 2 vols., 55-79.

5. Advertissement touchant les chants des Pseaumes, in Pseaumes octantetrois de David, mis en rime françoise par Clément MAROT et Théodore de BÈZE (Genève 1551 = New Brunswick, New Jersey 1973ʳ) V.iii.

6. LUTH: 'Daer wert om 't seerste uytgekreten...' 79-82, 91-92.

7. LUTH: 'Daer wert om 't seerste uytgekreten...' 117-119, 147-150, 422-433.

8. J.R. LUTH: Een bron over de gemeentezang uit het begin van de 17e eeuw, in Jaarboek voor liturgie-onderzoek 5 (1989) 227-253.

cially during the first half of the seventeenth century we read more complaints about Datheen's old fashioned language and the words he added than about the bad relation between melody and text.

During further research on Römeling's activities I discovered another still unpublished text from his hand. It consists of only three pages and is not printed, unlike the one already mentioned, but available only in manuscript form. It deals with the same question as the proposal he did at the National Synod of Dordrecht, but has at some points other emphases.[9] Römeling shows us the practice of congregational singing half a century after Datheen's metrical psalter was introduced. This makes it worthwhile to pay more attention to this little text.[10] We start with the main points.

In the first place, Römeling writes, he has changed the rhymed psalms of Marnix van St. Aldegonde in such a way that the number of melodies is reduced from 129 to 23. These melodies, which are not specified, are those best known and most simple in Datheen's psalter.[11] Among these melodies there is one that is moreover also the best known and the most important in the hymnbook of Emden.[12] The changes he made are small according to Römeling. A large number of psalms remained unchanged. In some psalms only a few syllables were changed and 18 psalms had received totally new versifications. The result is that with only 23 melodies all rhymed psalms and hymns in Marnix's psalter could be sung and also 70 hymns from the hymnbooks of Emden and Hamburg, and hymns that belonged to the rhymed psalter of Lobwasser. According to Römeling these changes made the rhymed version accessible even for the most simple people. In this respect, he thought, the psalter he changed in the way described is comparable with the English hymnbook, in which also many texts could be sung to a relative small number of melodies. Among the melodies which Römeling considered useful are, in contrast with Datheen's rhymed version, not only all twelve church-modes represented, but among them are also melodies in *tripla proportio*. Moreover Römeling brought all melodies into one clef. He wrote that he hoped that the synod was willing to publish a hymnbook of this kind and he offered his services.

In the second place, Römeling mentioned the most important reasons which made it necessary to change the existing rhymed version. First, in order that the simplest members of the church would have the possibility to sing the psalms and many other spiritual songs also outside the divine service. Secondly, because such a changed rhymed psalter would stimulate theologians

---

9. It is possible that Römeling wrote this short text for another synod than the National Synod, for instance for the synod of the province of Drenthe.

10. The manuscript is kept in the State Archives (*Rijksarchief*) in Groningen: Archief van het Provinciaal Kerkbestuur Groningen, nr. 031.1.47.

11. Datheen and Marnix used the same, Genevan, melodies.

12. Römeling calls it the *Martijnsche gesanckboock*. I have proved elsewhere that this is the hymnbook used by the Dutch congregation in Emden: LUTH: *'Daer wert om 't seerste uytgekreten...'* 119-122.

to make a more accessible psalter than Datheen's rhymed version in the future. Several times in the synod it had been pointed out that the great number of melodies was the reason why the hymnbook remained closed to most people. According to Römeling even organists and other musicians were able to acquire only a quarter of these melodies. For this reason a great number of faults entered congregational singing.

Römeling did not only discuss the rhymed version and the number of melodies, but also the manner of singing. He put some questions to the synod with marginal remarks, which inform us about the usage of his time. Römeling's main question is, whether the practice of slow singing in the Netherlands should be improved upon or not. He holds up as an example the German way of singing, which is faster. He mentions the following reasons why congregational singing has to be more rapid.

1. The slow way of singing conflicts with the nature of the melodies.
2. As a result of the slow *tempo* one cannot sing more than two or three stanzas. When the *tempo* would be faster, it should be possible to sing two or three complete psalms before and after sermon.
3. Rapid singing stimulates concentration, but slow singing relaxes it.
4. During the slow congregational singing no one can understand what is chanted, because people sing letters and not words. As an illustration Römeling gives a sentence from psalm 2 in Datheens rhymed version: *Wa-er o-m ra-est da-t vo-lck me-t so-lcke-n ho-och mo-et. Etc.* ('Why does this people rage with such a haughtiness').

In Römeling's opinion it is easy to raise the *tempo* of congregational singing. He mentions four possibilities to achieve this:
1. by playing the organ preludes faster;
2. by instructing the precentor to sing fast;
3. by teaching the children at school to sing more rapidly, in order that they can lead the singing in the same way as a precentor;
4. nature itself will be ready to help, because it is inclined to proportion and measure. Singing rapidly one can keep measure, singing slowly one cannot.
When we survey what Römeling brought forward, we see that for him the rhymed psalter of Marnix van St. Aldegonde was more important than Datheen's version. For several reasons Marnix's psalms, which were judged better than those of Datheen, were not introduced in worship.[13] But it is possible that this version was used, together with or instead of Datheen's psalms, in the North of the Netherlands, where Römeling lived and worked. The synod of Friesland, convening in Franeker in 1595, for instance decided to allow the use of Marnix's rhymed version of the psalms in worship.[14] Perhaps Römeling was hoping that Marnix's version would have a better chance, when

13. LUTH: *'Daer wert om 't seerste uytgekreten...'* 58-68.
14. J. REITSMA and S.D. VAN VEEN (eds.): *Acta der provinciale en particuliere synoden, gehouden in de Noordelijke Nederlanden gedurende de jaren 1572-1620* 6 (Groningen 1892-1899) 83, art. 9.

his proposal to revise the hymnbook was accepted. In any case it is remarkable that he thought it not necessary to elucidate the selfevidence with which he took Marnix's version as a starting point for a new rhymed version of the psalms.

It is also clear that the number of melodies in Datheen's rhymed psalter was a problem for congregational singing. On the basis of this experience Römeling wanted to reduce drastically the number of melodies. In his proposal a strong familiarity is visible with a number of North-German hymn-books, a familiarity which he presumed his readers, the members of a synod, would also have had!

From Römeling's other proposal which I described earlier, it is clear that in the North of the Netherlands hymns from these hymnbooks were sung on a large scale in Church.[15] The familiarity with these North-German hymns went so far, that in Römeling's proposal to change the rhymed psalms of Datheen, the application of a small number of melodies from German hymnbooks needed no defence. This fact is very important for the interpretation of de-cisions made by synods. As we saw several synods in the sixteenth century and the National Synod of Dordrecht in 1619 decided that only Datheen's psalms were allowed in worship. On this ground it has many times been asserted that Calvinists in the Netherlands did sing psalms only and no other chants. In Römeling's writings we see – and other sources affirm this – that decisions made by synods are not very good sources for our knowledge of actual liturgical practice. In many parts of the Netherlands congregations were sing-ing also hymns other than those of Datheen's psalter, mostly hymns of Lutheran origin, until far into the nineteenth century.[16] But even when we had no other sources than decisions made by synods, the facts would still be clear. For the more often a decision is repeated, the more probable it is that it was ignored. This means that when Dutch synods decided several times that Datheen's psalter should be used in the services, this repeated regulation was necessary in the opinion of the members of these synods to change a different practice! Such decisions are therefore not to be understood as a report of the actual situation.

Besides his orientation on Ostfriesland there is another remarkable fact in Römeling's information: about 50 years after Datheen's psalter was introduced in the liturgy it was still very difficult to sing the melodies and a very great part of the psalter was not used at all. For this reason England was a good example to look at, because there they used few melodies to sing many different texts. When we suppose that the church-modes in which the Genevan melodies were composed were an important reason why these melodies were hardly accessible, it is amazing that Römeling in his proposal for a new hymn-book introduced melodies among which all church-modes are present. This contradiction is difficult to explain. Probably it has to do with the inclination

---

15. See note 4 above.
16. LUTH: *'Daer wert om 't seerste uytgekreten...'* 117-127, 245-248.

of that time to understand church-modes as major and minor scales. If this is the case then the chosen melodies perhaps had modifications in this direction, so that the real characteristics of church-modes were less recognizable. It also appears that *tempus imperfectum diminutum*, the only *tempus* in the Genevan psalter, was experienced as monotonous. For that reason Römeling wanted to introduce melodies in *tactus proportionatus*.[17]

Another stumbling block seems to have been the notation of the melodies. Even if people were able to read it, the use of different clefs remained an obstacle. For that reason Römeling wanted to reduce their number and to maintain only one. Without these changes the hymnbook was hardly useful. For Römeling it was obviously normal that people in everyday life sang many hymns, partly derived from the New Testament. This again confirms the conclusion on the meaning of synod's decisions and the use of different hymn-books, viz. that in some regions of the Netherlands familiarity with hymns other than Datheen's was considerable, perhaps even greater than with those of Datheen. It is clear once more that synod's decisions in favour of Datheen's psalter were in fact efforts to keep out or to remove other hymns from the liturgy. It is also an interesting point in Römeling's arguments that he does not want a new psalter because of the way in which it is rhymed, but because of the great number of melodies. Not only for the congregation, but even for professionals it was too much to learn all these melodies. As a consequence melodies were changed in singing by the congregations. These changes Römeling considers to be faults.

The situation which is described at the end of Römeling's proposal, the slow *tempo* and the absence of rhythm, is undoubtedly a result of the problems mentioned. As far as we know at this moment Römeling is the first one who informs us that isometric singing was usual in that time and for this reason alone he is a very important source. It has always been assumed that isometric singing was introduced during the eighteenth century. This way of chanting in a very slow *tempo* had in Römeling's time as a result that the congregation could hardly sing two or three stanzas of a psalm. The Genevan principle of singing complete psalms as much as possible was impracticable in the Nether-lands. It is also interesting that Römeling thought that raising the *tempo* would not only make it possible to sing complete psalms, but also to sing them in a rhythm. Finally we can deduce from the possibilities to raise *tempo* which he mentioned that Römeling did not yet know the organ as an instrument for the accompaniment of congregation singing but only as an instrument to play preludes.

Because Römeling's claim that he is describing the situation not only in his own environment but for the whole country is confirmed by Isaäck Beeck-man, whom we already mentioned,[18] we may suppose that congregational singing was in the beginning of the seventeenth century at a low level. It is

17. In his first proposal he mentiones as an example *Allein Gott in der Höh sei Ehr*.
18. See note 8.

probable that the situation during the second half of the sixteenth century was not any better. Not only during the first 50 years after the introduction of the Genevan psalms, but until the end of the nineteenth century we read many complaints about congregational singing. In the opinion of several authors the congregation sang too loud and 'cried'. Efforts to change this by means of education have hardly had any result. The organ accompaniment that was introduced about 1630, and which in the opinion of Constantijn Huygens[19] could improve congregational singing, was for this purpose not succesful either.

A revival occurred during the second half of the eighteenth century in the time of the introduction of the *Statenberijming*, the rhymed version of 1773, the successor to Datheen's psalter. At that occasion attempts were made in several congregations to sing softer and in a kind of rhythm. The best known possibility was the *korte zingtrant* ('short way of singing'),[20] which consisted in making long the first and last note of a line and short the other notes. Of this usage we have several examples in chorale books from the second half of the eighteenth century.

During the nineteenth century the opinion that congregational singing needed improvement was gaining ground. Johannes G. Bastiaans, the organist of the *Grote Kerk* (St. Bavo's Church) in Haarlem around 1850 for instance suggested to pay more attention to the church-modes, and he wanted a harmonisation in accordance with these modes.[21] And the church historian J.G.R. Acquoy pleaded at the end of the last century for an improvement of the hymnbook, its notation and the manner of singing.[22] These efforts cannot of course be understood without the interest for history and the results of scientific research, which are very characteristic for the nineteenth century. A fundamental improvement we do not see however before the twentienth century. This improvement we owe especially to the work of Ds. ('the Rev.') H. Hasper and Ina Lohr. They asked each in their own way to pay attention to and to have consideration for the melodies of the psalms, for the characteristics of church-modes and for the chanting practice. They have had a great influence on the development of church music until today.

---

19. C. HUYGENS: *Gebruyck of ongebruyck van 't orgel in de kercken der Vereenighde Nederlanden (1641)*. Tekstverzorging en commentaar door F.L. ZWAAN (Verhandelingen der Koninklijke Nederlandse Akademie van Wetenschappen, afdeling letterkunde, nieuwe reeks 84) (Amsterdam-Londen 1974).
20. LUTH: *'Daer wert om 't seerste uytgekreten...'* 286-292.
21. J. BASTIAANS: *Vierstemming koraalboek voor koor (sopraan, alt, tenor, bas) en orgel of piano-forte, bevattende al de melodieën der Evangelische Gezangen, bij de N.H. Gemeenten in gebruik; ten dienste van kerk, zangvereeniging, school en huisgezin* (Arnhem 1852); J. BASTIAANS: *Vierstemmig koraalboek bevattende de nieuwe melodieën van de Vervolgbundel op de Evangelische Gezangen met voor-, tusschen- en naspelen voor het orgel tot begeleiding van het kerkgezang bij de Hervormde Gemeente of dezelfde melodieën met nieuwe woorden voor gemengd koor (sopraan, alt, tenor en bas) en orgel (ad libitum) tot algemeen gebruik in zangscholen, zangvereenigingen en huisgezinnen* (Haarlem 1869).
22. J.G.R. ACQUOY: De psalmwijzen der Nederlandsche Hervormde Kerk en hare herziening, in *Archief voor Nederlandsche Kerkgeschiedenis* 4 (1893) 1-84.

When we look back at what we have seen, the most remarkable point is perhaps this: when we compare the descriptions in the sources we have from past centuries with what we know of twentieth-century congregational singing, we must come to the conclusion that comparatively the singing is in this century at an acceptable level, although in our time education in church music, in contrast with the practice of the sixteenth until nineteenth century, is totally absent as an ordinary subject in schools. For, as we have seen, during four centuries the teacher and the precentor, usually the same person, taught children to sing the psalms and under his direction children went to church where they had fixed places to lead the congregation in singing.

The question why descriptions of congregational singing have been negative for so long is not easy to answer. For a long time it has been supposed that Datheen's rhymed version, which lacked a good relation between melody and text, was to blame for isometric singing. But what has stimulated the 'crying' and 'shouting' is not made clear, although we can imagine that the practice of using several rhymed versions at the same time in worship will have been instrumental. The explanation for the rise of isometric singing is however not to be sought in Datheen's rhymed version. Firstly because a relation between melody and text as in his psalter was not exceptional in the sixteenth century. Secondly because the first data we have do not point in the direction of the rhyme, but to the difficulty of the melodies. Moreover complaints concerning congregational singing in England and Germany, countries in which they had quite different hymns and rhymed versions, are exactly the same as in the Netherlands, and they were in those countries likewise repeated until far into the nineteenth century.[23]

Looking back at the available sources, we have to come to the conclusion that we can hardly say anything positive about the only real part the congregation had in the worship of the Dutch Reformed Church: congregational singing. That is: if we look with the eyes of those who inform us on this subject through the writings they have left us. We do not know much however about what the members of the congregations experienced, even though Römeling stated that they also had an aversion against the slow way of singing.[24] Surveying the history of congregational singing a question arises on the one hand: whether Calvin's successors did not aim too high when they introduced congregational singing, because the actual practice shows us quite a different picture than the one we would expect from Calvin's high theological ideals. But on the other hand: the Genevan melodies, which have been a stumbling block during centuries, are still used and today not only by Protestants. And it is a fact that, unlike the Church in the native country of the Genevan psalter, the Dutch Reformed Churches still retain all 150 rhymed psalms as a very important part of their hymnbook.

23. F. BLUME (ed.): *Die Musik in Geschichte und Gegenwart* 4 (Kassel 1949-1986) 17 vols., 1662-1675; N. TEMPERLEY: *The music of the English parish church* (Cambridge 1979) 2 vols.
24. LUTH: *'Daer wert om 't seerste uytgekreten...'* 179.

Liturgy and piety in the Netherlands during the seventeenth and eighteenth centuries[1]

TH. CLEMENS

In former times liturgy historians considered the period between the Council of Trent and the Second Vatican Council as rather devoid of interest. Once that the major liturgical books had been promulgated, nothing new happened for ages. Liturgy degenerated into ritualism, rubricism and legal quibblings.[2] In the celebration of the Eucharist the separation between priest and laity, which had become definite during the Middle Ages, was perpetuated. The *circumstantes* were at that time no more than lookers-on from a deferential distance. They were present but their devotions at Mass rather accompanied, than were derived from, the liturgical forms.[3] Their activities were judged to belong more to the field of piety and popular culture than to the domain of history of liturgy.

Nowadays this opinion is changing and not without good reasons. For, however it may be, only half of the history of liturgy is described, if its object is restricted to the history of the alterations in the formulas and rituals.[4] In this contribution a specific example will be discussed, showing how an unchanged supply during the post-Tridentine times did not lead to a uniform reception of it.

1. A NEW EDITION OF THE ANCIENT PICTORIAL MASS-BOOK

In Amsterdam, in 1651, a booklet was published under the title of *Misse. Haer korte uytlegginge/en godvruchtige oeffeninge onder de zelve. Neffens eenige besondere zegeninge: en het gebruyck der h.h. sacramenten/zoo die in de h. katholijcke apostolijcke roomsche kercke geoeffent worden.*[5] The author, at

---

1. I should like to thank drs. B. Loonen and dr. P. Raedts for the translation.
2. G. LUKKEN: *De onvervangbare weg van de liturgie* (Hilversum 1980) 113; H.A.J. WEGMAN: *Geschiedenis van de christelijke eredienst in het westen en in het oosten. Een wegwijzer* (Hilversum 1983²) 241-242.
3. WEGMAN: *Geschiedenis* 167-169, 239, 241-242. O. CHADWICK: *The Reformation* (The Pelican history of the Church 3) (Harmondsworth 1986) 293-294.
4. Cf. J. DE VIGUERIE: La dévotion populaire à la messe en France aux XVIIe et XVIIIe siècles, in *Histoire de la messe en France XVII-XIX siècles* (Paris 1980) 7-25; F.E. WEAVER: Liturgy for the laity: the Jansenist case for popular participation in worship in the seventeenth and eighteenth centuries, in *Studia liturgica* 19 (1989) 47-59. See also WEGMAN: *Geschiedenis* 5 (preface of the second edition).
5. I.e.: 'Mass. Its short explanation/and devout exercise during the same. Along with some special blessings: and the usage of the holy sacraments/as they are practiced in the holy Catholic apostolic Roman Church'. Amsterdam: voor den aucteur 1651 A⁸-Ff⁸. Cf. the illustrations on the next page for frontispiece and titlepage of this book.

197

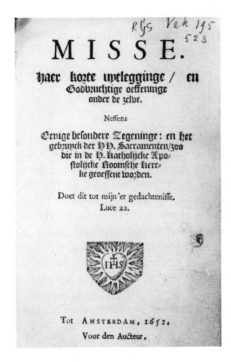

whose expense the book had been printed, was a secular priest, Andreas
vander Kruyssen, who at that time ministered to the town of Amsterdam.[6]
This relatively well preserved work marks a transition in the history of the
devotional life of the Dutch Mission. In one respect it is closely bound to a
time-honoured tradition and in another respect it offers something very new.

This second side does not show itself at once. The book starts with a way of
'hearing Mass', which is based upon the parallel depiction of scenes of
Christ's passion and of the different stages of the Mass. The first engraving
represents at a glance both the tools of the passion and ceremonial attributes
of the priest and the altar. On the second picture Christ is going to the Garden
of Olives, whereas the priest and his servers are approaching the altar.[7] So step
by step, with the aid of 37 illustrations, the priest's actions are related to
Christ's passion, death, resurrection and ascension, to Pentecost and to the
first public appearance of the apostles. The corresponding text supports this
relation, first by a short *aenmerckinge* (consideration), which draws the read-

6. *Nieuw Nederlandsch biografisch woordenboek* 9 (Leiden 1933) 185.
7. Cf. illustrations on the opposite page.

MYSTERIA PASSIONIS ET MISSÆ.

1.

I.

In 't oberdencken des Lijdens ons Zaligh-makers moeten dese vier punten oberwogen worden.

Ten eersten. Wie 'er lijdt : te weten Gods Zoon/ gelijck met den Vader : boben wien geen meerder/ geen beter/ geen uptnemender kan gebonden/ ofte gedocht worden.

Ten tweeden. Wat hy lijdt : te weten die ober-groote pijnen bol ban berswaetheydt : soo datze een yder/ dieze oberdenckt/ doen berschricken.

Ten derden. Voor wie hy lijdt : te weten boor my berworpen/en ondanckbare Schepsel: daer 'er geen berworpender / en ondanckbaerder onder den Hemel gebonden kan worden.

Ten vierden. Waerom dat hy lijdt : niet om dat hy dat ban noode had/ nochte dat hy per goedts in my boorzagh/ maer upt enckele liefde/ genegent-heydt/ en zijn onepndelijcke barmhartigheydt.

Instrumenten des Lijdens ons Zaligh-makers.
Priesterlijck/en Autaers Gewaedt.

Aenmerckinge.

A Enziet met welcke wapenen/ de Zalighmaker des werelts uwe verlossinge bebochten heeft.

't Gebedt.

C Hriste Jesu: die door ulw bitter lijden/in het H. Sacrificie der Misse afgebeelt/my gewaerdight hebt te verlossen: Jck bidde my soodanige gratie te willen berleenen/dat ick 't zelve waerdighlijck magh oberwegen. Amen.

A 4   Christus

SACERDOS INCHOAT SACRUM.

3.

3.

Christus bidt in 't Hofken.
De Priester begint de Misse.

Aenmerckinge.

L Et met aendachtigheydt hoe uwe Za-lighmaker zich tot het gebedt begeeft: Oock zijn liefste Discipelen een steen-worp achterlatende. Leert hier oock alle tijdte-lijcke bekommeringe ten tijde des Heyligen Dienst ter zyde te stellen.

't Gebedt.

C Hriste Jesu: die my/ hoe wel onwaer-digh in uwe tegenwoordigheydt ge-waerdight hebt te ontfangen: Verleent my dat ick alle wereltlijcke zorghvuldigheden/en verstroptheden buyten sluytende met uwe Majesteyt alleen/ gelijck ghy met uwen Hemelschen Vader in 't Hofken der Olyven dede/ ban mijn Salighheydt met aendaght magh handelen. Amen.

Christus

er's attention to what happened to the Saviour, and secondly by an appropriate *gebedt* (prayer) in which the praying user of the book involves himself in what is represented and asks for repentance, uprightness, and so on.

This manner of 'hearing Mass' is only new in so far as the author/editor has taken care to improve the engravings and the text of the considerations and prayers.[8] Otherwise it is no more than a variation upon a theme, dating back to the early Middle Ages. Commemorating-allegorical explanations of the Mass and of pictorial Mass-books had been published since the invention of the art of printing.[9] Consequently, it is clear that the *Misse* in its first pages represents tradition, and in doing so it was by no means the last of its kind, neither in the Netherlands, nor elsewhere.[10] For a long period the devotion to the passion dominated religious life and the connection between the sacrifice of the Mass and the sacrifice of the Cross can be found in a great number of post-Tridentine prayer-books.[11] The illustrated Mass was published up to the twentienth century. See for example *Christi bloedighe passie, verbeelt in het onbloedigh sacrificie der h. misse* by the Jesuit A. Poirters (1675),[12] the altered version of it in *Geest des gebeds* (1733) and *Gulden paradys* (1743),[13] *Dagelyksche oeffeningen en godvruchtige bemerkingen door den geheelen vasten op het lyden onzes Heeren Jesus Christus* (editions of 1752 and later) by Ambrosius vanden Bosch[14] and *Gebedenboekje voor roomsch catholyke christenen*, distributed in large numbers from 1832 to 1867 by Hanicq (after 1854 Dessain) in Mechelen.[15]

8. *Misse* preface.
9. M. SMITS VAN WAESBERGHE: De misverklaring van meester Simon van Venlo, in *Ons geestelijk erf* 15 (1941) 228-261 and 285-327; 16 (1942) 85-129. B. DE TROEYER: *Bio-bibliographica Franciscana Neerlandica saeculi XVI* 1-2 (Nieuwkoop 1969-1970) 1, 7-13 and 2, 105-115 for Gerrit vander Goude. G.M. OURY: Les explications de la messe en France du XVIe au XVIIIe siècle, in *Histoire de la messe* 81-93, pp. 82-85. A. COLOMBO: 'L'Explication de la messe' di P. Le Brun de l'Oratoire (1661-1729), in *Ephemerides liturgicae* 101 (1987) 425-442, pp. 427-431.
10. See for similar Mass-books elsewhere St. BEISSEL: Zur Geschichte der Gebetbücher, in *Stimmen aus Maria-Laach* 77 (1909) 28-41, 169-185, 274-289 and 397-411, pp. 403-404; DE VIGUERIE: La dévotion 18.
11. Th. CLEMENS: *De godsdienstigheid in de Nederlanden in de spiegel van de katholieke kerkboeken 1680-1840* 1-2 (Tilburg 1988) 1, 77-78, 95 and 167. Cf. M. THERRY: *De religieuze beleving bij de leken in het 17de-eeuwse bisdom Brugge (1609-1706)* (Brussel 1988) 128-139.
12. I.e.: 'Christi bloody passion, represented by the unbloody sacrifice of the holy Mass'. E. ROMBAUTS: *Leven en werken van pater Adrianus Poirters S.J. (1605-1674). Bijdrage tot de studie van de didactisch-moraliserende letterkunde in de XVIIe eeuw in Zuid-Nederland* (Ledeberg-Gent 1930) 79 and 278. Th. CLEMENS: La répercussion de la lutte entre jansénistes et antijansénistes dans la littérature de spiritualité depuis 1685 jusqu'à la fin du XVIIIe siècle, in E. VAN EIJL (ed.): *L'Image de C. Jansénius jusqu'à la fin du XVIIIe siècle* (Louvain 1987) 203-229, p. 220.
13. I.e.: 'Spirit of prayer' and 'Golden paradise'. CLEMENS: *De godsdienstigheid* 1, 83, 90, 108; 2, nos. 229, 333, 507.
14. I.e. 'Daily exercises and devout observations during the whole Lent on the passion of our Lord Jesus Christ'. Ieper: Th.Fr. Walwein 1752 (AntwRS); with reprints in the nineteenth and twentienth centuries.
15. I.e.: 'Prayer-book for Roman-Catholic Christians'. CLEMENS: *De godsdienstigheid* 1, 148 and 2, nos. 218.020-218.050; with eleven reprints and 58,700 copies. See also: *Het godvruchtig kind. Met de h. mis in 37 afbeeldingen*, i.e.: 'The devout child. With the holy Mass in 37 illustrations'. 's-Hertogenbosch 1878[16] and Amsterdam 1882[17].

What is the significance of the *Misse* as a pictorial Mass-book for the participation of the laity? One may assume that the engravings hardly encouraged its user to develop real interest in the liturgical celebration of the Mass. For it is obvious that not the Mass itself but the story of Christ's passion is the point of departure for the devotion. Every part of the Mass was connected with it, even if there were few or no links at all between both. So, the piety of the laity went its own way, following the actions of the priest, but not touched by their proper meaning or by the text of the lessons and prayers.

This way of 'seeing Mass' led in the *Misse* to a perhaps weekly repeated and therefore almost continuous confrontation with one's own sinfulness as a major cause of the passion. As such it was a permanent exhortation to repentance and to bear one's cross as the only way to heaven. Moreover, it urged on to faith, hope (expectation of joy after suffering) and charity and it insisted on improvement of life.

All considered, the illustrated Mass of the *Misse* must have contributed to perpetuate the late medieval concentration on the devotion of the passion and, implicitly, to favour an attitude alien to the liturgy among 'common' lay-men. It can hardly be accidental that in only a few engravings they appear together with the priest. His surroundings, which are quite changeable because of the somewhat inconsistent character of the pictures, are mainly populated with altarboys, assisting angels and, judging from their clothes, praying religious 'specialists'.[16]

There is no reason to be surprised at the appearance of this kind of book in 1651. In the art of the Counter-Reformation strong visuality and an allegorical spirit prevailed.[17] In post-Tridentine theology the Mass was predominantly considered as a sacrifice.[18] In the prayer-books of the time devotion to the passion stood at an unrivalled first place.[19] Yet, at the same time other ways of attending Mass were available as well, although those were not necessarily more liturgical.[20] Some impulses, however, to pay more attention to the liturgy did exist. The Council of Trent had ordered priests to explain the Mass to the people.[21] Moreover, some knowledge was necessary, especially in the Calvinist Republic, to enable the laity to defend the doctrine and the observances of their Church.[22]

So far, the literature that contributed to a better explanation of the Mass has hardly been the subject of systematic investigation. Despite of my pre-

---

16. Cf. illustrations on the next page.
17. B. KNIPPING: *De iconografie van de Contra-Reformatie in de Nederlanden* 1-2 (Hilversum 1939-1940) 1, 146.
18. H. BREMOND: *Histoire littéraire du sentiment religieux en France* 9 (Paris 1932) 136-155; DE VIGUERIE: La dévotion 21.
19. CLEMENS: *De godsdienstigheid* 1, 77, and 167. Cf. THERRY: *De religieuze beleving* 132.
20. CLEMENS: *De godsdienstigheid* 1, 76-77.
21. H. SCHMIDT: *Liturgie et langue vulgaire. La problème de la langue liturgique chez les premiers Réformateurs et au Concile de Trente* (Rome 1950) 95-155, esp. 148-151.
22. Cf. OURY: Les explications 85.

SACERDOS SIGNAT OBLATA.
21

21.

Chꝛiſtus woꝛt op 't kruys geſpijckert.
De Pꝛieſter zegent de Offerande.

Aenmerckinge.

Nauwelijcks is uwe Zalighmaker met groote moeyte en pijn op den bergh van Calvarien met zijn ſwaer pack gekroopen/ of die wꝛeede beulen rucken hem de kleede- ren/daer het bloedt nu in gebacken was/van de Schouderen af/ziet die wonden wederom geopent: overwꝛeeght eens hoe zy hem op het Hout neerſnijten/hoe zy hem recken/trecken/ die armen ſpannen/ die handen en voeten dooꝛbooꝛen/ die plompe ſpijckers daer dooꝛ ſlaen: raeckt dat uw hart niet? O Chꝛiſten Ziel/laet die wonden met den H. Franciſcus in uw hart gedꝛuckt zijn.

't Gebedt.

Chꝛiſte Jeſu / waerachtige Verzoen- boogh vooꝛ het menſchelijck geſlacht/die hier zoo uptgereckt en geſpannen woꝛt/raeckt en wondt mijn hart met de ſchichten van uw Goddelijcke liefde/ op dat ick met uw God- delijcke liefde vervult/alles om uwent wille magh lijden / en aen uw kruys gehecht blijven. Amen.

Chꝛiſtus

AD MEMENTO PRO DEFUNCTIS.
24

24.

Chꝛiſtus bidt vooꝛ 't menſchelijck geſlacht.
De Pꝛieſter bidt vooꝛ de overleden.

Aenmerckinge.

Ziet hoe uwe Zalighmaker in 't midden van alle zijn ſmart en verſmaetheydt in 't verbloecken en verfoepen der Joden/ ver- laten van zijn Apoſtelen/ noch vooꝛ u/ vooꝛ zijn vpanden/ja vooꝛ 't gantſche menſchelijck geſlacht zijn Hemelſchen Vader bidt; let hoe hy de booſheydt zijner vpanden tracht te verminderen: Hooꝛt hoe hy vooꝛ u bidt. Leert hier upt uwe vpanden upt gantſcher harten lief te hebben / vooꝛ hun Godt Al- machtigh te bidden/ en hun fouten/ tegen u begaen/ te vergeven.

't Gebedt.

Chꝛiſte Jeſu: die vooꝛ my aen het Kruys hangende uwen Hemelſchen Vader vooꝛ my / die u dooꝛ mijn booſheydt daer aen ge- hecht had/gewaerdight hebt te bidden: Ick/ uwen onwaerdige Dienaer/verklare in uw' Goddelijcke tegenwooꝛdigheyt/dat ick om de liefde van u upt gantſch mijner harte ver- geve allen die my miſdaen hebben/ en bidde u hun 't zelve oock te willen vergeven / op dat ick uwe genade hier namaels met alle geloo- vige Zielen deelachtigh magh weſen. Amen.

D 3   Bekeeringe

vious remarks it is also true that well before 1651 there was an unmistakable rise of more or less paraphrasing Mass texts in the vernacular prayer-books. I have even found a complete translation of the Mass in a booklet, published in Antwerp in 1647 under the title of *Cort verhael ende uytlegginghe van het heyligh sacrificie der misse soo de saecke selver, als de ceremonien betreffende. Mitsgaders een naeckte oversettinghe der woorden, die soo van de priester als van den dienaer worden ghesprocken.*[23] The author, who signs his name with the letters L.D.W., had included the translation, because, despite ample explanation, some people were irritated by the incomprehensibility of the Latin language.

The *circumstantes* of the mid-seventeenth-century obviously wanted a greater involvement for themselves than just watching. It was no longer enough to see the gestures. They wanted also to understand the words. This is the background of the 'other part' of the *Misse*.

2. THE TRANSLATED MASS

Turning over the pages of the *Misse* after the illustrated Mass one will soon discover that the engravings can be seen as a nicely restored ancient façade that hides a rather modern house. Without any elucidation or comment on the spot the book continues with 'the holy service of the Mass, and the ceremonies of the holy Church'. Christ's passion is in the centre in this second Mass too, but the frame-work is totally different. The devout exercise that follows after a short explanation of the word 'Mass', is, in fact, the ordinary of the Mass, enlarged with, among others, a part of the story of the passion of Our Lord according to St. John, all together both in Latin and Dutch.

This bilingual Mass has already been noticed and discussed, but, at least in my opinion, not properly rated. In his excellent manual of the history of the Catholic Church of the Netherlands during the eighteenth century P. Polman assumes first that translations of the Mass were in quite common use in the Dutch mission and secondly that the inclusion of a translation in the *Misse* was a result of apologetical instead of liturgical considerations.[24] Both assumptions seem untenable to me.

As to the common use of translated Masses, so far hardly any evidence of a wide circulation has come to my notice. They are not found in the prayer-books of the first half of the seventeenth century. Outside this kind of devotional books I only know of the above mentioned translation of 1647 and this did not originate from a city in the Dutch mission but from Antwerp in the Southern or Spanish Netherlands. Moreover, the existence of a lot of different

23. I.e.: 'Short story and explanation of the holy sacrifice of the Mass concerning the subject itself as well as the ceremonies. Together with a bare translation of the words which are spoken by the priest as well as by the servant.' Antwerp: Widow of Jan Cnobbaert 1647 165-(3) pp. (Utrecht, Library of the Old-Catholic Church of St. Gertrudis). See also *Bibliotheca Catholica Neerlandica impressa* 1500-1727 (The Hague 1954) no. 9894 for an edition of 1645.
24. P. POLMAN: *Katholiek Nederland in de achttiende eeuw* 1-3 (Hilversum 1968) 1, 128-129.

translated Masses older than 1651 seems to me unlikely, because the Jansenists did not refer to an older example than the *Misse* to prove their right to make full translations. This would certainly have happened, if they had been widely available.[25]

As long as conclusive evidence is not provided, I therefore prefer to suppose that Polman has been deceived by the author's preface, which is not very clear. From his own words one can derive that he did not act on his own initiative, but at the request of others, on which occasion he was handed over *verscheyde boecxkens* ('several booklets'). So far it is all clear. It is uncertain, however, in what degree the final result has to do with these exemplars. In the words *alzoo mijn meeninge alleenlijck was de plaetjens en gebeden wat te verbeteren, ben allencxkens verder in 't werk geraeckt* ('first, I only intended to improve the pictures and the prayers, but gradually I got more involved in the matter') I read that the author of the *Misse* did more than just choose from the material already available. If this interpretation is correct, then Vander Kruyssen's contribution is not necessarily restricted, as Polman thought, to adding the Latin text to the already existing Dutch Mass. Then the translation itself could be meant too. To solve this problem we need to know exactly what books the author has used. In other words, we need information which is not available. So, a definitive answer is impossible and that is sufficient for the moment to make Polman's first assumption at least less certain.

The same doubt, and more than that, rises when we investigate his second assumption. Did the bilingual Mass serve only apologetical purposes? It is true that the author gives, once more, cause to think so. He states in his preface that he added the Latin to the vernacular in order to give non-Catholics a better understanding of *de heerlijckheydt en eygen woorden van onze Moeder de Heylige Kercke* ('the glory and the proper words of our mother the holy Church'). On the other hand I notice that he also very much appreciates the prayers and ceremonies of the Church for internal use. I have even found a clear indication that his own fellow-believers were the people he was really thinking of, when he 'gradually got more involved' in his editorial work. In a autographic dedication of the *Misse*, which fortunately has been preserved, nothing is said of the liturgy to give better instruction to Protestants. On the contrary, the text of the dedication mentions the *luyster* [...] *van Godes wonderwerck (dat) nu niet verborgen blijft voor 't volck van Zijn Kerck* ('the glory of God's marvellous work that is no longer hidden to the people of his Church').[26]

Which of these statements is the most reliable? I should like to answer this question by asking another: why does he state here something which is so different from what he said in the preface of his book? I can only explain it by surmising that the author thought that the novelty which he wanted to introduce in his own community, was best safeguarded against criticism, if he

25. *Berigt over verscheide gebede-boeken* (S.l.: s.n. 1705) 1-2 (MaastrUL).
26. MaastrTL CB 135 E 10.

made use of a way of arguing which was generally accepted in the Counter-Reformation.[27]

The assumption of the author's real interest in liturgy is confirmed by the rest of his book. After the translated Mass another 300 pages follow with texts almost exclusively derived from Missal and Ritual. Successively the *Misse* contains a number of blessings (of salt and water, of candles on Candlemas, of ash on Ash Wednesday, of palms on Palm Sunday), the liturgy of Good Friday and Holy Saturday, the ritual of baptism (from the second edition including a blessing of mothers of new-born children), the confession (with penitential psalms and the litany of All Saints), the Communion (also for the sick), the extreme unction (with prayers for the sick, the dying and the deceased), the burial service and the litany of Our Lady of Loreto, the marriage service, (again from the second edition:) the vespers of Sundays and feast-days, and finally the Creed of pope Pius IV.

At a first glance all this has a timeless and impersonal character, because, as Polman rightly observes, 'it is only very rare that the author himself is speaking'.[28] Considering the historical context, however, it is the choice of the above-mentioned components, which is personal and more or less revolutionary, compared with the other prayer-books of the mid-seventeenth century. Whereas in the latter the devotion to the passion still largely consists of late medieval prayers and exercises, Vander Kruyssen connects this pious work exclusively with the Mass and with the liturgy of Good Friday. Whereas the existing prayer-books contain no more than two sacraments (confession and eucharist), the *Misse* appears to be an important step on the post-Tridentine way of the sacramentalization of piety.[29]

3. CONTEXT AND BACKGROUND

Books which stood the test of time are often and above all examined by a mere analysis of their contents. To assess their impact, however, attention should be paid to their origin, setting and destination as well. This applies to the *Misse*, too.

The book emanates from a Catholic Church which had to hold its own in a protestant State. During the preceding period the struggle to survive had not always been easy. Around the middle of the seventeenth century the period of the mobile and hidden mission work had passed and the Church had returned to the regularity of ordinary, established spiritual care. The positions of the several denominations had been set out. Although the author had asserted himself as a translator of polemic literature only a few years earlier,[30] in 1651

---

27. Cf. L.J. ROGIER: *Geschiedenis van het Katholicisme in Noord-Nederland in de zestiende en zeventiende eeuw* 2 (Amsterdam 1947²) 754-757.
28. POLMAN: *Katholiek Nederland* 1, 128.
29. CLEMENS: *De godsdienstigheid* 1, 77 and 165.
30. J.A. ALBERDINGK THIJM: *Volksalmanak voor Nederlandsche katholieken 1861* (Amsterdam) 271-272.

he explicitly stated in his preface that he refrained from controversial issues, because they had been dealt with so many times. It is also significant that his book was not published under a hiding address but with the name of Amsterdam on the title-page.

After 1648 the battle-cries stopped for a while and the extraordinary position of the Dutch Catholics can only be guessed at from the Creed of pope Pius IV and some short, almost casual remarks. For the latter the Good Friday service is a case in point: it ends up with stating that in Catholic countries a procession follows after the service (p. 192). Another case is the instruction, given at the end of the baptismal service that the parents should be careful in their choice of a wet-nurse to whom they, if necessary, board their child out (p. 235). In the prevailing Ritual (of 1622) the same instruction contains a blunt warning against heretic women!

Another important fact is that the author of the *Misse* was not just a well-meaning, but otherwise nameless and unassuming pastor in one of the many more or less hidden Catholic communities. Andreas vander Kruyssen came from a distinguished, ancient Amsterdam family and was at least on that account highly respected, even outside the circle of his fellow-believers.[31]

Moreover, he belonged to the leading lights among the clergy for several reasons. As a *doctor theologiae* (around 1650 only eleven in the Dutch Mission out of 370 priests) he belonged to the best educated pastors of his Church.[32] He enjoyed the confidence of the highest ecclesiastical leader of the Catholic Church in the area north of the great rivers, the vicar apostolic Ph. Rovenius. At least it was at his special request that Vander Kruyssen was admitted to the chapter of the vacant bishopric of Haarlem,[33] an institution which has been very important for the survival of Catholicism in the Republic which was dominated by Calvinism. At the time only the most distinguished, learned and influential priests were granted the honour of its membership.[34] Subsequently the canons showed him their recognition by appointing him first, on July 6, 1650, archpriest of Amstelland (the area around Amsterdam) and later, on January 16, 1653, of the city of Amsterdam as well.[35] In short, Andreas vander Kruyssen in every respect belonged to the élite of the Republic and of his Church.

Regarding this state of affairs, the *Misse* might well have been the fruit of a carefully considered ecclesiastical policy. The book, so the author himself states, came into being at the request of others. It is a known fact that the chapter of Haarlem supervised the Catholic booktrade and stimulated the

---

31. ALBERDINGK THIJM: *Volksalmanak* 203; *Nieuw Nederlandsch biografisch woordenboek* 9 (1933) 185.
32. ROGIER: *Geschiedenis* 2, 194.
33. J.J. GRAAF: Uit de akten van het Haarlemsche kapittel, in *Bijdragen tot de geschiedenis van het bisdom van Haarlem* 15 (1888) 352.
34. ROGIER: *Geschiedenis* 2, 94. J.C. VAN DER LOOS: *Vaderlandsche kerkgeschiedenis* 3 (Amsterdam 1949) 21.
35. GRAAF: Uit de akten 357 and 365.

publication of at least some works.[36] Did the request come from that side? It seems unlikely that the canons had no knowledge at all of the project of their colleague. Moreover, the ecclesiastical permission to publish the *Misse* was actually granted by Leonardus Marius at Amsterdam in spite of the signature of Henricus Franken (Sierstorff) dated June 20, 1651 at Cologne.[37] This Marius, an outstanding member of the chapter, is considered to be the most important man in the supervision of the Catholic booktrade. And in 1651 he also published (accidentally?) a revised edition of Mary's Office at his own expense.[38]

Further, the *Misse* excellently fits Rovenius' endeavours to introduce the Roman liturgy into the Netherlands. Particularly his abbreviated edition of the *Rituale Romanum*, promulgated in 1622 and at that time probably published for the first time, was (in its proper order) used by Vander Kruyssen as a starting-point for most of the pages after the translated Mass.[39] Besides, here another connection with the chapter of Haarlem might be conjectured. During the same meeting, in which Vander Kruyssen was inducted as a canon, the decision was taken to reprint the abbreviated Ritual in an amended version.[40]

Finally, the question of the translation of the liturgical books has to be placed in the wider context of the growth of vernacular tongues to the highest respectability. Around 1650 Latin was still the language of European scholarship, but it had ceased to be the language of everything else that mattered to the life of man.[41]

All things considered, the *Misse* should be seen as a product of the upper classes of society and the leaders of the Church. Was the book also meant for a small élite? On the face of it the presence of a pictorial Mass argues in favour of a large public. For especially the engravings enabled the numerous illiterates to follow the Mass, as J. de Viguerie has pointed out in his stimulating survey of the devotion to the Mass in seventeenth and eighteenth century France.[42]

This relation between illiteracy and the illustrated Mass seems self-evident, but I doubt whether, at the time, the pictures were exclusively meant for the common people and the words for a better educated élite. It can hardly be irrelevant that the captions of the prints were put in Latin! Of course, to someone

---

36. ROGIER: *Geschiedenis* 2, 95-97.

37. L. LEUVEN: *De boekhandel te Amsterdam door katholieken gedreven* (Epe 1951) 24.

38. *Kerkeliike getyden van den hoogwaerdige moeder Gods, zo als die in de roomsche kerk in 't gebruik zyn, met de uitlegging van die.* Antwerp: P.M. (voor den auteur) 1651. ROGIER: *Geschiedenis* 2, 96-97.

39. H.v.H.: *Batavia sacra* 1-3 (Antwerp for Chr. Vermey 1715-1716) 3, 281-285 (decree of 1622, March 15) esp. 283. See for a (incomplete and amendable) description of the history of this Dutch *Rituale* F.X. SPIERTZ: Liturgie in de periode van de schuilkerken, in J.A. VAN DER VEN (ed.): *Pastoraal tussen ideaal en werkelijkheid* (Kampen 1985) 121-132, esp. 125-128.

40. GRAAF: Uit de akten 353.

41. CHADWICK: *The Reformation* 298-299.

42. DE VIGUERIE: La dévotion 18.

completely illiterate it did not matter at all what language was used. But in that case the use of Latin exhibits a rather cynical attitude. Moreover, the original edition of the *Misse* does not look very cheap. The fine engravings and the entire lay-out do not suggest a popular publication. Certainly, it is possible that the author distributed his work for free to his poor parishioners, but this solution does not easily fit the solemn dedication (only in the second edition) to the honourable, virtous lady Geertrudis Vander Kruyssen. She was, being his cousin, of the same descent and by no means the prototype of an ordinary, illiterate woman. I assume, therefore, as original destination of the *Misse* the litterate rather than the illiterate. This does not imply that the book later on might not have become more widespread, as we will see in the next paragraph.

4. THE RECEPTION OF THE *MISSE*

In Polman's manual a number of twenty reprints of Vander Kruyssens' booklet is mentioned, equally divided between the seventeenth and the eighteenth centuries and as a rule made on an Amsterdam press.[43] From this it seems obvious that such works were far more appreciated in the northern than in the southern part of the Dutch-speaking regions. Consequently it seems clear that the qualification 'liturgical' is more appropriate to the piety of the Catholics in the Calvinistic Republic than to that of their 'brethren' in the more baroque Spanish, later Austrian Netherlands. But these conclusions are premature and need correction. In so far as data about the reception of the *Misse* are suitable to make general statements on the liturgical orientation of the Northern and Southern Netherlands, they sooner have a tendency towards denying than affirming the prevailing view.

First, I have to draw attention to the fact that the history of print and reprint is more extensive than Polman supposed. The appendix to this contribution lists more than sixty items instead of twenty. The number may be brought down, when the conjectures[44] and dubious cases[45] are removed, but even then the list is quite long. Moreover, the guesses, based upon the numbering of the reprints[46] and the granting of privileges,[47] show that what has been preserved, is not a true reflection of the original production. If one takes account of these and other indications (such as variety of pictures,[48] pagination,[49] title[50] and ec-

43. POLMAN: *Katholiek Nederland* 1, 127.
44. Cf. nos. 6, 7, 8, 11, 14, 22, 30, 31, 38, 45 and 50.
45. Cf. nos. 4 and 17.
46. The numbering of the editions is not very reliable. Some of them stay unchanged in spite of several reimpressions. Of others it is uncertain whether the publisher has counted for himself only or in connection with an already existing series of another publisher.
47. Privileges can indicate a profitable issue. Even if there are now no more copies available of an edition from the period of the privilege, then its existence can still be assumed. Cf. CLEMENS: *De godsdienstigheid* 1, 25-26 and 37-38; cf. also appendix, nos. 38 and 39.
48. Cf. the annotation of nos. 3, 23, 24, 43, 46 and 58. This point is not systematically examined. In reality the number of different series is considerable larger than I have registered in the appendix.
49. There are 16 different pagings.
50. Cf. nos. 30, 32 and 63.

clesiastical approbation[51] and the co-existence of reprint-series from several printers), it is even plausible that the real number of reprints was much higher than its registration suggests now. It is likely that it was nearer to a hundred than to fifty and even then this estimation is probably rather low.[52]

And yet, this is not the whole story of the reception of the *Misse*. Its Antwerp publisher, J. Woons, incorporated the above mentioned *Christi bloedighe passie* in his publisher's program in 1675. In this book the well-known pictorial Mass has been furnished with new texts (by Poirters) and combined with Vander Kruyssens' translated Mass, according to the subtitle 'to increase the devotion of those who are not versed in the Latin language'.[53] Along this by-way the Mass translation went through reprint after reprint, outside the original context. This even occurred in the name of a Jesuit, although he may never have been consulted about the desirability of the combination, for he was dead when the book was published.[54] The same translation was also inserted in the *Christelyke onderwysingen en gebeden*.[55] This prayer-book was composed on the initiative and under supervision of the vicar apostolic J. van Neercassel, and published for the first time in 1685. Many reprints of this preeminently biblical and liturgical work followed, especially between 1685 and 1713.[56]

Thus far the data concerning the reception of the *Misse* provide us with sufficient indications to justify the proposition that Vander Kruyssen's (and his circle's) endeavours to reform piety were not fruitless. The modern house behind the ancient façade clearly pleased not only its architect, but also attracted many inhabitants. The cheaper editions which were soon brought out even suggest that the *Misse* must have been used increasingly by people below the level of the élite.

If we consider the distribution in time[57] and place,[58] then the available reprint

51. Cf. nos. 1, 17(?), 22, 33, 43, 45 and 61. See on this subject Th. CLEMENS: De uitgavegeschiedenis van het kerkboek de *Christelyke onderwysingen en gebeden* en de implicaties ervan voor de geschiedenis van de vroomheid in de Nederlanden (1685-1894), in *Archief voor de geschiedenis van de katholieke Kerk in Nederland* 27 (1985) 215-253, esp. 217 and 250-253.
52. Cf. CLEMENS: *De godsdienstigheid* 1, 30-48.
53. Subtitle: *Midtsgaders de misse over-gheset in het duyts, tot meerder devotie der ghener die in de latijnse taele niet en zijn ervaren. Verçiert met printen, dichten, ende zeden-leeringhen* ('Together with the Mass translated in (Low) German, to increase the devotion of those who are not versed in the Latin language. Adorned with pictures, poems and moral lessons.').
54. CLEMENS: La répercussion 220. Poirters died in 1674. 'His' translated Mass was later a strong argument in favour of the Jansenist point of view: even a Jesuit had edited one. Cf. *Berigt* 2.
55. I.e.: 'Christian instructions and prayers'.
56. CLEMENS: La répercussion 209 and 217-218; CLEMENS: De uitgavegeschiedenis 218-225.
57. The problem of undated issues has been solved by taking the 'W'(ork)-year between the first and the last known activity of the publisher in question. Cf. CLEMENS: *De godsdienstigheid* 2, xi-xii.
58. The problem of the use of hiding-addresses by Catholics in the Northern Netherlands is solved by taking the place of residence of the bookseller. Cf. CLEMENS: *De godsdienstigheid* 1, 50.

data point into the direction of a longstanding success, culminating in the first half of the eighteenth century. The success, however, was not restricted, as Polman assumed, to the Dutch Mission. In absolute figures there are even more reprints in the Southern than in the Northern Netherlands! As the table shows, the *Misse* appears of little use as evidence for the supposed differences in piety between North and South.

Table. The editions of the *Misse*, 1651-1851

Years	Dutch Mission	Southern Netherlands	Total
1651-1675	3	4	7
1676-1700	4	4	8
1701-1725	8	5	13
1726-1750	2	12	14
1751-1775	1	5	6
1776-1800	4	3	7
1801-1825	1	-	1
1826-1850	2	-	2
1851-	1	-	1
Total	26	33	59

The history of the editions of this book is more likely to confirm the 'regression' of the Catholics in the Dutch Mission after the schism of 1723, which has been highlighted in a book on the vernacular prayer-books from the Netherlands.[59]

This conclusion requires some explanation, also from the printing-history of the *Misse* itself. Till 1698 Vander Kruyssen's book was reprinted almost without any substantial change. In the next edition which can be dated with certainty, the translated canon of the Mass suddenly appears to have been replaced by prayers not derived from the Missal. The intervention is not explained, nor is it clear exactly who was responsible for it. There might be a link, however, with the struggle at the time between Jansenists and anti-Jansenists. The fully translated text of the Mass, which had been totally acceptable during a half century within the framework of the Counter-Reformation, now, within a decade, became a sign of heretical inclinations. Against this background the almost simultaneous disappearance of the translated canon from the *Misse* as well as *Christi bloedighe passie* and the Flemish version of *Christelyke onderwysingen en gebeden* gives supplementary evidence of the anti-Jansenist victory in the Netherlands shortly after 1700.

In the area of the Dutch Mission, where the Jansenists, not in the least in defense of their biblical and liturgical orientation, went into a schism, their op-

---

59. CLEMENS: *De godsdienstigheid* 1, 98. Cf. for the traditional view on the spirituality of the Dutch catholics among others J.A. BORNEWASSER: The Roman Catholic Church since the Reformation, in *Lowland highlights. Church and oecumene in the Netherlands* (Kampen 1972) 40-48, esp. 41-42 and 45-46.

ponents, on the rebound, rather massively turned away from all suspect books. Their fellow-believers in the Southern Netherlands, however, succeeded in saving much of the new orientation, albeit in an adapted form. E.g. the book of lectures, grown into a missal, is a case in point, as well as the books for the liturgical celebration of Holy Week, Eastern and Whitsun, and last but not least the very successful Flemish varieties of *Christelyke onderwysingen en gebeden*.[60]

Finally a remark must be made about the printing history of the *Misse* after 1750. It is true that, at first, an effort to catch up was made in the Dutch Mission, but on the whole the declining line is unmistakable. Here the question rises whether this was caused by a decline in interest in the piety represented by Vander Kruyssen's book. To solve this problem we need more than just information about the history of one work. From 1651 the total supply of devotional books had altered. Meanwhile the *Misse* had become an ancient book. In the nineteenth century it would only prolong its existence in a version patched up by Bontamps.

If we take into account the broader field of the prayer-books, we can ascertain that after 1800 especially the Catholics in the North preferred contemporary works, mostly of German origin. At that time hardly any place was left for traditional books in the field of devotional literature. Those new prayer-books were not necessarily more liturgical, but at least some of them certainly were innovatory as here and there the translated Mass found a place once more, and the devotional life was set within the framework of the ecclesiastical year.

In the South on the other hand, the faithful, taken aback by the negative experiences with Enlightenment and Revolution, first reverted to those seventeenth century prayer-books to which the *Misse* already had wanted to offer an alternative. When this changed after 1825, it was more in favour of a private than of a liturgical piety.[61]

5. CONCLUSION

If attention is payed only to internal alterations, the liturgical books, published by order of the Council of Trent, seem almost to have transcended history. If their reception is studied, however, relevant developments do appear to have occurred after Trent. What it all boiled down to, was a better educated clergy which tried to make the faithful more *circumstantes* again. At first sight the *Misse* does not seem to contribute to this renewal. On further investigation, however, an innovatory content appears to be wrapped in a traditional cover. The reception of Vander Kruyssen's work shows that his (and others) endeavours were well received, possibly among the élite at first, but later also in wider circles. Among the 'Romanists' in the North this development

60. CLEMENS: La répercussion 225-227.
61. CLEMENS: *De godsdienstigheid* 1, 153-162.

was checked by the schism of 1723. In the South, on the other hand, it continued, albeit within the boundaries set by the struggle between Jansenists and anti-Jansenists. Henceforth the translation of the canon was excluded, but the popular devotion went on becoming more liturgical. By Enlightenment and Revolution this process was reversed. The South turned its back upon the liturgy and returned to a more private piety. The printing history of the book with which we have dealt here, has hardly anything to contribute, however, to the study of that development.

APPENDIX

SURVEY OF THE EDITIONS OF THE *MISSE* WITH THE MOST IMPORTANT VARIATIONS IN THE TITLE.

To shorten the list the following abbreviations are used to date and localize the copies registered here below:

A = Approbation   F = Frontispiece   f: = for:
fsa = for sale at   P = Privilege   s.a. = sine anno
s.l. = sine loco   s.n. = sine nomine   T = Title-page
W = Working around the year ...

Hiding-addresses (e.g. Antwerpen for Amsterdam) are mentioned in parentheses after the publisher's name.

References to libraries are composed of (abbreviated) city-names (Adam = Amsterdam, Antw = Antwerpen, etc.) and, if necessary, a specification, for example the sigla of an order or congregation (MSC, OSB, OSC, etc.), a library (CD = Catharinadal, FT = Faculty of Theology, LEA = Library of the Episcopal Archive, MA = Museum Amstelkring, MC = Museum Catharijneconvent, PL = Provincial Library, RL = Royal Library, RS = Ruusbroec-Society, TBI = Titus Brandsma Institute, TL = Town Library, UA = University of Amsterdam, UL = University Library) and a special collection (CT = Collection Thomaasse with A, AP, R and W for subcollections).

The archive of the Council of Brabant is in the General State Archives at Brussel.

1. Amsterdam: for the author,
T:1651 A: H. Franken, Keulen, 20 June 1651, 421 pp.
AdamUA, CuykOSC, GravhRL, LeeuwPL, MaastrTL, MaastrUL, NijmUL, TilbFT, UtrMC, UtrUL-CTR.

2. Second edition Antwerpen, fsa Amsterdam: Ph. van Eyck,
T:1657 A:1651, 524 pp.;
enlarged with the benediction of mothers of new-born children, vespers and complin.
AdamMA, AdamUA, HboschLEA, LeuvenUL, MaastrUL, UtrMC, UtrUL-CTR.

3. Third edition Antwerpen: C. Woons; fsa Amsterdam: J. van Metelen,
T:1657 A:1651 549 pp.;
new engravings with Dutch captions.
AdamUA, TilbFT.

4. Brussel: J. Mommaert,
1658. *Haarlemsche bijdragen* 57 (1939) 137: as work of C. Molina alias C. Vermeulen. Perhaps here Vander Kruyssens *Misse* has been confused with Vermeulen's *'t Heyligh sacrificie der misse, II. Eenighe andere kerkelycke zegeningen, diensten, en ceremonien. III. 't Catholyck kerkelyck gebruyck der meest-gemeyne hh.sacramenten: uyt de Latynsche, inde Neder-duytsche tale vergadert, vertaelt, en uyt-geleydt* door C. Molina. Antwerpen: C. Woons, T:1652, 342-(6) pp. *AntwRS.*

5. Third edition (!) Antwerpen: C. Woons,
T:1661 A:1651, 549 pp.
AntwRS, GentUL.

6. Fourth edition?

7. Fifth edition?

8. Sixth edition?

9. Seventh edition Antwerpen: s.n.,
T:s.a. A:1651, 485 pp.
DendermondeOSB (the pictorial Mass is removed).

10. Antwerpen: s.n.,
T:1680 A:1651, 550 pp.
AntwTL, NijmTBI.

11. Antwerpen: J. Woons,
P:22 Dec.1682, 9 years.
Council of Brabant, inv.no. 3677, f.50: note of a copy.

12. Antwerpen f: N. Braau (Haarlem),
T:s.a. W:1687 A:1651, 486 pp.
AntwRS, LeuvUL.

13. Tenth edition Antwerpen f: J. Stichter (Amsterdam),
T:s.a. F:1689 A:1651, 486 pp.
LeuvUL, UdenOSC, UtrUL-CTW.

14. Antwerpen: J. Woons,
P:19 Dec.1691, 9 years.
Council of Brabant, inv.no. 3677, f. 50^v.

15. Twelfth edition Antwerpen f: F. van Metelen (Amsterdam),
T:1692 F:1683 A:1651, 486 pp. (printed as 386!)
AntwRS.

16. Tenth edition Antwerpen f: W. van Bloemen (Amsterdam),
T:1698 A:1651, 486 pp. (?)
AntwRS, BrusselRL, LeuvUL.

17. Antwerpen,
A: A. Hoefslagh, Antwerpen, 28 Nov.1703? Cf. no. 33;
Hoefslagh died on 13 July 1702; this apparently false approbation is probaby derived from that of no. 22.

18. Tenth edition Antwerpen f: W. van Bloemen (Amsterdam),
T:s.a. W:1707, 404+ pp.
AntwRS (incomplete).

19. Tenth edition Antwerpen f: W. van Bloemen (Amsterdam),
T:1709 A:1651, 486 pp.
AntwRS.

20. Tenth edition Antwerpen f: W. van Bloemen (Amsterdam),
T:1712 A:1651, 486 pp.;
with a vignette like in no. 13.
AntwRS, AntwTL.

21. Tenth edition Antwerpen f: W. van Bloemen (Amsterdam),
T:171? (defective) A:1651, 486 pp.;
with a vignette like in no. 13; other edition than no. 20.
AntwRS.

22. Antwerpen: P. Jouret,
P:13 Dec.1713, 9 years: A: A. van Ertborn, Antwerpen, 28 Nov.1713 (cf. no. 23).
Council of Brabant, inv.no. 3678, f. 16: note of a copy.

23. Eleventh edition Antwerpen: P. Jouret,
F:1715 A:(1651) and 1713 P:1713, 486 pp.;
with ill. by P.B(outtats).
De Boo (Kwadendamme).

24. Tenth edition Antwerpen: J. van Soest,
T:s.a. W:1717 A:1651, 405 pp.;
with wood-engravings.
AntwRS (2 copies).

25. Twelfth edition Antwerpen: P. Jouret,
T:1719 F:1715 A:(1651) and 1713, 486 pp.
AntwRS.

26. Twelfth edition Antwerpen: H. van Metelen (Amsterdam),
T:s.a. W:after 1719? A:(1651) and 1713, 486 pp.;
different from no. 25.
AdamUA, AntwRS.

27. Twelfth edition Antwerpen: H. van Metelen (Amsterdam),
T:1722 A:(1651) and 1713, 486 pp.
Westmalle.

28. Antwerpen f: I. vander Putte (Amsterdam),
T:s.a. F:1724 A:1651, 487 pp.
Rotterdam (Old Catholic Parish).

29. Antwerpen f: Th. Crajenschot (Amsterdam),
T:s.a. F:1724 A:1651;
Crajenschot started as publisher in 1745!
AdamUA.

30. Antwerpen: F. van Soest,
P:28 July 1725, 6 years.
Council of Brabant, inv.no. 3679, f. 12^r.

31. Antwerpen: P. Jouret,
P:21 March 1727, 9 years.
Council of Brabant, inv.no. 3679, f. 50^r;
according a side-note P. Jouret and H. Verdussen have later on agreed to print and sell the *Misse* together.

32. Antwerpen: J.F. van Soest,
T: ? A:(1651) and 1713 P:12 Oct. 1727, 485 pp.
(without title-page; description is derived from the text of the privilege, granted for *Den gulden mis-boeck*).
AntwRS.

214

33. Antwerpen: J. van Soest,
T:s.a. A: H.A.D., Keulen, 20 June = H. Franken, 20 June 1651; A. Hoefslagh, Antwerpen, 28 Nov. 1703; J. vander Staack, Antwerpen, 4 July 1730; 487 pp.; with the title: *Den gulden misboeck*; with wood-engravings. At least the first two approbations do not fit in!
OosterhCD.

34. Thirteenth edition Antwerpen: P. Scheffers ('s-Hertogenbosch),
T:s.a. W:1734, 486 pp.
TilbFT (without last pages: the approbation is missing).

35. Antwerpen: J. Verdussen,
T:s.a. W:1738 A:(1651) and 1713, 487 pp.
UtrUL-CTW.

36. Eleventh edition Antwerpen f: Erfg. Wed. C. Stichter (Amsterdam),
T:1740 F:1689 A:1651, 486 pp.;
year also *in fine.*
AdamMA, TilbFT (title-page is missing).

37. Twelfth edition Antwerpen: M. Verdussen,
T:1740 A:(1651) and 1713, 486 pp.
UtrUL-CTA.

38. Antwerpen: M. Verdussen,
P:31 Jan. 1742, 9 years.
Council of Brabant, inv.no. 3680, f. 13.

39. Antwerpen: Wed. P. Jouret,
T:1743 A:1730 P:10 April 1743, 487 pp.
Council of Brabant, inv.no. 3680, f. 37;
AntwRS.

40. Antwerpen: A. Everaerts,
T:s.a. W:1745 A:1730 P:1743 (for Wed. P. Jouret), 487 pp.
AntwRS.

41. Eleventh edition Antwerpen: J.F. van Soest,
T:s.a. W:1746 A:(1651), 429 pp. (printed as 229!);
with the title: *Den gulden mis-boeck*; perhaps a part of the approbations is missing; F like F of Stichter; with wood-engravings.
MaastrUL.

42. Eleventh edition Gent: M. de Goesin,
T:s.a. W:1746 (A is missing *in fine*), 403 pp.;
with the title: *Den gulden mis-boeck*. After 1755? Cf. below no. 48: tenth edition and similar paging).
GentUL (defective).

43. Gent: M. de Goesin,
T:1747 A: J.F. Bruynsteen, Gent, 12 Aug. 1747, 395 pp.;
with ill. by Wauters of 1746.
AntwRS.

44. Twelfth edition Antwerpen: M. Verdussen,
T:1748 A:(1651) and 1713 P:s.d., 486 pp.
AntwRS, TilbFT.

45. Antwerpen: A.P. Colpyn,
P:15 Sept. 1751, 9 years, for: *Den gulden mis-boeck*. Perhaps with A:
J. vander Staack, Antwerpen, 1751 (cf. no. 59),
Council of Brabant, inv.no. 3680, f. 144.

46. Gent: J. Meyer,
T:s.a. W:1753 A:1747, 417 pp.;
with ill. by Kraft of 1732.
Breda (Museum).

47. Gent: J. Meyer,
T:1754 A:1747, 417 pp.;
with ill. by Kraft of 1732.
AntwRS, MaastrTL.

48. Tenth edition fsa Antwerpen: J.P. Willemsens,
T:s.a. W:1755 A:1751, 403 pp.
AntwRS.

49. Antwerpen f: G. Tielenburg (Amsterdam),
T:s.a. W:1758 A:1651, 487 pp.
AdamMA, AdamUA, MaastrTL (2 copies), *UtrUL-CTAP*.

50. Antwerpen: A.P. Colpyn,
P:1 June 1761, 9 years, note of a copy from 6 July 1762; for: *Den gulden mis-boeck*.
Council of Brabant, inv.no. 3680, f. 144.

51. Thirteenth edition Antwerpen f: Erfg. Wed. C. Stichter (Amsterdam),
T:1779 A:1651, 473 pp.
TilbMSC, TilbFT.

52. Fourteenth edition Antwerpen f: Erf. Wed. C. Stichter (Amsterdam),
T:s.a. A:1651, 486 pp.
AdamMA (with silvermark of 1754 or 1779).

53. Antwerpen: Henricus van Soest,
T:s.a. W:1780 A:(1651), 1703 and 1730, 487 pp.;
with the title: *Den gulden mis-boeck*; with vignette like in no. 13 and with wood-engravings.
UtrUL-CTR.

54. Tenth edition fsa Antwerpen: F.I. Vinck,
T:s.a. W:1783 A:1651, 405 pp.;
with wood-engravings.
Achel, AdamUA, AntwRS, MaastrUL, NijmTBI, TilbFT, Westmalle. In *AntwRS* 4 different copies!

55. Fourteenth edition Antwerpen f: Erfg. Wed. C. Stichter (Amsterdam),
T:1788 A:1651, 473 pp.
NijmUL.

56. Venlo; Gelder: Wed. H. Bontamps; F. en C. Bontamps,
T:1789 A:s.d.(1651) P:1789 for 20 years, 476 pp.;
with ill. by Wauters of 1746.
TilbFT, UtrMC, UtrUL-CTA, UtrUL-CTAP, UtrUL-CTW.

57. Gent: B. Poelman,
T:s.a. W:1800 A:1747, 417 pp.;
with ill. by Kraft of 1732.
GentUL.

58. Gent: J. Begyn,
T:s.a. W:1804 A:1747, 417 pp.;
with ill. by Boole of 1799.
GentUL, MaastrTL.

59. Twelfth edition Antwerpen: J.H. Heyliger,
T:s.a. W:1806 A: J. vander Staack, 7 Sept. 1751, 369 pp.;
preface signed by A.V.R. (= A.V.K.)
AntwRS.

60. Antwerpen f: G. Banning,
T:s.a. W:1813 A:(1651), 476 pp.
UtrMC.

61. Venlo: Wed. H. Bontamps,
A: 1844; cf. no. 63.

62. Second edition Venlo: Wed. H. Bontamps,
preface of 1848; cf. no. 63.

63. Fourth edition Amsterdam; Rotterdam: B. Lenfring,
T:s.a. A:1844 P:1789, 466 pp.;
with the title: *De heilige mis*. With preface by Wed. H. Bontamps for the second edition of 1848.
NijmTBI.

Child and Church, Communion and culture[1]

RUDOLF BOON

There were really no children present? Or did the artist perhaps overlook them, when he was drawing what happened before his eyes around the table of the Lord? Talented draughtsmen and engravers in the 'Siècle des lumières' however did not overlook even the very little ones, when they had a part in the scene. For these artists applied themselves to illustrate accurately with their prints what happened, e.g. in the more important ceremonials in the different Christian Churches, as may be seen in the plates which accompany this contribution, taken from the encylopedic standard work *Naaukeurige beschryving der uitwendige godsdienst-plichten.*[2] The images of the Communion are so very sharp, so real to life, that we can read from them the age structure of the congregation. The communicants, which the artist saw go up to the altar or sit down at the table for the Lord's Supper, did not form a grey-haired group at all. Apparently there were many young people among them. But children, no, they were not present.

Why is it that we look in vain for the child at the Lord's Supper? For its absence is certainly not a matter of course!

1. NO SEPARATE CHILD WORLD

In which area of daily life of the world of 'grown ups' do we not meet children in those days? From which events were the youngsters painstakingly kept away? Take the whole human existence between birth and death, at home and on the streets: everywhere the little ones were, so to say, on top of it. The extent to which children were familiar with death and to which they were aware of the shortness of life can be seen e.g. from two Dutch poems for children. The first is by Hieronymus van Alphen:[3]

1. This contribution was translated and edited from the author's Dutch manuscript by Marc Schneiders.
2. A fuller title of this six volume work is: *Naaukeurige beschryving der uitwendige godsdienst-plichten, kerk-zeden en gewoontens van alle volkeren der waereldt in een historisch verhaal* [...] opgeheldert en in kunstige tafereelen afgemaalt: geteekent door Bernard PICARD; uit het Fransch in Nederduitsch overgezet door Abraham MOUBACH ('s-Gravenhage-Amsterdam-Rotterdam 1727-1738). It is the Dutch version of Bernard PICART's *Cérémonies et coûtumes religieuses de tous les peuples du monde* [...] (Amsterdam 1723-1743) in 8 vols. The work was also published in English: *The ceremonies and religious customs of the various nations of the known world* [...] Illustrated with a large number of folio copper plates [...] designed by Mr. Bernard PICART [...] Faithfully translated into English by a gentleman, some time since of St. John's College in Oxford (London 1733-1739) in 7 vols.
3. Hieronymus van Alphen (1746-1803), lawyer and civil servant, is most famous for his poetry for children. He also wrote religious poetry and essays on art theory.

La COMMUNION des REFORMÉS.

La COMMUNION des ANGLICANS a SAINT PAUL.

La COMMUNION *des* LUTHERIENS *dans* L'EGLISE *des* MINORITES *à* AUGSBOURG.

La CENE *des* ANABAPTISTES *premiere figure.*

La CENE *des* ANABAPTISTES *seconde figure.*

La COMMUNION.

Ach! mijn zusjen is gestorven,
nog maar veertien maanden oud.
'k Zag haar dood in 't kistje liggen:
ach! wat was mijn zusje koud!
'k Riep haar toe: mijn lieve Mietje!
Mietje, Mietje! maar voor niet.
Ach! hare oogjes zijn gesloten;
schreijen moet ik van verdriet.[4]

Alas! she's dead, my little sister,
Fourteen months – and no more – old;
Stretched out in her tiny coffin,
Oh! she was so very cold!
Loud I called my darling Mary,
Mary, Mary, but in vain;
Closed for ever are those eyelids,
Cry I must with grief and pain.[5]

The second example is by Pieter 't Hoen.[6] To the question of his little sister:
'Why do you not play with me?', little Peter answers:

Neen, zei Pietje, al ben ik klijn,
Ligt kan mij op heden
Nog de dood vertreden.
Zou ik dan zoo dartel zijn?
Neen, ik zoek hier boven
Eeuwig God te loven.[7]

No, said Peter, I may be little,
But easy on this very day
Death may trample me.
How would I be playful?
No, I seek above us
To praise God eternally.

Toddlers were not addressed in 'child language'. If they happened to be present when the intimate affairs of human life were discussed, adults did not
change to whispering or limit themselves to hinting. The child should be part

---

4. From Hieronymus VAN ALPHEN: *Proeve van kleine gedigten voor kinderen* ('A sample of little
   poems for children'), originally published anonymously in three volumes in Utrecht between
   1778 and 1782. The text is printed here following J.I.D. NEPVEU's edition of the collected
   poems of Van Alphen: *Dichtwerken van Mr. Hieronymus van Alphen volledig verzameld en
   met een levensberigt van den dichter verrijkt* (Utrecht 1871) 265.
5. Translation from: *Poetry for children by Hieronymus van Alphen*. Translated into English
   verse by F.J. MILLARD (London 1856) 8.
6. Pieter 't Hoen (1744-1828), a journalist and editor, wrote poetry for children in imitation of
   Van Alphen and also some plays.
7. From Pieter 'T HOEN: *Nieuwe proeve van klijne gedichten voor kinderen* ('A new sample of
   little poems for children') (1778-1779) in 6 parts, with continuous pagination. The text cited is
   from the third impression of the first part (Utrecht 1778) 30.

of the adult life and find his place in society as soon as possible. That was the aim of every upbringing. In intellectual families it was not extraordinary when children of four years old were able to read and write. When they were twelve many could master French, Latin and Greek and produce their first literary achievements. And at the age of fourteen they started their university education, which they finished with the doctorate at seventeen. To illustrate this, we may take e.g. the poem *Aan een lieve kleine jongen* ('To a dear little boy') from the *Economische liedjes* ('Industrious songs') by Betje Wolff en Aagje Deken.[8] The accompanying print shows among the members of the family a little boy who is hardly able to look upon the table. Nevertheless, for him the time of playing is over:

Heintje, nu 's de tyd verscheenen
Dat men u de Taalen leert; – [...]
't Is of ik u al hoor zeggen:
Haut hoog, *Bas* laag; en zo voordt.
Ny zyt gy aan 't conjungeeren,
Of zoekt driftig naar een woord
In de groote *Dictionaire*,
't Zy van *Halma*, of *Marin*;
'k Weet, gy zult wel haast uw Vader
Iets vertellen in 't Latyn.
Lustig! nu aan Theemaas maken.
Help! daar komt het Grieks in 't spel;
Nu dat zal zich ook wel schikken
Doet gy slegts uw zaakjes wel. [...]
Dus verloopen deeze jaaren.
Gy zyt naarstig en te vreên.
En wat dan? zult gy my vragen:
Dan? naar 't Academie heen'. [...][9]

Henry, now the time has come
That they will teach you the languages. [...]
It is as if I already hear you say:
Haut high, *bas* low, and so forth.
Now you are busy with conjugations
Or looking hastily for a word
In your big *Dictionaire*,
That by Halma or Marin's.
I know, soon you will to your father

8. Betje Wolff (1738-1804) and Aagje Deken (1741-1804) were two female authors working and since 1777 living together. They published novels and volumes of verse, mostly jointly, which are generally considered to belong to the best that was written in the period.
9. Text according to the third, popular, edition: *Economische liedjes, uitgegeven door E. Bekker, weduwe A. Wolff en A. Deken* (s' Graavenhage 1785) 110-111. This and all other earlier editions do not contain the plates, which were printed for the first time between 1792 and 1798. Cf. P.J. BUIJNSTER: *Bibliografie der geschriften van en over Betje Wolff en Aagje Deken* (Utrecht 1979) 76.

Tell something in Latin.
Merry now doing an exercise.
Beware, Greek comes into play.
Well, this will also fit in,
If you only do your job well. [...]
Like this these years will pass.
You are industrious and content.
And after? you will ask me.
After: to the university! [...]

In our eighteenth-century society we quite often find talented young men of around twenty in leading positions.

The position of children and young people in the eighteenth century was not any different from that in the sixteenth and seventeenth centuries. Society took young people seriously. The period of being 'under age' was not long.

2. NO SEPARATE CHILD RELIGION

With this sort outline of the child in eighteenth century society in mind, we might suppose that the education which the Church provided for children corresponds with what we saw. And indeed it did. Let us limit ourselves to the Netherlands. Towards the end of the seventeenth century an enlightened man like Balthasar Bekker[10] accommodates the dear youngsters with his *Gerymde kinderleer of kort begrijp van den Nederlandschen catechismus. Tot behulp der memorie voor de kinderen en eenvoudigen gerymd* ('Rhymed doctrine for children or short summary of the Dutch Cathechism. Rhymed to assist the memory of children and simple folk').[11] For the very young pupils in religion he had compiled *LII vraagjes voor de kleyne kindertjes* ('52 little questions for the little children').[12]

These verses may be called simple without qualification. Still it must have taken the children some effort to learn the long drawn-out rhymed text by heart. Moreover, the contents are hardly what we could call 'a children's lesson'.

Eighty years later we find in the teaching room the *Groot A.B.C. boek. Zeer bekwaam voor de jonge kinderen te leeren* ('Large A.B.C. book: very efficient for children to learn').[13] The contents are:

–*Dat Vader Onze* ('The Lord's prayer');
–*De hoofdartijkelen onzes Christelijken geloofs* ('The main articles of our Christian religion');

10. Dutch Reformed divine (1634-1698), known especially for his combat against superstitious beliefs in devils and spirits. His ideas in these matters were heavily opposed and he was deposed as minister by the provincial synod of North Holland in 1692. But the Church of Amsterdam, which he served, kept his position open and continued to pay him his salary.
11. In: *De Friesche godgeleerdheid van Balthasar Bekker: begrijpende alle desselfs werken in Friesland uitg. en 't gene daar af geoordeeld en daar over voorgevallen is* [...] (Amsterdam 1693) 625-638.
12. *Friesche godgeleerdheid* 639-645.
13. This book was published in Amsterdam in 1774.

–*Van den heyligen doop* ('Of holy baptism');
–*De tien geboden des Heeren* ('The ten commandments of the Lord');
–*Van 't nagtmaal Christi* ('On the Lord's Supper');
–*Het morgengebed* ('Morning prayer');
–*Het avondgebed* ('Evening prayer');
–*Gebed voor den eeten* ('Prayer before meals');
–*Gebed naa het eeten* ('Prayer after meals');
and as a last item: *Christelijk A.B.C.* ('Christian alphabet').

Thus young children in the Netherlands receive for their first reading matter the classical texts as printed in the prayer books of the Reformed Church. In this way children are acquainted at an early age with the language of worship, in Church and around the table at home. The *Christelijk A.B.C.* is a collection of short and easy to memorise passages from Holy Scripture and pious sayings. We can imagine that children were looking captivated at the innumerable prints of Jan Luijken,[14] especially at his large scenes from the Bible. But did they also read the accompanying texts, the pious thoughts in *Het menselyk bedryf* ('The human trade'), *Het leerzaam huisraad* ('The instructive household belongings'), *Jesus en de ziel* ('Jesus and the soul') and in *Des menschen begin, midden en einde* ('Man's beginning, middle and end')?[15]

The answer to this question is given in the reprint of the last named title in 1824. 'This author', writes one of the editors, 'remembers, at the least, the pleasure with which he in his childhood looked at the pictures in father Luiken and how he learned some verses by heart'. And Betje Wolff, of whom we cited a poem for children earlier on, recalled how she as a little girl overcame her fear for the 'black man' and for darkness by repeating a verse from *Des menschen begin, midden en einde*:

Als 't Kindje vroom en schiklyk is,
En niet en speeld met stoute knaapen,
Zo mag het in de duisternis,
Na zijn gebed, gerust gaan slaapen;
Want wie by Jeugd de Deugd betracht,
Die heeft de Engelen tot wacht.[16]

If a child is pious and obedient,
And does not play with bold lads,
Then it in the darkness may
After his prayer sleep with peace.

14. Jan or Joan or Johannes Luiken or Luyken (1649-1712), a Dutch poet and engraver, is famous for his emblem books.
15. For the different editions of these works see: John LANDWEHR: *Emblem books in the Low Countries. A bibliography* (Utrecht 1970) nos. 347 ff.
16. H.C.M. GHIJSEN: *Betje Wolff in verband met het geestelijk leven van haar tijd. Jeugd en huwelijksjaren* (Rotterdam 1919) 2-3. Text of the poem cited from: Joannes LUIKEN: *Des menschen begin, midden en einde* [...] (Leiden [1888]) 65.

For who in his youth practises virtue,
Has the angels as his strength.[17]

We may add that Jan Luijken compiled the little book from which this text is taken for his grandson.

Considering all, we would really expect children[18] together with adults and adolescents at the Lord's Supper. We may return to our initial question: How to explain the absence of the child at the Communion?

3. THE AGE OF THE COMMUNICANTS INCREASES MORE AND MORE

The Church in late antiquity did not find any difficulty in taking in the baptized child into the community around the table. It is still the usage of the Eastern Orthodox Churches that infants and toddlers and even babies communicate. Child Communion was not a problem at all in the Western Church during the Middle Ages. But the Fourth Lateran Council (1215) implied that a child could receive the sacrament of the altar *postquam ad annos discretionis pervenerit*.[19] According to the general opinion children were considered to have reached these 'years of discretion' approximately at seven. At this age they would be capable of realising what the Mass is about.

In the days of the Reformation the youngest communicants are again a few years older. Calvin's opinion is that a child of ten is fit to be admitted to the Lord's table, after it has proven to have sufficient knowledge of the faith.[20]

At the 21st session (16 July 1562) the Council of Trent decided to stick to the rule of 1215: Children who have not reached the moment when they start using the faculty of reason, do not have to communicate. Reborn in the bath of baptism and incorporated in Christ, they cannot loose the grace of being a child of God, which they received, at that age.[21] That children should not receive the sacrament of confirmation before they have acquired the use of

---

17. Cf. also the second last line of the 8th stanza of Betje Wolff's poem *Het leestertje* ('The little girl reading') in de *Economische gedichtjes* (cf. above note 9): [...] *'k Lees ook Geestelyke boeken, En gebeden op myn tyd* [...] (p. 228) ('... I also read religious books and prayers at proper times...'). And in *Het dankbare kind* (pp. 83-86) ('The grateful child') included in the same work the little girl is overjoyed with a Bible, which she has received as a prize in school from the hands of a deacon.
18. Although it will most probably be superfluous, I like to stress, just in case some reader may be left uncertain about my intention, that the children I am talking about here are always baptized children.
19. Henricus DENZINGER and Adolfus SCHÖNMETZER: *Enchiridion symbolorum, definitionum et declarationum de rebus fidei et morum* (Barcinone-Friburgi Brisgoviae-Romae 1976^{36}) no. 812.
20. For the sources of the data in this paragraph, I refer the reader to the references in my: Lidworden van de kerk: van devaluatie naar revaluatie van de doop. Vraagteken rondom een (tamelijk recente) traditie, in *Eredienstvaardig* 2 (1986) 237-256.
21. Council of Trent, 21st session: *Doctrina de communione sub utraque specie et parvulorum*, c. 4 and canon 4.

reason, was added by the Catechism of the Council of Trent.[22] This council also decreed that at the least on Sundays and other feast days in every parish the children should be instructed in the rudiments of the faith and that obedience to God and their parents will be inculcated in them.[23]

A thorough catechesis to prepare children for confirmation requires time. Moreover, one may ask, whether a young child is capable to assimilate what is taught and to understand properly what the purport of confirmation is. And thus the age for confirmation and the first Communion is moved up slowly to the fourteenth year in the period of the Counter Reformation. Later on in the Reformed Church it will be usually young adults, who put in their names for *aanneming* ('confirmation').

When knowledge and understanding is required of those aspiring to communicate, these pupils in the faith certainly cannot be young children.

4. THE INFLUENCE OF RATIONALISM

For the ideas behind this moving up of the age of the youngest communicants a remark of Descartes is perhaps characteristic. According to this philosopher the childhood years are a period 'characterized by errors, springing from the mistake to regard sense impressions as the reality of things'.[24] Descartes does not have in mind here the incapability of the child to understand the mysteries of the faith. But if it is true that children do not come beyond the visible, how can they penetrate into the invisible and find communion with it? 'That we then may be nourished on the true heavenly bread Christ, let us not cling with our hearts to the outward bread and wine, but raise the same upwards into heaven, where Christ Jesus is...' (from the classical Reformed form for the Lord's Supper).[25] If the child with its visual focus cannot participate in this spiritual flight, how then will it be capable to 'discern' the body and blood of the Lord?

With Descartes, followed by Locke, we are at the beginning of the Age of Reason, which will see the elaboration of the idea of a 'natural religion'. Through the light of reason, says Locke, God has revealed to all men, at least if they make use of this light, that he is good and merciful. This natural light, coming from God, makes known to man his duties. It also makes him find the means to reconcile himself with the supreme Being and to receive his forgive-

---

22. *Catechismus ex decreto Concilii Tridentini ad parochos* II, 3, qu. 17 (ed. Ratisbonae 1911, p. 157).

23. 24th session: *Decretum de reformatione* c. 4.

24. *Les principes de la philosophie* 1, 71-72 (DESCARTES: *Oeuvres philosophiques* 3 (Paris 1973) 139-142).

25. The Dutch text from 1566, which is still used in the *Nederlandse Hervormde Kerk* (Dutch Reformed Church) in 'right wing' congregations, may be found in: Irmgard PAHL (ed.): *Coena Domini* 1. *Die Abendmahlsliturgie der Reformationskirchen im 16./17. Jahrhundert* (Spicilegium Friburgense 29) (Fribourg 1983) 533 and the German text on which the Dutch is based: PAHL: *Coena Domini* 1, 519-520.

ness of sins. These means, which the natural light imparts upon man, are the consciousness and the disapproval of sin, the prayer for forgiveness and the recognition that God's eternal unchangeable law is just and reasonable; and finally a serious resolution to live henceforth according to this law. In this law, which man is capable of knowing by the natural light of reason, God reveals himself to him, as the merciful, gracious and just. The Christian faith concurs with natural religion, but is, so to speak, a revelation which reaches further. To be a Christian you need to have the Bible, especially the teaching of Jesus and his apostles. To believe that Jesus of Nazareth is the Messiah, to confess Him as the Lord, to obey his commandments: these things make a man a Christian.[26]

In the days of the Enlightenment many took these views as the standard for the religious and moral formation of children. They will have limited themselves to the area of natural religion and have kept the catechesis of the Christian faith for those of somewhat higher age. To get an impression of what was imparted in the religious education of children, we have a look at the letter 'G' in the *Vaderlandsch A-B boek voor de Nederlandsche jeugd* ('National A.B.(C.) book for the Dutch youths'), written by the lawyer J.H.Swildens.[27] There we read:

'God is invisible and incomprehensible for us. From the existence of the visible world, we can prove with certainty the existence of one God. But the general knowledge of this most serious truth can be reached without a verbiage of proof. It belongs especially to the rational nature of man and is innate.' The Creator is the Lord of the universe and of our lives. 'God lets everything grow which is necessary for us to live healthy and happily. [...] A child which is properly reared will accept these truths immediately. [...] God's endless wisdom and goodness shine through all creatures, through the smallest as well as through the largest. But nowhere is God's omnipotence more remarkable than in the stars. [...] Such a remarkable great and glorious universe has God created from nothing and He continues to maintain and govern it. What a tremendous and glorious supreme Being God must be!' Because we, his creatures, belong to him in every way, we are 'undoubtedly obliged to serve Him'. [...] 'Religion consists of this: that we recognize God as the supreme Lord of the universe and do his will. God does not want anything but what is truly salutary for humanity.'

Below the first print at the letter 'G', a landscape with plants and animals, is printed this children's verse:

God is van dit alles Heer.
– Alles wat gy ziet,
Aarde, Hemel, 't gantsch Heelal
maakte God uit niet.

26. His ideas on natural religion and the Christian faith John LOCKE most comprehensively expounded in *The reasonableness of Christianity, as delivered in Scriptures* (London 1695). Pedagogical conclusions from these ideas he had already drawn in *Some thoughts concerning education* (London 1693).
27. This was published in Amsterdam in 1781. There is a reprint of the more interesting pages, including those cited further on in the text ('s-Gravenhage 1941).

God is Lord of all this.
Everything you see,
Earth, heaven, the whole universe,
God created from nothing.

And below a second plate, a landscape by night under the starry heaven:

God is van dit alles Heer.
– Leer hier welk een goed,
Wys en magtig Heer Hy is,
dien gy dienen moet.

God is Lord of all this.
Comprehend here what a good,
Wise and mighty Lord He is.
Serving Him you should.

Among the subjects in religious education based upon the ideas of 'natural religion', we will probably not find the Lord's Supper. For a subject like this, they say, a child is not yet ready and fit. And therefore it is not expected at the table of the Lord.

5. THE INFLUENCE OF PIETISM

The approach of altar or table had to be preceded by an inner preparation and selfexamination. A range of devotional writings assisted the communicants in this preparation. The writers of these texts do not leave us in any doubt to which denomination they consider themselves to belong. Nevertheless, despite denominational controversies, these writings show a remarkable unity in spirituality. It is a unity which has its origin in the congeniality, which is no less remarkable, of very diverging movements: the variegated British Puritanism, the Dutch Reformed *Nadere reformatie* ('Further Reformation'), German Lutheran Pietism and Jansenism in the Gallican Church. Far outside the boundaries of their parties they have influenced Western Christianity and have determined the religious climate to a large degree. Are perhaps these movements indicative for the spirit of the age? At any rate, all this 'piety' around the table of the Lord's Supper and the altar could be characterized as a spirituality of personal religious life. What is important in this spirituality is a personal involvement in the salvation which is preached and an inner assimilation of the doctrine which is taught; it is about being ready to examine oneself and a decision for a conversion to the 'new life', about the resolution to sanctify one's life and about being susceptible of a personal religious experience: the experience of God's work in one's personal life, which the Dutch call *bevinding*. To illustrate the concurrence of different denominations in this respect, I give two religious works for comparison. The first is a collection of meditations and prayers related to the Lord's Supper. Amongst this kind of texts it is a good example of material for meditation at a high level. It is called:

Het recht gebruyck van des Heeren h. avondmaal ('The right use of the Lord's Holy Supper'). In this collection, published in Amsterdam in 1700, we find for the preparation for the sacrament the following meditations:

–Ootmoedige sucht, om te bidden eer men aan de tafel des Heren gaat ('A meek sigh to pray before one approaches the table of the Lord');
–Sucht voor een swacke ziele tot Godt haren Vader ('Sigh for a weak soul unto God its Father');
–De vriendelijke noodiging van Jesus Christus, der zielen bruydegom ('The friendly invitation of Jesus Christ, the bridegroom of the soul') with the *Antwoord der boetvaerdige ziel* ('Answer of the penitent soul'), based on the Song of songs;
–Aendachtige versuchtingen, op de uyterlycke handelingen van het heylige avondmael ('Attentive sighs at the external actions of the Holy Supper');
–Klachte van een swaermoedige ziele over het gebruyck van des Heeren avondmael, met een nevens-gaende troost ('Lament of a melancholic soul about the use of the Lord's Supper, with an accompanying consolation').

The second collection, to compare with the Reformed one, is a product of the Gallican Church, translated into Dutch as *De geestelijke zielbestierder* ('The spiritual guide of the soul') and published in Utrecht in 1740. Let us choose from this little book the chapters for the inner preperation for Communion:

–Van de dorrigheden en verstrooidheden, welke in het gebed voorvallen ('Of the aridities and distractions, which happen during prayer');
–Van de boetoeffeningen der rechtvaerdigen ('Of the penitent exercises of the justified');
–Van de godvrugtigheid welke vereischt word om te communiceren ('Of the devotion which is necessary to communicate');
–Van de begeerte tot de h. communie ('Of the desire for holy Communion');
–Van de beletselen welke de daegelijksche zonden aan het dikmaels communiceren kunnen stellen ('Of the impediments which daily sins put against frequent Communion');
–Dat de geloovigen groote reden tot zugten hebben over de ellende van dit leven en over hunne afgescheidenheid van God ('That the faithful have ample reason to sigh on account of the misery of this life and their separation from God').

De geestelijke zielbestierder, originally published in 1689, brings us into a genuine Roman Catholic circle. Nevertheless the agreement with the Reformed meditations in the aspect of 'experience' (*bevinding* or *bevindelijkheid*) is really striking. In the Churches of Rome and Reformation the spiritual climate is strongly determined by this spirituality of a personal experience of God. Now, this 'secret familiarity' with the Lord, which we find in innumerous devotional tracts, in so many biographies and diaries of religious people, is unknown to the younger child.

It is this mood of pietism which dominates in the prints of the Communion, which accompany this contribution. Whether it is enacted in an Anglican, a Roman Catholic, a Lutheran or a Reformed Church, or in a Mennonite service, everywhere prevails the same mood of pious attention, of seriousness and reverence, of modesty and solemness. Is it perhaps because of the absence of the child that this solemness tends to become the graveness so typical for the adult world in the age of Enlightenment?

What caused the end to child Communion in this period? From what we have seen, I venture to conclude that influences of Rationalism on the one hand and Pietism on the other have played an important role.[28]

6. THE RISING CHILD CULTURE

Other influences followed. Seven years after the orthodox Reformed *Groot A.B.C. boek* the *Vaderlandsch A.B. boek voor de Nederlandsche jeugd* was published. We have seen both titles already. The *Vaderlandsch A.B. boek* is a beautifully illustrated little book in which the religious and moral ideals of the Enlightenment are voiced for young children. It belongs to a completely new type of literature: the book for children. In England it started with the books for children of John Newbery, the most well known of which is his *Goody two shoes*.[29] In the Netherlands it is Hieronymus van Alphen who set the *genre* going with his *Proeve van kleine gedigten voor kinderen*, immediately followed by *Nieuwe proeve van klyne gedichten voor kinderen* by Pieter 't Hoen. Above we have already seen poems from both works, which were published in 1778. At the same period we see for the first time a special fashion for children in clothing. The little boy is hardly ever dressed anymore to look like an adult of smaller proportions. In his 'fantasy outfit' according to the English cut he is clearly defined as a child.[30]

In the same period a new institution is born alongside of the Church: Sunday school. It was an initiative of the Evangelical revival in the Church of England. At first it was only an attempt to help the children of the lower classes, from non-Church-going groups, on Sunday afternoons. Those poor youths acquired a knowledge of the Bible and because child labour hindered them from attending an ordinary school regularly, they also received some primary education in Sunday school. Slowly however, Sunday school lost its 'poor man's' character and developed into a playing room alongside of the Church, in which for approximately a century and a half, generation after generation, practically every Protestant youth in the English speaking world and on the European continent, from toddler to adolescent, spent the Sunday morning.

7. NOT WELCOME IN CHURCH

A playing room alongside of the Church, or to put it sharply, aside from the Church. Sunday school now has its own liturgical apparatus: special versions

---

28. This assessment is confirmed by a parallel conclusion in my essay mentioned already in note 20. In this essay I argue that baptism has been devaluated in the Dutch Reformed Church under the influences of Rationalism and Pietism.
29. London 1765.
30. An interesting example of this may be seen in the picture accompanying the verse *Het blijde kind* in the *Economische liedjes* (cf. note 9).

of the Bible for the child, songs, prayers and stories, adapted to the world of the youths. Sunday school distributes numbers of books for children, a lot of playing material and also provides audio-visual means, detailed information and expert instruction for the teachers.

In Sunday school a tenor of language, tone and style has developed which is far apart from what happens usually around the pulpit. Looking from Sunday school the conventional preaching service is apparently intended for 'grown ups', something for the older people and thus 'old' and out of date.

And the ministration of the Lord's Supper? 'Hasn't this been from ancient times (as we now know) a ceremonial for the "tested" faithful? The child cannot nearly be ready for such a thing!' And thus the Lord's Supper disappeared from the field of vision of Sunday school. Mercilessly Sunday school reveals how things are between child and Church: the conventional Protestant preaching service and the ministration of the Lord's Supper are indeed an affair of 'grown ups'. At most children are tolerated at times for a while in Church, e.g. at the beginning of the service or at a baptismal ceremony. 'But after this they have to leave, be gone from the Church, back to Sunday school class. For how they do disturb, spontaneous and restless as they are, the adults in their attention to the sermon! Just imagine, they might even break the solemn tenor of the celebration of the Lord's Supper!'

8. OUTSIDE THE SERVICE: UNTIL RECENTLY

It started towards the end of the eighteenth century with a new view on childhood and the accompanying new approach to children. Names may be mentioned of influential men: Rousseau, Pestalozzi, Basedow, men set off by others from an earlier generation like Comenius, Locke, Vico. It would be a long history of all which has been thought, written and taught on childhood and of the many things which have been done with children according to those thoughts and doctrines. It reveals rather more about the adult world than about the child. This whole history seems to be a kind of mirror of the image of man which Western society moulded time and again, a mirror also of the patterns of its culture and its aims.

What has been said briefly about the relation of Church and Sunday school may suffice to indicate that the history of social sciences with regard to the child together with the application of the theories of these sciences has apparently hardly stirred the Church's services until the recent past.

I am aware that I have 'withdrawn' to Protestant terrain in my discussion of Sunday school. What happened to the relation of Church and child in the Roman Catholic Church since the eighteenth century? The answer to this question will be a story rather different from the one which has to be told of the Protestant side. More than an ordinary preaching service in one or other Reformed Church the Mass will have appealed to the imagination of the child. During the period of emancipation of the Roman Catholic Church in the Netherlands (c. 1850 until Vatican II) there must have been much to experience for children on all kind of holy days, both at home and in church. Has the relation of child and Church until this day among Roman Catholics seen a development without any problem? I like to leave the task of providing an answer to this question to Roman Catholic authors.

9. CULTURAL AND SOCIAL FACTORS OF TWO KINDS

Let us suppose for once that Sunday school could have grown not alongside or aside of the Church, but in its very middle. Let us accept moreover that people from the world of Sunday school would have tried hard to trace useful material in the 'scientific' reflections and treatments of the child. Would it then have been possible to break through the traditional rejection of the idea of child Communion and thus to smooth the way to the Lord's Supper for the child? I do not know. All I know is that if it would not have come to such a breakthrough in the supposed circumstances, it would have been owing to cultural and social factors of two sorts.

1. Reflections and treatments of the child of all kinds (behind which, as we did remark, images of man and definite aims are hidden in our modern society!) apparently have never been able to lead people in Sunday school and Church to the idea to reflect critically the traditional rejection of child Communion.

2. It has become clear that these historical reflections and treatments of the child have been influenced to a large degree by the (in many ways antagonistic) movements of Rationalism and Pietism. Certainly, both have given us the greatest minds, who have bequested ideas which remain important for our generation and, we may hope, for many generations to come. But as forms of believing and experiencing, of thought and act, reflexion and impression, Rationalism and Pietism are dated, dated by the time and culture from which they sprang and in which they grew: the Western Christian society of the seventeenth and eighteenth centuries.

10. 'SUFFER LITTLE CHILDREN TO COME UNTO ME AND FORBID THEM NOT'[31]

The Church has not known any period in which culture and society had not a voice in the chapter within its walls. But both culture and society should never impede us to carry into effect what the Lord has commanded. How then is it possible that the young 'called' are hindered from participating at the Lord's Supper on no other grounds than cultural and social factors, even if these factors are partly interwoven into traditions of an honourable *praxis pietatis*?

31. St. Matthew 19:14; St. Mark 10:14; St. Luke 18:16.

Active participation as the gateway towards an ecclesial liturgy

J. LAMBERTS

'Active participation' of all the faithful is undoubtedly one of the main aims of the Constitution on the sacred liturgy *Sacrosanctum Concilium*. The term occurs no less than twenty-five times in the text.[1] H. Schmidt calls it in his commentary the refrain of the Constitution.[2] It may be seen as the recognition and the ratification of the struggle of the Liturgical Movement, which had made active participation its goal. This does not mean that the Liturgical Movement has lost its reason for existence after Vatican II. On the contrary, more than ever it has to be zealous for the realization of what, in contrast with a mere clerical liturgy, we might call an 'ecclesial liturgy'. Active participation is in this sense the gateway towards such an ecclesial liturgy.

1. ACTIVE PARTICIPATION AS AIM OF THE LITURGICAL MOVEMENT

1.1. The question concerning the beginning

At the beginning of the Liturgical Movement and its endeavour for active participation we prefer to place Dom Lambert Beauduin (1873-1960), a monk of Mont-César (Louvain), although the tendency to see Dom Prosper Guéranger (1805-1875), the restorer of the French Benedictine Congregation at Solesmes, as the pioneer, still persists.[3] Indeed, Guéranger already used the expression 'liturgical movement' in his *Institutions liturgiques*.[4] Maybe his role in, what we prefer to call, the 'liturgical revival' is underestimated by some previous scholars. But the question is: what do we understand by 'liturgical movement'? The liturgical movement is the movement which aims at real and active participation of the faithful in the liturgy. Three words are to be focussed on here: movement, liturgy and active participation.

1.2. Liturgical movement throughout history

In a sense we can say that there has always been movement in worship, but this movement has not always resulted in a more active participation of the faith-

---

1. Cf. *Sacrosanctum Concilium* art. 11, 12, 14 (twice plus heading), 17, 19, 21, 26, 27, 30, 33, 41, 48, 50, 53, 55, 56, 79, 90, 106, 113, 114, 121, 124.
2. H. Schmidt: *Constitutie over de heilige liturgie. Tekst, genese, kommentaar, documentatie* (Antwerpen 1964) 208.
3. Cf. recently R.W. Franklin: The people's work: anti-Jansenist prejudice in the Benedictine movement for popular participation in the nineteenth century, in *Studia liturgica* 19 (1989) 60-77.
4. P. Guéranger: *Institutions liturgiques* (Paris 1840-1851) 3 vols. (2nd edition: Paris 1878-1885, 4 vols.) 3 (1851) 171 (= 1883², 167).

ful. The early Church's practice shows us a worshipping congregation in which all were involved. There was a diversity of functions but the liturgy was evidently experienced as a common celebration. It should be remembered that in order to attain a celebration at the people's level, without loosing sight of the substantial core of Christian worship, the Church welcomed under certain conditions, what was good and noble in pagan religions. Not only in the East but also in the West there were other rites besides the Roman.[5]

Enamoured of the Roman liturgy and dreaming of a new Christian Roman empire, Pepin and Charlemagne (742-814) imported the Roman rite and practically abolished the vivid Gallican liturgy. However, what is actually called the Roman liturgy as determined in the Tridentine liturgical books, had assumed many Gallican, Celtic and even Germanic elements, when the Ottonian emperors brought the Roman Franco-Germanic liturgy back to Rome in the tenth and eleventh centuries.[6] The Celtic liturgy only began to disappear from Ireland in the twelfth century, while the Visigothic rite remained in use even until the fifteenth century in southern Spain, which was dominated by the Moors. However, when the Church began its great missionary activity in the sixteenth century, it neglected to adapt liturgy to the geniuses of the newly-discovered peoples. In those days liturgy had become an inflexible clerical activity. This led e.g. to the Chinese rite controversy, a tragedy which meant the loss of China for the Church.[7]

Indeed, liturgy had become an inflexible clerical activity; the rubrics appointing what the clerics had to do and say were strictly fixed in the Tridentine liturgical books, and the Congregation of Rites (established in 1588) looked after a punctual, even scrupulous observance. But in defence of the Council of Trent (1543-1563) we have to take a few things into consideration.

1.3. Trent and liturgy

As J.A. Jungmann has pointed out, the fourteenth, fifteenth and part of the sixteenth centuries mark the decline of liturgical life. This situation was prepared during the preceding centuries.[8] At the eve of the Reformation, liturgy was characterized by a contradictory situation: on the one hand an abundance of liturgical ceremonies marking social life, on the other hand the erosion of liturgical life and many abuses. Liturgy was celebrated with pomp and splendour in the many ornate churches built in this period. The dominical Eucharist was the *missa cantata*. The many holy days ordered social life, being days of rest; holy days became holidays. And in addition to having their proper liturgies these days gave rise to devotional practices, such as processions,

---

5. Cf. e.g. A.A. KING: *Liturgies of the past* (London 1959).
6. H.A.J. WEGMAN: *Christian worship in East and West* (New York 1985).
7. F. BONTINCK: *La lutte autour de la liturgie chinoise aux XVIIe et XVIIIe siècles* (Louvain 1962).
8. J.A. JUNGMANN: The state of liturgical life on the eve of the Reformation, in J.A. JUNGMANN: *Pastoral liturgy* (London 1962) 64-80. Cf. J. HUIZINGA: *The waning of the Middle Ages* (London 1924 = 1976ʳ) 182-205.

veneration of relics and pilgrimages, often jointly with public amusements and fairs. The rhythm of the day was fixed by the hours of the divine office, announced by the bells. A crowd of clerics took care of the many liturgical ceremonies. Besides the parish churches and the monasteries with their own services there were the colleges of canons and priests who were engaged in the solemn services in cathedrals and collegial churches, completed by the multitude of altarists who had only to say low Mass and pray the breviary.

People assisted at the main ceremonies and made possible the other services by foundations. In spite of the people's presence these ceremonies had become a mere clerical affair. Between people and clergy there was a gap, expressed by the choir screen which partitioned choir and nave. Since the unfamiliarity with Latin was already a hindrance for active participation, the people's part was nil: the faithful were only silent spectators. At the end of the Middle Ages the dialogue between celebrant and congregation no longer existed, while the choir had taken over the common singing. The choir began to sing more difficult pieces, so that liturgy was indeed more solemn but without any participation of the faithful. While the main altar disappeared in the apse, side-altars came for the altarists. Those altars and even chapels and oratories were dedicated mostly to the patron saint of the guilds, brotherhoods and rich families and were intended for private worship.

So the community broke up into smaller groups with their own devotions. The belief that each Mass gives its fruits brought also an increase in the number of Masses; people wanted to 'buy' this *fructus missae*. Holy Communion during the Eucharist was rather the exception. On the other hand, there was a strong desire to see and to adore the Host. People believed that they would receive many graces by doing so. The eucharistic movement in those days did not aim at participation in the eucharistic celebration, but at veneration of the holy Sacrament. The Sacrament was exposed even during Mass and was carried around for many purposes. Besides adoring the Host, people had their devotions, such as meditating on the events of Christ's life, especially on his passion. Therefore the allegorical explanation of the ceremonies of the Mass was helpful. Thus it was not the memorial of the paschal mystery but a multitude of separated mysteries connected with the different ceremonies of the Mass to which the people were expected to pay attention. These mysteries were seen more as a past event to be contemplated than as a present mystery in which one should participate. Even the liturgical books reflected the evolution of liturgy in those days and for lack of control many texts and ceremonies of superstitious character were to be found in them.

In the period preceding the Council of Trent there were some attempts to curb abuses and to reform the clerical liturgy in order to realize the active participation of all the people.[9] This stream, however, was mainly canalized

9. See e.g. R.B. BOND: *The efforts of Nicholas of Cusa as a liturgical reformer* (Salzburg 1962); J.L. CONNOLLY: *John Gerson, reformer and mystic* (Louvain 1928); L. PRALLE: Die volksliturgischen Bestrebungen des Georg Witzel, in *Jahrbuch für das Bistum Mainz* 3 (1948) 224-242.

within the Reformation, but there it came not only to specific realizations; it was especially connected with dogmatic positions. Where the Reformation obtained a firm footing, the faithful experienced especially the liturgical changes, which perhaps met the people's wishes, but were also hiding the positions of the Reformation for the same people.

It cannot be maintained that Trent in its reaction against the Reformation has disregarded liturgy, on the contrary, liturgy was much discussed. Trent saved some valuable traditions by codifying existing liturgical usages, avoiding novelty as well as archaeologism and purifying the Roman rite of its medieval abuses. But Trent did not succeed in such a liturgical reform or adaptation as could be the answer to the question of the particular place of the lay people in the liturgy of the Church. As new situations arose, liturgy proved inflexible and unconscious of the new factors. Nevertheless – and this is sometimes forgotten – incentives for a more active participation of the faithful are to be found in some Tridentine decrees. There is the stimulation of liturgical catechesis in the vernacular during the celebration, the appeal for a frequent sacramental Communion and the not-fundamental character of the refusal of Communion under both kinds.[10] In the liturgical praxis after Trent this was almost completely neglected. The faithful remained in their role of silent and passive spectators. Also the liturgical books, revised after Trent, sanctioned the clerical liturgy. One example: the missal, completely drafted from the role of the priest-celebrant, made no provision for the Communion of the faithful. When the faithful wanted to receive Communion, one had to appeal to the *Rituale Romanum*, in which directions for Communion without Mass were to be found.

1.4. Attempts to reform the liturgy

In the centuries before ours a few attempts were made to reform the liturgy in order to promote the active participation of the faithful, but they did not have the desired results. In the spirit of the Enlightenment and against the Baroque, the neo-Gallican liturgies arose in France, under the influence of Jansenism and Gallicanism. It was not only an attempt to revive the ancient Gallican liturgy; apart from the political overtone it possessed, the movement was a trend towards making the official prayer of the Church the substance of the prayer of the laity.[11] It represented a desire to return to the original status of

10. For the use of the vernacular: Henricus Denzinger and Adolfus Schönmetzer (eds.): *Enchiridion symbolorum definitionum et declarationum de rebus fidei et morum* (Barcinone-Friburgi Brisgoviae-Romae 1976[36]) no. 1749 and Council of Trent, 24th session, *Canones reformationis generalis*, canon 7. We may note that P. Guéranger assumed that Trent had dogmatically connected liturgy and the sacred languages (Guéranger: *Institutions* 3 (1883[2]) 51-215. Frequent communion: Denzinger and Schönmetzer: *Enchiridion* no. 1747; Communion under both kinds: Denzinger and Schönmetzer: *Enchiridion* nos. 1726-1733.

11. Cf. the first translations of the missal and the breviary: J. Voisin: *Le missel romain selon le réglement du Concile de Trente, traduit en français, avec l'explication de toutes les messes* (Paris 1660); N. le Tourneux: *Bréviaire romain, traduit en français* (Paris 1655); very important was: N. Pavillon: *Rituel romain du pape Paul V à l'usage du diocèse d'Alet, avec les instructions et les rubriques en français* (Paris 1667); further: the missals of Paris (1684), of Meaux (1709) and of Troyes (1736).

liturgical pluralism. To realize an active participation of the faithful liturgical texts were translated and the vernacular received a place in liturgy, the ceremonies were simplified, original Gallican prayers and ceremonies were adopted. To give a few examples: the *canon* was prayed aloud; people could give their assent by saying *Amen*; the celebrant did not repeat in silence what was read or sung by others; the Communion of the faithful was part of the celebration; the readings formed a thematic unity; the number of feasts of saints was reduced in favour of the proper of the season, celebrating the annual circle of Christ's mysteries.[12] In the campaign against the neo-Gallican liturgies Dom P. Guéranger played an important role, and about 1870 the Tridentine Roman rite was 'restored' in France.

Pope Benedict XIV (1740-1758), a liturgical scholar, also intended to reform the liturgy, but did not succeed.[13] Important, but without any result, was his proposal that the faithful should receive the Lord's Body after the priest's Communion under elements consecrated during the same Mass.[14]

At the initiative of bishop Scipione Ricci (1741-1810) and grand duke Leopold of Tuscany the Synod of Pistoia (1786) proposed drastic liturgical reforms.[15] We enumerate some decrees: active participation of the faithful; parish celebrations; only one altar in each church; primacy of the Sunday by reducing the feasts of saints; use of the vernacular; reading of the entire Sacred Scripture within a year; Communion of the faithful during the Mass from elements consecrated during the same Mass; reform of popular devotions.

Because of their Jansenist, Gallican and Josephinist backgrounds pope Pius VI condemned in 1794, not without some hesitation, 81 theses of the Synod.[16] But this background alone does not explain the failure of the Synod; its reforms, valid in themselves, were imposed on clergy and people who were not prepared for them.

From these historical facts the Liturgical Movement has learnt at least two things:
– liturgical reform can only succeed when the people are formed in the authentic spirit of the liturgy, in what we are doing when we gather as the priestly people of God to be sanctified, to manifest it and to perform full public worship;
– liturgical reform can only have a lasting effect when such a reform is carried out in ecclesiastical unity.

---

12. These examples are taken from the missal of Meaux. In this missal we also find this formula at Communion: 'The body of Christ. Amen.' The missal of pope Paul VI (1970) has borrowed several elements from the neo-Gallican liturgies; cf. P. JOUNEL: Les sources françaises du missel de Paul VI, in *Questions liturgiques* 52 (1972) 305-316.
13. Cf. J. HERMANS: *Benedictus XIV en de liturgie. Een bijdrage tot de liturgiegeschiedenis van de moderne tijd* (Brugge 1979).
14. BENEDICT XIV: *Certiores effecti* (1742) 3.
15. C.A. BOLTON: *Church reform in 18th century Italy (The Synod of Pistoia, 1786)* (Den Haag 1969).
16. *Auctorem fidei*, in DENZINGER and SCHÖNMETZER: *Enchiridion* nos. 2600-2700.

The Liturgical Movement, which began in 1909, has really taken these two points into account. This is the first reason why we want to reserve the name 'Liturgical Movement' to the movement started by Lambert Beauduin. A second reason is the way in which liturgy was approached and treated in this Liturgical Movement.

1.5. The use of the term 'liturgy'

The use of the term 'liturgy' is rather recent in official documents of the Roman Catholic Church, and from the beginning of our century an important evolution in the meaning of 'liturgy' came about.

In contrast with the East, the Latin-speaking West used other words to indicate worship, in the first place Eucharist, and the accompanying acts: *ministerium, officium, munus, ritus, actio, opus, celebratio, mysterium, sacramentum, servitium, sollemnitas.* In the sixteenth century the term 'liturgy' was generally adopted by Humanists. In 1551 the Dutch scholar G. Cassander used the term for the first time in his work *Liturgica de ritu et ordine dominica coenae quam celebrationem Graeci liturgiam, Latini missam appelarunt.* But in the 'official' Church the word was not used for many years. In 1588 the Congregation which should take care of the correct liturgical observance as prescribed in the liturgical books received the name *Congregatio pro sacris ritibus et caeremoniis.* Only from 1832 did this Congregation speak of *libri liturgici* and in 1898 about *de usu linguae slavicae in sacra liturgia.* The *Codex iuris canonici* of 1917 acknowledged in canon 1257 the term by appointing *unius Apostolicae Sedis est tum sacram ordinare liturgiam, tum liturgicos approbare libros.*

But what was meant by *sacra liturgia*? This has not always been what we presently understand by it. In an article in the important periodical *Études* from 1913 J. Navatel called liturgy 'the perceptible, ceremonial and decorative part of Catholic worship'.[17] This was the current idea of 'liturgy' during the first decades of this century. The Liturgical Movement had to resist this idea.

1.6. The work of Dom Prosper Guéranger

This brings us back to the question of the beginning of the Liturgical Movement. As we have already said, there is a tendency to see Dom Prosper Guéranger as the pioneer of the Liturgical Movement. Three arguments should confirm this opinion:
- he drew attention to liturgy as the core of ecclesial life;
- he was the first to use the term 'liturgical movement';
- he made the Benedictines promotors of the liturgical movement.

These arguments cannot however convince us.

Born in 1805, Guéranger had from his youth a great admiration for liturgy, which – *nota bene!* – was in those days in France the neo-Gallican liturgy. He

---

17. J. NAVATEL: L'apostolat liturgique et la piété personelle, in *Études* 137 (1913) 449-476, p. 452.

came in touch with the Roman missal only in 1827 when he was ordained a priest. From 1828 he published in the periodical *Mémorial catholique* under the inspiration of F. de Lammenais, the leader of the Ultramontane party. In his articles *Considérations sur la liturgie catholique* he defended the Tridentine Roman rite against the neo-Gallican missals and breviaries. His thesis was that an authentic and legitimate liturgy must have four characteristics: ancient origin, universality, authority and solemnity. The Roman liturgy of Trent had these characteristics in an eminent way but they were not to be found in the recent liturgies. Seized by the Romantic tendency towards restoration he bought in 1832 the Benedictine abbey of Solesmes, abandoned since the French Revolution, and with a few other priests he began to live according to the Rule of St. Benedict, in which liturgy takes precedence.

After many difficulties he became abbot on October 10, 1837 and received from Rome the task to restore the Benedictine order and to promote the study of ecclesiastical antiquity and the liturgy.[18] Guéranger intended to write a liturgical *summa* entitled *Institutions liturgiques*. This plan was not completely realized.[19] In the foreword we can already hear his polemic intentions:

Soyons sincères, notre désir de perfectibilité Liturgique ne nous a-t-il pas insensiblement réduits à l'état que saint Pie V reprochait à nos pères, au seizième siècle? Qu'est devenue cette unité de Culte que Pépin et Charlemagne, de concert avec les Pontifes Romains, avaient établie dans nos Eglises; que nos Evêques et nos Conciles du seizième siècle promulguèrent de nouveau avec tant de zèle et de succès? Dix bréviaires et dix missels se partagent nos Eglises, et le plus antique de ces livres n'existait pas à l'ouverture du dix-huitième siècle; il en est même qui ont vu le jour dans le cours des quarante premières années du siècle où nous vivons.[20]

The first volume of the *Institutions* deals with the history of the liturgy until the reform of the sixteenth century which gave the Roman liturgy its definitive form. The second volume, which is extremely polemic, treats of the origins of the neo-Gallican liturgies. Guéranger speaks about a coalition between parliament and clergy to avert Roman influence and to make the Church subservient to the State under the mask of Gallican freedom. He mentions bishops overstepping their authority and introducing innovations. But he points his finger in particular to Jansenist influence. This second volume aroused a significant protest,[21] but it was especially the younger and lower clergy who made this book into their controversial pamphlet for 'returning to Rome' and to introduce the Roman liturgical books. As we know, their success was such that in 1870 the Roman liturgy was completely restored in France.

In the meantime Guéranger had started on another work: *L'année litur-*

---

18. GREGORY XVI: Breve *Innumeras inter* (1 September 1837).
19. In the foreword of the first volume Guéranger wrote: *L'ouvrage entier formera de six à huit volumes.* (GUÉRANGER: *Institutions* 1 (1840) XXIII).
20. GUÉRANGER: *Institutions* 1, X.
21. A survey of the polemics may be found in A. GUÉPIN: Préface de cette nouvelle édition, in GUÉRANGER: *Institutions* 1 (1878²) XXV-LXVI, pp. XLVII-LIX.

gique.[22] His intention was to give the faithful a deeper understanding of the different liturgical feasts, so that they could appreciate the beauty and sublimity of the liturgy.[23] People could bring this book to church, where it could replace all other prayer-books.[24] The work gives at every turn a detailed explanation of the liturgy of the day but never a literal translation, certainly not of the *canon*.

We want to point out that the significance of Guéranger is connected with two elements: first, the renewed interest in the liturgy and especially in liturgical science, and secondly, the restoration of the Benedictine order. We have some critical questions about his idea of liturgy and his one-sided refusal of all neo-Gallican elements, the systematic disparagement of everything not strictly 'Roman'. We take into account the fact that he was a child of his age and therefore influenced by the spirit of Restoration and Romanticism.

Solesmes became the centre of the monastic revival, of the intense way of celebrating the liturgy and of liturgical science. There J. Pothier (+ 1924) and A. Mocquereau (+ 1930) began the difficult restoration of Gregorian chant. We may put together this work and the *motu proprio* on Church music of pope Pius X (1903-1914), in which the expression 'active participation' appears, and to which the Liturgical Movement constantly referred.

From Solesmes the Abbey of Beuron was founded in 1863. From Beuron were established Maredsous (1872) and Maria Laach (1892). From Maredsous the Abbey of Mont-César (Louvain) was founded in 1899. It was a monk from this Abbey who started the Liturgical Movement proper.

Dom Guéranger revived the flourishing liturgical science of the seventeenth and eighteenth centuries. He wanted to restore liturgy to the core of ecclesiastical life. Perhaps his significance in a period of religious indifferentism, Liberalism, Atheism, Anti-clericalism, Materialism and Communism is sometimes underestimated.[25] This is right: that is the reason why we prefer to speak of a *réveil liturgique*, a liturgical revival. In the second part of the nineteenth century different works were published, but most of them did no more than glorify the esthetic value of the liturgy as it was then celebrated. Nevertheless, the way was paved for the scientific liturgical study of which we may presently reap the fruits. It was through returning to the fathers and to the different liturgical traditions that the authentic spirit of the liturgy was found.

The spirit of Restoration in the nineteenth century drove Guéranger into a

22. P. GUÉRANGER: *L'année liturgique* (Le Mans-Paris 1841-1866) 9 vols. The work was not completed by Dom Guéranger; 6 other vols. were edited by his pupil L. FROMAGE.
23. GUÉRANGER: *L'année* 1, XIX-XX.
24. Thus the introduction to the second edition: *Il sera destiné à aider les fidèles dans l'assistance aux offices divins; on pourra le porter à l'église, et il y tiendra lieu de tout autre livre de prières.* (GUÉRANGER: *Institutions* 1 (1878²) LXXIX.)
25. R.W. FRANKLIN e.g. tried to give a more balanced judgement (see note 3 and R.W. FRANKLIN: Guéranger: a view on the centenary of his death, in *Worship* 49 (1975) 318-328; R.W. FRANKLIN: Guéranger and pastoral liturgy: a nineteenth century context, in *Worship* 50 (1976) 146-162).

return to the uniform Roman liturgy, which had reached its summit in the Middle Ages. The clerical liturgy of the Middle Ages as 'the separation of the liturgical community'[26] can hardly be seen as an ideal. His Ultramontane spirit forced him to repudiate the local liturgies. Our view of liturgy, according to which the local congregation of the faithful is the subject of liturgical action, makes it very difficult for us to call Guéranger's abolition of all local liturgy the beginning of the Liturgical Movement. A critical research of the neo-Gallican liturgies proves that Guéranger was wrong when he wanted to change presumed Gallican, Jansenist or Protestant practices for presumed Roman usages. He obviously did not recognize as one of the basic elements in those liturgies the solicitude to bring people to a more active participation in liturgy. Indeed he was no supporter of a full explanation of the liturgical texts and rites to the laity: liturgy should be kept concealed under the veil of mystery. For Guéranger active participation was out of the question; liturgy is a clerical affair, carefully fulfilled by the clergy, while the faithful come to admire in veneration and love the veiled mystery and to nourish their devotion.

In the introduction to *Institutions liturgiques* he wrote:

Ce livre où sont racontées les mystérieuses beautés et les harmonies célestes que l'Esprit Saint a répandues sur les formes du Culte divin.[27]
La liturgie, considerée en général, est l'ensemble des symboles, des chants et des actes au moyen desquels l'Eglise exprime et manifeste sa religion envers Dieu.[28]

In other words: liturgy is mainly seen as an esthetic whole of external ceremonies. We are still far away from the idea of liturgy as the praising and thanksgiving celebration of our salvation by the local congregation of the faithful. Guéranger may have used the term 'liturgical movement',[29] but he did not mean what we presently understand by it.

1.7. Dom Lambert Beauduin and the beginning of the Liturgical Movement

So, as we have already said, we prefer to speak about a *réveil liturgique* and reserve 'Liturgical Movement' for the movement which started with Lambert Beauduin. Of course this Liturgical Movement is tributary to the liturgical revival of Guéranger. At the same time it should be emphasized that it was also influenced by the theological rediscovery of the sacramental nature of the Church. We might mention theologians such as J.A. Möhler (+ 1838) and M. Scheeben (+ 1888) as the 'precursors'.

The work of Dom Lambert Beauduin should be seen as the beginning of the Liturgical Movement proper, beause he gave the liturgical revival its definitive parochial and pastoral dimension, moving it away from its rather monastic ethos. Beauduin, who as a priest first was a member of the *Aumôniers du Tra-*

---

26. Th. KLAUSER: *Kleine abendländische Liturgiegeschichte. Bericht und Besinnung* (Bonn 1965) 95.
27. GUÉRANGER: *Institutions* 1, V-VI.
28. GUÉRANGER: *Institutions* 1, 1.
29. See note 4 above.

vail, a social organization founded as a concrete result of the encyclical letter *Rerum novarum*, maintained his social endeavour when he entered the Benedictine Abbey of Mont-César in 1906. There he discovered liturgy and even while he was still a novice he said:

Quel dommage que cette piété demeure l'apanage d'une élite; nous sommes les aristocrats de la liturgie; il faudrait que tout le monde puisse s'en nourir, même les gens les plus simples; il faudrait démocratiser la liturgie.[30]

With Beauduin this did not remain wishful thinking; he took action.[31] Already on May 27, 1909 he wrote a letter to explain his plan to Beuron where the general chapter was to take place, and on July 7, 1909 also to cardinal Mercier, archbishop of Malines.[32] The following quotation is illustrative:

Aux messes basses, si les assistants pouvaient s'unir à l'acolyte pour dialoger avec le prêtre et également réciter avec le prêtre les parties de la messe que le peuple peut chanter aux messes solennelles, à savoir le Gloria, le Credo, le Trisagion et l'Agnus Dei. Tout au moins ne pourrait-on obtenir cette autorisation pour les communautés réligieuses et pour les maisons d'éducation? Quelle communion s'établirait ainsi chaque matin, sans allonger l'office, à la messe basse, entre le directeur et ses élèves, ou mieux encore entre le pasteur et le troupeau; quelle participation active des fidèles au sacrifice; et combien se généraliserait rapidement la connaissance des évangiles et des épitres! Seulement cette autorisation effrayerait peut-être la Congregation des Rites. Mais, introduite par vous, Eminence, cette demande recevrait certainement un accueil favorable. Surtout qu'elle réaliserait parfaitement les désirs du Souverain Pontife: 'La participation active des fidèles aux mystères sacro-saints et à la prière publique et solennelle de l'Eglise' dont il parle et où les fidèles doivent 'puiser le véritable esprit chrétien à sa source première et indispensable' – ensuite la communion fréquente qui serait le complément naturel d'une participation plus active et plus intelligente au saint sacrifice. Ne pourrait-on dans ce domaine, tenter l'essai de missions liturgiques? Quelques Pères se rendraient pour la durée habituelle d'une mission (huit à quinze jours) dans une paroisse et y organiseraient matin et soir des offices liturgiques avec participation active des fidèles et distribution à tous des chants et prières traduits et précédemment expliqués. Pendant la journée, les Pères se partageraient les gens d'église, les enfants et les personnes moins occupées pour les initier à la liturgie, les exercer au chant et les préparer aux offices du matin et du soir. De la sorte, le mouvement liturgique serait imprimé à la paroisse et le premier pas qui effraie plusieurs prêtres laissés à eux-mêmes, serait fait. Je ne fais qu'ébaucher le projet, Eminence, mais il ne me paraît pas utopique. Et si vous me permettez en passant une réflexion intéressée: quelle occasion opportune pour les moines de prendre une part active à votre oeuvre de restauration liturgique![33]

This letter is typical of what would become the working method of the Liturgical Movement: to propose elaborated liturgical projects to Rome through the episcopate.

30. O. Rousseau: Autour du jubilé du mouvement liturgique, 1909-1959, in *Questions liturgiques* 40 (1959) 203-217, p. 208.
31. B. Botte: *Le mouvement liturgique. Témoignage et souvenirs* (Paris 1973) 18-19.
32. Both letters may be found in A. Haquin: *Dom Lambert Beauduin et le renouveau liturgique* (= Recherches et synthèses, section d'histoire 1) (Gembloux 1970) 234-237, 80-88.
33. Haquin: *Dom Lambert Beauduin* 83.

At the fifth *Congrès National des Oeuvres Catholiques* in Malines on September 23, 1909 Beauduin was able to present a paper *La vraie prière de l'église* in the subsection *Liturgie et musique sacrée* of the fifth session *Oeuvres scientifiques, artistiques et littéraires*, after all not very favourable for his liturgical preoccupation.[34] Beauduin began with the words of pope Pius X, who had said that 'the first and indispensable source of the true Christian spirit is to be found in the active participation of the faithful in the liturgy of the Church'. To realize this active participation he saw two primary means: the comprehension of the liturgical texts and the common chant. In his paper he wanted to treat of the first means. Therefore he demonstrated the necessity of liturgical renewal and proposed some practical means to circulate translated liturgical texts. In this way the faithful should no longer have recourse only to devotional practices, but could follow the priest and pray with him, in one word: be involved in the common prayer. To make the people's devotions more liturgical, Beauduin also wanted to promote the participation at parish Mass and vespers.

What Lambert Beauduin proposed did not remain confined to an academic speech. Although few people were present and some of them pronounced their scepsis, a number of like-minded men did find each other and were willing to support Beauduin's plan. In the Abbey of Mont-César each monk was engaged in preparing the booklets for Advent 1909. The booklets, published monthly, contained the liturgical texts of the Sundays and a supplement with explanations about the importance of liturgy, the significance of the Sunday, the liturgical year, etc. They were published in French with the title *La vie liturgique* and in Dutch as *Het kerkelijk leven* ('ecclesial life'). In December 1909 they had a press run of 45,000 and in June 1910 of 70,000 copies!

The circulation of missals for the people was not a completely new idea. In the middle of the nineteenth century we already find such missals in France and England.[35] The French *Paroissien* contained the translation of the proper, but the ordinary of the Mass was paraphrased in accordance with the prohibition to translate it by pope Alexander VII in 1661.[36] In Maredsous (Belgium) Dom Gerard van Caloen published his *Missel des fidèles* in 1882, and in Beuron (Germany) Dom Anselm Schott published his *Meßbuch* in 1883. For Dom Beauduin the publishing of missals in monthly instalments was part of a bigger plan of action.

---

34. The text of the paper was printed in *Questions liturgiques* 40 (1959) 218-221. We note that Beauduin, fearing an unfavourable reception of his paper, asked G. Kurth to say something about the necessity of liturgical life for the faithful in his opening address.
35. There were also the translations of the missal in the period of the neo-Gallican liturgies, e.g. Voisin: *Le missel*. This translation was the reason for the prohibition of pope Alexander VII in 1661.
36. Alexander VII: *Ad aures* (1661): *...et ita sacrosancti ritus majestatem latinis vocibus comprehensam dejicere et proterere, ac sacrorum mysteriorum dignitatem vulgo exponere temerario conatu tentaverint...* The prohibition was repeated by pope Pius IX in 1851, 1854 and 1858.

In 1910 he transformed the previous supplements of the liturgical booklets into bimonthly reviews *Les questions liturgiques* in French and *Liturgisch tijdschrift* (afterwards *Tijdschrift voor liturgie*) in Dutch. With these reviews he wanted to reach the priests, because he thought that changing anything in the liturgical life of the faithful had to start with the priests. The priests had to be convinced that liturgy is not so much a body of rites which one had to fulfil scrupulously and circumstantially, but more the *fons vitae* for them and for the faithful.[37] In order to educate the priests in liturgics he had a plan to found a high school for liturgy in Louvain, where the leaders of the Liturgical Movement and the professors of liturgy in the seminaries would receive their formation.[38] This school however was never founded.[39] On the other hand, the Liturgical Weeks for priests, organized from 1910 onwards both in Dutch and French, enjoyed great success.[40]

In 1913 the Liturgical Movement also started in Maria Laach with Dom Ildefons Herwegen. The link with L. Beauduin is clear. Maria Laach was certainly not unaware of Beauduin's letter to Beuron. And a monk from Maria Laach, Dom Kunibert Mohlberg (1878-1963), the famous liturgical scholar, was staying in Mont-César for his theological studies at the University of Louvain from 1905 to 1911. We may suppose that he was seized by the fresh enthousiasm of the Liturgical Movement and brought it to Maria Laach.[41] From there, in the aftermath of the First World War, his younger friend Romano Guardini (1885-1968) brought the liturgical spirit to the young students. In the first period the liturgical action at Maria Laach did more aim at an élite of university scholars, not without some interest for the artistic side of liturgy.[42] In a way Maria Laach remained mainly a centre of liturgical science, which later on would prove, however, to be extremely important for the liturgical renovation. In addition to K. Mohlberg we only have to mention the work of Dom Odo Casel (1886-1948). Beauduin's idea of 'democratization' of the liturgy came at the heart of the German liturgical movement in the third decade of our century. The pastoral solicitude of Pius Parsch (1884-1954) and

---

37. *Questions liturgiques* 1 (1910-1911) 1-3.
38. In a letter of July 2, 1910 to Beuron we find also a few names of potential professors: C. Callewaert, P. Batiffol, F. Cabrol, J. Pothier, A. Cauchie.
39. Some possible reasons for this are given in Haquin: *Dom Lambert Beauduin* 145-148.
40. Reports on these weeks and most of the papers read were printed in *Questions liturgiques* and *Tijdschrift voor liturgie*.
41. B. Fischer: Dom Lambert Beauduin et le mouvement liturgique en Allemagne, in J. von Allmen (ed.): *Veilleur avant l'aurore. Colloque Lambert Beauduin* (Chevetogne 1978) 79-93, p. 81. In the introduction to the *Festschrift* for Mohlberg on his 70th birthday we read: *Neque est oblivioni tradendum Patrem Mohlberg, tempore quo Lovanii in coenobio 'Regina Caeli' Montis Caesaris commoratus est, fuisse ex primis et ardentissimis qui liturgicae renovationis studia in Belgio inchoaverint et adiuverint. Ex Lovanio deinde incitamenta plurima ad patrium coenobium Lacense transmisit ibique eodem tempore renovationem spiritus S. Liturgiae urgebat.* (*Miscellanea liturgica in honorem L. Cuniberti Mohlberg* 1 (= Bibliotheca 'Ephemerides liturgicae' 22) (Roma 1948) X).
42. Already in 1912 I. Herwegen gave a conference about liturgy as a work of art.

even of J.A. Jungmann (1889-1975) were very similar to Beauduin's care.[43] To realize their aim both got in touch with the Abbey of Maria Laach. For the idea to circulate the translated Mass texts P. Parsch said to be obliged to Wilhelm Schmidt, who probably had the idea from Maria Laach.[44] P. Parsch himself confessed that he was a pupil of Maria Laach.[45] J.A. Jungmann published his *Habilitationsschrift* in the collection *Liturgiegeschichtliche Forschungen* (as it was then called) of Maria Laach.[46] While already on August 6, 1921 Maria Laach had its first *missa recitata*, Pius Parsch only began with his, more parochial, *Chormesse* on Ascension day 1922. To indicate his pastoral aim, accepting the way they were working in Maria Laach, he entitled his work with a pleonasm, intentionally chosen: *Volksliturgie* ('popular liturgy'). In reality, Maria Laach and Klosterneuburg became the two important centres of the Liturgical Movement in the German speaking countries. They influenced each other, stimulated many promotors of the Liturgical Movement and prepared the definitive period of this movement in the years between the Second World War and Vatican II, the period of the International Liturgical Congresses, where on a scientific, historical, theological and pastoral level the liturgical renovation was elaborated which Vatican II should demand.

1.8. Pius X and active participation

But now we have to return again to the beginning of the Liturgical Movement. In his paper read at the Congres of Malines in 1909 L. Beauduin referred to the *motu proprio Tra le sollecitudini* of pope Pius X, in which we find the famous expression 'active participation'.[47] Afterwards the Liturgical Movement always quoted these words to provide a papal basis for their endeavour for the active participation of the laity in the liturgy, and proclaimed Pius X the great sponsor of the Liturgical Movement.[48]

43. N. HÖSLINGER and T. MAAS-EWERD (eds.): *Mit sanfter Zähigkeit. Pius Parsch und die biblisch-liturgische Erneuerung* (= Schriften des Pius Parsch-Institut 4) (Klosterneuburg 1979); B. FISCHER and H.B. MEYER (eds.): *J.A. Jungmann. Ein Leben für Liturgie und Kerygma* (Innsbruck 1975).

44. *P. Schmidt hat das Verdienst, die Idee des Messtextes gefunden zu haben. Ich möchte ihm dies neidlos zuerkennen. So ist also P. Schmidt einer der Väter der volksliturgischen Bewegung.* (P. PARSCH: Drei Jubilare der volksliturgischen Bewegung, in *Lebe mit der Kirche* 14 (1948) 182. See also: W. GLADE: Pius Parsch und Wilhelm Schmidt SVD, in HÖSLINGER and MAAS-EWERD: *Mit sanfter Zähigkeit* 273-278.)

45. P. PARSCH: Die liturgische Aktion in Oesterreich, in *Questions liturgiques* 15 (1930) 351-363, p. 354; P. PARSCH: Zum Geleit, in *Bibel und Liturgie* 12 (1938) 361-362, p. 362. See also: E. VON SEVERUS: Pius Parsch, ein Schüler des Abtes von Maria Laach, in HÖSLINGER and MAAS-EWERD: *Mit sanfter Zähigkeit* 257-263.

46. J.A. JUNGMANN: *Die Stellung Christi im liturgischen Gebet* (= Liturgiegeschichtliche Forschungen 7-8) (Münster 1925). See also E. VON SEVERUS: Aus dem Briefwechsel mit Abt Ildefons Herwegen, in FISCHER: *J.A. Jungmann* 140-143. For the relation between Jungmann and Parsch, see: N. HÖSLINGER: Der 'Volks'-Liturgiker, in FISCHER: *J.A. Jungmann* 78-81.

47. PIUS X: *Tra le sollecitudini*, in *Acta Sanctae Sedis* 36 (1903) 329-339. See J. LAMBERTS: Paus Pius X en de actieve deelneming, in *Tijdschrift voor liturgie* 71 (1987) 293-306.

48. See e.g. the paper of Cardinal Giacomo Lercaro on the Liturgical Congress in Assisi in 1953 (J. LERCARO: Tätige Teilnahme. Das Grundprinzip des pastoral-liturgischen Reformwerkes Pius X., in *Liturgisches Jahrbuch* 3 (1953) 167-174).

The liturgical efforts of Pius X, who received his education in the middle of the nineteenth century, sprang in our opinion from his rather supernatural disposition, Romanticism as a reaction to Rationalism, his interest in Church music,[49] his experience with the political cauldron of nineteenth-century Italy and not the least his pastoral career.[50] His device *Omnia restaurare in Christo* is on a par with these facts: he wanted to arrive at the heart of being Church, there where the Church really lives its essence in its liturgical-sacramental life, where the mysteries of faith are proclaimed and celebrated. But there is still more: Piux X was a providential person in whom the Divine Spirit was acting to bring the faithful together in a rediscovered and about-to-be restored liturgy. Pius X made a beginning with liturgical reforms which have contributed to the great liturgical reform of our time: not only the renewal of sacred music, but also a first restoration of the proper of the season and the liturgy of the Sunday as the day of the Lord,[51] and his decrees on frequent Communion and the Communion of children.[52] But the decree on frequent Communion was not fully understood in all its implications; the prevailing idea of Communion as a rite almost independent of the Mass and also administered apart from the liturgical event of Communion persisted for some decades.

Dom Beauduin made a phrase from the *motu proprio* of 1903 into a watchword of the Liturgical Movement:

Essende infatti Nostro vivissimo desiderio che il vero spirito cristiano riforisca per ogni modo e si mantenga nei fedeli tutti, é necessario proveddere prima di ogni altra alla santità e dignità del tempio, dove appunto i fedeli si radunano per attingere tale spirito dalla sua prima ed indispensabile fonte, che è la 'partecipazione attiva' ai sacrosanti misteri e alla preghiera pubblica solenne della Chiesa.[53]

We translate the last sentence into English: 'Active participation in the sacred

---

49. Giuseppe Sarto (born 1835), the later pope Pius X, was *sotto-maestro* of the *schola cantorum* in the seminary of Padua. As chaplain and parish priest he continued conducting a choir. As early as 1893 he wrote a *votum* in connection with an inquiry of the Congregation of the Rites on sacred music. As patriarch of Venice he issued in 1895 a pastoral letter on sacred music. These texts may be found in F. HAYBURN: *Papal legislation on sacred music: 95 A.D. to 1977 A.D.* (Minnesota 1979) 195-219.

50. G. Sarto was successively chaplain in Tombolo (1858-1867), parish priest in Salzano (1867-1875), canon and vicar in Treviso (1875-1884), bishop of Mantua (1884-1893), cardinal and patriarch of Venice (1893-1903) and pope (1903-1914).

51. In the apostolic constitution *Divino afflatu* we read: ...*dein vero ut in sacra Liturgia Missae antiquissimae de Dominicis infra annum et de Feriis, praesertim quadragesimalibus, locum suum recuperarent.* (PIUS X: *Divino afflatu*, in *Acta Apostolicae Sedis* 3 (1911) 633-646). This reform was to some extent undone by the institution of many feasts during the following three pontificates.

52. The decree *Sacra Tridentina Synodus* in *Acta Sanctae Sedis* 38 (1905-1906) 400-406; the resolution of the Congregation of the Council in *Acta Sanctae Sedis* 39 (1906) 499-511; the decree *Quam singulari* in *Acta Apostolicae Sedis* 2 (1910) 577-583.

53. PIUS X: *Tra le sollecitudini* 331. Although it was intended for the whole Church the document was written in Italian!

mysteries and in the solemn prayer of the Church is the first and indispensable source of the true Christian spirit.' Here we find for the first time the words 'active participation'. Yet it is striking that the Latin translation of the *versio fidelis* only speaks about *participatio* and the *versio authentica* about *actuosa communicatio*.[54] *Actuosa participatio* has become the usual phrase in Latin later on.

The term 'active participation' indicates one of the main aims of the Liturgical Movement. But, of course, *partecipazione attiva* in the *motu proprio* did not yet have completely the theological content it would have in the days of Vatican II. Many years of theological reflection on the nature of liturgy and of the sacraments had to pass before these two words, enriched and deepened, became the indispensable expression of the particular task of all the faithful in liturgy.

Pius X probably thought of the patristic idea of *participatio* (*metalèpsis*), which means to partake in what is present in the celebrations of the Church, which could explain the translation *communicatio*. Such participation can be achieved to a greater or lesser degree. It is especially sacramental: in the eucharistic celebration the faithful participate in the mystery of Christ, especially, although not exclusively, by partaking of the consecrated gifts. Precisely through this participation, in which there is no fundamental distinction between clergy and lay people, the faithful obtain the Christian spirit as a fruit of the sacrament celebrated within liturgy. To realize this active participation, the liturgy and especially liturgical chant was, according to Pius X, to be cleansed of the theatrical veil, and the churches were to be cleansed from all Baroque bombastry. Only then could people participate more consciously. To achieve full, active participation he wanted to stimulate the Communion, the summit of sacramental participation. In this approach liturgy is seen as an action of the official Church, performed by a mandated hierarchical minister, according to fixed rules, on behalf of the faithful, who should join (participate) in the happening at least in a spiritual way and if possible, sacramentally, in order to receive the fruits of the celebration. Here active participation (hence in Latin indicated by *actuosa* rather than *activa participatio*) does not yet have the meaning of cooperating in the celebration by the laity, but of joining the liturgical action performed by the official Church as intensely as possible.

Within the Liturgical Movement the term gradually received a different content and began to indicate more precisely the particular role of the faithful, distinguished from that of the clergy. Liturgy indeed was experienced as a mere clerical affair, at which the faithful were only silent spectators. This had to be changed, not only by explaining the given liturgy to the faithful, but especially by making them conscious of their own role as belonging to the people of God called to worship and by making them accomplish their own

---

54. A Latin *versio fidelis* in *Acta Sanctae Sedis* 36 (1903) 387-395 and a *versio latina authentica* in *Ephemerides liturgicae* 18 (1904) 129-149.

task in the celebration which is by definition a common celebration. Active participation did not however yet have this present-day meaning in the days of Pius X. This may appear from the fact that the faithful could not yet sing the Gregorian chant. This would become possible under pope Pius XI, but he was walking in the footsteps of Pius X![55] For Pius X the Gregorian chant still belonged to the choir, but the restoration of this chant he considered to be a service to the faithful 'in order to obtain the true Christian spirit, to participate more actively in the ecclesial services as it used to be before'.[56] Here the first step was taken to realize that the worshipping community could again participate in the liturgical chant. The wish for the use of the vernacular, which was later on one of the most important objects of the Liturgical Movement, was not admitted by Pius X. He firmly stated that Latin is the proper language of the Roman liturgy.[57] On the other hand, the changes in the eucharistic discipline, although not completely understood at that very moment, had a deeper significance for the people's participation. The liturgical reform initiated, a redistribution of the Psalms in the hours of the divine office and the pruning of the calendar to give precedence to the Sunday and to the proper of the season, were seen by Pius X as 'the first step towards the emendation of the Roman breviary and missal'.[58] He recognized that:

a long period of years must pass before the liturgical edifice, which the mystical spouse of Christ has formed in her zeal and understanding to proclaim her piety and faith, may again appear splendid with dignity and harmony, cleansed of the accumulations of age.[59]

1.9. Active participation and the request for liturgical reform
As the pastoral approach of the Liturgical Movement grew, it also became

55. On the occasion of the 25th anniversary of the *motu proprio* of 1903 Pius XI wrote: *Quo autem actuosus fideles divinum cultum participent, cantus gregorianus, in iis quae ad populum spectant, in usum populi restituatur. Ac revera pernecesse est ut fideles, non tamquam extranei vel muti spectatores, sed penitus liturgiae pulchritudine affecti, sic caeremoniis sacris intersint – tum etiam cum pompae seu processiones, quas vocant, instructo cleri ac sodalitatum agmine, aguntur – ut vocem suam sacerdotis vel scholae vocibus, ad praescriptas normas, alternent; quod si auspicato contingat, iam non illud eveniet ut populus aut nequaquam, aut levi quodam demissoque murmure communibus precibus, liturgica vulgarive lingua propositis, vix respondeat.* (Pius XI: *Divini cultus*, in *Acta Apostolicae Sedis* 21 (1929) 33-41, p. 40.) See J. Lamberts: Paus Pius XI (1922-1939) en de liturgie, in *Tijdschrift voor liturgie* 73 (1989) 292-301.
56. Pius X: *Tra le sollecitudini* 333, note 3. We have to mention here the importance of the Associations of St. Gregory (*Gregoriusvereniging*) founded in the Netherlands in 1878 and in Belgium in 1880. See also J. Overath: *Der Allgemeine Cäcilien-Verband für die Länder der deutschen Sprache. Gestalt und Aufgabe* (Köln 1961).
57. Pius X: *Tra le sollecitudini* 336, no. 7.
58. *Quoniam vero Psalterii dispositio intimam quandam habet cum omni Divino Officio et Liturgia coniunctionem, nemo non videt per ea, quae hic a Nobis decreta sunt, primum Nos fecisse gradum ad Romani Breviarii et Missalis emendationem...* (Pius X: *Divino afflatu* 636). See also note 51 above.
59. Pius X: *Abhinc duos annos*, in *Acta Apostolicae Sedis* 5 (1913) 449-451.

more and more evident that a liturgical reform was necessary. Indeed, as instruction of the faithful was undertaken, it was seen that the actual liturgical ceremonial was out of tune with modern society and asked too much historical knowledge of the ordinary faithful to appreciate it and to make this way of worshipping their own. The study of the history of liturgy showed that reform and even variety had always existed until the unification and fixation after the Council of Trent. The Roman liturgy appeared to be one possible way of Christian worshipping among others and historically and culturally defined.

So in the years before the Second World War in the German speaking countries some extremist promotors of the Liturgical Movement were not satisfied with liturgical instruction of the faithful, singing the Gregorian chant, dialoging with the priest and stimulating frequent Communion. They wanted a real renovation and began arbitrarely with some innovations and changes. Their action however provoked opposition and caused controversy: the crisis of the German Liturgical Movement.[60] This crisis was so grave that in 1943 Rome asked the episcopate for a report about the liturgical question, but – and this is important – also gave to understand its willingness to grant privileges in this area if the episcopate decided to ask them. The German episcopate sent a report to Rome and did ask for some privileges. As early as December of the same year they received a favourable reply from the papal secretary in Rome. The letter approved many of the positive changes encouraged by the Liturgical Movement except for the fact that such changes were made arbitrarily. The so-called *Gemeinschaftsmesse* and *Betsingmesse* were approved and the *Deutsches Hochamt* was tolerated. This letter indicated the direction which the Liturgical Movement was to follow in the years after the war. It was to some extent as a result of the liturgical question in Germany that pope Pius XII felt obliged to issue his encyclical letter *Mediator Dei et hominum* in 1947, which was received as the *magna charta libertatis* of the Liturgical Movement.[61]

Indeed, in the years after World War II, encouraged by papal approval, the Liturgical Movement entered a new and decisive period to realize its fundamental aim: the active participation of the faithful. While Pius XI established in 1930 within the Congregation of the Rites a new section *Per le cause storiche dei Servi di Dio e l'emendazione dei libri liturgici*,[62] it was not until 1948 that Pius XII created a pontifical commission for the general restoration of the liturgy. This commission revised the rite of the Easter vigil on an experimental basis in 1951, then all Holy Week services in 1955, produced decrees simplifying the rubrics in 1955 and codifying the kinds of liturgical participation of the faithful in 1958.[63] There were also the bilingual rituals, in which the

---

60. Th. MAAS-EWERD: *Die Krise der Liturgischen Bewegung. Studien zu den Auseinandersetzungen um die 'liturgische Frage' in Deutschland und Österreich von 1939 bis 1944* (= Studien zur Pastoralliturgie 3) (Regensburg 1979).

61. PIUS XII: *Mediator Dei et hominum*, in *Acta Apostolicae Sedis* 39 (1947) 521-595.

62. PIUS XI: *Già da qualche tempo*, in *Acta Apostolicae Sedis* 22 (1930) 87-88.

63. PIUS XII: *De solemni vigilia paschali instauranda*, in *Acta Apostolicae Sedis* 43 (1951) 128-

vernacular might be used in part of the sacraments.[64] Evening Masses were introduced and the eucharistic fast was shortened.[65] It is important to note that most of these changes are the result of proposals from the leaders of the Liturgical Movement brought up to Rome by different episcopates.

In this new succesful phase of the Liturgical Movement the leading centres were the *Liturgisches Institut* at Treves and the *Centre de Pastorale Liturgique* in Paris. Their contacts led to the International Liturgical Congresses, where specific liturgical questions were discussed by the most important liturgists from divers countries.[66] Also many bishops supported the movement and were sometimes present at the Congresses. So theologically, historically and also pastorally justified motions were formulated and sent to Rome as the wishes of episcopates throughout the world. The essential elements for the liturgical renewal of Vatican II were conceived during these Congresses.

A far-reaching development was also the contribution of the young Churches, in those days still called 'missions', during these Congresses. Already in the third Congress in Lugano in 1953 there was a modest intervention from the young Churches. For many of the participants in this Congress the contact with the particular liturgical problems of the missions was a revelation. The question rose whether the proposals of liturgical renovation did not start from the Western European way of thinking only and thus forgot the needs of the world Church.[67] Here the foundation was laid for what we may now call a pluriform liturgy. Here the idea grew that we must return to the original simplicity and clarity of the Roman rite, so that, when this was given, we should be able to adapt it to various cultures, traditions and even situations. Only in this way active participation could become possible. In different Congresses bishops and theologians from the young Churches took the floor and pointed out the necessity of a fundamental liturgical renewal, so that the worship of the local congregated people of God would take place by the real active participation of all involved. A culminating point was the Liturgical Congress in Nijmegen-Uden in 1959, where the theme was 'Liturgy and missions'.[68]

129. *Rubricae sabbato sancto servandae si vigilia paschalis instaurata peregatur*, in *Acta Apostolicae Sedis* 43 (1951) 130-137. *Maxima redemptionis nostrae mysteria*, in *Acta Apostolicae Sedis* 47 (1955) 838-847. *Cum nostra hac aetate*, in *Acta Apostolicae Sedis* 47 (1955) 218-224. *De musica sacra et sacra liturgia*, in *Acta Apostolicae Sedis* 50 (1958) 630-663, esp. 637-639.
64. Already a week after *Mediator Dei*, on November 26, 1947, France received the first (limited) bilingual ritual. Cf. De indulto Ritualis Romani lingua Latina et Gallica exarati, in *Ephemerides liturgicae* 62 (1948) 280-281. Germany received its (more ample) bilingual ritual on March 21, 1950. Cf. *Ephemerides liturgicae* 65 (1951) 116.
65. Cf. the apostolic constitution *Christus Dominus*, in *Acta Apostolicae Sedis* 45 (1953) 15-24.
66. After a first meating of the leaders of both Institutes in Luxembourg in 1950, the first International Liturgical Congress was organized at Maria Laach in 1951. The other Congresses were in Mont Sainte-Odile (1952), Lugano (1953), Louvain (1954), Assisi (1956), Montserrat (1958) Nijmegen-Uden (1959) and Munich (1960).
67. See e.g. the evidence given by Dom Botte in BOTTE: *Le mouvement liturgique* 106.
68. J. HOFINGER (ed.): *Liturgy and missions. The Nijmegen papers* (New York 1960).

2. VATICAN II: FROM ACTIVE PARTICIPATION TO ECCLESIAL LITURGY

When in 1959 pope John XXIII announced his plans for the Second Vatican Council, the problems facing liturgical renewal in order to realize the active participation of all the faithful of all cultures were already well formulated and could be discussed by the universal Church, thanks to the groundwork of the Liturgical Movement. When on December 4, 1963 the solemn promulgation of the Constitution on the sacred liturgy made active participation a *conditio sine qua non* for all real liturgy, the way was opened towards what we prefer to call an ecclesial liturgy.

2.1. Liturgy presupposes active participation

Articles 5-13 of *Sacrosanctum Concilium* give the theological basis of the Constitution by concluding to the importance of liturgy in the life of the Church from the nature of liturgy itself. God, who wishes all persons to be saved, sent his Son, anointed by the Holy Spirit, to preach the Gospel and to bring salvation. As *Mediator* between God and humanity He brought the fullness of divine worship, principally by the paschal mystery. This work is now accomplished by the Church, especially in its liturgical celebrations. Christ always associates the Church with Himself in the truly great work of giving perfect praise to God and making humanity holy.

Rightly, then, the liturgy is considered as an exercise of the priestly office of Jesus Christ. In the liturgy the sanctification of man is manifested by signs perceptible to the senses, and is effected in a way which is proper to each of these signs; in the liturgy full public worship is performed by the Mystical Body of Jesus Christ, that is, by the Head and his members.[69]

The centre of liturgy is the celebration of Christ's paschal mystery as the perfect glorification of the Father and the sanctification of humanity. This priestly office is exercised by the Mystical Body of Jesus Christ, the Head and his members. This means by Christ and those associated with Him in his Church. It is the people of God, gathered by the Holy Spirit and together with their Chief, that is seen here as the subject of liturgical action. It is good to stress that in this presentation of liturgy the distinction is not made between the priest and the faithful, but between Christ, the High Priest and the celebrating community. Only when the Constitution formulates its concrete norms does it speak about the different liturgical services in what is in essence

69. *Merito igitur Liturgia habetur veluti Iesu Christi sacerdotalis muneris exercitatio, in qua per signa sensibilia significatur et modo singulis proprio efficitur sanctificatio hominis, et a mystico Iesu Christi Corpore, Capite nempe eiusque membris, integer cultus publicus exercetur.* (*Sacrosanctum Concilium* 7.) Cf. the definition of *Mediator Dei*: *Sacra igitur Liturgia cultum publicum constituit, quem Redemptor noster, Ecclesiae Caput, caelesti Patri habet; quemque christifidelium societas Conditori suo et per ipsum aeterno Patri tribuit; utque omnia breviter perstringamus, integrum constituit publicum cultum mystici Jesu Christi corporis, Capitis nempe membrorumque eius.* (PIUS XII: *Mediator Dei* 528-529.)

a common celebration. Such an approach to liturgy requires by definition the active participation of all those who belong to the celebrating community. This participation is presupposed by the nature of liturgy itself. In a certain sense there is no real liturgy if only some are involved while others are only spectators. Liturgy is not only an activity for the people but also an activity of the people. It is not only a realization of salvation for the faithful by the appointed priest in the name of Christ and of the Church but also an activity of thanksgiving and praise by the faithful.

So article 11, the first article of *Sacrosanctum Concilium* in which we find the term 'active participation', states:

But in order that the sacred liturgy may produce its full effect, it is necessary that the faithful come to it with proper dispositions, that their thoughts match their words, and that they cooperate with divine grace lest they receive it in vain. Pastors of souls must therefore realize that, when the liturgy is celebrated, more is required than the mere observance of the laws governing valid and licit celebration. It is their duty also to ensure that the faithful take part knowingly, actively and fruitfully.

These words are a reaction against the mere ceremonial view of liturgy. The Constitution does not deny the importance of liturgical norms, but points out that pastors of souls have to take care of the active participation of the faithful. In other words, where before the priests applied themselves to the correct observance of the rubrics in order to make liturgy valid and licit, the Constitution asks that they will apply themselves at least in the same measure to realize the active participation of the faithful in the liturgy, which is the work of the whole people of God. Not only the observance of the rubrics, but also the active participation of the faithful is a necessary and constituent element of liturgy.[70]

2.2. Active participation by reason of baptism

Such full, conscious and active participation of the faithful, demanded by the very nature of liturgy, is based on baptism, by which men are designated as Christian people. 'Such participation by the Christian people as "a chosen race, a royal priesthood, a holy nation, a purchased people" is their right and duty by reason of their baptism.'[71] We note that the expression *vi baptismatis* is an addition to the original text put to the vote on December 3, 1963 and approved with 2096 for, 10 against and 7 null.[72] This article indicates that the

---

70. Article 11 of *Sacrosanctum Concilium* is undoubtedly a reaction to the mere ceremonial conception of liturgy. From the beginning the Liturgical Movement had to defend itself against those who see liturgy only in a rubrical way. In 1913 there was already a polemic on this question between L. Beauduin and J. Navatel. NAVATEL: L'apostolat liturgique; L. BEAUDUIN: Mise au point nécessaire: réponse au P. Navatel, in *Questions liturgiques* 4 (1913) 83-104. See note 17 above.

71. ...*et ad quam populus christianus, 'genus electum, regale sacerdotium, gens sancta, populus adquisitionis', vi Baptismatis ius habet et officium.* (*Sacrosanctum Concilium* 14.)

72. The original text: *Nihil carius habet Ecclesia quam ut fideles universi ad plenam illam, consciam atque actuosam liturgicarum celebrationem participationem ducantur, quae ab ipsius*

ecclesial community and not only the clergy are the subject of the liturgical action. The faithful have the right and duty to participate actively in virtue of their baptism and not by canon law or by any mandate of the Church. This affirmation is the opposite of what we still find in the instruction *De musica sacra et sacra liturgia* of September 3, 1958.[73] This document, although it takes over the definition of *Mediator Dei* that liturgy is the full public worship performed by the Mystical Body of Jesus Christ, that is by the Head and his members, calls readings, chants and other services clerical ministries, that can be committed to laypersons only by delegation (*servitium ministeriale delegatum*). The Constitution on the Liturgy says in article 29 that servers, lectors, commentators and members of the choir exercise a genuine liturgical ministry, while article 28 states that 'in liturgical celebrations, whether as a minister or as one of the faithful, each person should perform his role by doing solely and totally what the nature of things and the liturgical norms require of him'. So the nature of the liturgy presupposes the active participation of all the gathered faithful in virtue of their baptism, while liturgical laws indicate the particular functions and ministries.

The whole assembly is involved in the liturgical event, but we can discern degrees and ministeries: I can participate as a baptized person, or in virtue of my ordination as a bishop, priest or deacon; I can have a function as a servant, lector or member of the choir; I can participate very actively by praying, answering, singing, and receiving Communion or I can remain a silent spectator.

2.3. Common priesthood

By reason of their baptism the Christian people are a royal priesthood. Article 10 of the Dogmatic Constitution on the Church *Lumen gentium* speaks about the common priesthood of the faithful.[74]

Liturgiae natura postulatur et ad quam populus christianus, 'genus electum, regale sacerdotium, gens sancta, populus adquisitionis', ius habet et officium. The spokesman of the commission, F. Grimshaw, explained the modification as follows: *...Nempe ut fundamentum sacramentale participationis liturgicarum celebrationem verbis exprimatur, vestigia sequendo beati Thomae Aquinatis et praesertim Litterarum Encyclicarum Mediator Dei, ubi habentur haec verba: 'Baptismatis enim lavacro generali titulo christiani in Mystico Corpore membra efficiuntur Christi sacerdotis, et charactere qui eorum in animo quasi insculpitur, ad cultum divinum deputantur'. Emmendatio ergo est: 'vi Baptismatis'.* (*Acta synodalia* vol. 1, pars 4 (Civ. Vaticana 1971) 170-171.) See e.g. the intervention of archbishop M. Oloechea Loizaga: *...ut pulchris et utilis doctrina 'de actuosa participatione prosequenda' in hac paragrapho proposita roberetur, nonnulla addere oportet circa fundamentum sacramentale huius participationis? Sumerer ergo verba tam S. Thomae quam Encyclicae Mediator, ubi dicitur: 'Christiani vero omnes baptismatis lavacro, generali titulo in Mystico Corpore membra efficiuntur Christi sacerdotis et charactere qui eorum in animo quasi insculpitur, ad cultum divinum deputatur; atque adeo ipsius Christi sacerdotio pro sua conditione participant.* (*Acta synodalia* 1, 5, 495.)

73. *De musica sacra et sacra liturgia.*
74. Although the correct term is 'common priesthood' (*sacerdotium commune fidelium*) many authors still use 'universal priesthood' (*sacerdotium universale fidelium*). The change was made already in July 1964. See G. ALBERIGO and F. MAGISTRATTI: *Constitutionis dogmaticae Lumen gentium synopsis historica* (Bologna 1975) 48, c. 3.

Though they differ from one another in essence and not only in degree, the common priesthood of the faithful and the ministerial or hierarchical priesthood are nonetheless interrelated. Each of them in its own special way is a participation in the one priesthood of Christ.

One difference is that the baptismal or common priesthood is a collectivity and not an additive sum of individual priests, while the ministerial priesthood is realized in a personal charism institutionalized by the Church. A second difference is that the ministerial priesthood presupposes the common priesthood and has the mission and task to form and rule the priestly people in their communication with Christ.

The Church, the people of God, constituted by faith and baptism, participates as a community in the unique priesthood of Christ and is in this way the subject of liturgy. A repartition of the community in two well-differentiated classes, clergy and lay persons, priests and spectators, makes no longer sense. In this way the priests are 'brethren between the brethren'. Christ wanted the Church as a community, and this community participates by reason of baptism in the unique priesthood of Christ: the common or baptismal priesthood. But it is a structured community, which he wanted. Within and not above this community we can see some ministries for its edification and functioning: the ministerial priesthood. By ordination the Spirit creates a particular relation within the community on behalf of the common priesthood. On the one hand the ministry expresses in an explicit way the priestly mission of the whole ecclesial community: *repraesentatio ecclesiae*. On the other hand, the priest is ordained by a special and personal charism to the sacramental representation of Christ amidst the community: *repraesentatio Christi*.

In virtue of baptism the Spirit animates the assembly and by a charism *sui generis* He allows the priest to represent Christ in order that the *ecclesia* could really be sacrament of Christ in the execution of its priesthood. The role of the priest is especially ecclesial, and when he carries out his ministry among the community this is really the *ecclesia* and it may execute its priestly function: celebrating the mysteries of the faith, the gathered people of God performing full worship to the Father, through Christ, in the Spirit. This way of treating the question no longer makes a separation between priest and faithful. On the contrary, it explains how the role of the priest is really a *diaconia*, a *ministerium*, a service to the common priesthood of the people of God. Thus the priest is the president of the assembly, as Justin expressed it: *ho proestôs*.[75]

2.4. Liturgical catechesis and restoration

All of this is the reason why article 14 states firmly:

In the restoration and promotion of the sacred liturgy, this full and active participation by all people is the aim to be considered before all else.

75. JUSTIN: *Apologia* 1, 67, 5 (Edgar J. GOODSPEED: *Die ältesten Apologeten* (Göttingen 1914 = 1984ʳ) 75).

To achieve this active participation more attention must be given to liturgical instruction of both priests and faithful (articles 14-20), while a general restoration of the liturgy itself seems to be necessary (article 21). How important the restoration may be, we think that too little attention is still given to liturgical instruction.

The resolutions for restoration can be reduced to the following six:
- the use of the vernacular;[76]
- the simplification of liturgy;
- the stimulation of the common celebration;
- a more ample, more varied and more suitable reading from Sacred Scripture;
- the return to the roots of liturgy;
- the adaptation of the liturgy to the geniuses and traditions of peoples.

To attain this restoration the liturgical books are to be revised (article 25).

The general introduction of the vernacular into the liturgy is undoubtedly one of the most important means to realize active participation, but the end is not attained by a mere translation of the Latin texts.[77] What we need is a new redaction of the prayers in fidelity to the real liturgical spirit but also with respect for modern conceptualities, the modern way of thinking, the particular linguistic patterns of a people. Our texts seem sometimes strange, far away from daily life, and make it difficult to respond with *Amen* to what is said. The formulation of the penitential rite e.g., and of the general intercessions is mostly indoctrinating and reprimanding.

However, when real efforts are made on this level, one may not forget that liturgy is not only a matter of language. The revaluation of the vernacular seems to make liturgy too talkative, while the gestures and rites are mostly underestimated. Although this was certainly not intended, the simplification of the liturgy led to a loss of *decorum* in our celebrations. Our liturgy is often a cold, cerebral liturgy, where talking and singing are emphasized, but the corporal, the expressive and ceremonial elements are neglected. And this in a time in which outside the liturgy corporal, expressive and creative elements are being rediscovered.

Nevertheless, the Constitution on the liturgy stated:

In this restoration, both texts and rites should be drawn up so that they express more clearly the holy things which they signify. Christian people, as far as possible, should be able to understand them with ease and to take part in them fully, actively and as befits a community. (article 21)

We may not forget that the words, rites and gestures all belong to the liturgy itself. That is the reason why we find them also in the definition of liturgy:

76. J. LAMBERTS: Vatican II et la liturgie en langue vernaculaire, in *Questions liturgiques* 66 (1985) 125-144.
77. Cf. H. WEGMAN: De Romeinse euchologie in de quadragesima: verandering van paradigma?, in *Jaarboek voor liturgie-onderzoek* 4 (1988) 5-40.

...the sanctification of man is manifested by signs perceptible to the senses, and is effected in a way which is proper to each of these signs. (article 7)

We think that in order to achieve an active participation more must be done for the common actions and postures, for all the expressive elements. We even think that the restoration of the liturgy to its Roman genius of simplicity was to give it the semblance of a universal rite, which is flexible enough to admit variations according to different cultures. In this sense the resolution of simplification must be seen together with that of adaptation to the geniuses and traditions of peoples and also with that of returning to the roots of the liturgy. In order to make the liturgy more available and accessible, adaptations must be based on the authentic Roman form rather than on local modifications of the Roman liturgy.[78] Active participation indeed requires a certain transparency of rites. Therefore the liturgical reform should bring the Roman rite back to its pristine simplicity and clarity. But this is not sufficient: not only to exuberant people will this simplicity appear cold and anemic. Hence the simplicity of the reformed Roman rite has a relative value and is not a guarantee for the intended active participation. More is required to ensure that the liturgy will become a real ecclesial liturgy, this means a festive celebration of the paschal mystery by this gathered local community of faithful. Returning to the simplicity of the Roman rite is not a question of historical romanticism, but is intended to provide a liturgical form that could be effectively adapted not only to the culture of various peoples but also on behalf of this concrete congregation. This is the meaning of the articles 37-40 of the Constitution on the liturgy, which have to be related to article 34. This is also the meaning of the revised liturgical books. These are intended as *editiones typicae*, typical editions,[79] in which we find the substantial unity of the Roman rite and in which the cases of adaptations by episcopal conferences are laid down. Some of these books even distinguish between *aptatio* and *accommodatio*: here *accommodatio* refers to the competence of individual ministers to adapt to the concrete congregation. Not without importance for a more active participation, offering the possibility for a cordial and more personal atmosphere in the liturgical celebration of this local manifestation of the *ecclesia*, are some details in the rubrics such as: 'the priest addresses them in these or similar words'. We think that in this area – at least in our countries – too little is done, and we have to complain too often about a cold, cerebral and anemic liturgy.

78. A. CHUPUNGCO: *Cultural adaptation of the liturgy* (New York 1982) 31.
79. As to the word 'typical', the discussion about the *missa normativa* is very instructive. This denomination suggested by *Coetus* X preparing the new *ordo missae* (see De missa 'normativa', in *Notitiae* 3 (1967) 371-380) was a translation of the German *Rahmenmesse*: *Normativa proinde indicat solummodo hanc formam Missae esse normam seu 'guide' (non lex, comma, praeceptum) ad alias formas instruendas. Missa 'typica' est nomen minus aptum: typus est quid fixum et immutabile; norma applicari et accomodari potest adiunctis. 'Missa exemplaris' est nomen insufficiens, 'Missa paroecialis' nomen incompletum.* (De missa 'normativa' 371) At the Synod of 1967 the significance of *missa normativa* was not understood by most bishops. The spirit of rubricism still persisted and they thought *normativa* meant this way and not otherwise. See De liturgia in Primo Synodo Episcoporum, in *Notitiae* 3 (1967) 353-370.

On the other hand we think too often that the liturgy is a strange world for the faithful because the rites and signs it uses are no longer understood by the people. It may be. On the base of article 21 of the Constitution one is sometimes tempted to change or to abolish these rites and signs. Indeed, article 21 says:

For the liturgy is made up of unchangeable elements divinely instituted, and elements subject to change. The latter not only may but ought to be changed with the passing of time if features have by chance crept in which are less harmonious with the intimate nature of the liturgy, or if existing elements have grown less functional.

It is not always easy to tell the difference between form and content, between what is determined by Christ and by the Church and the historical or cultural conditioning. When it is not completely clear that a rite can be changed without loosing the full content, an absolute fidelity must be demanded. Here we find the necessity of liturgical catechesis or instruction. One of its aims is precisely to bridge the gap between our time, our culture and the historical, cultural and biblical background of the liturgy.

In addition we must take into account what is stated in article 23 of the Constitution. Progress, accommodation and creativity for the sake of popular understanding must be tempered by theological, historical and pastoral research so that sound tradition may be retained, and any new forms should in some way grow organically from forms already existing. We just mentioned the biblical background. This brings us to the fourth of the six resolutions for restoration enumerated above. As article 24 puts it:

Sacred Scripture is of paramount importance in the celebration of the liturgy. For it is from Scripture that lessons are read and explained in the homily, and psalms are sung; the prayers, collects, and liturgical songs are scriptural in their inspiration, and it is from Scripture that actions and signs derive their meaning. Thus if the restoration, progress, and adaptation of the sacred liturgy are to be achieved, it is necessary to promote that warm and living love for Scripture to which the venerable tradition of both Eastern and Western rites gives testimony.

Active participation in the liturgy as a celebration of the paschal mystery is impossible without providing that richer fare for the faithful at the table of God's Word (article 51). We really think it would be futile to entertain any hope of realizing any level of active participation without cultivating our conviction that here we are dealing with the very Word of God Himself. Non-biblical readings draw the people's attention away from God's Word and will not ensure that the faithful take part knowingly, actively and fruitfully.

3. ACTIVE PARTICIPATION AS THE GATEWAY TOWARDS AN ECCLESIAL LITURGY

Active participation was the aim of the Liturgical Movement. The Constitution on the liturgy declared the necessity of active participation for a real liturgy. In order to obtain this active participation it insisted on liturgical catechesis and on liturgical reform. But this is not the end: our worship has to grow into a real ecclesial liturgy. Active participation is the gateway towards such a real ecclesial liturgy.

When we speak about an ecclesial liturgy we want to say many things at the same time. By this expression, however pleonastic it may seem, we want to emphasize the full ecclesial dimension of the liturgy, the involvement of all the faithful present, and this as opposed to a mere clerical liturgy. Since the Constitution on the liturgy clerical liturgy is a *contradictio in terminis*. Article 11 of the Constitution says that active participation is supposed by liturgy itself. Article 14 calls this participation, demanded by the very nature of the liturgy, a right and a duty by reason of baptism. Article 26 states that liturgical services are not private functions but celebrations of the whole body of the Church. And article 7 underlines that every liturgical celebration is an action of Christ the Priest and of his Body the Church. So the *ecclesia*, the celebrating community, is the subject of liturgy.[80]

In a certain sense 'active participation' is not so apt an expression of what the gathered people of God are doing in the liturgy.[81] This is the reason why we like to see active participation as the gateway towards an ecclesial liturgy. The term 'active participation' has a taint of the time in which it was used for the first time. In those days one started from the liturgical action of the priest and wanted the faithful to take part in it as actively as possible. Hence the expression still makes a distinction between priest and faithful. By using the term 'ecclesial liturgy' we want to avoid this distinction. First of all the liturgy is a celebration of the people of God as a whole, and only on a secondary level we must discern different ministries and functions which exist to make the common celebration possible. But this does not mean that active participation is outstripped and that the Liturgical Movement has lost its meaning. On the contrary: to arrive at an ecclesial liturgy people must be made aware of their own role in the liturgy, which is to be done by the call for active participation. And as we have shown, because there is still much to do to attain the active participation of all involved in the celebration of our salvation and worshipping of God, the Liturgical Movement has to continue.

By using the term 'ecclesial liturgy', we bring together the renewal of ecclesiology and sacramental theology. As K. Rahner said already in 1960, 'Church' and 'sacrament' are interrelated.[82] We cannot understand the essence of the Church without thinking about the sacraments and our comprehension of the sacraments depends on our idea of what the Church really is. Precisely in the sacraments we express that we are the Church. The sacramental celebrations are privileged moments which make us sensitive, motivate us and strengthen us in our being *ecclesia*. In the liturgy the Church manifests in a paramount way that it is an assembly, the people of God, con-

---

80. Y. CONGAR: L'ecclesia ou communauté chrétienne, sujet intégral de l'action liturgique, in *La liturgie après Vatican II. Bilan, études, prospective* (= Unam sanctam 66) (Paris 1967) 241-282.
81. P.M. GY: Liturgie, in *Dictionnaire de spiritualité* 6 (Paris 1976) 911-912.
82. K. RAHNER: *Kirche und Sakramente* (Fribourg 1960).

voked by Christ to listen to the Word, to celebrate in thanksgiving his coming in his paschal mystery, and to be transformed in communicating with Christ and animated by the Spirit in order to be the Body of Christ on earth.

Vatican II has valued the local Church as manifestation of the universal Church.[83] The Church is viewed in the first place as an event, realizing its sacramentality *hic et nunc*. The Church is not an abstract idea but a concrete reality: it is to be found in the first place where the faithful are gathered around their pastors in the name of Christ. The Dogmatic constitution on the Church *Lumen gentium* says:

This Church of Christ is truly present in all legitimate congregations of the faithful which, united with their pastors, are themselves called Churches in the New Testament. (article 26)

Such an accentuation of the local Church as the subject of the liturgical celebration presupposes by definition the active participation of all those who belong to the concrete community. Each of them has his task and responsibility to realize that ecclesial liturgy. By praying, singing, answering, giving assent, acclamations, communicating, by actions and postures, even by a common silence, all contribute to an atmosphere in which the assembly can meet God in actualizing the sacramental presence of Christ in his paschal mystery. Some have a more specific ministry as a lector, servant, member of the choir, priest etc., but always on behalf of the celebrating community.[84]

By speaking about ecclesial liturgy we also want to emphasize the role of the Holy Spirit in the liturgy. The *ecclesia* was born when the apostles were anointed with the Spirit (Acts 2). God has sent the Spirit of his Son into our hearts, crying: Abba, Father (Galatians 4, 6). Filled with the Spirit we address one another in psalms and hymns and spiritual songs (Ephesians 5, 19). No one can say 'Jesus is the Lord' except by the Holy Spirit (2 Corinthians 12, 3). When we let ourselves be animated and stimulated by the Spirit, the Church can be the Body of Christ, sacrament of divine salvation. Not only Church and sacrament are interrelated, but also Church and Spirit. With W. Kasper we call the Church: sacrament of the Spirit.[85] Article 48 of *Lumen gentium* states:

Christ, having been lifted up from the earth, is drawing all men to himself (St. John 12, 32). Rising from the dead (cf. Romans 6, 9), He sent his lifegiving Spirit upon his dis-

---

83. K. Rahner called this the most new contribution of Vatican II to ecclesiology (K. RAHNER: Das neue bild der Kirche, in *Schriften zur Theologie* 8 (Einsiedeln 1967) 329-354, p. 333). See also B. NEUNHEUSER: Église universelle et église locale, in G. BARAUNA (ed.): *L'église de Vatican II* (= Unam sanctam 51b) (Paris 1966) 607-638.
84. It is significant that in the second edition of the new *Missale Romanum* the word *celebrans* is changed into *sacerdos celebrans*: so the priest is not the only celebrant. For the history of *celebrare* see B. DROSTE: *'Celebrare' in der römischen Liturgiesprache. Eine liturgietheologische Untersuchung* (München 1963).
85. W. KASPER: Die Kirche als Sakrament, in W. KASPER and G. SAUTER: *Kirche. Ort des Geistes* (Fribourg 1976).

ciples and through his Spirit has established his Body, the Church, as the universal sacrament of salvation.

In her liturgical celebrations the Church has to implore the Spirit in order to be really the Body of Christ in this world.[86] An important consequence is that each participant of the ecclesial liturgy has to let himself be animated by the Spirit in order to make concrete by his own responsibility and in his own situations this Church as Body of Christ, as sacrament of salvation for all people. In this way celebrating liturgy can never be without engagement.

---

86. See J. LAMBERTS: Eucharistie et Esprit Saint, in *Questions liturgiques* 67 (1986) 33-52.

De strijd rond een modern altaarstuk te Nuenen

REGN. STEENSMA

In 1973 maakte Hugo Brouwer in opdracht van het kerkbestuur een drieluik voor de altaarwand van de St. Andrieskerk in Nuenen. De inhoud van het werk wil de mens aan de hand van figuren en symbolen voor de keuze stellen om ja of nee tegen God te zeggen. De vormgeving toont enige verwantschap met het kubisme terwijl Brouwer koos voor vrij directe, felle kleuren.

Het werk wekte naast bewondering ook veel tegenstand. De bezwaren richtten zich zowel tegen de inhoud, als ook tegen de vormgeving van allerlei details. Daarnaast hadden velen moeite met het werk doordat het meer op een verstandelijke dan op de gevoelsmatige beleving gericht was, zoals men over het algemeen gewend is bij kunst in katholieke kerken.

Na tien jaar van vaak felle discussies werd het drieluik in 1984 uit de kerk verwijderd en vervangen door een aantal textiel-panelen die zowel naar inhoud als voorstelling geheel traditioneel zijn. In 1986 werd het drieluik weer opgehangen maar nu tegen de zijmuur.

1. HUGO BROUWER

Hugo Brouwer werd geboren in 1913 in 's-Gravenhage. Hij werd opgeleid voor onderwijzer en gaf ook enkele jaren les, maar dat voldeed hem niet. Hij wilde kunstenaar worden en kreeg onderricht aan de Academie van Beeldende Kunsten in Den Haag, de Akademie in München en de Kunsthochschule te Berlijn. Als beeldend kunstenaar maakte hij gebruik van diverse technieken. Hij vervaardigde glas-in-lood ramen, gevelreliëfs, mozaïeken, sculpturen, olieverfschilderijen en tekeningen. In de jaren vijftig en zestig kreeg hij vele monumentale opdrachten met name in het zuiden van het land, zowel voor kerken als voor profane gebouwen.

Volgens I. Everaers kunnen er in zijn glazenierswerk drie fasen worden onderscheiden.[1] Aanvankelijk werkte hij realistisch figuratief en gebruikte hij veel grisaille, bijvoorbeeld bij het doopraam en het St. Jozefraam uit 1954 in de St. Catharinakerk in Eindhoven. Vrijer van opzet zijn de 18 ramen in de St. Lidwinakerk te Schiedam uit 1955 met 9 oudtestamentische en 9 nieuwtestamentische voorstellingen. Deze ontwikkeling wordt voortgezet bij de vijf ramen met oudtestamentische voorstellingen in de Eindhovense St. Catharinakerk. De derde fase is het abstracte werk: 'In zijn nonfiguratieve ramen gaat het om het spel van lijn en vlak, van lood en kleur.'[2] Voorbeelden van dit werk

---

1. I. EVERAERS: Hugo Brouwer, in C. HOOGVELD (red.): *Glas in lood in Nederland 1817-1968* ('s-Gravenhage 1989) 217.
2. EVERAERS: Hugo Brouwer 217.

zijn de ramen in de Fatimakerk te Weert (1956-1960) en de glaswand in het gezondheidscentrum voor dieren in Boxtel uit 1964.

C. Hoogveld karakteriseert het werk van de Zuidnederlandse glazeniers uit deze periode als gloedvol in het kleurgebruik met vaak een blauwe en rode grondtoon.[3] Volgens Hoogveld hanteerden veel kunstenaars een hiëratisch byzantijnse of anecdotisch romaanse of vroeggotische vormentaal en zij geeft daarvan als voorbeeld de Christus Pantocrator van Brouwer op een van zijn ramen in Schiedam.

Naast de ramen kreeg Brouwer wat het monumentale werk betreft vooral bekendheid door het grote wandmozaïek dat hij maakte voor het priesterkoor in de kerk van Onze Lieve Vrouwe van Fatima in Weert. Het werk is 32m breed, 8m hoog en heeft 255m² aan oppervlak. Na drie jaar werk kwam het gereed in 1966. In een tamelijk lineaire stijl verwerkte Brouwer van links naar rechts de volgende onderwerpen: het levensscheepje, Christus als verlosser staande in een straal van licht, Petrus wegzinkend in de golven als symbool van de geloofscrisis van onze tijd, het kruis als teken van verlossing (precies in het midden achter het altaar), de ark als symbool van de kerk, de triomferende Christus en tenslotte het apocalyptische visioen waarin Christus de eindstrijd aangaat met zonde en dood. In de stilering van de personen en de indeling in kleurvlakken is een overgang merkbaar van de ramen naar het drieluik in Nuenen. Hans Redeker merkte bij dit werk op dat Brouwer een eigen iconografische oplossing concipieerde, 'een persoonlijke interpretatie van bijbelse motieven, waarbij naast de compositorische eenheid vooral één gedachte leidinggevend was: de directe, eenvoudige leesbaarheid van de symboliek als een taal voor de gewone mens en als achtergrond van het liturgische gebeuren'.[4]

Brouwer wilde in zijn werk verstaanbaar zijn voor de gewone gelovige. Toen hij zeventig werd zei hij in een interview:

Ik voel me nog steeds een revolutionair in de frontlinie, die religieuze schuttingkunst maakt, maar mijn werk is in elk geval begrijpelijk. Ik spreek de taal van een gelovige en als iemand zich er aan ergert, is dat niet mijn fout.[5]

In 1955 verhuisde Brouwer van Den Haag naar Nuenen waar hij de bloei van zijn leven en kunstenaarsbestaan beleefde. Rond 1973 raakte hij in een crisissituatie o.a. door het overlijden van zijn vrouw en het sterk teruglopen van het aantal monumentale opdrachten. Dit laatste was mede het gevolg van het feit dat er weinig nieuwe kerken gebouwd werden. In 1980 nam Brouwer afscheid van Nuenen en verhuisde hij naar Uithuizermeeden, waar hij woonde tot zijn dood op 19 augustus 1986.

---

3. C. HOOGVELD: Monumentale beglazingen gedurende de periode 1945-1968, in HOOGVELD: *Glas in lood* 177.
4. H. REDEKER: Hugo Brouwer en het Weerter koormozaïek, in *Algemeen Handelsblad* 13 april 1966.
5. Krant in familiedossier zonder naam en jaartal.

2. HET DRIELUIK

Het drieluik in de St. Andrieskerk werd in 1973 door Hugo Brouwer geschilderd met olieverf op hout. De hoogte bedraagt 3.51m, de breedte 2.28m en de breedte met opengeslagen luiken 4.56m. Deze afmetingen werden bepaald door J. de Jong, de architect van de kerk, die als aanhanger van de Bossche School veel waarde hechtte aan de verhouding drie op vier.

In dichtgeslagen toestand is beneden een doolhofachtige plattegrond te zien die het lichaam van een monsterdier vormt met beneden twee klauwen en boven twee horens en ogen op steeltjes. Het monster heeft in elke klauw een mensfiguur en de staart in de vorm van een vuist omklemt eveneens een mens. Rechts boven bevindt zich een geblinddoekt hoofd met erboven een neerdalende duif met nimbus, symbool van de Heilige Geest. Onder het hoofd een sleutelgat en een sleutel met daarbij een vraagteken. Midden boven is in een ellips of mandorla een naakte vrouw afgebeeld met een druiventros in haar hand en een tros als schaamblad voor haar geslachtsdeel. Achter haar staat een satyrachtige figuur met horens en staart die haar omarmt. Links boven houdt een hand een lantaarn vast, waarin een kaars brandt. Het licht van de lantaarn dringt binnen in een zwart vlak met daarin een plus- en een minteken. Pastoor Van Oosterhout zegt hiervan in zijn beschrijving:[6]

De voorkant van het drieluik stelt een zoekend mens voor met vele vragen omtrent het leven en zijn bestemming. Dat wordt uitgedrukt met de vraagtekens, de plus- en mintekens, het brandend lampje en de blinddoek. Zal hij de goede weg blijven volgen, of zal hij in de greep van het kwade verstrikt raken. De H. Geest, in de gedaante van een duif boven het hoofd geeft de hulp van God aan. De zoekende figuur staat met de benen in de doolhof die wordt voorgesteld als een verslindend beest. Het antwoord, op het alsmaar zoeken naar de betekenis van het leven, is misschien te vinden als men het drieluik openslaat. Dat wordt aangeduid door de sleutel en het sleutelgat ('maak open').

In opengeslagen toestand is op het middenpaneel centraal de omtrek van een menselijke figuur geschilderd met hoofd, hals en bovenlichaam, voor het grootste deel in de kleur geel. In het gezicht is op de plaats van het oog aan de linkerzijde een menselijke figuur geschilderd, terwijl op het voorhoofd twee rondjes ook iets van ogen suggereren. De cirkel rond het hoofd roept reminiscenties aan een nimbus op. Centraal in de figuur staat een opgeheven hand met daarin een meetlat. Onderaan bevindt zich een kleine mansfiguur gekleed in colbertcostuum met das, met als bijschrift 'Jezus'. Hij heeft een nimbus rond zijn hoofd en rode vlammen om hem heen. Met zijn rechterhand wijst hij naar boven en met zijn linker naar het rechter zijpaneel. Rechts van hem is een blauwe baan weergegeven met daarin vijf sterren en een cirkel met een gezicht, wat kan duiden op de zon en/of de maan, of mogelijk een komeet. Links van Jezus is een gebouwtje te zien, waarschijnlijk een huis, met daarboven een vliegtuig. Rechtsboven Jezus twee groene planten en linksboven een dier dat naar boven loopt.

6. 'Even praten'. Kerkblad St. Andriesparochie oktober 1977.

De beschrijving van pastoor Van Oosterhout luidt:

Als het drieluik geopend is ziet men in het middenpaneel God oprijzen als een vage menselijke figuur die ook iets van een berg heeft. De Bijbel zegt: 'De Heer is als de berg Sion, vanaf zijn hoogte ziet hij de kinderen der mensen'. De mensen ziet men als kleinere bergjes (ze hebben ogen en oren). De Schepper draagt in zijn hoofd de hele schepping zoals Hij ze gedacht heeft. Dit goede leven biedt God de mensen aan, waarbij Hij de maatstaf blijft (deze maatstaf draagt Hij in zijn hand). Onder die hand kan men de figuur van Jezus zien die het leven van de Schepper op de aarde verkondigt. Een leven dat men kan aanvaarden of niet.

Het linkerpaneel toont de figuur van een vrouw, die met haar ene voet de onderkant van de schildering raakt en met haar hoofd bijna de bovenrand. Ze is naakt waarbij het bovenlichaam groen geschilderd is met uitzondering van de rechterborst die een gele kleur heeft. Aan de rechterzijde heeft de vrouw drie armen die naar boven gericht zijn en aan de linkerzijde een arm die naar beneden wijst. In de bovenste hand rechts houdt zij een brandend hart en in de middelste een T-teken. Haar rug en hoofd zijn omgeven door veren of vlammen. Onder de buik van de vrouw is een kind geschilderd met het hoofdje naar beneden en onder het kind een rode bloem op een steel. Links onderaan steekt een slang de kop op.

Van Oosterhout schrijft over dit paneel:

De figuur links (vanuit de kerk gezien) aanvaardt het leven zoals het voortkomt uit de hand van de Schepper. Daardoor is de mens in staat zelf leven te scheppen. Het kind dat uit de schoot springt stelt voor de energie, de daadkracht, de goedheid van zovele mensen die Gods mededelende liefde in zich opnemen. Tegelijk doet deze figuur denken aan Maria die de slang afwijst; de roos van weelde bloeit op. Ze heeft geen handen genoeg om Gods schepping te aanvaarden en op een van haar handen draagt ze haar hart. Ze zegt duidelijk tegen de schepper: 'Yes – Ja'.

Het rechterpaneel toont een verwrongen figuur waarvan alleen de armen en benen herkenbaar zijn. De benen lopen uit op boomwortels. Aan het rechterbeen zit een kraantje waaruit druppels naar beneden vallen. Waar de benen samenkomen is een doodskop geschilderd met rechts erboven het woord NO in een cirkelvormige omlijsting. Het bovenlichaam bestaat uit een skeletachtige ribbekast met links een blote vrouwenborst en rechts een arm met hand die naar een gezicht gericht is. Boven dit gezicht bevindt zich een lange uitgestrekte arm met een hand en op de plaats van de elleboog een oog.

Van Oosterhout merkt hierbij op:

Aan de rechterzijde daarentegen ziet men een figuur die 'No – Nee' zegt tegen het leven van de Schepper. Zij straft daarmee zichzelf, want daardoor heeft ze géén leven. Zij weet niet te aanvaarden uit Gods hand. Zij miskent de oorsprong van haar bestaan. Ze wordt op zichzelf teruggeworpen en is slechts een karikatuur van de mens die ze zou moeten zijn. Haar leven stroomt weg zonder iemand iets te bieden.

De vormgeving doet denken aan het kubisme waarbij de verschuiving van vlakken ten opzichte van elkaar door Brouwer met name bereikt wordt door de kleurkontrasten. Sommige onderdelen van het werk wijzen op invloed van Picasso, met name het bovendeel van het rechterpaneel en het hoofd van de vrouw op het linkerpaneel, terwijl de doolhof op het gesloten paneel reminiscenties aan Dubuffet oproept. De figuren en vlakken op het werk zijn strak omlijnd en de kleuren zijn fel en direct.

3. DE INTENTIE VAN DE SCHILDER

Bij het gereedkomen van het werk maakt Hugo Brouwer een gedicht waarin hij zijn bedoeling toelicht.

Een lied over het drieluik
Door de schilder ervan: Hugo Brouwer

Van dit drieluik, dames en heren,
van dit drieluik aan de wand
kunt u echt nog heel wat leren,
mits u kijkt met uw verstand.

Op de voorkant van het drieluik
ziet u het grote doolhof-dier
Leven is soms als een doolhof,
menigeen verdwaalde hier.

Boven ziet u 't goede leven
't leven vol vermaak en sier
Onder ziet u het nare leven,
onder dreigt het doolhof-dier.

Wat moet nu de ziel wel denken?
Is het Yes of is het No.
Hij vraagt aan zijn klein lichtje.
Is het zus of is het zo?

Als men nu het drieluik opent,
ziet men God in 't centrum staan.
Wie dat doet in eigen leven,
heeft de juiste keus gedaan.

Links ziet u de ziel die 'ja' zegt
tegen God, die hij ontmoet
in zichzelf en in 't leven
als de bron van alle goed.

Doolhof houdt hem niet gevangen,
geloof bevrijdt hem van de dood.
God, de maatstaf aller dingen
is de redder uit zijn nood.

266

Rechts de ziel die niet kan geloven.
Zij zegt 'nee', ik zie het niet.
Velen, kúnnen niet geloven,
Velen leven in verdriet.

Het leven sijpelt uit hun wezen,
en de dood huist in hun geest.
Nergens zien zij meer een uitkomst,
totdat God ook hen geneest.

Ja, de schilder die dit maakte
gelooft met Jezus, onze Heer,
dat de dood wordt overwonnen
door het leven, altijd weer.

En hij schilderde dit drieluik
denkend aan zijn lieve vrouw,
die nu lachend op hem neerziet
uit de hemel, zonder rouw.

Uit het gedicht blijkt dat Brouwer persoonlijk sterk bij dit werk betrokken was. Het had te maken met zijn geloof, met de boodschap die hij aan de mensen wil meegeven en met het sterven van zijn dierbare vrouw. De voortdurende discussies over het werk en de verwijdering hebben hem diep aangegrepen. Toen hij bij gelegenheid van zijn zeventigste verjaardag werd geïnterviewd zei hij hierover:[7]

'Dit drieluik, en ik verklaar dit zonder enige terughoudendheid als mijn oprechte mening, is misschien het enige echte eigentijdse stuk actuele kerkelijke kunst dat in de tweede helft van deze eeuw in ons land is ontstaan. Dit werk ademt echter zó realistisch Christus' geest, dat de beminde-gelovigen-met-te-weinig-geloof die geest daarin niet terugherkennen en het daarom afwijzen.'
Hugo Brouwer windt zich weer op als hij nog eens voor de geest haalt hoe hij destijds als kunstenaar en gelovig christen tot in het diepst van zijn ziel gekrenkt is in zijn vorige woonplaats Nuenen. Daar heeft hij indertijd in opdracht een majestueus drieluik – 'zonder één voorwaarde vooraf' – geschilderd voor de St. Andrieskerk. Het werd een werk in, zoals hij dat zelf betitelt, 'schuttingkunst van het betere soort'. Inderdaad niet een schildering met een versieringsfunctie, maar een provocerende uitstraling; geen braaf 'plaatje' dat men na een keer bekijken al niet meer werkelijk ziet, maar een stuk dat aandacht blijft vragen.
'Het was van mij een cri du coeur, een gebed', zegt Hugo Brouwer. 'Niet een schilderij met sinterklazen of soepjurkenparade van heiligen in de stijl van Joep Nicolas, Charles Eyck en zo. Ik heb daarin mijn religieuze ideeën en gevoelens verkondigd, recht uit het hart. Een radicale prediking – in dit geval in lijnen en kleuren – zoals naar mijn mening Jezus gehouden zou kunnen hebben.
Dat drieluik kreeg een centrale plaats in de lichte, kale kerk: boven het altaar. Een

7. B. WUNDERINK: Hugo Brouwer wordt zeventig. Beter soort schuttingkunst, in *Eindhovens dagblad* 23 april 1983.

kleurexplosie in een maagdelijk witte ruimte. Och mens, er is vier jaar door vóór- en tegenstanders strijd geleverd over dit werk. Uiteindelijk is, na een algemene rondvraag, besloten het drieluik ergens achter in de kerk weg te stoppen. Boven het altaar hangt nu een braaf wandkleed met gestyleerde plompebladen. Kunnen de gelovigen onder de Mis weer verder dommelen.'

4. PLAATSING, VERWIJDERING EN HERPLAATSING

Het initiatief voor de opdracht aan Brouwer om een drieluik te maken ging uit van J.F.M. van Oosterhout, sedert 1961 pastoor van de St. Andriesparochie. De kerk kwam gereed in 1964 en ontbeerde tot 1973 een altaarstuk. Tegen de aandachtswand hing een kleed in overwegend blauwe tinten. Van Oosterhout beschikte over een geldbedrag dat bijeengebracht was met giften van parochianen in de twaalf jaar dat hij in Nuenen had gewerkt. Dikwijls gaven de mensen hem geld met de opmerking: 'Dat is voor de kerk; u ziet maar wat u ermee doet'. De opdracht werd aan Brouwer gegeven omdat deze in de parochie woonde en Van Oosterhout bewondering had voor zijn werk. Brouwer maakte eerst een ontwerpschets en liet die aan het kerkbestuur zien. De kerkmeesters hadden er veel moeite mee, en ook de meningen in de parochieraad waren zeer verdeeld: men vond het werk te modern, maar Van Oosterhout zette door omdat het werk hem wel aansprak. Hij had zich primair ten doel gesteld dat er iets inspirerends zou moeten komen en dacht daarbij bepaald niet aan een bekende traditionele voorstelling. Hij had vertrouwen in Brouwer en liet hem geheel vrij bij ontwerp en uitwerking. Hij vond de symboliek aansprekend en de vormgeving boeiend. Brouwer schilderde het stuk in de kerk en gedurende drie maanden konden de parochianen zien hoever het werk gevorderd was. Eind 1973 kwam het drieluik gereed en hing sindsdien tegen de wand achter het hoofdaltaar.

De bewondering van Van Oosterhout werd niet door alle parochianen gedeeld en er kwam van verschillende kanten kritiek. Van Oosterhout dacht eerst dat de mensen op den duur wel aan het kunstwerk zouden wennen en dat daarmee de kritiek zou verstommen, maar dat gebeurde niet. De discussies laaiden steeds weer op: in de parochieraad, in het kerkbestuur en in individuele gesprekken.

In september 1976 werd in de parochie een uitgebreide enquête gehouden waarin de mening gevraagd werd over allerlei aspecten van kerkgebouw, eredienst en parochieleven.[8] Er werden 2100 formulieren verspreid, waarvan er 387 ingevuld werden. Op de vraag 'Hoe beoordeelt u de aankleding van het kerkgebouw?' antwoordde 43 procent goed; 28,4 procent matig; 18,6 procent onvoldoende en 10 procent blanco. Men kon bij deze vraag ook opmerkingen

---

8. Gaarne betuig ik mijn dank aan C.H.A.S. van Schaik die uit het parochieblad *'Even praten'* en uit de notulen van de parochieraad over de jaren 1976 tot 1986 alle opmerkingen over het drieluik vergaarde.

maken en verscheidene parochianen maakten van die gelegenheid gebruik om hun afkeuring over het drieluik kenbaar te maken en dat vaak in krasse bewoordingen. Opvallend is dat niemand van degenen die tevreden zijn met de aankleding van de kerk zich positief uitlaat over het drieluik.

Herhaaldelijk komt daarna het drieluik ter sprake in de parochievergadering. Op 24 oktober wordt besloten de schilder te vragen om de kleuren wat te verzachten, maar Brouwer is hiertoe niet bereid. De negatieve kritiek hield aan ondanks een artikel van pastoor Van Oosterhout in het parochieblad en zijn herhaaldelijke mondelinge toelichting en verdediging. Op 20 november 1978 besloot het kerkbestuur om het drieluik aan het gezicht te onttrekken door het wandkleed voor het gesloten drieluik te hangen. Men sprak wel af na een jaar de situatie opnieuw te bezien, maar de praktijk was dat het kleed tot november 1984 voor het drieluik bleef hangen. In oktober 1980 werd een verfraaiings-commissie ingesteld met als taak het onderzoeken van de mogelijkheden van een verdere aankleding van het kerkgebouw, welke aankleding 'moet dienen tot ondersteuning van de liturgische handelingen en bevordering van de devotie bij de kerkbezoekers'.

De nieuwe commissie kwam in mei 1982 met het voorstel het drieluik te vervangen door zes kleden in appliqué-techniek. In november 1984 waren twee textiel-panelen gereed en zij vervingen toen het drieluik. De andere vier panelen waren met pasen 1985 klaar. Men stond toen echter voor de vraag wat te doen met kleed en drieluik. Op 26 februari 1985 besloot de parochievergadering dat het kleed in de crypt zou worden opgehangen en het drieluik een plaats zou krijgen tegen de rechterzijmuur bij de ingang. Op 16 oktober 1986 werd dit besluit uitgevoerd.

5. HET VERVANGENDE KUNSTWERK

De zes kleden die sinds 1985 tegen de wand achter het altaar hangen, werden vervaardigd door dames uit de parochie naar een ontwerp van mevr. Ilse de Kort-Claassen, lerares textiele vaardigheden. Door middel van appliqué-techniek zijn de kleden van voorstellingen voorzien. Het grote verticale paneel in het midden (hoog 2.50m, breed 1.90m) toont de opgestane Heer, terwijl het horizontale paneel daaronder (hoog 1.40m, breed 1.90m) twee vrouwen bij het lege graf laat zien. Links en rechts van het verticale middenpaneel hangen twee kleinere verticale panelen, elk hoog 2.15m en breed 1.40m. Ter linkerzijde toont het ene paneel de annunciatie met de engel bij Maria, en het andere Bethlehem: voor Jozef en Maria met het kind knielt een koning neer met een geschenk in zijn hand; boven hen prijkt een ster. Ter rechterzijde heeft het ene paneel een zittende figuur die een voor hem knielende persoon de hand op het hoofd legt, terwijl een andere persoon erachter staat, kennelijk een vrouw: Jezus zegent een jongen die door zijn moeder bij hem gebracht is. Op het meest rechtse paneel is de kruisiging afgebeeld, waarbij het opvallend is dat Jezus geheel gekleed aan het kruis hangt. Met de figuur die voor het kruis knielt, is Maria bedoeld. Maria is steeds gekleed in een gewaad met identieke licht- en donkerrode tinten; daarentegen heeft Jozef een gewaad met dezelfde bruine kleuren die ook de kleren van Christus kenmerken. Opvallend is de Chinees aandoende uitdrukking van de gezichten. Naast de personen zijn de panelen leeg: er is geen landschap getekend. De horizon die vrij hoog in de voorstellingen is geplaatst, loopt omhoog van de zijpanelen naar het midden-paneel en benadrukt daardoor de verrezen Christus. De houdingen en gebaren zijn volgens het gebruikelijke patroon in de traditionele katholieke kerkelijke kunst.

Voordat de kleden ontworpen waren had de commissie als uitgangspunt gesteld dat de vormgeving duidelijkheid en devotie als kenmerk zou moeten hebben met een uitvoering in warme kleuren.[9] De Kort-Klaassen schrijft in de toelichting bij haar ontwerp dat haar uitgangspunten waren:
– de wandversiering moet warmte, zachtheid uitstralen en gekozen wordt daarom voor textiel;
– uitgebeeld moet worden een aantal belangrijke momenten uit het leven van Jezus op afzonderlijke panelen;
– de afbeeldingen moeten herkenbaar zijn voor iedereen;
– de belangrijke rol van Maria in het leven van Jezus moet herkenbaar zijn;
– het geheel moet een vage kruisvorm hebben.
In september 1982 hield de commissie een enquête aan de hand van een maquette van de kerk met de ontwerpen op schaal. Er kwamen 87 antwoorden waarvan 59 zich voor het ontwerp uitspraken en 28 tegen, dus 2/3 voor en 1/3 tegen. De commentaren op de nee-formulieren waren o.a.: huidige situatie met kleed is ideaal (10 ×); liever weer het drieluik (7 ×); Christus is teveel monnik (3 ×); Christus gekleed aan het kruis is onjuist (2 ×); te dominerend, massaal, teveel aandacht trekkend (3 ×); kleuren te zwak (2 ×). Ook bij de voorstemmers werden opmerkingen gemaakt over de uitvoering van Christus. De commissie was van mening in de tweederde meerderheid voldoende steun te hebben en ging tot uitvoering van het plan over.

6. DE BEZWAREN TEGEN HET DRIELUIK VAN BROUWER

Volgens Van Oosterhout richtten de bezwaren zich in de eerste plaats inhoude-lijk tegen diverse onderdelen van de voorstelling. Men had grote moeite met de blote borsten, met het voor de buik te voorschijn springende kind, met de dikke buik van de vrouwenfiguur, met de doodskop op de plaats van het ge-slachtsdeel, met de simpele kleding van Jezus die men ook te klein vond afge-beeld, en met de omarming van de naakte vrouw door een satyr.

Daarnaast waren er ook bezwaren tegen de vormgeving. Men vond dat het kind een te groot hoofd had, dat het niet juist was dat het kind op de bloem viel en dat het hoofd van de figuur op het rechterpaneel geheel vertekend was. Ronduit belachelijk vond men de voeten als boomwortels en het kraantje aan

---

9. Gaarne betuig ik mijn dank aan F.M.A. Poppe die de stukken over het werk van deze commis-sie bijeenzocht.

270

het been. Verder richtten de bezwaren zich ook tegen de felle kleuren en het telkens verspringen van de kleuren bij de vele vlakken.

De opmerkingen in de enquête van 1976 luidden:

Weg!
Te druk, schreeuwend, afschuwelijk.
Draagt niet bij tot vroomheid en inkeer.
Irriterend, te rationeel, te schetterend, leidt af, storend.
Te grof, voorkant storend, te fel.
Geen succes, te bont en te dominerend, doet afbreuk aan het geheel, de kleuren vliegen je aan, onrustig, te modern, overheersend, verschrikkelijk, doorn in het oog.

Op 14 september 1989 had auteur dezes een gesprek met een zestal leden van de parochie, zowel voor- en tegenstanders van het drieluik, geselecteerd door de pastoor. Daarbij kwamen o.a. de volgende argumenten naar voren. Mevr. H.H. Trum-Smeenge: 'Religieuze kunst in de kerk moet begrijpelijk zijn, moet rust geven en het werk van Brouwer deed dat beslist niet.' F.M.A. Poppe: 'Religieuze kunst moet stichtend en dienend zijn en dat was het werk van Brouwer niet.' F.J.H. Vinke: 'Het drieluik vroeg te sterk de aandacht en vormde daardoor een concurrentie voor de liturgie.' Een andere mening was mevr. E.C.J. Sterenborg-Peters toegedaan:

Van het gebouw op zich gaat voldoende rust uit en het drieluik riep mij op tot het uit-dragen van het evangelie in dit leven. Mijn godsbeeld is in de loop der jaren niet gelijk gebleven maar gewisseld en ik vond dat mijn geloofservaring door het werk van Brou-wer goed werd uitgedrukt. Ik had er zeker in het begin ook wel moeite mee, maar ik leerde in een groeiproces om er met andere ogen naar te kijken.

In zijn algemeenheid merkt Van Oosterhout op dat de symboliek door velen als moeilijk werd ervaren:

Ik heb het idee dat de mensen te veel moesten nadenken. Men is dat niet gewend, want velen zijn tevreden met een gevoelsmatige geloofsbeleving. Het werk van Brouwer stel-de de mensen voor vragen en daar heeft men gewoonweg vaak geen zin in. Ook begreep men verschillende facetten van de voorstelling niet ondanks het feit dat ik het vaak uit-gelegd heb, zowel in de preek als in gesprekken. De kleden die nu in de kerk hangen hebben bekende voorstellingen zodat men er niet bij hoeft na te denken. Vorm en inhoud sluiten aan bij een gevoelsmatige geloofsbeleving zoals men dat in het verleden gewend was. Ze storen niet maar roepen ook niets op. Het is dan ook begrijpelijk dat de bezwaren in hoofdzaak van ouderen kwamen en veel jongeren wel positief oordeel-den.

Volgens Van Oosterhout liep de scheidingslijn tussen voor- en tegenstanders dwars door de verschillende maatschappelijke geledingen in de parochie, die voor ca. 10 procent uit autochtonen bestaat en voor ca. 90 procent uit nieuw-ingekomenen. Tot de laatste groep horen vele forenzen naar Eindhoven, waar-onder een groot aantal met een hogere opleiding. De bezwaren kwamen dan ook zowel van arbeiders als van hoogleraren.

7. CONCLUSIES

Het werk van Hugo Brouwer kan beschouwd worden als een waardevolle poging tot vernieuwing van de kerkelijke kunst. Uitvoering en inhoud hebben verschillende facetten, die het werk voor een katholieke parochiekerk in zekere zin baanbrekend maken. Het is een oproep tot bekering, wijst op de levendmakende kracht van het evangelie en doet dat in een hedendaagse artistieke vormentaal.

Het is echter de vraag of een dergelijk stuk geschikt is voor de aandachtswand waar iedere kerkganger elke zondag naar kijkt. De mensen komen niet alleen in de kerk voor een oproep tot bekering, maar ook voor rust, troost en meditatie en dat laatste is bij dit werk niet direct voor de hand liggend. Was het stuk een oproep tot bekering in oude vertrouwde vormen dan zou het wel geaccepteerd zijn, want het merendeel van de bezoekers is wat kunst betreft gewend aan een landschap of portret en in de kerk aan een barokke Golgothascène of een devoot Maria-beeld. Het is begrijpelijk dat de combinatie van de vorm, de inhoud en de plaats boven het altaar voor de meesten te veel was.

Helaas is men met de zes textielpanelen wel naar het tegendeel doorgeslagen. De commissie had als doelstelling: duidelijkheid en devotie, terwijl de ontwerpster als uitgangspunten nam: warmte, zachtheid, herkenbaarheid en de nadruk op belangrijke momenten uit het leven van Jezus en de rol van Maria. Men koos voor bekende beelden uit de geloofsbeleving. Dat stelt echter hoge eisen aan de artistieke uitvoering om het voorgestelde te laten doordringen tot de beschouwer en het telkens weer tot leven te laten komen, iets wakker te roepen. Als een kunstwerk met een overbekende voorstelling onder de maat blijft, loopt het snel het gevaar nauwelijks meer te zijn dan een vertellend plaatje, waar men snel op uitgekeken raakt. Helaas is dat bij deze panelen die niet meer zijn dan een goedbedoelde blijk van textiele vaardigheid het geval. Terecht merkte pastoor Van Oosterhout hierover op: 'Het stoort niet, maar roept ook niets op.' Het is de gekroonde gezapigheid. Parochie en kerkgebouw hadden beter verdiend.

SUMMARY

A CONTESTED MODERN ALTAR PIECE IN NUENEN (THE NETHERLANDS)

In 1983 Hugo Brouwer received an assignment to make a triptych for the Roman Catholic Church of Saint Andrew in Nuenen (province of Noord-Brabant) from the Church Council. The artist explained the purpose of the triptych in a poem, which begins:

From this triptych, ladies and gentlemen,
from this triptych on the wall
you really may learn a lot,
if you look intelligently.

The triptych is somewhat related to cubism. It is painted in vivid colours. Brouwer's work aroused not only admiration but also objection. Those who had objections against his work took offence at both 'content' and the styling of certain details. Many people, moreover, were troubled because the work was designed more for an intellectual apprehension than for the 'sensitive' experience which people expect in Catholic churches and to which they are accustomed.

In 1984, after ten years of discussions which were often passionate, the triptych was removed from the church. It was replaced by a number of textiles which are traditional both in content and representation. In 1986 the triptych was restored to the church, but not to its original place behind the altar. It was put up on one of the side walls.

We can understand that the combination of form and content of Brouwer's triptych and the central place where it was displayed above the altar were too much for most people. The textiles which have replaced the triptych have completely turned the scale. As works of art they are very inferior. They are no more than 'pictures' which tell a 'devotional' tale.

1. Drieluik van Hugo Brouwer tegen de altaarwand: 1973 tot 1983.

2. Het geopende drieluik.

274

3. Drieluik in gesloten toestand.

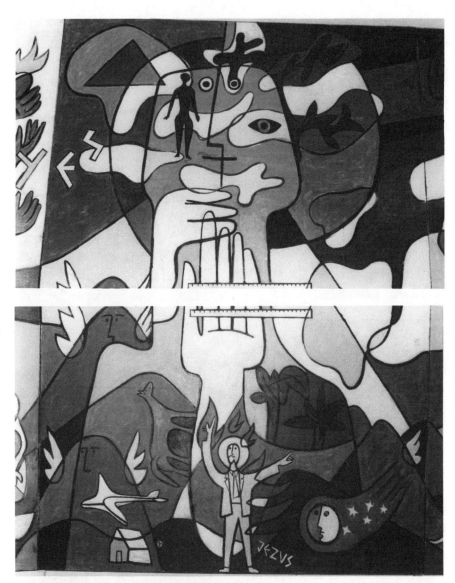

4.-5. *Details van het middenpaneel van het drieluik.*

6. Linkerpaneel van het drieluik.

7. Rechterpaneel van het drieluik.

277

8. De textielpanelen, ontworpen door I. de Kort-Claassen.

9. Twee textielpanelen: annunciatie en aanbidding door een koning.

278

Zeitgemäße Liturgie und klassische Polyphonie[1]

AD BLIJLEVENS

Als ein Theologe, dessen Dissertation 'das Gebet als Lobpreisung in Lehre und Praxis der Kirche' zum Inhalt hatte und der sich ständig mit diesem 'Thema mit Variationen' beschäftigt, berührte es mich sehr, als im Jahre 1985 im Saal des Gemeindehauses von 's-Gravenhage eine 1935 gemalte Inschrift wieder sichtbar gemacht wurde mit dem Text:

Ehre dem göttlichen Licht in den Offenbarungen der Kunst.

Zurecht sagt der holländische Kunsthistoriker C. Peeters, daß dies sehr feierliche Worte seien und daß die Besucher einer Kirche oder eines Museums häufig diesen Erfahrungsprozeß nicht begreifen könnten.[2] Ebenso richtig weist er darauf hin, daß die Kirche diese alte Weisheit in ihr Gedankengut aufgenommen und verbreitet habe. Offensichtlich vollbringt die Kirche dies hauptsächlich in und durch ihre Liturgie. Andererseits hat Peeters auch wieder Recht, wenn er darauf hinweist, wie wenig Beachtung offenbar Amtsträger und andere Gläubige oft dieser Angelegenheit schenken. Selbst in theologischen Ausbildungseinrichtungen scheint das Vorhaben 'Liturgie und Kunst' noch immer einer stiefmütterlichen Behandlung zu unterliegen.

Letzteres ist umso erstaunlicher, als wir es heutzutage mit einer Erscheinung zu tun haben, die Peeters einen 'umgekehrten Bildersturm' nennt: 'Wir werden durch alle Kommunikationsmittel und durch die Reklame mit Bildern bestürmt.'[3] Projektionsleinwände, Kinderzeichnungen, Fotomaterial, Zeitungsausschnitte, Textilienaufschriften zeugen davon. Darunter läßt sich wirklich manch Gutes finden. Über den Schönheitswert solcher Ausdrucksformen kann man sich ja wenigstens manchmal streiten. Wir müssen allerdings anerkennen, daß auch dem Formenspiel der Liturgie wieder viel Aufmerksamkeit gewidmet wird. Zugleich müssen wir aber auch zugeben, daß es unseren liturgischen Feiern oft sehr an Formen mangelt. Letzteres ist umso erstaunlicher, da ja Kunstäußerungen historisch gesehen in und aus der Liturgie entstanden und gewachsen sind. In solchen Ausdrucksformen stilisiert, ritualisiert der Mensch sein Verhalten, womit sich oft das schöpferische Wort verbindet. Darin kann der Mensch vor allem seine tiefste Wirklichkeit erfahren und zum Ausdruck bringen. Dies gilt auch im Hinblick auf die christliche Liturgie, in welcher diese tiefste Wirklichkeit neue Namen erhält.

1. Übersetzung aus dem Niederländischen von Wolfgang Kreilinger.
2. Vgl. C. PEETERS: Kerkelijke kunst en religieuze kunst, in *Religieuze kunst vandaag* (= Brabantse lezingen 3) ('s-Hertogenbosch 1987) 11-30, S. 30. [Herausgegeben von: Het Noordbrabants Genootschap, Postfach 1104, NL-5200 BD 's-Hertogenbosch.]
3. Vgl. PEETERS: Kerkelijke kunst 28-30.

An diese Tatsachen muß ich denken, wenn wir uns mit dem Verhältnis zwischen klassischer Polyphonie und zeitgemäßer Liturgiefeier beschäftigen, was ja oft genug ein Spannungsverhältnis ist. Obwohl in liturgischer Hinsicht zeitgenössische Künstler und Künstlerinnen Werke zustande gebracht haben, die unsere Bewunderung verdienen, werden wir zur gleichen Zeit mit einer Barbarei konfrontiert, der auf dem Gebiet der Kirchenmusik kaum etwas oder auch nichts entgegengesetzt wird. Oft wird wertvolles Traditionsgut *ad acta* gelegt. Gleichzeitig greifen offenbar manche Kirchenchöre wieder auf dieses Traditionsgut zurück, was wiederum Spannungen hervorruft im Hinblick auf das notwendigen Streben nach einer Liturgie, in welcher beispielsweise die aktive Teilnahme aller mitfeiernden Gläubigen hinreichend zu ihrem Recht kommt. Dies alles regt mich in aller Bescheidenheit zu nachfolgenden Überlegungen an.[4]

Persönlich halte ich sehr viel von klassischer Polyphonie. Diese Vorliebe rührt noch aus meinen Jugendjahren in der Pfarrei zum Hl. Sakrament in Breda her. Der damalige Kirchenchor sang fast ausschließlich gregorianische Gesänge und klassisch polyphone Stücke, dies unter Leitung des bekannten Komponisten und Dirigenten Louis Toebosch. Ihm gelang es, die fließende Transparenz, den kristallklaren Charakter und die Ehrfurcht vor dem Wort, die diesen Stücken zu eigen sind, sauber und doch festlich zum Klingen zu bringen. Während meiner Ausbildung im Seminar der Redemptoristen, aber auch später, als ich in Nimwegen im Studentenchor Alphons Diepenbrock und im Kammerchor von Hoensbroek sang, wuchs diese Verbindung. Immer stärker konnte ich erfahren, wie das humanistische Interesse an den Gesetzen der Betonung und der Silbenzahl lateinische Polyphoniker wie Giovanni Pierluigi da Palestrina und Orlando di Lasso beeinflußt hatte und wie wir bei ihnen in der Regel eine wortgenaue Deklamation der Texte finden, die sich übrigens keineswegs individualistisch und genausowenig prahlerisch gebärdet. Ich hielt und halte sie als Musiker denjenigen Mystikern für ebenbürtig, die ihre Glaubenserfahrungen im gesprochenen oder geschriebenen Wort äußerten oder noch äußern.

---

4. Für diesen Beitrag zogen wir folgende Publikationen heran:
  –hinsichtlich Liturgie und Kunst im Allgemeinen: A. ADAM und R. BERGER: *Pastoralliturgisches Handlexikon* (Freiburg i.Brsg. 1980) Stichwort Kunst und Liturgie 292-293; H. BECKER und R. KACZYNSKI (Hrsg.): *Liturgie und Dichtung. Ein interdisziplinäres Kompendium* (= Pietas liturgica 1-2) (St. Ottilien 1983); *Concilium* 7 (1971) Nr. 2; *Kosmos en Oekumene* 17 (1983) Nr. 3; H. VAN DER LAAN: *Het vormenspel der liturgie* (Leiden 1985); *La Maison-Dieu* 159 (3. Trim. 1984); *La Maison-Dieu* 169 (1. Trim. 1987) namentlich den Artikel von Constantin ANDRONIKOF: L'art pour la liturgie 49-60; *Sacrosanctum Concilium* Nr. 122-129 mit Kommentaren;
  –hinsichtlich Liturgie und Musik: Kommentare zum neuen *Ordo Missae*; J. GÉLINEAU: *Chant et musique dans le culte chrétien. Principes, lois et applications* (Paris 1962) 102-114; J. SCHMITZ: Die musikalische Gestaltung der Gemeindeteile in der Meßfeier, in *Musica Sacra* 97 (1977) 180-192; M. GREGOR-DELIN: *Heinrich Schütz. Sein Leben, sein Werk, seine Zeit* (München-Zürich 1984) (namentlich über das Verhältnis zwischen Wort und Musik); A. VERNOOIJ: Het gezongen Ordinarium slechts wisselgeld naar de koren?, in *Werkmap voor Liturgie* 23 (1989) 223-232.

Gleichzeitig entwickelte sich in mir das Verlangen, die Liturgie in einer Weise zu feiern, die sowohl den verschiedenen Funktionen der Gesänge in liturgischen Zusammenkünften gerecht wird, aber auch denen, die zusammengerufen wurden oder sich versammelt haben, um hier und jetzt Gott zu loben und anzubeten.

Geht es hier um ein 'entweder-oder' oder um ein 'sowohl-als auch'? Diese Frage untersuchte ich in mehreren Arbeiten über die Eignung oder Nicht-Eignung der klassischen Polyphonie – ihr widmen wir in diesem Beitrag unsere Aufmerksamkeit – für die Feier einer zeitgemäßen Liturgie.

Im Rahmen dieser Sammlung, in der die Bedeutung von *Omnes circumadstantes* aus verschiedenen Blickwinkeln beleuchtet wird, gehen wir im Nachstehenden wie folgt vor. Erst nehmen wir die Grundbegriffe der musikalischen Formgebung in den 'Gemeindeteilen' der Liturgie unter die Lupe. Hierbei beleuchten wir besonders die ästhetischen Voraussetzungen und danach theologische bzw. liturgische Grundlagen. Im zweiten Teil konkretisieren wir dieses hinsichtlich der klassischen Polyphonie und im Hinblick auf die oben gestellte Frage. Wir betonen natürlich, daß wir keineswegs den Ehrgeiz haben, vollständige Antworten anzubieten. Es geht uns vielmehr darum, Anstöße zu einer weiteren Betrachtung zu geben mit der Blickrichtung auf Theorie und Praxis.

1. GRUNDLAGEN MUSIKALISCHER FORMGEBUNG IN DEN 'GEMEINDETEILEN' DER LITURGIE

1.0. Vorbemerkungen

Wenn wir in diesem Beitrag den Ausdruck 'Gemeindeteile' gebrauchen, meinen wir damit nicht nur die Gesänge, die normalerweise durch die Gemeinde gesungen werden, sondern auch diejenigen, die der Kirchenchor vorträgt. Der genannte Begriff berücksichtigt die Tatsache, daß es keinen Gesang gibt, der allein dem Kirchenchor vorbehalten ist. Der Chor bildet ja keine eigene Gruppe über oder neben den anderen Gläubigen, sondern er ist Bestandteil der feiernden Gemeinde.

Im Folgenden werden wir der Feier der Eucharistie besondere Aufmerksamkeit widmen. Wir wollen damit keinesfalls unterstellen, daß andere Formen liturgischer Feiern deswegen weniger wert sind. Wir sind aber der Ansicht, wegen des beschränkten Umfangs dieses Beitrags diese Einschränkung auf jeden Fall machen zu müssen. Wir hoffen, daß dadurch der weite Horizont des liturgischen Feldes, in dem die Eucharistiefeier selbstverständlich einen zentralen Platz einnimmt, nicht aus dem Auge verloren wird.

1.1. Ästhetische Voraussetzung: Kirchenmusik muß den Forderungen künstlerischer Qualität entsprechen

Wenn wir für die Kirchenmusik ein ästhetisches Prinzip zu formulieren versuchen, dann soll man es einem Liturgiker nicht übelnehmen, wenn er beabsichtigt, den Dingen auf den Grund zu gehen und eine klare Vorstellung vom

Begriff der Kunst zu erlangen. Ich gebe gerne zu, daß ich mich dabei als Nicht-Kirchenmusiker unter Umständen auf's Glatteis begebe. Ich bin aber der Meinung, daß man doch einiges deutlich machen sollte.

Zunächst scheint mir der Aspekt 'Form' wichtig zu sein. Kunst ist ja immer auch Formgebung, sei es innerlicher oder äußerlicher Art. Das bringt mit sich, daß es bedeutsam ist, Proportionen von Rhythmus und Form ernstzunehmen, auch die Wirkung von Maßen und Farben sowie den Zusammenhang zwischen der Form und dem ins Auge gefaßten Ziel. Man kann sich dabei die Frage stellen, ob nicht mancher Künstler oder manche Künsterlin mehr oder weniger unbewußt und in kleinerem oder größerem Ausmaß an einem Kunstbegriff festhält, der sich im neunzehnten Jahrhundert entwickelt hat und der neben (!) der Güte der Form als zweite wesentliche Komponente die Autonomie des Kunstwerks umfaßte. Wenn wir das auf die Kirchenmusik beziehen wollen, dann schließen wir uns der Aussage von Johannes Aengenvoort an, der sagte:

> Für liturgische Musik, die sich ihrer Zielsetzung nach in die Struktur des Gottesdienstes, das heißt auch: in die aktiven und passiven Mitvollzugsfähigkeiten der jeweils den Gottesdienst feiernden Gemeinde einfügen will, gelten zweifellos weitgehend die Formprinzipien funktionsgebundener Kleinformen, also der Werkkunst; daran vorbei Musik zu machen, würde also die künstlerische Qualität solcher Musik bereits in Frage stellen. [...] Hier wird 'Güte gegenüber dem Nächsten', gegenüber dem Mitmenschen, den man sich nicht aussuchen kann, [...] zum mitkonstituierenden Teilelement der 'Güte der Form'. [...] Ohne Güte zum Nächsten keine Güte der Form.[5]

Hierbei wird ja sicher deutlich, daß es *in concreto* nicht so einfach zu beurteilen ist, ob und inwiefern Güte der Form, musikalische Qualität und Kraft vorhanden ist oder nicht.

1.2. Theologische bzw. liturgische Grundlagen

Als theologische bzw. liturgische Grundlagen können wir uns im Rahmen dieses Beitrags auf die im Folgenden kurz dargestellten beschränken. Wir glauben, auf eine weitergehende Ausarbeitung verzichten zu können.

1.2.1. Die ganze Gemeinde vollzieht die Feier der Liturgie. Die Forderung nach (innerer und äußerer) Teilnahme aller versammelten Gläubigen hat ihren Ursprung im Wesen der Glaubensgemeinschaft, der Kirche nämlich, und hebt auf eine Praxis ab, die damit übereinstimmt.

1.2.2. Das liturgische Handeln der feiernden Gläubigen besitzt eine 'innere' und eine 'äußere' Seite, die zueinander in einem qualitativen Gleichgewicht stehen müssen. Menschen sind ja Wesen aus Geist und Körper, und eine gleichartige Struktur finden wir auch in der Kirche vor. Wir sprechen hier von einem qualitativen Gleichgewicht: nicht sosehr das quantitative Verhältnis verdient unsere Aufmerksamkeit, vielmehr das qualitative.

---

5. J. Aengenvoort: Liturgische Musik im Umbruch der Zeit: Fortschrifft oder Verfall?, in *Musik und Altar* 24 (1972) 150-158, S. 156-157.

1.2.3. Die feiernde Gemeinde hat Gliederungen mit verschiedenen Aufgaben. Auf letzteres gehen wir in Verbindung mit unserem Vorhaben etwas näher ein.

Welche Gaben und Aufgaben bei einer liturgischen Zusammenkunft zur Geltung kommen bzw. kommen müssen, ebenso in welchem Maße und auf welche Weise, hängt von der konkreten Liturgiefeier ab. Das Zweite Vatikanische Konzil hat in *Sacrosanctum Concilium* als grundlegende Regel für das harmonische Zusammenspiel der Teilnehmer folgendes ausgesagt: 'Bei den liturgischen Feiern soll jeder, sei er Liturge oder Gläubiger, nur das und all das tun, was ihm aus der Natur der Sache und gemäß den liturgischen Regeln zukommt.'[6] Der Begriff 'Natur der Sache' zielt hier zweifellos nicht allein auf das Wesen der konkreten Handlung, sondern es werden hiermit auch die Bedürfnisse der liturgiefeiernden Gemeinde angedeutet. So sollen Hauptgebete zumindest überwiegend durch den Gemeindevorsteher gesprochen werden und sollen Elemente, die als singbar vorgeschlagen werden, nach Möglichkeit gesungen werden. Die Art und Weise, auf die der Sängerchor an der Gestaltung der liturgischen Feier teilnehmen kann und muß, wird in erster Linie an den Bedürfnissen der Gemeinde ausgerichtet. Wir müssen dabei ja bedenken, daß uns die besonderen Geistesgaben zwecks Dienst an der Glaubensgemeinschaft verliehen worden sind. Die Ausgangssituation gleich welcher Gemeinde fordert vom Sängerchor immer: Unterstützung des Gemeindegesangs, z.B. beim Einüben neuer Lieder; der Sängerchor soll der Gemeinde als Partner dienen, indem er dazu beiträgt, daß die Feier durch verschiedene Formen des Wechselgesangs reicher und lebendiger wird und indem er möglichst die Voraussetzungen für eine Vertiefung der inneren Anteilnahme bei allen Anwesenden schafft; der Sängerchor muß die Gemeinde stellvertretend darstellen können, indem er unter Ausnutzung seiner Möglichkeiten den Glauben der Gemeinde umfassender zum Ausdruck bringt.

Gehen wir auf letztgenannte Funktion etwas näher ein. Auf welchen Gebieten der Sängerchor oder einzelne Sänger oder Sängerinnen stellvertretend für die Gemeinde auftreten können, hängt mit der Art des Geschehens zusammen. Es wird abgegrenzt durch Handlungen, die speziell der Gemeinde als solcher zukommen. Gemäß den Nummern 14-16 der 'Allgemeinen Einleitung' zum römischen Meßbuch wird eine Teilnahme der ganzen Gemeinde in jeder Eucharistiefeier gefordert bei: den Akklamationen (z.B. beim einleitenden Dialog zur Präfation), den Antworten auf den Gruß des Vorstehers, den Antworten auf die Hauptgebete (d.h. das eucharistische Hochgebet und die Orationen), dem Schuldbekenntnis, dem Glaubensbekenntnis und den Fürbitten. Danach werden in Nummer 17 Handlungsteile aufgeführt, zu denen nicht alle Beteiligten zwingend beitragen müssen, sondern die auch von einem Chor, einer Schola, einem Kantor oder einer Kantorin vorgetragen werden können. Hierzu gehören: *Gloria*, Antwortpsalm, *Halleluja* und Vers vor dem Evange-

---

6. *Sacrosanctum Concilium* Nr. 28; Deutsche Übersetzung aus Heinrich Rennings und Martin Klöckener (Hrsg.): *Dokumente zur Erneuerung der Liturgie 1. Dokumente des Apostolischen Stuhls 1963-1973* (Kevelaer 1983) 49-50.

lium, *Sanctus*, Akklamation nach den Einsetzungsworten, Gesang nach der Kommunion, Eröffnungsgesang, Gesang zur Gabenbereitung, Gesang zur Brotbrechung (*Agnus Dei*) und zur Kommunion. Wenn wir das alles näher betrachten, wird deutlich, daß die genannte Einteilung in zwei Kategorien nicht konsequent durchgeführt wird und einige Ungereimtheiten beinhaltet. Dies betrifft die Akklamationen. Unter Akklamationen verstehen wir Antworten der Gemeinde, die in der Art eines Sprechchors gegeben werden. In der Eucharistiefeier sind Akklamationen beispielsweise die Rufe 'Lob sei dir, Christus' vor dem Evangelium und 'Wir haben sie beim Herrn' vor der Präfation. Akklamationen sind aber auch das *Kyrie*, das *Sanctus*, die Antwort der Gemeinde auf die Einsetzungsworte und das *Agnus Dei*. Wenn nun also nach der in den genannten Nummern 14 und 15 aufgeführten Regel die Akklamationen zu den Teilen der Eucharistiefeier gehören, die der Gemeinde vorbehalten sind, werden in Nummer 17 ausdrücklich das *Sanctus*, die Akklamation nach den Einsetzungsworten und das *Agnus Dei* zu den anderen Elementen gerechnet, die einer bestimmten Gruppe vorbehalten bleiben können. Wir stellen hier also einen Widerspruch zwischen den Nummern 14 und 15 auf der einen Seite und Nummer 17 andererseits fest. Letztgenannte Nummer steht außerdem noch in Widerspruch zu anderen Bestimmungen, die wir in der Einführung zum römischen Meßbuch finden.

So wird in Nummer 30 über das *Kyrie* gesagt, daß es normalerweise von allen gesungen wird. In Nummer 108 steht, daß der Priester zusammen mit seinen Assistenten und dem Volk das *Sanctus* betet oder singt (vgl. hierzu Nummer 55b). Nummer 55h bestimmt, daß alle unter anderem durch die Akklamationen, die zum betreffenden Ritus selbst aufgeführt sind, am eucharistischen Gebet teilnehmen sollen. Schließlich wird das *Agnus Dei* während der Brotbrechung und während des Ritus der Mischung von Brot und Wein durch den Sängerchor oder durch einen Kantor gesungen oder laut gebetet, während das Volk darauf antwortet: so will es Nummer 55e. Wenn wir also den verschiedenen Bestimmungen gerecht werden wollen, können wir folgendes sagen. Zu den Gesängen, die der Sängerchor oder einzelne Personen stellvertretend für die Gemeinde vortragen können, gehören laut diesen Bestimmungen:
das Eingangslied;
das *Kyrie* (nur in Ausnahmefällen);
das *Gloria*;
der Antwortpsalm nach der ersten Lesung;
das *Halleluja* und der Vers vor dem Evangelium;
der Gesang zur Gabenbereitung:
die *Sanctus*-Akklamation (nur in Ausnahmefällen);
der Gesang zur Brotbrechung (nur in Ausnahmefällen);
der Gesang zur Kommunion;
der Gesang zur Danksagung nach der Kommunion;
das Schlußlied;
darüber hinaus kann nach dem Evangelium oder nach der Homilie ein Lied gesungen werden.

Diese Aufzählung läßt erkennen, daß die Eucharistiefeier einer musikalischen Gestaltung durch einen Sängerchor oder durch einzelne Sänger oder Sängerinnen viel Raum läßt, daß aber auch bestimmte Teile – wir nennen sie nicht noch einmal – auf jeden Fall durch die Gemeinde selbst gesungen werden sollen.

2. KLASSISCHE POLYPHONIE

2.1. Klassische Polyphonie und die ästhetische Voraussetzung, wie wir sie formuliert haben

Über die Ästhetik der Renaissance-Musik könnte man sehr vieles sagen. Ich denke beispielsweise an himmlische Harmonie, das Gegenwärtigmachen des Vollkommenen, aber auch an den großen Werkumfang und an die Mehrstimmigkeit. Wir wollen hier nur folgendes anmerken.

Der Text, der vertont wird, ist nicht allein ein geschriebenes Wort, sondern ein lebendiger Körper: hinter dem Geschriebenen steht der Mensch, der ganze Mensch. Ein Kirchenmusiker greift das geschriebene Wort als solches auf und versucht, ihm auf den Grund zu gehen. Auch in der klassischen Polyphonie taucht jedesmal das 'Ich' wieder auf, sei es betend, flehend, klagend, dankend und lobend oder verkündigend. In diesem Sinne fühlt der Komponist sich dem Redner verwandt; wollen doch beide dasselbe erreichen. Für den Komponisten allerdings ist es nur der Ausgangspunkt für den melodischen und rhythmischen Ausdruck, wenn er dem Redevortrag des Textes folgt. Der Komponist setzt mit eigenen Mitteln den Prozeß der oratorischen Vergegenwärtigung fort. Von diesem Augenblick an wird der Text vom Denken und Fühlen – wir können auch sagen: von der Spiritualität – desjenigen her, der ihm musikalische Gestalt gibt, zum Ausdruck gebracht. Namentlich bei der Kirchenmusik und *a fortiori* bei liturgischer Musik im engeren Sinne ist es dann von Belang, daß das 'Ich' des Komponisten als des Übersetzers des Glaubens der Kirche Jesu Christi gegenwärtig ist. In der klassischen Polyphonie finden wir zweifellos eine Spur des Strebens nach einer Wortvertonung, die nicht subjektivistisch ist, sondern eher dem Objektiven zuneigt. Ich persönlich vermute, daß wegen dieses Markenzeichens die klassische Polyphonie in der Kirchenmusik ihre ganz spezifische Entwicklung erfahren hat.

Wir sollten hierbei meines Erachtens folgendes nicht verhehlen. Gerade wegen den soeben vorgestellten Tatsachen, aber auch, weil die klassischen Polyphonisten ihre Stücke für Berufsmusiker und berufsmäßig Vortragende geschrieben haben, kann mancher Kirchenchor leicht zu hoch greifen, wenn er klassische Polyphonie zu Gehör bringen will. Wir müssen uns auch deshalb vor Konzertneigungen hüten. Diesbezüglich ist es sicher oft schwierig, ein Gleichgewicht zu finden zwischen gerechtfertigtem Bedürfnis nach liturgischer Musik, an der ein Sängerchor wegen ihres hohen ästhetischen Wertes sein Herz erfreuen kann, und einer liturgischen Musik mit etwas bescheidenerem musikalischen Inhalt.[7]

7. Vgl. VERNOOIJ: Het gezongen Ordinarium.

2.2. Klassische Polyphonie und theologische beziehungsweise liturgische Grundlagen

Wenn wir die klassische Polyphonie den von uns dargelegten theologischen Grundlagen gegenüberstellen, sollten wir das sehr fein abstufen und sollten wir Wege suchen, um zwischen der Szylla und Charybdis von Dogmatismus und von *laissez faire, laissez aller* hindurchzufahren. Im Nachfolgenden versuchen wir daher nur, einige Wegmarkierungen zu setzen.[8]

Die Entwicklung der Polyphonie und ihre liturgische Anwendung haben – jedenfalls in der römisch-katholischen Kirche und in ihren westlichen Riten – in hohem Maße eine Praxis der Kirchenmusik bestimmt, die bis heute fortgesetzt wird. Diese Praxis findet nicht zuletzt ihren Ausdruck in dem, was man kurzgefaßt oft 'Messen' oder 'Musikmessen' nennt. Obwohl das Repertoire sich über alle liturgischen Gesänge, die nicht besonders dem Vorsteher und seinen Assistenten vorbehalten sind, erstreckt, hat sich diese Praxis vor allem darin entwickelt, was man gemeinhin das *Ordinarium Missae* nennt, das heißt die sogenannten festen Gesänge der Messe: *Kyrie, Gloria, Credo, Sanctus* und *Agnus Dei*. Tatsächlich bedeutet dies unter anderem, daß der liturgische Gesang der eigentlichen Gemeinde ganz oder überwiegend von einer hierfür mehr oder minder spezialisierten Gruppe (dem Chor oder der Schola) übernommen wird. Seit der Renaissance wurde dieses zur zumindest 'normalen' Praxis in den Kirchen, die über eine solche Gruppe verfügten oder noch verfügen.

Aus dem bislang Dargelegten möge deutlich werden, daß wir diese Entwicklung, durch welche der Gesang der feiernden Gemeinde an sich – vorsichtig gesagt – zum Vorteil einer tatsächlich oft bemerkenswert hochstehenden Chormusik starr eingegrenzt wird, nicht als richtungweisend betrachten sollten. Dies wird zur Selbstverständlichkeit, wenn wir ernstnehmen wollen, was es bedeutet, daß die ganze Gemeinde die Feier vollzieht und daß es hinsichtlich der einzelnen Glieder der Gemeinde eine Vielfalt von Aufgaben gibt. Ob wir es angenehm finden oder nicht: hier stellt uns die klassische Polyphonie vor Probleme. Auf einige davon wollen wir näher eingehen.

Wir haben durchblicken lassen, daß als *Ordinarium Missae*-Gesänge nicht mehr ausschließlich der bekannte Fünfklang (*Kyrie, Gloria, Credo, Sanctus, Agnus Dei*) gelten kann. Will man eine sozusagen 'durchkomponierte Messe' gestalten beziehungsweise entwerfen, dann muß man sowohl die Teile berücksichtigen, welche unseres Erachtens ebenso Sache der Gemeinde sind – wir denken hierbei an die in diesem Fünfklang nicht genannten Akklamationen –, als auch veränderten Erkenntnissen Rechnung tragen hinsichtlich der Aufgabe(n), der Form(en) und der Ausführungsweise(n) verschiedener Gesänge.

Dies stellt uns vor Probleme hinsichtlich der 'polyphonen Messen'. Sie schließen ja nicht mehr passgenau an das an, was nach dem neuen römischen Meßbuch für die betreffenden Gesänge gelten soll. Wir können uns vorstellen, daß man die Gemeinde das *Gloria* manchmal nur anhören läßt; es wird aber

---

8. Vgl. VERNOOIJ: Het gezongen Ordinarium.

unseres Erachtens dem Charakter dieses Lobgesangs nicht gerecht, wenn diese Praxis einen zu großen Umfang hat oder erhalten soll. Eine sehr unglückliche Entwicklung ist weiterhin die Tatsache, daß hier und da das *Sanctus* (einschließlich des *Benedictus*) nur durch den Chor gesungen wird. Wie soll man da von aktiver Teilnahme am Herzstück der Eucharistie sprechen!? Gegenwärtig findet man auch manchmal die Gewohnheit vor, das *Sanctus* oder den einen oder anderen sonstigen Gesang (zum Beispiel das *Gloria* oder das *Agnus Dei*) zum Kommunionritus zu singen. Man sollte sich doch davor hüten, in den Kommunionteil Gesänge zu 'stopfen', denen irgendwo anders ihr eigener Platz zukommt und die eigentlich im Kommunionritus nichts zu suchen haben. Man sollte doch auch diesen an sich schon überladenen und manchmal auch unruhigen Teil nicht noch mehr belasten und dadurch noch unübersichtlicher machen. Außerdem: wenn schon das *Kyrie* und die anderen Gesänge wirklich 'durchkomponiert' sind und das genau in der zugeordneten Reihenfolge, durchbricht man dadurch nicht die vom Komponisten beabsichtigte musikalische Einheit?

Was soll man noch sagen hinsichtlich anderer Gesänge der klassischen Polyphonie? Manche können tatsächlich zu einer Eucharistiefeier passen. Wir müssen aber auch dabei ernstnehmen, daß die Inhalte, die Aufgaben und die Formen sowohl durch die Feier in ihrer Gesamtheit bestimmt werden als auch durch ihre jeweiligen Abschnitte. Wir können uns vorstellen, daß man unter Berücksichtigung dieser Vorgaben im Zusammenhang mit der Verkündigung des Evangeliums oder von seiner Verkündigung ausgehend oder auch während der Gabenbereitung oder/und während der Kommunion eine Motette singt, die inhaltlich dazu paßt und die in der Art einer Meditation oder Verkündigung gesungen beziehungsweise angehört werden kann. Auf jeden Fall sollte dann für die lauschende Gemeinde eine Übersetzung des lateinischen Textes zur Hand sein. Hier sei übrigens angemerkt, daß eine solche Übersetzung nur eine relative Bedeutung hat. Wir wollen gegenüber letztgesagtem übrigens behaupten, daß das Charisma, das in dem jeweiligen polyphonen Gesang zu Ausdruck kommen kann, auch so tiefgreifend wirken kann, ohne daß man bis in die Einzelheiten dem genauen Text folgen muß.

Es gibt ja noch ein breites Spektrum anderer Liturgiefeiern wie: Wortgottesdienste und Schriftgottesdienste, Andachten, Meditationen, Kantaten, 'Musikalische Vespern', Kommunionfeiern (bei letzteren würde ich übrigens einen größeren Vorbehalt geltend machen) und so weiter.[9] Hier können wir vielleicht der klassischen Polyphonie einen eigenen Platz einräumen, insbesondere dann, wenn man auf das musikalische Element einen besonderen Wert zu legen wünscht. Wir müssen natürlich auch dann, je nach dem jeweiligen Charakter des Gottesdienstes, die Gemeinde das singen lassen, was zu singen ihr zukommt. Ebenso müssen wir die Aufgabe(n) deutlich machen, welche die

---

9. Hierüber publizierte der Autor u.a.: Stellenwert und Gestalt nicht-eucharistischer Gottesdienste, in Martin KLÖCKENER und Winfried GLADE (Hrsg.): *Die Feier der Sakramente in der Gemeinde (Festschrift H. Rennings)* (Kevelaer 1986) 384-402.

jeweiligen Gesänge im Einzelnen haben, wie beispielsweise: Verkündigung, Gebet und/oder Meditation. Bei alledem müssen wir auch die konkrete Situation berücksichtigen, in der die Liturgiefeier stattfindet: welche Gläubigen, welche äußeren Umstände (hinsichtlich Raum und Teilnehmer) und welcher Anlaß.

3. SCHLUßWORT

Es möge klar sein, daß auch im Hinblick auf unser Vorhaben die Entwicklung der 'Gabe der Unterscheidung' in höchstem Maße bedeutungsvoll ist. Gerade heutzutage, wo auf dem Gebiet von Liturgie und Musik, nicht zuletzt auch hinsichtlich ihres wechselseitigen Verhältnisses, soviel in Bewegung geraten ist, bedarf man auch in diesem Zusammenhang einer gut fundierten Kritik, sei sie positiv oder negativ. Diese Kritik erstreckt sich auf die verschiedenen Formen der Liturgie, sei es, wie sie angeboten beziehungsweise vorgeschrieben wird, sei es, wie sie tatsächlich vollzogen wird. Selbstverständlich sollte diese Kritik konstruktiv sein und aus allen Gliedern der Glaubensgemeinschaft her vorkommen. Stärker, als das oft geschah oder geschieht, muß dabei die liturgische Musik unter die Lupe genommen werden. Dabei sollte man es nicht bei (mehr oder minder) abstrakten Betrachtungen oder Behauptungen bewenden lassen, sondern man sollte sich auf konkrete Tatbestände beziehen. Nicht zuletzt wird die 'Gabe der Unterscheidung' durch und in der täglichen Praxis entwickelt. Liturgie ist ja vor allem *actio*, ist Glaubensleben und Glaubensäußerung *in actu*.

Hintergrundfragen sind: Wie und inwiefern widerspiegelt die Liturgie, nicht zuletzt in ihren musikalischen Dimensionen, als gläubiges Kunstwerk *in concreto* den Glauben der Orts- und der Universalkirche, widerspiegelt sie die Offenbarung als Begegnung zwischen Gott und den Menschen und zwischen den Menschen untereinander, die Bezogenheit der Menschen aufeinander und – *last but not least* – die kontemplative Dimension, in der Christen auf dem Weg der Suche nach sich selbst und nach Gott sind? Man kann dies manchmal unter den tatsächlichen Umständen wirklich nicht einfach beurteilen, ob überhaupt und in welchem Maße konkrete Formen gut sind. Aber umso größer ist die Herausforderung, es dennoch zu unternehmen, damit der Begriff *Omnes circumadstantes* mit Inhalt versehen wird.

Mit der Bearbeitung dieses Themas haben wir die Absicht verfolgt, ein gemeinsames Fundament für Gespräche zwischen Kirchenmusikern und anderen für die Liturgie Verantwortlichen aufzuzeigen. Unsere Betrachtungen konnten nur einige Aspekte beleuchten, die für eine sinnvolle musikalische Gestaltung der Liturgie wichtig sind, namentlich auch im Hinblick auf eine verantwortliche aktive Teilnahme aller zur Feier vereinten Gläubigen. Wir wollen keinesfalls zu einer Verflachung des liturgischen Gesangs beitragen – die instrumentale Musik ließen wir bewußt außer Betracht – und wir wollen alles dafür geben, daß Schönheit und Stil unsere liturgischen Zusammenkünfte kennzeichnen. Die Tatsachen, daß veränderte Blickwinkel in Richtung auf unsere christliche Liturgie auch in kirchenmusikalischer Hinsicht Konsequenzen nach sich ziehen, sollte man keinesfalls als nachteilig ansehen. Im Gegenteil: Gerade auch im Zusammenhang mit unserem Vorhaben können wir sagen: Die Geschichte der Kirchenmusik lehrt uns, daß empfangsbereite und schöpferische Menschen es als Stimulans ihrer Kreativität erfahren haben, neue Aufgaben zu erfüllen. Das Wort 'Ehre dem göttlichen Licht in den Offenbarungen der Kunst' bleibt auch in dieser Hinsicht aktuell.

Praedicatio Verbi divini verbum populi?

ANTON H.M. SCHEER

1. EINLEITUNG

Auf Anregung Herman Wegmans will ich versuchen, meinen Beitrag im Geiste der volksbezogenen Liturgie zu liefern. Dieser Aufsatz beabsichtigt, ein besonderes Augenmerk auf die Predigt zu werfen, die wohl den am meisten dem Volk zugewandten Teil der liturgischen Riten bildet. Dabei setze ich voraus, daß die Homiletik, wie auch z.B. die Sakramentenlehre, zur Liturgiewissenschaft gehört.

Indem ich die Predigt als Thema wähle, riskiere ich gewissermaßen, mir selbst zu widersprechen. In meinen Vorlesungen versuche ich meine Studenten davon zu überzeugen, daß die Predigt jedenfalls nur einen Teil des ganzen Ritus bildet, der da stattfindet. Im Prinzip sollte man sie gemäß ihrem syntachmatischen und paradigmatischen Charakter betrachten, d.h. in Beziehung zu den anderen Teilen des rituellen Geschehens.

Daß ich mich in diesem Aufsatz dennoch auf die Predigt konzentriere, folgt aus dem Zweck dieser Arbeit. Sie soll eine Vorstudie sein für eine empirische Befragung der Person, die den Gottesdienst leitet. Sein/ihr Funktionieren möchte ich in einer bestimmten Hinsicht untersuchen. Es handelt sich dabei um die Frage nach dem hermeneutischen Prozeß, den er/sie entwickelt, um die Verbindung zwischen Botschaft und Existenzsituation in einem Kommunikationsgeschehen der Liturgie herzustellen. Wird diese Beziehung hergestellt, so geschieht dies in welchem Masse, auf welche Weise, mit welchen Hilfsmitteln und mit welcher Absicht? Dies gilt zwar für jegliches liturgisches Handeln des Pfarrers und für alle Phasen und Stadien seines Vorgehens. Ich meine aber, man könne anhand der Verkündigung im strengsten Sinn, also der Predigt, diese Beziehung exemplarisch entwickeln und näher bestimmen.

2. KENNZEICHEN DER PREDIGT

Der Titel dieses Aufsatzes ist eine gewagte Änderung der klassischen Aussage der Reformation, sogar von Luther selbst: *Praedicatio Verbi divini verbum divinum*. Ich habe das letzte Wort *divinum* durch *populi* ersetzt und ein Fragezeichen hinzugefügt. Damit will ich die Dialektik zwischen dem Sprechen Gottes und dem Sprechen der Gemeinde andeuten, also zwischen dem Wort der Bibel und dem der Existenzerfahrung, zwischen dem gegenseitigen Sprechen und Hören. Dieser Dialog, diese Wechselrede im Glauben, vollzieht sich namentlich im Prediger.

Wir setzen voraus, daß er/sie bei der Ausübung seines/ihres Amtes fortwährend, bewußt oder unbewußt, explizit oder implizit, absichtlich oder
unbemerkt damit beschäftigt ist die Botschaft und die Existenzsituation aufeinander zu richten und miteinander zu verbinden. Man darf behaupten, daß
das Predigeramt gerade in dieser hermeneutischen Tätigkeit zugunsten der
Glaubensbestätigung der Individuen, der Gruppen und der Gemeinschaft
besteht. Diese Aktivität erhält bei eben der Predigt einen eigenen Akzent.

Erstens gilt die Predigt als eine pastorale Arbeit, die sich selbstverständlich
an die Glaubensgemeinschaft richtet. Sie ist ein öffentliches Sprechen zu einer
Vielfalt von Menschen: ein Sprachakt als Anrede an Gläubige.

An zweiter Stelle ist die Predigt ein pastorales Handeln, in dem der Glaube
der Gemeinschaft von neuem Erzählung oder Text wird. Sie vollzieht sich auf
der Basis der Glaubensgemeinschaft und zu deren Förderung. Es handelt sich
ja um die Gemeinde selbst, um ihre Identität, und sie wird als solche angesprochen: es ist also ein Sprachakt als Ansprache an die Gemeinde.

An dritter Stelle ist die Predigt ein pastorales Tun, das auf Anregung der
Glaubensgemeinschaft stattfindet, weil diese erkennt daß sie wesentlich auf
das Hören angewiesen ist. Dies ist nicht bloß ein Hören auf sich selbst bis in
die Tiefen des Glaubens, sondern vor allem ein Hören auf Aussicht, auf
Erneuerung und Befreiung hin. Predigt ist Aufruf zur Transformierung,
Selbstkritik und Bekehrung. Sie ist kein Zwischenfall oder zufälliges Sprechen. Die Predigt ist vielmehr ein Sprechen im Auftrag der Gemeinde, ein
officium, zu dem sie sich strukturell und institutionell bekennt. Die Predigt ist
ein offizielles Sprechen zu der und an die Gemeinde, wovon diese erkennt, daß
es in ihrem Namen und zugleich ihr selbst gegenüber geschieht.

Schließlich ist die Predigt eine seelsorgliche Arbeit, in der bewußt, hoff-
nungsvoll, explizit und absichtlich die Glaubenssachen des Alltags verbal ausgedrückt werden: wie wir zusammen Menschen Gottes, Leib Jesu Christi,
Tempel des heiligen Geistes, Diener des Reiches Gottes sein können. Die Predigt verwurzelt den biblischen Glauben in die Existenzsituation und setzt das
begrenzte, situationshafte Dasein in das Licht der Schrift, damit Konfron-
tation, erhellende Einsicht und Läuterung zugunsten der gläubigen Existenz
geschieht. Somit ist die Predigt ein Sprachakt als eine maßgebende Anrede: sie
ist Widerrede.

Im Vorhergehenden haben wir vier formelle Kennzeichen und Aspekte des
Predigtaktes angedeutet, die an sich operationalisiert werden könnten, um
untersuchen zu können, inwiefern sie tatsächlich vom Prediger erkannt, erlebt
und in seiner Predigt aktualisiert werden.

3. WESENSELEMENTE DER PREDIGT

Namentlich in Kreisen der Reformation hat man vielfach und tiefschürfend
über das Wesen und die Wirkung der Predigt nachgedacht. Man könnte die
Predigt den Kristallisationspunkt der Theologie und der Liturgie nennen. Dieser Auffassung entspricht ein tiefes Erleben bei dem Prediger und der Gemein-

de. Was bei der reformatorischen homiletischen Reflexion auffält, ist der Vorzug und der Primat der Bibel (oder besser des Wortes Gottes). Gott spricht zur Gemeinde, redet die Gemeinde an, setzt die Gemeinde unter sein Wort und bestimmt ihr Wesen zum Hören. Überdies: ohne das Wort keine Verheißung, sondern ein bleibender Sündenbestand. Wer aber das Wort Gottes annimmt, kann zur Einsicht gelangen, daß er/sie in der Unheilslage steht, aus der nur Gott befreien kann.

Wer aus tiefer Seele hört, darf auf die Verheißung hoffen, die vorzüglich – nämlich menschgewordene – Gestalt erhalten hat in der Person und den Worten Jesu von Nazareth. In dessen Tod und Pascha sind Tod und Sünde überwunden. Es gilt also, diese Quelle der Rechtfertigung immer wieder zu erschließen und durch Menschen und Welt fließen zu lassen. Deshalb stehen Predigt und Liturgie so zentral im reformatorischen Glaubenserleben und in ihrer Spiritualität: Gottes Evangelium und die Menschen begegnen sich, und so werden diese von Gott zu freien Menschen gemacht, nachdem und weil sie ihre existentielle Gefangenschaft, ihre Isolierung und Selbstorientierung genügend erkannt haben, blind für das irdische Leben und der Welt abgewandt. Der Mensch steht zwischen Welt und Gott, folglich in der Angst vor dem Tod und der Auslieferung an das Nichts, zur Absurdität verurteilt.

Liturgie und Predigt beabsichtigen, diese Unheilsaussicht abzulenken und zu vernichten. Sie können das nicht auf eine momentane, wunderhafte Weise erreichen, sondern nur mittels eines Hörvorganges, durch eine fortwährende Verkündigung und Ermutigung mit immer der gleichen Tendenz: Bruch mit der Angst und der Sünde, Aussicht auf Erlösung und Verheißung. Dies alles kraft des Wortes Jesu von Nazareth, besiegelt in seiner österlichen Lebenshingabe als Protest gegen die Herrschaft von Sünde und Tod; und nicht nur das, sondern auch: 'Seht, ich mache alles neu' (Offenbarung 21, 5). Ich möchte diese reformatorische Einsicht und Gewißheit als Ausgangspunkt für eine weitere Bearbeitung des Phänomens Predigt nehmen, wobei ich in diesem Aufsatz jede Apologetik oder Polemik übergehen möchte.

Apologien und Polemiken auf dem Gebiet der Homiletik sind übrigens an der Tagesordnung, nicht zo sehr in bezug auf die herausragende Stellung des Wortes Gottes und der Schrift in Predigt und Homilie, sondern mehr im Zusammenhang mit oben erwähnter Existenzsituation, und wenn man sich Fragen stellt über die Wirkung (In-, Durch- und Auswirkung) der Predigt als Heilswirksamkeit oder als Zeugnis des Heiligen Geistes.

4. DIALEKTIK ZWISCHEN EVANGELIUM UND EXISTENZSITUATION

Im allgemeinen verstehen wir hier unter Existenzsituation den Komplex psychischer, physischer, persönlicher und sozialer, ideologischer und technologischer, wahrnehmbarer und unbemerkter Faktoren und Einflüsse, die das tägliche Leben der Individuen und Gruppen dermaßen bestimmen, daß sie als Kontext mit der Person gegeben und verwoben sind. Diese Verwobenheit ist so umfangreich und tiefgreifend, daß man den Subjektkern des Individuums oder der Gruppe nicht ohne sie erhalten kann. Formuliert man den Menschen als ein freies Wesen mit Verantwortung und Zielbewußtheit, so soll man dabei die wesentliche Konditioniertheit mit einkalkulieren. Es handelt sich eben um Freiheit, Verantwortung und Sinngebung im Kontext, und deshalb um ein fragmentarisches Subjekt. Im Rahmen einer Untersuchung nach dem Handeln von Predigern ist die Existenzsituation einer der zentralen Begriffe, die eine angewandte und eingehende Operationalisierung fordern.

Mit Bezug auf das Verhältnis zwischen Evangelium und Existenzsituation treten in der Theorie – und wohl auch in der Praxis – drie Möglichkeiten auf.

4.1.

Dominanz der Schrift in bezug auf die Existenzsituation, insofern Mensch und Welt in ihrer Säkularität der Schrift unterstellt sind und demnach zu profanen Größen gemacht werden: zu empfangenden Subjekten, bei denen die Empfänglichkeit sich auf die Abwesenheit von *obices* und auf Hörbereitschaft beschränkt. Die Rezeptivität enthält in diesem Licht ein Mindestmaß an Intersubjektivität, insofern der Mensch sich als Sünder weiß und grundsätzlich zu Gott keinen Zugang hat; es gibt keine Möglichkeit, Gott näher zu kommen. Die Heilsmöglichkeiten beschränken sich auf den Willen und auf das Maß dieses Könnens. Das Subjekt ist der Heilsbedürftige, der Bittsteller, der Mensch als elementare Bitte um Gnade. Man kennzeichnet diese Sicht auch als die Vertikalität der Schrift auf der Horizontalität von Mensch und Welt. In der homiletischen Literatur nennt man diese Art Predigt wohl die orthodox-reformatorische, weil sie sich dem Gedankengut der Reformation anschließt. Die Schrift steht an erster Stelle, am Anfang, im Zentrum und am Schluß der Predigt: *praedicatio Verbi divini verbum divinum*. Die Schrift ist unablässig und unabkömmlich zugegen; im Zentrum das menschgewordene Heilsangebot Jesu des Herrn, der in sich selbst Angst und Tod überstand und besiegte.

4.2.

Dominanz der Existenzsituation der Schrift gegenüber, insofern Mensch und Welt hier grundsätzlich Ausgangspunkt und Endpunkt der Predigt sind. Der Prediger spricht ausdrücklich aus der Gemeinschaft der Gläubigen heraus, zu ihr und für sie, und hat den Aufbau und die Kontinuität des Einzelnen und der Gruppe im Auge. Diese Zielsetzung duldet keine Schattierung und Abschwächung, auch nicht von seiten des Wortes Gottes. Dies folgt aus dem Wesen der Schrift, die sich an die Menschen aller Zeiten und Orte wendet und ihnen zuredet. Die Schrift hat keinen wesentlichen Wert an sich, sondern sie ist für Menschen auf göttliches Geheiß Träger der Wahrheit, der Güte und Redlichkeit. Dieses 'auf göttliches Geheiß' der biblischen Wahrheiten, Normen, Aussichten usw. verdient die volle Betonung, weil dies das *proprium* der Predigt bildet. Aber trotzdem bleibt die Predigt den Menschen zugewandt. Das Wort Gottes ist im höchsten Maß ein *verbum humanum*, kein *verbum hominis* in dem Sinn, daß die Predigt von einem Menschen gesprochen und in Worte gefaßt wird, sondern ein menschliches Zeugnis, in dem ausgesagt wird, was der Mensch ist und wie er sein könnte und sein sollte. Diese Würde der Schrift ist der reinen Inspiration zu verdanken. Die Urquelle ist Gott in seiner Dreieinigkeit; sie wird aber durch die wahrhafte und unbegrenzte Menschlichkeit des Wortes vermittelt. Primär und exklusiv, so erkennen wir, ist die Predigt auf Menschen gerichtet. Der Historizität der Bibel – als Symbol der historischen Gestalt Jesu Christi – entspricht die Historizität der Predigt: sie betrachtet all das, was des Menschen ist und was des Menschen sein könnte, Erlösung die zum Frieden führt. In dieser Sicht ist der Unterschied zwischen personbezogene oder gesellschaftbezogene Predigt nicht relevant. Die Diagnostik der Existenzsituation unter den Normen der Schrift bestimmt die nähere Klassifizierung der Predigt.

4.3.

Die Äquivalenz der Schrift und der Existenzsituation in der Predigt, insofern man beide als zwei Pole in wechselseitiger Dialektik verstehen soll. Die Homilie steht in einem dialektischen oder dialogischen Prozeß, in dem Gott und Mensch zur Sprache kommen. Einseitige Polarität stört das Gleichgewicht im Glauben, wie sich das in der Geschichte öfters herausgestellt hat: der Neo-Chalcedonismus, der Gott auf Kosten des Menschen vorzieht; der Pelagianismus, der das Gegenteil tut. Aufgabe der Verkündigung und der Liturgie ist es, zwischen dem Göttlichen und dem Menschlichen Mittler zu sein. E. Schillebeeckx benutzt, wenn er über das Gebet spricht, die harmonisierende Terminologie der 'indirekten Direktheit'. Nicht die Konkurrenz zweier Pole ist wichtig, sondern deren Berührung, Verflechtung, Harmonie und Korrelation, ohne daß man übrigens das grundsätzliche Anderssein verneint oder ignoriert. Dank ihres Andersseins behaupten beide Partners, Gott und Mensch, ihren Platz, so daß sie sich an einander wenden und einen Dialog führen können. Schon dieser tatsächliche Dialog stellt den Menschen in eine kritische Lage: er dialogisiert wirklich mit Gott. Die Unbestimmbarkeit dieses Partners bewirkt jedoch eine entsprechende Relativierung der bruchstückhaften Bestimmtheit der Existenzsituation der Menschen und der Gemeinde. Das Evangelium Jesu Christi setzt den üblichen Lebensmaßstab um oder dehnt diesen ins Unvermutete aus, so daß die bedingte Lebensweise als Mangel oder Anschein aufleuchtet. Der Predigt wird eine reformierende Kraft zuerkannt, wenn der Dialog aufrichtig und wahrhaft geführt, gehört und angeeignet wird.

In der Folge dieses Aufsatzes wählen wir die Ausarbeitung dieses dritten dialektischen Modells als die ideal-typische Predigtart. Neben dem Vorhergehenden wird diese Wahl deswegen genommen, weil diese Predigtart in der heutigen Praxis am meisten vorkommt. Es ist ja unsere Absicht, uns bei der Untersuchung möglichst der pastoralen Predigtpraxis anzuschließen.

5. WIRKUNG DER PREDIGT

Man kann auf mancherlei Weise die Grundform oder die Wirkung der Predigt betrachten. Es gibt da große Unterschiede. Das hängt mit der Auffassung zusammen, die man vertritt, inwiefern eine Handlung sinnvoll oder wirksam ist. Fallen Sinn und Effektivität zusammen, bestimmen sie einander notwendigerweise oder sind sie voneinander unterschieden. Wiederum gibt es hier drei denkbare und ausführbare Stellungnahmen.

5.1.

Die systematische theologische Literatur bezügiich der Wirkung der Liturgie ist geneigt, sich letzten Endes für den Unterschied zwischen Sinn und Effekt zu entscheiden. Eine Handlung kann als sinnvoll betrachtet werden, auch wenn ihr erfahrungsgemäß keine Folgen entsprechen. Dies bedeutet, daß die Handlung als solche einen Wert had, einzig und allein durch die Tatsache, daß sie begangen wird. Die liturgischen Symbol- und Metapherakte werden auf diese Weise qualifiziert und gewertet. Bei dieser Stellungnahme spielt die Diskussion über die Wirkung des menschlichen Verhaltens eine entscheidende Rolle. Zur Diskussion stehen einerseits der sogenannte Funktionalismus, Pragmatismus und Produktionismus, andererseits der Symbolismus, die Versinnbildlichung und Ritualisierung. Man hebt das funktionalistische Prinzip der Produktivität und Nützlichkeit gegen das symbolistische Prinzip der Unentgeltlichkeit ab. Auf die Liturgie angewandt behauptet man, daß diese gläubige Handlung einen unentgeltlichen Charakter hat, nicht gemessen werden kann mit den Maßstäben des Produktionismus, und daß es sich wesentlich um die Beteiligung selbst an der Handlung handelt. Man zieht Parallelen mit dem Genuß einer Feier oder dem Erleben von Kunst und Liebe. Bezieht man diese Gedanken auf die Predigt als liturgische Handlung, so gilt diese schließlich als ein kultisches, rituelles und metaphorisches Sprechen vom Glauben aus und auf den Glauben hin. Das Ohr der Zuhörer soll genau auf die religiösgläubige Wellenlänge eingestellt sein. Aus Forschungsergebnissen zeigt sich, daß Gläubige die Predigt hoch bewerten, ohne sich nachträglich mindestens der Kerngedanken und der Grundworte zu erinnern oder sie wiederholen zu können.

5.2.

Die entgegengesetzte Sicht bezüglich der Auswirkung der Predigt, wonach Sinn und Effekt zusammenfallen, findet man gleichfalls in der systematischen theologischen Literatur. Sie erscheint da im Rahmen bestimmter Thematiken, wie der Akkulturation der Liturgie, der Beteiligung der Gemeinde, der Relevanz der Liturgie im Verhältnis zu anderen Formen pastoralen Handelns. Die Liturgie mit ihren Eigenheiten und typischen Charakterzügen darf nicht so fremdartig, weit entfernt und eigentümlich sein, daß sie für den heutigen Menschen unzugänglich und irrelevant wirkt. Dieses Risiko besteht durchaus. Je mehr man die Unersetzlichkeit und den Wiederholungscharakter der liturgischen Riten betont, desto mehr kann das Bild einer Verbindlichkeit, Schablonenhaftigkeit und Unabänderlichkeit dieses Handelns entstehen. Das Gewordensein der Dinge konkurriert dann mit dem Werden, demzufolge das Heute und die Zukunft verbarrikadiert werden. Nun denn, die Liturgie soll primär den Erwartungen der Teilnehmer entsprechen. Ihre Lebensumstände sind eine Richtlinie für die liturgische Praxis, so daß sie von vornherein in ihrer gläubigen Identität angeredet werden. In prägnanter Weise gilt dies für die Predigt, die ja als Ansprache und Aussprache dargeboten wird. Die gläubige Deutung ihrer Existenz soll die Erfahrungen der Hörer berühren, mit ihnen rechnen und sie ordnen. Deshalb soll die Predigt bei ihnen einen kognitiv-emotionellen Prozeß in Gang bringen, der zum Betrachten und Nachdenken führt. Sollte die Predigt dies nicht beabsichtigen, so mangelt es ihr an der richtigen Zielsetzung und verliert sie ihren Sinn, ist sie nicht mehr sinngemäß. Die liturgische Handlung, konkret die Predigt, bezweckt ganz entschieden Effekt bei den Hörern: Seele und Leib werden geistig angeregt, die Glaubenserfahrung zu aktualisieren.

5.3.

Die dritte Sicht entscheidet sich für das Zusammengehen von Symbolismus und Funktionalismus, von Sinn und Effekt. Sie setzt voraus, daß namentlich auf dem Gebiet der religiösen bzw. liturgischen Ausdrucksform und Sprache kein Keil getrieben werden darf zwischen die zwei dem Menschen eigenen Wahrnehmungsfelder und Perzeptibilitäten: *animal rationale et symbolicum.* Das liturgische Erleben soll so aktiviert werden, daß die Vernunft mit der Phantasie zur Einheit gebracht wird und die gläubige Gesinnung bestimmt. Diese Gleichgewichtssicht soll man bevorzugen, nicht bloß aus liturgischen Erwägungen, sondern auch im Licht der Beschaffenheit des heutigen Menschen, dessen Lebensführung in starkem Maß einseitig durch die Betonung der Funktionalität belastet ist. Letztere soll aber nicht verdrängt, sondern durch das Erleben der Symbole und Metaphern korrigiert und ergänzt werden. Eben wegen ihres hochkommunikativen Charakters in den Arten der Ansprache und Zusprache muß die Predigt dazu geeignet sein – ideal-typisch gesehen – Sinn und Effekt miteinander zu verbinden, also sinnvoll und funktionell zu sein.

6. EINIGE DATEN AUS EINER ERFAHRUNGSUNTERSUCHUNG

Im Rahmen dieses Aufsatzes habe ich auch einige Daten aufgenommen, welche die empirische Untersuchung eingebracht hat. Bei der Wiedergabe beschränke ich mich auf die Charakteristika der Zuhörer, des Predigers und der Predigt selbst.

Das Auditorium ist eine alternde Gruppe, bei der Höhergebildete prozentual zu stark vertreten sind und zu der nicht wenige Langzeit-Fernsehzuschauer gehören. Hieraus schließt man, daß die ersten über eine größere Aufnahmefähigkeit verfügen und die zweiten sich durch einen weltanschaulichen Pluralismus auszeichnen. Dem Glauben steht man freier gegenüber als einstmals. Die Gruppe ist ziemlich zusammengewürfelt: Es gibt große Unterschiede bezüglich Kirchenbindung, Status, Frequenz der Kirchenfeier und Bekanntschaft mit dem Pfarrer. Im allgemeinen will man eine lebensnahe Predigt, die mit dem Alltag zu tun hat und in der Umgangssprache gehalten wird. Inhaltlich bevorzugt man als Thema die Nächstenliebe und das Verhältnis zu anderen. Auch der Sinn des Glaubens und der trostspendende Wert der Predigt kommen gut an, weniger aber bei Jugendlichen und bei denen, die nur selten an der Liturgie teilnehmen; für diese zwei Gruppen stehen die an das Leben gesetzten Erwartungen vornan. Das Interesse für Ordnung ist bezeichnend für die Älteren. Im allgemeinen findet man die identitätsfördernde Funktion der Predigt: Sie soll dazu beitragen, das Leben zu verstehen und neue Perspektive zu eröffnen, die ein richtiges Verhalten ermöglichen. Man sucht eine Beziehung zwischen Religion und Ethik. Von geringerer Bedeutung ist meistens das politisch-soziale Handeln. Diejenigen, die nur wenig mit der Kirche zu tun haben, möchten Kontakt und Diskussion mit dem Prediger und sind empfänglich für politisch-soziale Themen. Die moralische Funktion der Predigt wird von den Älteren und Mindergebildeten geschätzt, während die Jüngeren, die Höhergebildeten und die zur Randgruppe der Kirche Gehörenden sie stark ablehnen. Was die biblische Orientierung betrifft, so ist diese für die meisten kein Ziel an sich, sondern bloß funktional; sie soll sich der täglichen Lebensführung anschließen. Die Bibel gibt der Lebenserfahrung eine Deutung und führt zu einem wohlüberlegten Handeln. Übrigens wird Bibelauslegung von den Älteren und den Wenigergebildeten höher geschätzt. Aus all dem ergibt sich, daß das Alter der Zuhörer die wichtigste Variabel ist; dann folgen Ausbildung und kirchliche Beteiligung.

Den Prediger betrachtet man als jemanden, der sein Amt persönlich und glaubhaft ausübt. Er genießt das Vertrauen der Zuhörer. Die Höhergebildeten sehen ihn als einen Diskussionspartner; die Wenigergebildeten wahren ihm gegenüber den Abstand. Die Beziehung der Zuhörer zur Kirche wirkt auf ihre Beurteilung der Predigt ein. Wer nur selten der Liturgie beiwohnt, schenkt dem Prediger eine geringere Autorität, akzeptiert ihn aber als Gesprächspartner; die kirchlich Beteiligten sind eher ausgerichtet auf das Amt und die Verkündigung als an der Person orientiert. Es hat den Anschein, daß je weniger die Predigt kulturell als selbstverständlich erfahren wird, um so stärker die persönliche Perzeption des Predigers unterstrichen wird: Man hört kritischer zu; was hat diese Person mir zu sagen?

Die Zuhörer bevorzugen keinen bestimmten Predigttypus: weder den persönlich-dialogalen Typus mit der Kommunikation an erster Stelle, noch den dogmatisch-bekennenden Typus, bei dem die Inhaltsübertragung betont wird. Letzterer scheint in etwa eher für die Diskussion geeignet zu sein, d.h. die Lebenspraxis zu beeinflussen, und wird von den Hörern eher beifällig aufgenommen. Je inniger sie mit der Kirche verbunden sind, um so mehr sind sie einer Meinung mit dem, was gepredigt wird. Formgebung und Vortragsweise werden ebenfalls hoch bewertet. Der persönlich-dialogale Typus wird nicht besser verstanden und zwiespältig erlebt: lebens- und personsnäher, aber weniger klar und deutlich. Von jeder Predigt erwartet man, daß die Relevanz der christlichen Tradition in Worte gefaßt wird.

7. PREDIGT ALS INTERRELATIONELLE KOMMUNIKATION

Bis jetzt habe ich einige Kennzeichen der Predigt gesammelt und einige skizzenhafte Angaben über das Wesen der Predigt gegeben; ich bin schematisch auf zwei homiletische Fragen eingegangen, nämlich auf das Verhältnis zwischen Schrift und Existenzsituation und auf die Problematik betreffs der Effektivität der Predigt. Auch habe ich eine Anzahl Daten aus einer empirischen Untersuchung, die für diesen Aufsatz illustrativ und informativ sein können, herbeigetragen. Nun möchte ich zu einer Beschreibung übergehen, wie die Predigt ein relativ dauerhaftes, verbales, kommunikatives Handeln bildet, in dem Prediger und Glaubensgemeinschaft durch den Austausch und die Aufnahme von Glaubensfragen eine Beziehung unterhalten.

Die homiletische Kommunikation – beispielhaft für die liturgische Kommunikation – kennzeichnet sich an erster Stelle als ein sprachliches Geschehen, bei dem zwar vielfache Ausdrucksformen angewandt werden, in dem aber der sprachliche Aspekt dominiert. Dieses Sprechen geschieht nicht nur innerhalb eines räumlichen Ambiente mit eigenen Bedingungen, sondern vollzieht sich in einer bestimmten Zeitspanne. Es bietet eine ziemlich lange Gelegenheit, eine geordnete Reihe von Dingen in Worte zu fassen, die alle zusammen die Predigt bilden. Außer durch die Dauerhaftigkeit kennzeichnet die Predigt sich meistens dadurch, daß sie von einer Person gesprochen und von vielen angehört wird: Prediger und Gemeinde. Daher die Frage der Interaktionsfähigkeit der Predigt. Der Kommunikationsprozeß zwischen Prediger und Gemeinde wird tatsächlich in hohem Maß durch dieses Sprech-Hör-Verhältnis bestimmt. Wir lassen uns nicht weiter auf die Folgen ein. Zwar nehmen wir an, daß nicht bloß von Einbahnverkehr die Rede ist, und daß jedenfalls Elemente des Austausches, der Rücksprache, des Einvernehmens während der Predigt stattfinden. Wir stellen diese dauerhafte, vor allem sprachliche Glaubenskommunikation bildlich dar durch eine lange dicke Waagerechte P (Prediger) und G (Gemeinde) und nennen sie die x-Achse. Es ist die Kommunikationsachse, auf der mit Pfeilen angedeutet wird, daß diese Verbindung in Großem Maß vom Prediger bestimmt wird und in geringerem Maß von der Gemeinde.

Die Predigt ist aber nicht nur eine Kommunikationsmöglichkeit zwischen P und G, sie zeichnet sich auch aus durch die Tatsache, daß der Glaube verbal explizitiert wird: Sie erwirkt einen Austausch grade auf Glaubensniveau, vom Glauben aus und im Hinblick auf den Glauben der Menschen: P und G. Dazu markieren wir auf der x-Achse den Mittelpunkt – Symbol des zentralen Elementes in der homiletischen Kommunikation – und ziehen durch diesen Punkt eine Senkrechte hinauf und hinunter. Beim Gipfel kommt eine E (Evangelium), das auch gilt für Bibel, christliches Glaubensgut, usw.; beim Tiefpunkt kommt das S (Situation der Existenz). Es sind dies die zwei Kernbegriffe, über die wir vorhin schon im Zusammenhang mit dem Wesen der Predigt sprachen. Beide sind auf einander gerichtet, und zwar so, daß eine Integration entsteht: eine inhaltliche Kommunikation in Worte gekleideter Wahrheiten, Werte, Normen Überzeugungen, Wünsche, Attitüden und Gefühle von im Glauben stehenden Menschen. Diesen inhaltlichen Interaktionsprozeß nennen wir die y-Achse, die Korrelationsachse gemäß der von uns aufgestellten Meinung zum Verhältnis zwischen Evangelium und Existenzsituation in der Predigt. Diese Korrelation bezeichnen wir mit einer Reihe aufwärts und abwärts gerichteter Pfeile. Indem wir die beiden Achsen abstecken, benennen und richten, und indem wir die vier Hauptelemente – P und G als persönliche Kommunikationspartner und E und S als inhaltliche Kommunikationspaare – innerhalb eines Feldes bezeichnen, sind damit die Basiselemente der Predigt mit ihren gegen- und wechselseitigen Beziehungen gegeben.

Figur 1

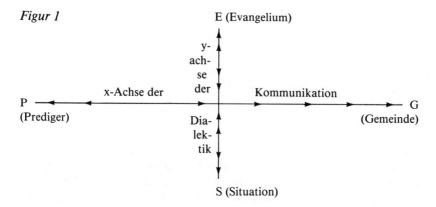

8. DIE PREDIGT ALS KONTEXTUALISIERTE KOMMUNIKATION

Von nun an spitzt sich meine Fragestellung bezüglich einer homiletischen Untersuchung zu. Obige Abbildung (Figur 1) ist ja – mit alle ihren Hypothesen und Positionsmöglichkeiten – noch immer strikt formaler Art. In Wirklichkeit ist die Predigt aber ein lebendiges Geschehen, von Menschen vollzogen, die in einem eigenen persönlichen Kontext stehen.

Der Prediger z.B. ist durchaus kein unbeschriebenes Blatt. Er gilt als einer, der das Evangelium kennt, damit umgeht und daraus auf persönliche Art lebt. Anders formuliert: Er hat mit der Schrift eine wechselseitige Beziehung. Er bestimmt durchaus die Deutung der Schrift und läßt sich durch die Schrift etwas sagen. Zwischen ihm und der Bibel gibt es eine interpretative Relation, die in der Predigt in Worte gefaßt wird. Wir bezeichnen diese Relation mit einer Linie zwischen den Punkten P und E (Figur 2). Der Prediger steht aber nicht nur in einem biblischen, sondern auch in einem sozial-kulturellen Kontext, von uns angedeutet mit dem Grundbegriff Existenzsituation. Hier liegen Faktoren gelagert wie Persönlichkeit, Geschichte, Familie, Ausbildung, Arbeit, soziale Umwelt, gesellschaftliches System usw., ein sehr komplexes und umfangreiches Ganzes von Voraussetzungen, die alle zusammen den Menschen ausmachen, so wie er ist, wie er geworden ist und wie er werden wird. Auch angesichts der sozial-kulturellen Wirklichkeit hält der Prediger unvermeidlich und fortwährend eine Beziehung der Wechselseitigkeit instand.

Der Kontext bezeichnet ihn als diesen Menschen, und er selbst bewirkt auch, daß dieser Kontext zustande kommt. Mit anderen Worten: Es gibt einen stetigen Austausch zwischen Person und Situation, wobei unablässig, implizit oder explizit, unbewußt oder bewußt, Abwägungen und Wahlen getroffen werden: eine interpretative Relation, die in der Predigt verbal ausgedrückt wird. Diese Verbindung wird mittels einer Linie zwischen den Endpunkten der x- und y-Achse P und S angedeutet. P (Prediger) wird in der Figur als interpretierender Handelnder bezeichnet, in dem E (Evangelium) und S (Situation) sich treffen und durchdringen. Der Prediger füllt den Raum des Dreiecks P-E-S aus und steht vor der Aufgabe, interpretierend in sich selbst die Korrelation (y-Achse) zwischen Schrift und Situation zustande zu bringen und diese dann (oder besser gleichzeitig) in Worten der Homilie auszudrücken (x-Achse).

Die gleiche Beschreibung soll man auch für die Zuhörer, die Gemeinde benutzen. Sie wird mit Recht als Glaubensgemeinschaft zu- und angesprochen, aufgrund und zur Neuerlebung ihres Glaubens. Auch sie steht in und lebt aus der Bibel; aus diesem Grund ist sie anwesend und zum Hören motiviert. Sie pflegt also eine interpretative Relation mit der Schrift, ist in ihrer Geschichte durch das Wort Gottes bestimmt und sucht Inspiration zur Kontinuierung ihrer Lebensführung. Wir geben dies mit einer Linie an zwischen den Endpunkten der x- und y-Achse G und E. Die Gemeinde hat nicht bloß eine Verbindung mit ihrem biblischen Glaubenskontext sondern auch mit ihrem sozial-kulturellen Kontext. Im Grunde spielen hier die gleichen Faktoren eine Rolle, die wir beim Prediger aufgezählt haben. Beide – Prediger und Gemeinde – sind Menschen dieser Welt und Zeit, sie sind unablässig in einem Interpretationsprozeß bezüglich der sozial-kulturellen Realität, in der sie leben, verwickelt. Deshalb ziehen wir in der Figur 2 auch eine Linie zwischen den Endpunkten der x- und y-Achse G und S. Die Gemeinde als Auditorium wird in der Figur also als Dreieck G-E-S angedeutet. Sie soll die Erwartung und die Aufgabe erfüllen, beim Hören der Predigt (x-Achse) in sich selbst die Korrelation (y-Achse) zwischen Schrift und Situation herzustellen.

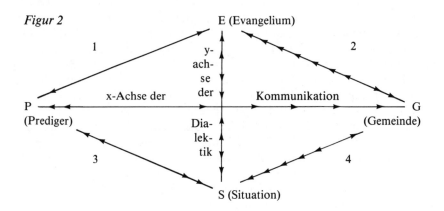

Figur 2

9. DIALEKTIK ZWISCHEN PREDIGER UND GEMEINDE

Es stellt sich also heraus, daß die figurative Abbildung des homiletischen Handelns eine Komposition zweier Dreiecke bildet, deren zwei personale Pole P und G einander auf der Korrelationsachse E und S völlig berühren: Dies ist kennzeichnend für die Kommunikation der x-Achse. Überdies zeigt sich aus der Figur, daß das Predigtgeschehen aus vier interpretativen Relationen aufgebaut ist, 1-2-3-4, die alle auf das Zustandekommen der Korrelation E und S bei dem Prediger und der Gemeinde gerichtet sein sollten; das Idealbild.

Wir müssen aber noch auf eine wichtige Komplikation hinweisen, die in der Gemeinde gelegen ist. Bis jetzt wurde die Gemeinde als eine Einheit in der Einzahl typisiert. Tatsächlich besteht sie aber aus vielfältigen Personen mit dementsprechend einer Vielzahl von Glaubens- und Existenzhorizonten. Die Predigt fungiert eben als ein liturgischer Vermittler, um das Viele zur Einheit zu bringen, aus den zahlreichen Hörern ein Auditorium zu machen. Konkret bedeutet dies, daß wir mit den Interpretationsachsen 2 (zwischen G und E) und 4 (zwischen G und S) rechnen müssen, die eine große Vielfalt von Interpretationen enthalten, in Einklang mit der Identität der Gemeindemitglieder selbst. Der Prediger spricht im Namen Vieler und zu Vielen. Hier liegt eine von der schier unlösbaren Komplikationen der Verkündigung, die wir in der Figur mit einer Vielfalt von Pfeilen angedeutet haben, die auf den Interpretationslinien 2 und 4 in die Richtung des Predigers zeigen. In ihm/ihr konzentriert sich also die Predigtproblematik.

Diesem Aufsatz habe ich den riskanten Titel *Praedicatio Verbi divini verbum populi* gegeben: Kann die Verkündigung des Evangeliums tatsächlich das Wort der Gemeinde sein? So müßte es sein. Können die Voraussetzungen geschaffen werden, die dieses Ideal ausführbar machen? Ich habe versucht, die komplexe Fragestellung in groben Zügen anhand der Literatur darzustellen und zu schildern. Allmählich komme ich dann zum Verkehr zwischen dem Prediger und der Gemeinde, in dem sie versuchen, Glauben und Leben mit einander zu verweben. Aber letzten Endes komme ich in Gespräch mit dem Prediger, der Wortführer im Namen der Gemeinde und für sie ist. Er/sie ist wie kein anderer der Vermittler des Wortes Gottes und zugleich das Wort von Menschen: Er/sie ist *dialogos in persona*, der personifizierte Dialog. Seine/ihre Hermeneuse bestimmt die Predigt und das Hören der Gemeinde: ein komplexes und heikles Geschehen. Ich bin deshalb der Meinung, daß, im Lichte der heutigen Lage des Glaubens und der Gesellschaft, vorzugsweise er/sie Subjekt einer pastoral-liturgischen Untersuchung sein soll, zur Förderung des homiletischen Handelns für Menschen von Gott.

LITERATURVERZEICHNIS

O. HAENDLER: *Die Predigt* (Berlin 1960).

Th. KAMPMANN: Das Wesen der christlichen Predigt, in *Liturgie: Gestalt und Vollzug. Joseph Pascher zur Vollendung seines 70. Lebensjahres von Schülern und Freunden gewidmet* (München 1963) 154-170.

Handbuch der Pastoraltheologie, Band I (Freiburg 1964) 220 ff.

J. GÉLINEAU: L'homélie, forme plénière de la prédication, in *La maison-Dieu* 21 (1965) Nr. 82, 29-42.

K. BARTH: *Homiletik. Wesen und Vorbereitung der Predigt* (Zürich 1966).

C.J. STRAVER: *Massa-communicatie en godsdienstige beïnvloeding* (Hilversum 1967).

E. LANGE: Zur Theorie und Praxis der Predigtarbeit, in *Predigtstudien* Beiheft 1 (Stuttgart 1968).

B. DREHER, N. GREINACHER und F. KLOSTERMANN (Hrsg.): *Handbuch der Verkündigung* 1-2 (Freiburg 1970).

H. ARENS: *Die Predigt als Lernprozess* (München 1972).

H.-R. MÜLLER-SCHWEFE: *Die Praxis der Verkündigung* (Hamburg 1973).

R. BOHREN: *Predigtlehre* (München 1974).

W. TRILLHAAS: *Einführung in die Predigtlehre* (Darmstadt 1974).

Fr. WINTER: *Die Predigt. Handbuch der Praktischen Theologie* 2 (Berlin (DRR) 1974) 197-312.

J. STERK: *Preek en toehoorders* (Nijmegen 1975).

E. HENAU: *Inleiding tot de praktische homiletiek* (Averbode 1976).

J.-M. MARCONOT: *Comment 'ils' prêchent... Analyse du langage religieux* (Paris 1976).

H.-Br. PIPER: *Predigtanalysen. Kommunikation und Kommunikationsstörungen in der Predigt* (Göttingen 1976).

M. BOLKENSTEIN: *Zo wordt er gepreekt* ('s-Gravenhage 1977).

St. VAN CALSTER: *Bijbel en preek* (Brugge 1978).

H.J.C. PIETERSE: *Skrifverstaan en prediking* (Pretoria 1979).

K.-Fr. und A. DAIBER: *Predigen und Hören. Ergebnisse einer Gottesdienstbefragung* 1. *Predigten: Analysen und Grundauswertung* (München 1980).

H. ALBRECHT: *Arbeiter und Symbol. Soziale Homiletik im Zeitalter des Fernsehens* (München 1982).

W. LOGISTER: De prediking als oorsprong van christelijk ervaren, in *Tijdschrift voor theologie* 22 (1982) 3-23.

G. SCHÜEPP (Hrsg.): *Handbuch zur Predigt* (Köln 1982).

E.H. VAN OLST: *Bijbel en Liturgie* (Baarn 1983).

K.-Fr. und A. DAIBER: *Predigen und Hören. Ergebnisse einer Gottesdienstbefragung* 2. *Kommunikation zwischen Predigern und Hörern. Sozialwissenschaftliche Untersuchungen* (München 1983).

F. MILDENBERGER: *Kleine Predigtlehre* (Stuttgart 1984).

J. THOMASSEN: Überlegungen zur Heilswirksamkeit der Verkündigung, in L. LIES (Hrsg.): *Praesentia Christi* (Düsseldorf 1984) 311-320.

H.J.C. PIETERSE: *Communicative preaching* (Pretoria 1987).

Praktische theologie 14 (1987) nr. 2 (S. 121-234): Preken: een verhaal op zich.

Index of names

Aaron, 126, 127, 130, 131, 140, 143
Abraham, 140
Acquoy, J.G.R., 195
Adam, A., 11, 280
Adam of Bremen, 148
Adam, Paul, 155, 158, 163, 166-168, 170
Addai and Mari, 8, 73-76, 80, 85
Adelbert II of Mainz, 151
Adler, M.N., 136
Adolfsson, H., 152
Aeneas, 149
Aengenvoort, J., 282
Agneta, St, 161
Alberdingk Thijm, J.A., 205, 206
Alberigo, G., 254
Albinus, 122, 124, 125
Albrecht, H., 302
Alexander VII, 244
Alexandrescu, S., 29, 30
Allmen, J. von, 245
Alphen, Hieronymus van, 218, 222, 231
Amalarius of Metz, 113, 119, 140
Ambrose, St, 4, 103
Anchises, 149
Andrew, St, 53, 162
Andrieu, M., 107, 108, 110, 111, 114, 120, 124, 125, 134, 176
Andronikof, Constantin, 280
Anne, St, 40
Anselm of Mainz, 151
Arens, H., 302
Ariès, Ph., 43, 173, 174
Artonne, André, 155
Aspren, St, 150
Aston, T., 50
Athanasius of Alexandria, St, 82, 84, 96, 97
Athanasius of Napels, St, 149-151, 154
Aubry, J., 2
Auf der Maur, Hansjörg, 10, 43, 102, 103, 109, 112, 118

Augustine, St, 5, 27, 103
Avril, Joseph, 155-158, 168
Axters, Steph., 174
Baker, D., 50
Bandmann, G., 144
Bange, P., 169
Barauna, G., 260
Barnard, Willem, 8, 11, 12
Baron, H., 149
Barth, K., 302
Bartholomew, St, 162
Bartsch, 37
Basedow, 232
Basil, St, 81, 82, 88, 89, 95-98
Bastiaans, Johannes G., 195
Batiffol, P., 245
Bauer, W., 55
Baumstark, A., 49, 119
Bavo, St, 147
Beauduin, Lambert, 234, 239, 242-247, 253
Beck, E., 70, 73
Becker, H.J., 115, 280
Becket, St Thomas, 149
Beckmann, Joachim, 87
Beeckman, Isaäck, 190, 194
Beissel, St., 200
Bekker, Balthasar, 224
Bekker, E., 223
Beld, J.B. v.d., 1
Bell, C., 35
Benedict Canonicus (of St Peter), 125
Benedict XIV, 131, 132, 137, 238
Benjamin of Tudela, 136
Berg, P.J.M. van den, 3
Berger, R., 280
Bernardus, prior of the Lateran, 122, 124, 125, 142
Bertrand, D.A., 6
Betz, J., 52, 54
Bèze, Théodore de, 190

The contributors

Sible de Blaauw (1951) studied medieval history at the State University of Groningen. In 1987 he obtained his doctorate at the Faculty of Arts of the State University of Leiden with a dissertation on architecture and liturgy in Rome in Late Antiquity and the Middle Ages. Subsequently the Netherlands Organization for Scientific Research (NWO) granted him a C. and C. Huygens fellowship for a continuation of the research on liturgical dispositions and functions of church buildings in Rome from Antiquity to Renaissance. The author published on themes related with this project and on Neo-Gothic architecture in the Netherlands.

Ad Blijlevens (1930) entered the Congregation of the Redemptorists and studied philosophy and theology in Wittem (Limburg). After his ordination and three years of experience in pastoral work, he continued his studies in Nijmegen and Münster/W. He received a doctorate in theology from the Catholic University of Nijmegen (*Gebed als lofprijzing in leer en praktijk van de Kerk* (Nijmegen 1968)). He taught at the *Theologisch-Katechetisch Instituut* in Sittard, of which he was also director. At present he is professor in liturgy and *rector* of the *Universiteit voor Theologie en Pastoraat* in Heerlen. Publications in many periodicals and books, i.a. in *Praktische theologie*, *Tijdschrift voor liturgie* and in volumes in the series of the *Universiteit voor Theologie en Pastoraat*.

Joh.P. Boendermaker (1925) studied theology in Amsterdam, Erlangen and Heidelberg. From 1951 until 1968 he was a pastor of the Evang. Lutheran Church in the Netherlands. He received a doctorate in 1965 for a dissertation on Luther's Commentary on Hebrews. Since 1968 he is professor of theology in the University of Amsterdam and the Lutheran Seminary for Lutheranism and liturgy. Publications in both fields. Member of the international Roman Catholic-Lutheran Joint Dialogue Commission.

Rudolf Boon (1920) received his academic training at the Universities of Amsterdam and Utrecht. He did research in the field of Church history at the Union Theological Seminary, New York (from which he received his master's degree in 1949), Mansfield College, Oxford, New College, Edinburgh. In 1951 he obtained a doctorate in theology in Utrecht with a thesis on the early history of American Protestantism (Pilgrim Fathers, Puritans, and their background in the English Reformation). Dr Boon published many books and articles on ecumenics (Anglicanism, Methodism, Congregationalism, iconography of the early Church and Orthodoxy), the Reformation (the Reformed tradition, ecclesiology, the ministry and the sacraments), Judaica (in particular the relations between Judaism and Christianity), philosophy of culture (Renaissance, Enlightenment, secularisation), and liturgics (e.g. on the Jewish matrix of Christian worship). Dr Boon is still active as a professor in liturgical studies at the Free University, Amsterdam.

Charles Caspers (1953) studied at the *Theologische Faculteit Tilburg* and specialized in the history of Church and theology. He graduated in 1985. He published about the history of popular religion in several volumes of collected studies, and with Harry Peeters and Marcel Gielis: *Historical behavioural sciences. A guide to the literature* (Tilburg 1988). As a research assistant of Herman Wegman at the *Katholieke Theologische Universiteit Utrecht* he is working on a doctoral dissertation about the eucharistic devotion and the feast of Corpus Christi in the Low Countries during the later Middle Ages, which he expects to complete in 1991.

Th. Clemens (1948) studied theology at the *Theologische Faculteit Tilburg* and specialized in Church history. He graduated in 1975 and took his doctoral degree in 1988. The subject of his dissertation were the Dutch Catholic prayer-books between 1680 and 1840. He is lecturer in Church history at the *Katholieke Theologische Universiteit Utrecht* and i.a. editorial secretary of *Archief voor de geschiedenis van de katholieke kerk in Nederland*. For publications, see notes 10, 11 and 50 to his contribution in this volume.

Jozef Lamberts (1940) studied philosophy and theology at the Catholic University of Leuven (Louvain) and obtained the doctoral degree in theology from the same university for a dissertation on active participation. At present he is lecturer in liturgy and sacramental theology at the *Universiteit voor Theologie en Pastoraat* in Heerlen. Dr Lamberts is a member of the editorial board of *Questions liturgiques. Studies in liturgy*. He published approximately 30 articles, mainly in liturgical periodicals, and *De vernieuwde liturgie van de eucharistieviering en de actieve deelneming* (Leuven-Amersfoort 1985), as well as *Geborgen in zijn liefde. Het sacrament van de zieken* (Tielt 1987).

Gerard Lukken (1933) is professor for liturgy and sacramental theology at the *Theologische Faculteit Tilburg*. He studied at the Diocesan Seminary in Haaren (Noord-Brabant), the *Pontificia Università Gregoriana* in Rome, and the *Institut Liturgique* at Paris. He finished his studies at the Gregorian University with a doctoral dissertation under the supervision of H. Schmidt in 1966 (*Original sin in the Roman liturgy* (Leiden 1973)). He published many articles in liturgical journals and *De onvervangbare weg van de liturgie* (Hilversum 1984²), *Geen leven zonder rituelen* (Hilversum 1988³).

Jan R. Luth (1951) studied theology at the *Theologische Universiteit van de Gereformeerde Kerken (Vrijgemaakt) Kampen (Broederweg)*, and organ at the *Muzieklyceum* in Hilversum. In 1986 he received a doctorate from the University of Groningen for a dissertation on congregational singing in Dutch Reformed Protantism (see note 4 to his contribution). Since 1980 he has been lecturing on liturgical studies, especially on hymnology, at the *Instituut voor Liturgiewetenschap* of the University of Groningen. Dr Luth is also teaching at the conservatoire of Groningen, and active as an organist specialized in the performance of music from the French and German Baroque. He published i.a. in *Bulletin Internationale Arbeitsgemeinschaft für Hymnologie, Jahrbuch für Liturgik und Hymnologie, Mededelingen van het Instituut voor Liturgiewetenschap* and *Jaarboek voor liturgieonderzoek*.

Paul Post (1953) studied theology in Utrecht (*Katholieke Theologische Universiteit Utrecht*) and Christian art and archaeology in Rome (*Pontificio Istituto di Archeologia*

Cristiana). He obtained his degree in 1977. From 1980 until 1988 he lectured on the study of liturgy at the *Universiteit voor Theologie en Pastoraat* in Heerlen. He completed his doctoral dissertation under the supervision of professor Herman Wegman (*De haanscène in de vroeg-christelijke kunst. Een iconografische en iconologische analyse* (Utrecht-Voerendaal 1984)). Since 1988 he has been head of the Department of Folklore/European Ethnology of the P.J. Meertens-Institute (*Koninklijke Nederlandse Akademie van Wetenschappen*) in Amsterdam. He specializes in liturgy and Christian art, and liturgy and popular religion.

Dr Post published articles in national and international journals (apart from those mentioned in notes 4 and 6 to his contribution in this volume, in *Bijdragen. Tijdschrift voor filosofie en theologie, Nederlands theologisch tijdschrift, Praktische theologie,* and *Rivista di archeologia cristiana*) and (with M. Menken and H. van de Spijker (eds.):) *Goede herders* (=HTP-studie 5) (Averbode 1983); (with A. Blijlevens a.o. (eds.):) *Ruimte voor liturgie. Opstellen m.b.t. de restauratie van de Sint-Servaaskerk te Maastricht* (Maastricht 1983); (with H. Evers:) *Historisch repertorium m.b.t. Wittem als bedevaartsoord* (=HTP-katern 2) (Heerlen 1986); *De Collectie C.M. Kaufmann van de Katakomben-Stichting Valkenburg* (Valkenburg 1988).

Peter Raedts, S.J., (1948) studied history and theology at Utrecht and Amsterdam. He took a D.Phil. in medieval history at Oxford in 1983. His thesis was published under the title *Richard Rufus of Cornwall and the tradition of Oxford theology* (Oxford 1987). At present he teaches Church history at the *Katholieke Theologische Universiteit Utrecht*. He is working on the history of the image of Jerusalem in the Middle Ages, about which he published in *Bijdragen. Tijdschrift voor filosofie en theologie* 50 (1989) and in *Publications of the Sir Thomas Browne Institute* (1990).

Gerard Rouwhorst (1951) studied theology at the *Katholieke Theologische Universiteit* of Utrecht. Further studies at Rome and Paris resulted in a doctoral dissertation (*Les hymnes pascales d'Ephrem de Nisibe* (Leiden 1989)), which was prepared under the direction of professor Wegman. He also published some articles, mainly on the liturgical traditions of the Syriac-speaking Christianity and on the Jewish roots of Christian liturgy. Since 1985 he is teaching liturgy at the *Katholieke Theologische Universiteit* of Amsterdam.

Anton H.M. Scheer (1934) is professor of liturgy at the Theological Faculty of the Catholic University of Nijmegen. Publications about the history of liturgy and the theory of liturgical practice.

Marc Schneiders (1960) entered the Norbertine (Premonstratensian) community of De Essenburgh (Hierden-Harderwijk) in 1979. He studied theology at the *Katholieke Theologische Universiteit Utrecht* and specialized in the history of liturgy. He graduated in 1988. At present he is preparing a doctoral dissertation on the litugical year in Ireland under the supervision of professor Wegman. His work is supported by the Foundation for Research in the Field of Theology and the Science of Religions in the Netherlands (STEGON-NWO). Publications mainly on Irish liturgy, i.a. in D. Edel, W. Gerritsen and K. Veelenturf: *Monniken, ridders en zeevaarders* (Amsterdam 1988) and *Archiv für Liturgiewissenschaft* 30 (1988) and 31 (1989).

Regnerus Steensma (1937) studied theology at the State University in Groningen and received a doctorate in 1970 for a dissertation in the field of ecclesiastical history. At present he is lecturer in Church architecture and the use of the church-building at the *Instituut voor Liturgiewetenschap* in Groningen. His publications include: *Opdat de ruimten meevieren. Een studie over de spanning tussen liturgie en monumentenzorgh bij de herinrichting van monumentale Hervormde kerken* (Baarn 1982) and *In de spiegel van het beeld. Kerk en moderne kunst* (Baarn 1987).

Louis van Tongeren (1954) studied theology at the *Katholieke Theologische Universiteit Utrecht* and specialized in the history of liturgy and in semiotics. He graduated in 1981. Since 1983 he has been teaching liturgy and theology of the sacraments at the *Theologische Faculteit Tilburg*. He is preparing a doctoral dissertation about the feast of the Exaltation of the Cross under the supervision of professors Wegman and Lukken. His publications are about the application of semiotics (according to the Paris School of A.J. Greimas) on liturgical texts, and about today's liturgy and liturgical music.

Tabula gratulatoria

Gian Ackermans, Nijmegen
T.H.M. Akerboom, Nijmegen
Revd Dr. Solomon Amusan,
Birmingham, United Kingdom
Ariënskonvikt, Utrecht
Prof. Dr. H.J. Auf der Maur, Institut für
Liturgiewissenschaft, Wien, Austria
Joseph Avril, Charenton-le-Pont, France
T. Baarda, Amstelveen
Abt A. Baeten, Abdij van Berne,
Heeswijk-Dinther
Prof. Dr. L.A.R. Bakker, Amsterdam
Dr. J.H. van de Bank, Ede
Khajag Barsamian, New York, U.S.A.
Prof. Dr. Jakob Baumgartner, Fribourg,
Switzerland
Prof. Dr. Dr. Hansjakob Becker, Mainz,
Germany
John De la Bere, Member of Prayer Book
Revision Commission of New Zealand,
Christchurch, New Zealand
Biblioteca Pontificia Facoltá Teologica S.
Bonaventura, Roma, Italy
Bibliotheek Katholieke Theologische
Universiteit Amsterdam
Bibliotheek Nationale Raad voor
Liturgie, Zeist
Bibliotheek der Rijksuniversiteit te
Utrecht
Bibliotheek van het Seminarie,
Antwerpen, Belgium
Bibliotheek St. Paulusabdij, Oosterhout
Bibliotheek Theologische Faculteit
Tilburg
Bibliothèque du Centre National de
Pastorale Liturgique, Paris, France
Paul B. van den Biggelaar, Vught
Sible de Blaauw, Leiden
Ad Blijlevens, Heerlen
J.W.M. Bluyssen, 's-Hertogenbosch
Antoine Bodar, Amsterdam

Joh.P. Boendermaker, Hilversum
Rudolf Boon, Amsterdam
J.A. Bornewasser, H. Landstichting
Prof. Dr. G.J.F. Bouritius, Tilburg
Heinzgerd Brakmann, Bonn, Germany
A.H. Bredero, Dongen
Drs. A. Breukelaar, Leiden
P. Dr. Lucas Brinkhoff OFM, Trier,
Germany
R. van den Broek, Ravenswaaij
G. Broekhuijsen, Breda
Frans Brouwer, Utrecht
Gerhard M. Cartford, Saint Paul,
Minnesota, U.S.A.
Charles Caspers, Tilburg
Th. Clemens, Zeist
Paul De Clerck, Bruxelles, Belgium
T.E.H.M. Coenen, Baexem
Emmanuel Cutrone, Venezia, Italy
A.C. van Dam, Kampen
Margret Dekker, Gorredijk
Rev. Msgr. Alan F. Detscher,
Washington DC, U.S.A.
Deutsches Liturgisches Institut, Trier,
Germany
Drs. J.G.M. Droste, Gendt
Thomas Egloff, Liturgisches Institut,
Zürich, Switzerland
Prof. Drs. A.D.M. Elders, Amsterdam
Tom Elich, Brisbane, Australia
Drs. B.A. Endedijk, Kampen
J.H.M. Evers, Heerlen
René van Eyden, Zeist
Fr. John A. Frendo O.P., Dominican
Priory, Fatima Sanctuary, G'Mangia,
Malta
W.Th.M. Frijhoff, Rotterdam
Genootschap voor Liturgiestudie te
Utrecht/Zeist
C.A.F.M. van Gessel, Utrecht
Marian Geurtsen, Utrecht

317

Rev. Michael Gilligan, Ph.D., American Catholic Press, South Holland, Illinois, U.S.A.

André Goossens, Antwerpen, Belgium

Prof. Dr. C. Graafland, Gouda

Prof. Dr. F. de Grijs, Zeist

G.B. Groener, Nijmegen

Lucas Grollenberg, Nijmegen

Hetty en Aart de Groot-Dorlas, Zeist

B.L. de Groot-Kopetzky, Nijmegen

Revd John A. Gurrieri, Los Angeles, California, U.S.A.

F. Haarsma, Nijmegen

Dr. Werner Hahne, Bildungszentrum Propstei, Wislikhofen, Switzerland

Leo O. Harris, Hampton, Connecticut, U.S.A.

Henri W.M. ten Have, Utrecht

P.T.M. van Hezik, Boxtel

Rijcklof Hofman, Utrecht

P.G. van Hooijdonk, Amsterdam

A.W.J. Houtepen, Utrecht

The Revd Patrick Irwin, Oxford, England

Joost H.G.M. Jansen, Bergeijk

Peter Jeffery, Newton, Massachusetts, U.S.A.

E.P. de Jong, Driebergen

Klaas-Willem de Jong, Oudega

M.B. de Jong, Amsterdam

Prof. Dr. M. de Jonge, Leiden

Prof. dr. J.A.B. Jongeneel, Bunnik

J. Joosse, Rotterdam

Drs. J. Kerklaan, Noorden

R. van Kessel, Harmelen

Ad de Keyzer, Arnhem

Pater J. van Kilsdonk SJ, Amsterdam

Dr. Martin und Karin Klöckener, Trier, Germany

Prof. Dr. F.R.J. Knetsch, Eelde

H.W. de Knijf, Utrecht

M. van Knippenberg, Nijmegen

G.L.N. Kock, Veghel

Prof. Dr. Franz Kohlschein, Bamberg, Germany

Dr. J.A. de Kok OFM, ep. aux., Utrecht

A. van der Kooij, Theologisch Instituut, Leiden

J. Körver, Eindhoven

Prof. D. Georg Kretschmar, Ottobrunn, Germany

Walter Krikilion, Abdij Postel, Mol, Belgium

Theo C. de Kruijf, Zeist

José de Kwaadsteniet, Driebergen

Jaap H. van der Laan, Kampen

J. van Laarhoven, Nijmegen

J. Lamberts, Mechelen, Belgium

Gordon W. Lathrop, Philadelphia, Pennsylvania, U.S.A.

Prof. Dr. Lambert J. Leijssen, Leuven, Belgium

Gerard Lössbroek, Bergeyk

Gerard Lukken, Tilburg

Drs. J.P. Lutgerink, Deil

Jan R. Luth, Tolbert

Drs. J.J.C. Maas, Dussen

Prälat Prof. Dr. Theodor Maas-Ewerd, Walting, Eichstätt/Bayern, Germany

Prof. Patrick Mc Goldrick, St. Patrick's College, Maynooth, Ireland

H. Manders CSSR, Wittem

Dr. Gerrit Manenschijn, Amstelveen

William Marrevee, Ottawa, Ontario, Canada

Joska van der Meer, Geldrop

P.J. Meertens-Instituut, Amsterdam

Dr. A.K. de Meijer O.S.A., Eindhoven

Theo H.G. Menting OP, Utrecht

L. Meurders, Nuth

Drs. D.E. Mooij-Kemp, Maarssen

P.C.A. Morée, Utrecht

Dr. Jac. Mulders SJ, Den Haag

W.A.J. Munier, Valkenburg a.d. Geul

Nederlands Instituut voor Kerkmuziek, Utrecht

Nederlands Instituut te Rome, Italy

Jeanet Niemeyer, Nijmegen

Mgr. J.B. Niënhaus, Maarn

Dr. Peter J.A. Nissen, Heerlen

Dr. A. Noordegraaf, Ede

Rev. David A. Novak, Shaker Heights, Ohio, U.S.A.

Hans van Oort, Zeist

G. Oostvogel OP, Bilthoven

Ds. W.G. Overbosch, Amsterdam

Varghese Pathikulangara CMI, Dharmaram College, Bangalore, India

Paul Van Peteghem, Cuijk

Drs. A.P.G.M. Peters OFM, Utrecht

Pontifical Institute of Mediaeval Studies, Library, Toronto, Ontario, Canada

Paul Post, Naarden

Prof. Dr. G.H.M. Posthumus Meyjes, Oegstgeest

M.B. Pranger, Amsterdam

Drs. J. Rademaker, Oosterhout (Gld)

Peter Raedts, Utrecht

W.M. Reedijk, Utrecht

Janneke and Jan van Reenen, Driebergen

Hans van Reisen, Utrecht

Han Renckens, Amsterdam

J.E.H. van Renswoude, Apeldoorn

P. Rentinck, Utrecht

Revd Ian Hugh Robertson, Cumbria, United Kingdom

Dr. E. Roebroeck OSA, Utrecht

Susan Roll, Faculteit der Godgeleerdheid, Leuven, Belgium

Gerard Rouwhorst, Nieuwegein

Drs. H. Richard Rutherford C.S.C., Portland, Oregon, U.S.A.

Th.A.M. Salemink, Gendt

Drs. H.C. van der Sar, Zoetermeer

Anton H.M. Scheer, Rosmalen

Corry Schellekens, Beesd

Marc Schneiders, De Essenburgh, Hierden

Ted Schoof, Nijmegen

H.J.M. Schoot, Utrecht

I.A.M. Seeboldt, Egmond-Binnen

Sint-Adelbertabdij, Egmond-Binnen

Panagiotis Skaltsis, Thessalonika, Greece

Silveer De Smet, Heverlee-Leuven, Belgium

F. Smit, IJmuiden

Dr. Marjan Smolik, Ljubljana, Yugoslavia

Dr. G.J.C. Snoek, Aalsmeer

Prof. Dr. A.M.J.M. Herman van de Spijker, Heerlen

Dr. W. van 't Spijker, Apeldoorn

Regn. Steensma, Kollum

Wim en Bertie Steunenberg, Kampen

Stiftsbibliothek Abtei St. Bonifaz, München, Germany

Studia liturgica, Wiebe and Cornelia E. Vos, Grave

Drs. A.J.M. Sturkenboom, Driebergen-Rijsenburg

Thomas J. Talley, Forest Hills, New York, U.S.A.

Rev. Dr. Jacob Thekeparampil, Kottayam, Kerala, India

Theologisch Seminarium Hydepark, Doorn

Louis van Tongeren, Tilburg

E. Trietsch, Hilversum

Trinity College Library, Victoria, Australia

Rev. Dr. D. Tripp, West Midlands, England

Universiteit voor theologie en Pastoraat, Heerlen

The Ushaw Bookshop, Ushaw College, Durham, England

Pim Valkenberg, Utrecht

Mevr. Drs. V.M.M. van Valkenhoef, Driebergen-Rijsenburg

Kees Veelenturf, Zoeterwoude-Dorp

Prof. Dr. H. Vekeman, Erftstadt-Lechenich, Germany

R. Veldhuis, Groningen

Wil Veldhuis, Utrecht

Prof. Dr. W.H. Velema, Apeldoorn

Drs. Jeroen M.M. van de Ven, Boxtel

Die Vereinigten Seminare des Fachbereichs Katholische Theologie, Bibliothek, Münster, Germany

G.C.A. Vergouwen OFM, Hilversum

Ambroos Verheul OSB, Abdij Keizersberg, Leuven, Belgium

Jan Visser, Zeist

Drs. N.W. Visser, Den Dolder

P. Ewald Volgger Ot, Wien, Austria

Dr. Antonie Vos Jaczn, Bilthoven

A. de Vos-Berends, Bemmel

J.P.F. Waegemakers, 's-Hertogenbosch

J. Wagner, Kampen

B. Wallet, Utrecht

Dr. F. Ellen Weaver, Notre Dame, Indiana, U.S.A.

C.E.A. Wegman c.s, Ruurlo

Tamis Wever, Amsterdam

Prof. James F. White, Department of Theology, Notre Dame, Indiana, U.S.A.

319

Bert Wirix, Leuven, Belgium
Mevr., Drs. M.E.F. Wisse, Vriezenveen
Dr. J.B.M. Wissink, De Meern
J.B.J. de Wit, Ambt Delden

C.A Zunneberg, Amsterdam
Dr. H. Zunneberg, Warnsfeld
M.A. van Zutphen, Waalwijk
Th. H. Zweerman, Megen

320

DATE DUE

HIGHSMITH 45-220